WORKPLACE FLEXIBILITY

Workplace Flexibility

Realigning 20th-Century Jobs
for a 21st-Century Workforce

**Edited by
Kathleen Christensen and
Barbara Schneider**

ILR PRESS

AN IMPRINT OF

CORNELL UNIVERSITY PRESS   ITHACA AND LONDON

First published 2010 by Cornell University Press
First printing, Cornell Paperbacks, 2010

Printed in the United States of America

Library of Congress Cataloging-in-Publication Data
Workplace flexibility : realigning 20th-century jobs for a 21st-century workforce / edited by Kathleen Christensen and Barbara Schneider.
    p. cm.
  Includes bibliographical references and index.
  ISBN 978-0-8014-4860-7 (alk. paper) — ISBN 978-0-8014-7585-6 (pbk. : alk. paper)
  1. Flexible work arrangements—United States. 2. Work and family—United States. I. Christensen, K. (Kathleen) II. Schneider, Barbara L. III. Title.
  HD5109.2.U5W67   2010
  331.20973—dc22   2009032784

Cloth printing   10 9 8 7 6 5 4 3 2 1
Paperback printing   10 9 8 7 6 5 4 3 2 1

Contents

Preface

The rise of dual-earner households, as well as single-parent, single-earner households and older couples facing joint retirements, has significantly changed the relationship between work and family life in the U.S. and other nation states. No longer dominant is the family in which one parent goes out to work and one stays home. Yet even in the early 1990s, these demographic changes eluded the attention of scholars and public policymakers. In 1994 the Alfred P. Sloan Foundation chose to address explicitly this major social and economic sea change. The foundation sought to understand what was happening within working families at all stages in their lives, as well as within the workplaces in which they were employed. In focusing on the workplace, Sloan was interested in learning to what extent American employers were responding to this increasingly diverse workforce, in terms of both their business objectives and the organizational structure of the workplace, including provisions related to time and space. Sloan chose to develop funding strategies that would have the potential to affect how our society navigates these major social and economic changes by identifying what steps might be beneficial for the future.

The Sloan Foundation's vision was articulated by Kathleen Christensen, who was recruited to spearhead and direct a program on workers and their working conditions. She established four principles to guide Sloan's grantmaking in the area of working families and the workplace. These principles are: (1) supporting the production of high quality, multidisciplinary research to identify the critical issues faced by workers and their families over the course of their lifespans; (2) communicating these research findings beyond the academy to business leaders, policymakers, and the media to increase public understanding of problems faced by workers, particularly their need for workplace flexibility; (3) forming a coalition to launch and execute a national initiative to make workplace flexibility a compelling national issue and the standard way of working; and (4) funding parallel tracks for achieving success by increasing voluntary employer practices and building bipartisan support for a national policy on workplace flexibility. The resulting funding model is one of the few philanthropic efforts committed to an integrated program that supports collaborative work in three arenas: research, private sector practices, and public policy.

Informed by these principles, Christensen supported more than four hundred grants totaling $120 million over the course of more than a decade. The results of the program are significant in three distinct areas: producing work-family scholarship, improving media understanding of work-family issues, and executing the National Workplace Flexibility Initiative. This book is a culmination of these efforts and addresses each of these areas, not only from a U.S. perspective but from a global one as well. The intent is to interface issues of policy and practice with research as a way of understanding how to achieve workplace flexibility across the life course. The origins of the book came from a conference that was held at the University of Chicago's Center on Parents, Children, and Work, which was a Sloan Center on Working Families and for which Barbara Schneider was a cofounder and director.

The chapters in this book reflect the strategic principles that Christensen developed for the Sloan grantmaking program. Specifically in the area of work-family scholarship, Sloan grants supported the publication of over six hundred peer-reviewed articles, over a third of which are in the top journals of their respective disciplines, and over one hundred scholarly and commercial books. Through Sloan's establishment of six Centers on Working Families, each of which had a strong training component, the first generation of work-family scholars was created, with over 180 completed doctoral degrees and 70 post-doctoral fellowships. Nearly 60 percent of these scholars now hold tenure-track positions or tenured lines, ensuring subsequent generations of researchers focused on work-family issues. Through its grantmaking, Sloan has been instrumental in building infrastructure for the community of work-family scholars and practitioners. Much of the work from the research program has been collected and is now available through Boston College's Sloan Work and Family Research Network, widely recognized as the premier online destination for current, credible, and comprehensive research and information on work and family issues, which serves a global community of academics, human resources practitioners, and state legislators.

One of the four pillars of Christensen's model, the National Workplace Flexibility Initiative, has as its overarching goal to promote workplace flexibility as a compelling national issue. This is an essential step to achieving the long-term goal of making workplace flexibility the standard way of working in the United States. Since its inception in 2003, the initiative has pursued two fundamental strategies: to increase voluntary employer adoption of workplace flexibility, and to position ideas for comprehensive federal legislation on workplace flexibility. Through the efforts of the Families and Work Institute (FWI), a grassroots movement to promote workplace flexibility has effectively been seeded as a strategic means of achieving business goals. To do this, FWI has used a rigorously competitive business awards program to raise awareness, nurture local business leaders, and benchmark applicant companies against national norms. In 2008 there were more than one million media impressions based on the promising practices identified through the awards program. As part of the Sloan grant program, FWI continues to field the *National Study of Employers,* which provides national baseline data for scoring the Sloan awards. Included in this book are examples of these award-winning initiatives.

As part of the National Workplace Flexibility Initiative, Workplace Flexibility 2010 (WF2010) at Georgetown University, with support from the New America Foundation, anchors Sloan's efforts to lay the groundwork for federal policy in this arena. At the time WF2010 was initially funded, the term "workplace flexibility" was not in use and partisanship was so intense that there was no discussion across the aisle on issues related to the need for flexibility. Five years later, and due to their strategic efforts, the term workplace flexibility is not only in use but is the flagship term signaling an entirely new policy initiative on Capitol Hill. A platform of policy ideas was published in May 2009, having been vetted by members of political parties, key business groups, special interest groups, and relevant stakeholders. Active conversations by groups that previously were not engaged with one another now regularly take place and are essential to moving any bill through Congress.

Although the workplace flexibility community has grown in number and impact much remains to be done, particularly in light of the current economic crises we face. Christensen's integrated funding model of working with scholars, policymakers, and businesses will serve us well as we strive to solve the problems of workers who need and want more flexibility than is currently available. Research must continue to draw on the talents and wisdom of people from many disciplines, it must continue to reach beyond the walls of the academy to the broader public, and it can and must continue to forge paths for action by business and government. Only through these effective partnerships will the work that academics have so painstakingly pursued over the past decade and a half begin to bear witness to the changes that the American family has experienced and to the ways that American workplaces must change to address the needs of employees with family responsibilities, as well as the needs of their employers.

Kathleen Christensen
Barbara Schneider
New York City
July 2009

Acknowledgments

The idea for this book was generated by a conference held at the University of Chicago in 2006 on "Workplace Flexibility in a Global Context" that was funded by the Alfred P. Sloan Foundation. Many of the authors in this book made presentations at this meeting and it was their insights and critiques that underscored the fundamental issue of the mismatch between twenty-first-century workers and their twentieth-century jobs. We would like to thank the conference presenters and participants, the University of Chicago for hosting the meeting, and Demetria Proutsos, who had the major responsibility for organizing this conference and encouraging the participation of the contributing authors. We are also appreciative of Michigan State University, and particularly Vice President Ian Gray, for their support of research programs dedicated to working families. We also are extremely grateful to Anne Nelson for her careful editorial assistance and to Leigh Ann Halas, who managed the organization of this book from author correspondence to reference checking and formatting—not an easy task given the number of tables and figures constructed by scholars in several different countries. Our greatest thanks, however, is to the Alfred P. Sloan Foundation who had the foresight and resources to invest in perhaps one of the most critical issues facing U.S. dual-earner families, that is, the need for more workplace flexibility in our rapidly changing technological global society. The contents of this book, however, remain the position of the authors and not that of the Foundation.

WORKPLACE FLEXIBILITY

INTRODUCTION

Evidence of the Worker and Workplace Mismatch

Kathleen Christensen and Barbara Schneider

The American way of life has undergone profound changes over the last thirty years. More changes are likely, given the current Great Recession that is likely to be deep and long. This book was written before the onset of this current economic crisis and its potential effects on working families and workplace flexibility are unknown, as we have yet to experience a crisis of this magnitude in contemporary times. This economic situation raises a new set of questions: With high unemployment, will those with jobs be working more, or less? Will more parents be at home taking care of children, though with higher stress levels? Will workplace flexibility programs be cut back, especially those that cost money, as opposed to those that do not? Or will the economic downturn actually improve the chances for flexibility because there is less work overall and maybe more voluntary part-time work? Are workers in a better, or more compromised position to obtain individual or collective flexibility arrangements? Will corporations be in a stronger position to impose involuntary flexibility arrangements that benefit them, and not workers? What incentives will corporations offer in this market? Although we cannot predict what will happen in this decade and the next, this book provides compelling evidence as to how changes in the composition of the workforce exert new demands on employers and the organization of work in time and space. Understanding the potential for a new era of workplace flexibility can address some of the problems that are emerging from these economic times.

Today, record numbers of women, particularly middle-class mothers, have entered—and stayed in—the workplace. As a result, the majority of American families with children are now headed by dual-earner parents or single-parent, single-earner parents. But as the American family has changed, the American workplace has not, largely retaining its traditional structure.

1

The resulting one-size-fits-all workplace, with its full-time, full-year, year-in and year-out jobs, as well as its rigid, linear career paths, remains the norm of American workplaces, resulting in a profound structural mismatch between the way work is organized and the needs of a changing workforce. American working parents and older workers are paying the price for this structural mismatch and private sector employers in the United States, while slow to respond to this mismatch, are creating opportunities for more flexibility in how work is organized in time and space. But lessons may be learned from what is happening in other countries, particularly those that have been important partners in our global trade, that have relied to varying degrees on the state to restructure the organization of work. The challenge for this book, therefore, is to examine how, in the United States and abroad, organizing work more flexibly can realign the structure of work to the needs of workers, while meeting the goals of business. In meeting this challenge, there are roles for both the state and the private sector.

For most of the twentieth century, the one-size-fits-all workplace suited the needs of most of its workers. At mid-century, the typical middle-class American worker was a male breadwinner with a stay-at-home wife who cared for the home, family, and community. His job required full-time, full-year work. It offered little to no time off, and provided maximum opportunities for paid overtime, thus requiring these men to focus almost exclusively on their work, but enabling them to earn a family wage and support their wives and children. Federal laws, particularly the Fair Labor Standards Act (FLSA) passed in the late 1930s, codified this workplace structure. It set the standard workweek at forty hours and made provisions for overtime compensation. No safeguards regarding compensation were put into place for those who worked part-time or part of the year.

By the late twentieth century, however, the one-size-fits-all workplace that once so well fulfilled the needs of American workers became profoundly *mismatched* to the needs of the increasingly diverse and varied U.S. workforce. In 2009, the typical worker is as apt to be female as male. Due to declining real wages, he or she now lives in a household in which both parents need to work in order to support their families. Over 70 percent of married couples are dual-earners (Bianchi, Robinson, and Milkie 2006), resulting in a profound change in the arithmetic of the family.

The traditional American family followed the basic arithmetic of two adults and two jobs—the ratio of resources to demands being in balance, with each adult holding one job, either breadwinning or homemaking. But in the dual-earner families of today, the same two adults now share *three jobs,* two as breadwinners and one as homemaker. In other words, while the number of adults has remained constant over time, the number of jobs, and their cumulative demands, has increased dramatically, far outstripping the adult resources. This is evident in the number of paid hours worked. Nearly 70 percent of today's dual-earner households, on average, work eighty or more paid hours a week (Jacobs and Gerson 2004), compared to the forty-three average paid hours worked by traditional families in 1960.

In the United States, we typically view the challenges faced by the *three jobs–two adult families,* as well as the *two jobs–one adult families,* as private problems, to be solved by individuals acting privately and alone. For many of the adults in these stretched households, the solution to reducing the demand of the three jobs has been to purchase or rely on *care replacement services.* These services are either purchased at market rates or provided free or at subsidized rates by employers. A small percentage of typically large firms offer concierge systems, dependent care services, or sick-child care back-up systems. The basic rationale for employer-provided care replacement services is that they can free workers to work longer and harder. Services not provided by the employer are increasingly made available by the market, enabling parents with the financial wherewithal to outsource domestic work, including childcare, housecleaning, or gardening services, or to rely on online purchasing of goods and home deliveries. Relying on care replacement services to reduce the demands of the three jobs can constitute a legitimate solution to the "three job–two adult" work overload, but it is not the only solution.

Although relying on the market to fulfill the demands of what had been the unpaid homemaking job is one solution, another can be found in rethinking how work can be restructured in time and space to provide working parents with the time they need and want to care for their families and fulfill their work responsibilities. Thinking in terms of a structural solution to the structural problem of the workplace/workforce mismatch focuses attention away from work-family problems as only private, individual problems that require private, individual solutions. Providing workplace flexibility constitutes a critical means of realigning the workplace to the needs of the changing workforce.

Quality workplace flexibility programs, offered without penalties, would free working parents to devote more time to their families. But working parents are not the only ones who would take advantage of this type of opportunity. Indeed, increasing evidence shows that although many older workers want and need to work beyond conventional ages of retirement, they do not necessarily want full-time, full-year work. Research reveals that workplace flexibility, when properly designed and implemented, is not only good for business but also for workers and their families (Corporate Voices for Working Families 2005). In effect, workplace flexibility can realign the structure of work to the needs of an increasingly diverse workforce.

In the United States, however, there is considerable controversy over how to achieve workplace flexibility to meet the needs of today's workers. Should workplace flexibility be a mandated federal policy that requires employers to allow all employees, not only those with children, extended periods for personal leave time? Should employers be given incentives to adopt flexibility voluntarily? Should there be some combination of policy and voluntary adoption?

In 2003, the Alfred P. Sloan Foundation, a private, philanthropic organization, launched a collaborative initiative to make workplace flexibility the standard practice in the American workplace. The National Workplace Flexibility Initiative supports a variety of projects at the national, state, and local levels that bring together business, labor, government, and advocacy groups to work collaboratively on activities that advance workplace flexibility. Organized around a common set of principles, the initiative maintains that change should occur not only at the federal level but also at the state and local levels; that flexibility should be proportionately fair to both employees and employers; and that policies should be responsive to different income levels and take into account the changing needs of workers throughout their professional and personal lives.[1]

Defining Workplace Flexibility

The Sloan initiative identifies several different categories of work situations that require workplace flexibility policies including: (a) *short-term time off,* for workers who need time off because of illness or other extenuating family circumstances (e.g., a family member is ill, a school conference is scheduled, there is a death in the family, there is an emergency home repair); (b) *full-time scheduling flexibility* for workers who desire to work full-time (forty hours per week for the full year) but in remote locations or on nontraditional schedules; (c) *reduced hours* for employees who need to work fewer than forty hours per week or less than a full year; (d) *extended time off* for workers who need to take an extended time off for health conditions or the needs of family members; (e) *career exit and reentry* ramps allow workers to take time off from the workforce entirely, but makes it possible for them to reenter the workplace at a later time without career penalties. Of these five arrangements, only one, extended time off, is currently mandated by federal law under the Family and Medical Leave Act (FMLA).

The range of workplace flexibility policies are intended to meet several purposes. From an employer's point of view, flexibility can achieve a number of goals when properly implemented, including improving recruitment and retention; reducing paid time off; and improving performance, including turnaround times (Corporate Voices for Working Families 2005). Workplace flexibility can achieve numerous benefits for the workers.

Short-term time off (STO) typically involves having the employer pay for the worker to have five days or fewer off to address unexpected issues that can occur (e.g., because a child is sick, a parent needs to attend a school event, or there is some pressing household need). Today in the United States, most working families work a combined average of 63.1 hours per week and almost 70 percent of them work more than eighty hours per week (Jacobs and Gerson 2004). These dual-career couples, most of whom have children and many of whom have older parents or relatives, are increasingly likely to have caretaking responsibilities for family members and friends (National Alliance for Caregiving and AARP 2004). These changing demographics raise the importance of permitting workers the option to leave their workplace unexpectedly because of pressing concerns.

Currently short-term time off is provided by employers through a variety of employer-sponsored benefit packages and government regulations. However, access to STO varies greatly between and within organizations depending on an organization's size and industry, and a worker's occupation, employment status, and socio-economic status. Most firms employing more than five hundred workers provide paid holiday leave, paid bereavement leave, short-term disability, paid vacation, and paid sick days. There are fewer benefits for paid family leave or paid personal days. These types of leave tend to be disproportionately available to full-time but not to part-time workers.[2]

The value of short-term time off is fundamentally obvious: workers need flexibility to help resolve conflicts that can occur because often there are not enough persons and resources to cover the unexpected events and needs that occur in everyday life. On the employer side, these STO benefits are commonly perceived as relatively low cost, as an incentive for higher productivity, and as contributing to a healthier workforce. However, there are always concerns that such a flexibility option will be a drain on resources because employees may overuse the benefit and it may create a reduction in morale and an undesirable work ethic. These concerns notwithstanding, STO appears to be a practice in which many firms engage, although the benefit is often not extended to part-time employees.

Episodic time off (EPTO) is an extension of STO and deals with the recurring need for *extended time off* (ETO) that a flexible work arrangement cannot solve. This particular option was developed in response to the growing number of U.S. workers with disabilities and chronic or other medical conditions that are likely to need such an option. Among the fifty-eight million adults in the United States, it is estimated that at least 33 percent of adults between the ages of eighteen to sixty-five have at least one chronic health condition. One major concern in the United States is the aging workforce; the number of workers fifty-five years old and older will grow by 50 percent over the next decade (Toosi 2004). Diseases such as cancer, multiple sclerosis, and depressive disorders afflict a large number of workers and the treatments for these conditions require extended periods of time off from work.

The Family and Medical Leave Act is the first federal law to require flexibility through *extended time off* (ETO) in the private sector. The Act, enacted in 1993, allows employees to take time off from work to care for family members or themselves. The FMLA allows up to twelve weeks per year of unpaid, job-protected leave for employees to care for a newborn child (as well as a newly adopted child or a newly placed foster child) or for a child, spouse, or parent with a serious health condition. To be eligible for FMLA, employees must work for private companies with more than fifty employees or for federal, state, or local government agencies. Employees eligible for such leaves must have worked for their employer for at least one year and for over 1,250 hours during the last year and not be in positions considered essential to the firm.

As might be expected, those who have the greatest need for paid extended time off are the least likely to have access to such benefits. For example, based on a survey conducted in 2000, only about 60 percent of employees in the United States who work for employers that are covered by the FMLA are eligible to receive such benefits. The majority of workers in these businesses (78%) report that they are financially unable to take advantage of unpaid FMLA leave (Cantor et al. 2001).

Full-time flexible scheduling in time and space, as well as reduced hours (e.g., part-time or part-year work or job shares) constitute other forms of work flexibility options. Full-time flexible scheduling can include flextime—adjusting arrival and departure times; new standard work hours (e.g., beginning earlier on two days of the week and starting later the three other days; voluntarily working nonstandard hours, such as evenings to serve customers in other time zones); and compressed workweeks, in which the forty-hour week is worked on fewer than five days a week (e.g., ten-hour days, four days a week; changing the hours over a two-week period so that every other Friday the worker is off).[3] Some organizations have made these standard policies whereas others allow for flexible schedules with respect to shifts and breaks (e.g., altering the schedule for an employee who has to care for an elderly parent so that the individual does not have to work an evening shift). In all of these arrangements employees continue to work on a full-time and, typically, a full-year basis.

The more organizationally challenging flexibility option is *reduced hours,* over the period of a week or a year, involving adjusting the period of employment and amount of hours worked. From the employees' side, there can be multiple reasons for hour reductions. For example, a worker phases into retirement and is allowed to remain at the job working thirty hours a week over the subsequent two to three years. Other examples include a worker who has been through a traumatic life event and decides to return to work on a part-time basis or an accountant who works for a firm just for the tax season. Job sharing, in which two people share one job, has been in place for over thirty years, but it has been minimally used, in large part because the same purposes can be achieved with two or more part-time workers, without constraining the workplace to the formula of two people equaling one head count for human resources purposes.

From the perspectives of both the employer and employees, a major problem associated with telecommuting or reduced hours might be the real hidden costs to the social capital found in relationships among workers. Through such network relationships, important information is sometimes not explicitly stated but communicated more informally through gossip or other informal interactions. Loyalty, trust, and bonds of reciprocity are enforced when workers interact with one another. When individuals are in the workplace for only two or three days a week, it may be difficult to establish strong network ties and the meaningful relationships that help to create group camaraderie. This is especially the case for reduced-hour workers or telecommuters.

These flexibility arrangements often come with high costs both to the individual and businesses that employ them. The situation is not ideal and is exacerbated by the dynamic challenges most employees face in their work and home lives. The complexity of these challenges and how U.S. twenty-first-century workers and their employers are coping with them are the major focus of this book. The United States is not alone in trying to meet the needs of its workers; other nations are also engaged in various policies and practices to enhance workplace flexibility. Examining the policies of several other nations highlights the opportunities and problems these solutions present to the employees, employers, and the governments that support their implementation. By including some of these examples we gain important insights into some of the solutions and challenges the United States faces as it redesigns the workplace for this century's workers.

Making the Case for Flexibility

This book is organized into four major sections with a concluding chapter that addresses how to solve the workplace flexibility mismatch. The first section includes three chapters that address what life is like for today's working families. Section two includes three chapters that concretely describe how workers are unable to customize their lives to fit into twentieth-century jobs. Section three contains four chapters that discuss various types of voluntary employer practices to provide workplace flexibility to their employees. The last section includes six chapters that review both voluntary employer and state initiatives designed to enhance flexibility in Europe, Australia, and Japan.

Twenty-First Century Workers and Family Life

The first chapter, "The Long Reach of the Job: Employment and Time for Family Life," by Suzanne Bianchi and Vanessa Wight, focuses on two-parent dual-earner families with children and how much time they spend on paid work, childcare and housework, and leisure time, and the pressures they feel about allocating their time to these different activities. Data from the new American Time Use Survey (ATUS) collected by the Bureau of Labor Statistics and the 500 Family Study, funded by the Alfred P. Sloan Foundation, show that time for children, spouse, and self are often compromised by work time and parents often express conflict and pressure regarding their choices. Working long hours for both fathers and mothers is unquestionably having a toll on families, and it is not clear how to reduce the number of paid and unpaid work hours. Fathers in good jobs are reluctant to reduce their hours and incur the penalties to their pay and career options, and mothers who have shortened their hours subsequently often feel the need to work more hours outside the home to compensate or to simply to make ends meet.

One way mothers are coping with these demands is through multitasking. "Multitasking among Working Families: A Strategy for Dealing with the Time Squeeze," by Shira Offer and Barbara Schneider, uses time diary data from the 500 Family Study, funded by the Sloan Foundation, to examine how frequently dual-earner families with children multitask, what activities they are engaged in while multitasking, and how they feel about it. Parents multitask about half of their waking time, the equivalent of eight additional hours a day, suggesting that multitasking is the way things are done in contemporary working families. Multitasking occurs more often at home whereas multitasking at work is less prevalent and it tends to be on another work-related activity. Multitasking at home is more often undertaken by mothers, and while mothers and fathers feel productive when doing so, mothers are more likely to feel irritated, frustrated, and stressed. Although multitasking may help mothers manage the demands of work and home, the physical and psychological stress associated with it suggests that they pay a heavy emotional toll for this time-saving strategy.

Another domain where time constraints affect family life is the family dinner hour. In the next chapter, "Coming Together at Dinner: A Study of Working Families," Elinor Ochs, Merav Shohet, Belinda Campos, and Margaret Beck use extensive video-recorded data on the lives of thirty families from the UCLA Sloan Center on Everyday Lives of Families (CELF). These anthropologists investigate two popularized antithetical views on American dinner, the first, that regular family dinners continue to characterize American family life, the second, that family dinners have all but disappeared from the lives of working families. The evidence shows that most families in this study did not regularly eat dinner together; even when they were in the house together, they often ate dinner at different times and in different spaces. Eating dinner together remains a strong family desire but work schedules often prevent these families from engaging in this sociocultural ritual that is widely recognized as promoting family cohesion and child well-being.

The Misfit between Old Workplaces and a New Workforce

Phyllis Moen and Qinlei Huang begin the second section with their chapter, "Customizing Careers by Opting Out or Shifting Jobs: Dual-Earners Seeking Life Course 'Fit,'" which shows the implications of the mismatch between work and family and job security. Based on longitudinal data from the Ecology of Careers Study of 983 dual-earner couples, funded by the Sloan Foundation, the authors demonstrate how dual-earners customize their exits from the workforce in an environment where formal retirement policies and practices do not exist and those that are in place run counter to conventional understandings of when and how one retires. Retirement is often given as the rationale for leaving one's employment at a certain age even though the termination may be the consequence of forced layoffs or buyout packages. The authors recommend that the workplace needs to be responsive to life course constraints, customizing policies and practices that would allow for the successful integration of work and family life, especially in our interdependent global economy.

For women the decision to leave the workforce is often a complex one, and the next chapter, "Keeping Engaged Parents on the Road to Success," by Sylvia Ann Hewlett, describes through extensive case studies and survey data some of the reasons women leave the labor force (popularly referred to as "off-ramping"), why they return, and the policies several companies have instituted to keep women from opting out and to enable them to successfully progress in their careers. Hewlett's work documents the harsh realities, compromises, and sacrifices professional women face in leaving their careers and the difficulties they encounter when attempting to return to work, often resulting in downsizing vocational aspirations and remaining in jobs for which they are overqualified. In order to stem the loss of talented women, some companies have begun offering workplace flexibility options including working from home, job sharing, telecommuting, and short stints at the office.

It is not only women who face making difficult choices about their careers; elder workers are also making them. What is not clear is why the elderly work or do not work. This is the question analyzed in the chapter "Elderly Labor Supply: Work or Play?" by Steven Haider and David Loughran. Using data from the Current Population Survey and the Health and Retirement Survey, they explore whether the elderly who keep working do so because of financial pressures or because they enjoy it, and whether those who are not working are choosing to leave the workforce or being forced to do so. Not surprisingly, the most educated, the wealthiest, and the healthiest older individuals tend to work, and at the hours and level of effort they prefer but for comparatively low wages. There is some indication that the employment opportunities of those who left the labor force were more constrained than were those who continued to work. It may be that more elderly workers would continue to work if the jobs accommodated their needs. For low-skilled elderly workers, who are most likely to need the income, this seems an unlikely possibility. What remains unanswered is whether the elderly switch jobs for the flexibility they desire or if they work only in those jobs that are available.

Workplace Flexibility: Voluntary Employer Practices in the United States

The next section describes how flexibility arrangements are being forged by market conditions in the private and public sector and some of the advantages and constraints these options pose for workers and their employers. Ellen Galinsky, Kelly Sakai, Sheila Eby, James Bond, and Tyler Wigton, in their chapter, "Employer-Provided Workplace Flexibility," illustrate some of the promising practices of flexibility in action using data obtained through a nationally representative study of employees, the National Study of the Changing Workforce and a parallel study of employers, the National Study of Employers. Promising flexibility practices, the authors argue, must benefit both the employer and employee.[4] Profiling over a dozen companies combined with survey data, Galinsky et al. show that among those surveyed the majority of employees feel they do not have enough time for themselves, their partners, or children, and are dissatisfied with their jobs. However, there are new alternatives for structuring the workplace that not only engage workers to feel more satisfied and committed to their jobs but also maximize the productivity of the companies in which they are employed.

Robert Hutchens and Patrick Nolen look more specifically at employer workplace flexibility practices regarding childcare in their chapter, "Will the Real Family-Friendly Employer Please Stand Up: Who Permits Work Hour Reductions for Childcare?" Surveying a random sample of 947 firms, they examine what types of employers allow employees to take reduced hours for childcare and whether those offering these options also offer other workplace flexibility policies such as paid maternity and paternity leave. Large organizations are more likely than smaller ones to provide paid maternity and paternity leave, which can be partially explained by cost. The cost of an individual on leave is lower for a large organization than for a smaller one. On the other hand, smaller organizations are better equipped to allow for part-time work in order to care for a child, as they can schedule workloads around such changes, which in a larger organization with many employees would be extremely difficult to coordinate and implement. Part of the reason large companies engage in these policies may also be tied to their public image, where practices are visible and verifiable to outside parties. The authors conclude by recommending that workplace flexibility practices need to be customized to different types of employers with the ultimate goal of providing similar benefits to employees across both large and small companies.

One of the largest employers in the United States is the federal government. In "Workplace Flexibility for Federal Civilian Employees," Kathleen Christensen, Matthew Weinshenker, and Blake Sisk review the adoption and implementation of workplace flexibility by the federal government for its own workforce. The federal government was one of the initial adopters of flextime, compressed schedules, the accumulation of sick leave for family reasons, telework, and part-time work. The forerunner among employers in providing flexibility provisions for employees, it has also created a legal environment that supports flexibility in private employment. In thinking about what the federal role should be in enacting workplace flexibility legislation, it is important to underscore those practices the federal government affords its employees as a model for other not-for-profit organizations as well for as the private sector.

The final chapter in this section, "The Odd Disconnect: Our Family-Hostile Public Policy," by Joan Williams, draws upon a compilation of research studies and case law to show how workplace flexibility has been defined through various policies and illustrated in the media. Her analyses suggest that workplace flexibility has been portrayed as primarily a woman's issue and existing policies are more likely to benefit high-income dual-earner families and are least responsive to those working families with incomes below the national average. Williams points out that the individualistic ideology that characterizes much of American politics, federal legislation, and corporate practices is in sharp contrast to other countries where national legislation appears easier to mandate and enforce. The last section of the book examines the efforts of other countries to legislate workplace flexibility, demonstrating both the opportunities and limitations of national government policies.

Workplace Flexibility: Practices from Abroad

Turning first to Europe, Janet Gornick, in "Limiting Working Time and Supporting Flexibility for Employees: Public Policy Lessons from Europe," presents an overview of selected public policies that shape the work hours of workers in Belgium, France, Germany, the Netherlands, Sweden, and the United Kingdom. Relying on data from several sources, including the Luxembourg Income Study, Gornick discusses some of the critical policies that shape work time, including establishing a standard for the workweek, entitlements for paid days off, and paid leaves. The regulation of work time, she explains, has been a key feature of European countries, in contrast to the United States, where there is less regulation and effective lobbying efforts by businesses to keep it so; deeply embedded norms within the United States that stress the value of working long hours; and, among some religious groups, having mothers refrain from employment, especially when their children are young. The United States would be well served by an intensive examination of workplace flexibility policies in other high-income countries and an exploration of the possibilities for their successful adoption in the United States.

Several of the conflicts that have arisen from state regulation of workplace flexibility in several European and two postcommunist countries are reported in "Parents' Experiences of Flexible Work Arrangements in Changing European Workplaces," by Suzan Lewis and Laura den Dulk. Their data were obtained from the project Gender, Parenthood and the Changing European Workplace, designed to learn how women and men negotiate motherhood and fatherhood and work-family boundaries in different countries with varying degrees of state and employer support. Results indicate that the implementation of policies, whether government mandated or voluntary, is seriously undermined by the changing nature of work, including intensified workloads, the fast pace of change, and the consequences for job instability. Even with managerial training and support, the growing intensification of long work hours thwarts effective workplace flexibility options. The authors contend that good workplace flexibility practices are complex and dependent on the context in which the employees work. Changes in policy practices require not only state-supported mandates but also need to be accompanied by strategic efforts at multiple layers including but not limited to the employer, managers, and work group the employee is a part of if such policies are to be effective.

Robert Drago and Mark Wooden turn our focus to Australia in "Work Hours Mismatch in the United States and Australia," in which they compare actual and preferred work times in the two countries, using data from the National Study of the Changing Workforce in the United States and the Household, Income and Labour Dynamics study in Australia. Findings from the two studies underscore the mismatch between the preferences workers have for the hours they would like to spend at their jobs and hours they actually spend. The problem is more acute in the United States, where workers who spend long hours at their jobs would prefer to work less and workers who work few hours would prefer to work longer. Unions in both countries appear to protect members from both short hours and underwork, but not overwork. Overwork appears more concentrated in the United States, especially among managers and professionals, whose behavior appears closely tied to their perceptions of the ideal worker, that is, one who is willing to work long hours and stay committed and dedicated to their job. With respect to gender, mothers in Australia are more likely than those in the United States to work part-time and to have that option supported by the government. However, there are more part-time women workers who do not have children in Australia, suggesting that gender discrimination may indeed exist in this country independent of motherhood.

The next chapter, "Renewed Energy for Change: Government Policies Supporting Workplace Flexibility in Australia," by Juliet Bourke, reviews the history and critiques some of the policies Australia is implementing to lessen the hourly mismatch problems and the government's initiatives to provide additional support for working parents. Recent approaches to Australia's workplace flexibility policies, she maintains, grew out of the country's history, beginning in the 1970s and escalating in the 1990s, to promote work-family balance and gender equity. Bourke argues that the current WorkChoices legislation, when evaluated against four criteria—access to flexible work practices and leave without disadvantage, reasonable and predictable hours, legal redress when companies do not follow the law, and structural support for real choices—only minimally addresses work-family balance and fails to meet the aspirations of the Australian government. The 2007 national elections in Australia, she contends, were influenced in part by the winning Labor Party's promises to move the work-family agenda forward.

Japan has also adopted a set of government policies that support working family needs, including measures to shorten working hours and provisions for childcare and eldercare. The last two chapters, "Flexible Employment and the Introduction of Work-Life Balance Programs in Japan," by Machiko Osawa, and "Government Policies Supporting Workplace Flexibility: The State of Play in Japan," by Sumiko Iwao, address how the government is responding to the declining birthrate by supporting workplace flexibility. Osawa's chapter takes on the issue of part-time work and her analysis concludes that part-time employment in Japan is not designed to accommodate worker preferences, but rather is a means for the prevailing employment system to compensate for its high costs and inflexibility. The shift has been away from regular workers to nonregular workers, introducing a high degree of employment instability, especially among young workers. She argues that the government needs to introduce more flexible work arrangements on more favorable terms, especially for women who are most likely to have multiple household responsibilities as wives, mothers, and caregivers for elderly parents.

Iwao begins by defining flexibility in Japan where *workplace flexibility* policies are developed to benefit employees, whereas *flexible employment* benefits the employers and refers to explicit government support designed to assist employers in implementing work flexibility practices; all of these initiatives fall under the umbrella of work-family compatibility. Her chapter describes the policies Japan has recently implemented to increase workplace flexibility including improving the treatment of part-time workers, promoting childcare leave and reentry into the labor force, financially supporting employers who offer assistance for childcare, and altering the practice of long working hours and encouraging workers to take annual leave. To help employers better understand the laws and implement practices in their firms, the Japanese government has created and sponsored an extensive education program for employers. This has been complemented by a series of financial support measures for employers and employees, including the creation and operation of on-site daycare and childcare leave for mothers and fathers. Although there are limitations with some of the current programs, such as the lack of penalties if firms do not comply with the new laws, the Japanese government has embarked on a program of evaluation of business workplace flexibility and subsequent public disclosure of firms undertaking exemplary practices and those failing to comply. These actions, as Iwao states, indicate a strong concrete movement toward setting national goals and policies that support working families; however, they are mainly in response to demographic problems. She concludes by calling for workplace flexibility practices that can provide a more meaningful life to citizens and work-family well-being, a message that, while intended for Japan, applies to other countries as well.

The concluding chapter, "Solving the Workplace/Workforce Mismatch," by Kathleen Christensen and Barbara Schneider, reiterates the need to realign the structure of work in time and place with the needs of the changing workforce and argues that there is not an easy solution to creating and implementing workplace flexibility practices, either in the United States or abroad. The situation is critical for twenty-first-century workers, who are likely to be in dual-earner families with children and working long hours in jobs that provide few options for maintaining control over their work and family lives. The available options often come with great economic and personal costs. Working parents at all stages of the life course who opt to reduce work schedules may do so at the expense of their salary, while those choosing to take on more responsibility may find themselves emotionally drained, stressed, and resent the burden of being a working parent.

Overall, the voluntary business response to the issue of implementing workplace flexibility options has been uneven. Even though the benefits of having flexible workplaces for employees could be viewed as a mechanism for firms to be strategically competitive, presently flexibility is not viewed in that light and it remains more a concept than a reality in most businesses. The burden of redesigning the American workplace around issues of flexibility cannot be borne only through the voluntary efforts of businesses, nor solely by government. As other countries have shown, laws can be mandated, but if not carefully and systematically designed, such regulations can reduce productivity to the point that businesses find alternatives that undermine the very laws that are put in place to achieve a work-life balance for today's workers. Yet, the imperative for changing the temporal conditions of the jobs of U.S. workers so they can become more aligned with their twenty-first-century lives is one that cannot be ignored, as the authors conclude by offering some recommendations for how government regulations and voluntary programs can meet these challenges.

Part 1

TWENTY-FIRST-CENTURY WORKERS AND FAMILY LIFE

THE LONG REACH OF THE JOB
Employment and Time for Family Life

Suzanne M. Bianchi and Vanessa R. Wight

There is considerable debate over the amount of time that Americans spend working. Some argue that paid work hours have increased (Schor 1991), while others find that the amount of time Americans devote to market work has actually declined (Robinson and Godbey 1999). For those in their prime working years, ages twenty-five to fifty-four, with a college degree or employed in professional and managerial occupations, work hours have increased (Coleman and Pencavel 1993a, 1993b; Rones, Ilg, and Gardner 1997). Indeed, long work hours are one gauge by which a firm measures work commitment among those employed in the most highly skilled and remunerated occupations (Blair-Loy 2003; Jacobs and Gerson 2004). On the other hand, among workers with a high school education or less, there is evidence of a decline in work hours—signaling underemployment for these workers who often cannot get the amount of work they want.

Jacobs and Gerson (2004) argue that the work hours problem is one of bifurcation, with too much work for some workers at some stages of the life course and too little for others. Too few hours are problematic, as they leave individuals and families with insufficient income to meet their needs, and, indeed, much research focuses on the problems of low-income individuals and families. However, too many work hours can also be a problem because time is finite, and the more hours devoted to market work, the fewer hours are available for other things. This latter set of issues is the focus of this chapter.

Parents represent a group that might be particularly concerned about long paid work hours "crowding out" other uses of time. Parents have a particularly important alternative use of their time—rearing their children. When long work hours become commonplace, jobs may strain a mother's and a father's ability to spend adequate time with their children, with each other, or in family activities. According to the 1997 National Study of the Changing Workforce, about one-quarter to one-third of workers report feeling that they do not have enough time for themselves or their family because of their jobs (Jacobs and Gerson 2004). In addition, many parents say that they would prefer to work fewer hours per week and fewer weeks during the year (Christensen 2005; Reynolds 2005). The trend toward desiring fewer hours has been increasing among mothers over the last decade. According to a recent 2007 report by the Pew Research Center, about 21 percent of mothers report that full-time work is the ideal situation for them (down from 32% in 1997), whereas 60 percent of mothers today prefer part-time work (up from 48% in 1997; Taylor, Funk, and Clark 2007). Research indicates that the desire to reduce work hours stems from a number of factors reflecting both job demands and personal and family life considerations (Reynolds 2005).

The tension between work and family may be especially pronounced in the United States. American workers dedicate more hours to paid work than do their European counterparts. American parents vacation less, work the longest annual hours, and have the highest percentage of dual-earner couples who work long workweeks compared with parents in other countries (Gornick and Meyers 2003). Jobs requiring long hours may exacerbate tendencies toward gender specialization in the home, with the result that women lose out in terms of market equality. But men suffer losses as well. They may end up with more distant relationships with their children, and the sense later in life that they "overinvested" in market work to the detriment of important relationships in their lives.

This chapter focuses on married mothers and fathers in two-parent families with children under age eighteen. This group was chosen because these are the parents who negotiate employment, caregiving, and the gender division of labor. Despite changing demographic patterns in family formation, two-parent families remain the most common family type for rearing children, especially middle-class children (Casper and Bianchi 2002). In addition, married parents negotiate with each other over who will provide time and who will provide money to the family; research suggests that marital status matters when considering time-allocation behavior (Bianchi, Robinson, and Milkie 2006; Sayer, Passias, and Casper 2006). By focusing on married parents, the confounding effect of being a single parent on time use is minimized, and the association between paid work and other domains of family life, including time with a spouse, is examined.

Data from the Current Population Survey (CPS) is used to get an overview of trends in average hours of paid work for married fathers and mothers, as well as the change in the percentage of couples who both work at least thirty-five hours a week (full-time employment) and who work especially long hours (fifty or more hours a week). Two recent time diary data collections are used—the new American Time Use Survey (ATUS) collected by the Bureau of Labor Statistics, and the 2000–2001 National Survey of Parents (NSP), collected with funding from the Sloan Workplace,

Work Force, and Working Families Program—to assess time allocated to paid work, nonmarket activities such as childcare and housework, free time, and parents' feelings of time pressure. The total workloads (i.e., the amount of paid work and unpaid caregiving) of couples where the wife is not employed outside the home are compared to those in couples where she is employed part-time (i.e., less than thirty-five hours per week). This chapter also examines the overall workloads of subgroups of employed mothers and fathers where both spouses work at least thirty-five hours per week and where both spouses work fifty or more hours per week. For all these groups, three additional dimensions of time use are explored: (a) a parent's own rest and relaxation and sense of time pressure, (b) time spent with children and its perceived adequacy, and (c) time spent with a spouse.

Background

Long work hours are often associated with good things. For example, jobs that require long hours often pay well and provide good benefits and complex, intellectually challenging work. Workers in these jobs report less boredom or depression and greater motivation, commitment, and job satisfaction (Barnett 1998). Indeed, in a representative sample of the employed British population, Green (2004) found that working forty-six or more hours per week was associated with a higher assessment of job satisfaction than working 30–45 hours.

Longer work hours have also been linked to better physical and mental health. In a sample of time diaries from the 1981 Study of Time Use, Bird and Fremont (1991) found that longer work hours were associated with higher levels of self-reported health. Longer work hours are also associated with lower levels of psychological distress (Hughes and Galinsky 1994) and less anxiety (Kohn and Schooler 1982).

Time, however, tends to be a "zero-sum game." Time devoted to any one activity can increase only if another activity suffers an equal loss—unless individuals engage in large-scale multitasking, a stressful proposition. Thus, when jobs demand long work hours, family life frequently suffers. Long work hours have been associated with difficulty scheduling time with family and increased perceptions that work interferes with family time (Staines and Pleck 1983). Heavy workloads have also been associated with feelings of work-family strain and conflict (Golden and Wiens-Tuers 2006; Gutek, Searle, and Klepa 1991; Keith and Schafer 1980; Marshall and Barnett 1993). Further, long paternal work hours and high paternal work overload are related to both fathers' and adolescents' reports of lower levels of acceptance and greater conflict in the father-adolescent relationship (Crouter et al. 2001).

Parents, especially mothers, may not be able to commit large amounts of time to market work and still maintain a reasonable family life. Indeed, for mothers, what often gives in the face of trade-offs between work and family is their labor force activity—suggesting that women still remain bound to some degree by the norm of "intensive mothering" and an "ideology of domesticity" that places women's primary place in the home (Hays 1996; Williams 2000). Mothers, even highly educated mothers in good jobs, tend to cut back their hours of work, change to less demanding jobs, or drop out of the labor force for one or more years to care for their families (Blair-Loy 2003).

Men, on the other hand, typically do not curtail employment to meet family demands: fathers' labor market hours do not vary much by the number or ages of their children (Bianchi and Raley 2005). If anything, men work more hours for pay when they become fathers (Lundberg and Rose 2002). As a result, gender specialization in the home and gender inequality in labor market outcomes persist. Women and men reach midcareer with women having less labor market experience, holding positions with less responsibility and authority, and earning lower incomes than men. Jobs that require long hours and complete devotion are difficult to mesh with childrearing, because raising children also demands a great deal of time and a high level of commitment (Blair-Loy 2003). According to Joan Williams (2000), anyone who devotes significant time to caregiving cannot perform as an "ideal worker" in the workplace and has difficulty remaining in the best jobs in the American economy.

For those who work long hours and occupy good jobs there are trade-offs. For example, employed mothers spend less time doing housework, sleeping, and in volunteer and leisure activities when compared with nonemployed mothers (Bianchi 2000; Bianchi, Robinson, and Milkie 2006). Paid work is the activity most strongly (and negatively) correlated with sleep: more paid work is associated with less sleep, whereas most other activities have either no or a weak relation with time spent sleeping (Dinges 2005). There is also evidence that as work hours increase, the overall quantity and quality of leisure time decreases. Working more hours is associated with shorter leisure episodes and a decrease in the amount of pure, uninterrupted leisure time and adult-oriented leisure activities (Mattingly and Bianchi 2003).

Of course, without knowledge of parents' preferences and their need for income—two important factors that influence decisions about when and how much to work—it is difficult to ascertain *why* some parents seem willing to finance long work hours with debits to personal and family time, while other parents cut back on paid work. Some may curtail their work hours because they have small children at home, whereas others may work fewer hours because, despite their preferences or income needs, they are unable to find a job with longer work hours. On the other hand, some parents who work long hours may do so because their lifestyle requires the income generated by these hours, while others may do so because they love their work or prefer more hours at work than at home (Hochschild 1997).

A Note on Nonstandard Work Hours

Although this chapter focuses primarily on *how much* parents work, another important factor when considering the long reach of the job is *when* those hours are worked. Both long work hours in jobs with standard schedules as well as jobs with irregular or nonstandard schedules can spill over into parts of the day often reserved for family time (e.g., evenings), and restrict parents' traditional "downtime" activities that provide rest and relaxation. Recent research on nonstandard workers underscores this point.

In the United States, a standard workweek is generally conceived as one that is thirty-five to forty hours, Monday through Friday, and it is generally assumed that these hours are worked mostly during the day. There is a sizable portion of the employed population, however, who work most of their hours outside the general daytime schedule. About one-fifth of employed Americans work more than half of their hours *outside* the 8:00 a.m. to 4:00 p.m. standard daytime hours, work a rotating schedule, or report that their hours vary (Presser 2003).

Recent evidence from the American Time Use Survey on this population of nonstandard workers (restricted to those who work most of their hours outside the 8:00 a.m. to 4:00 p.m. standard daytime schedule) suggests that parents who work nonstandard hours experience losses in time for themselves, with their spouse, and with their children (Wight, Raley, and Bianchi 2008). Mothers who work most of their hours in the evening spend less time in routine childcare activities, such as bathing children and providing medical care, relative to mothers who work most of their hours during the day. Mothers with nonstandard work hours also are less likely to read to their children. Fathers who work evenings or nights actually spend more time in routine childcare than their counterparts who work daytime hours. Although those who work in the evening are more likely to eat breakfast with their children, evening work schedules reduce the likelihood of being present at the dinner table. Nonstandard workers, regardless of whether they work most of their hours in the evening or at night, spend significantly less time than their standard daytime counterparts with a spouse, and less time watching television and sleeping (Wight, Raley, and Bianchi 2008).

These results underscore an obvious point: when work hours intersect with culturally sanctioned "nonwork" periods of the day, whether as a result of nonstandard work schedules or long standard daytime schedules, the ability to engage in nonwork activities is limited. In short, long hours of employment that bleed into nonwork segments of the day may disrupt other activities, much as they do for workers with nonstandard work schedules.

Time with Children

Early time use research by Nock and Kingston (1988) found that long workweeks were associated with reductions in time with children, but that parents curtailed activities in which children were only peripherally involved, instead of activities where children were the center of attention. The number of work hours also does not appear to diminish parents' knowledge of their children's daily experiences. For example, in a small local sample of predominantly dual-earner, two-parent families, mothers who worked longer hours knew as much about their children's daily experiences as did mothers who worked fewer hours (Crouter et al. 1999; Crouter and McHale 2005).

Mothers' longer work hours are also associated with the increased involvement of fathers in children's lives. Husbands who were part of an intact, dual-earner family and who were married to women with longer work hours had more "parental knowledge" than husbands whose wives worked fewer hours (Crouter et al. 1999). This point parallels findings on nonstandard work hours. Fathers in dual-earner couples in which the wife works a nonstandard shift are more likely than fathers in other dual-earner couples to participate in childcare (Casper and O'Connell 1998; Presser 1988).

Time with a Spouse

Recent research indicates that increases in both individual work hours and the combined work hours of a couple are associated with declines in marital quality (Barnett 2004). Similarly, feelings of role overload or not having enough time for oneself are associated with lower levels of marital quality (Crouter et al. 2001). Among a sample of white, married, middle-class professionals, an increase in work hours was associated with higher reports of family-role difficulty and higher levels of marital tension (Hughes, Galinsky, and Morris 1992). In a sample of 190 dual-earner families, the more hours a husband worked, the less time he spent with his wife (Crouter et al. 2001).

The effect of employment on a couple's marital relationship may be patterned along gender stereotypic lines with longer work hours among wives, rather than husbands, associated more strongly with divorce. Using panel data from the 1991–93 Survey of Income and Program Participation, Johnson (2004) finds that the incidence of divorce is greater when both spouses are employed. Furthermore, women's hours of employment are more highly correlated with divorce than the work hours of men. Among parents, an additional hour of employment by a father is linked to a lower probability of divorce, whereas an additional hour worked by a mother is associated with a higher risk of divorce (ibid.). Lower marital quality and a heightened likelihood of divorce are also found to be associated with certain nonstandard work schedules (e.g., working nights; Presser 2000, 2003).

Rest and Relaxation Time

Work hours can spill over into evening hours, with potential implications for time typically reserved for rest and relaxation, or what might be considered "downtime." Opportunities for relaxing in front of the television, stopping by the gym on the way home, or even volunteering in the evenings may suffer when work hours encroach on the otherwise few free hours left over between work and sleep. Furthermore, feelings of "time pressure" may be heightened when long work hours curtail time for rest and relaxation (Bianchi, Robinson, and Milkie 2006; Nomaguchi, Milkie, and Bianchi 2005).

Data and Measurement

Data

To assess the "long reach of the job," this study draws on trend data from selected years of the March Current Population Survey; data from the 2003–06 American Time Use Surveys, a nationally representative time diary data collection sponsored by the Bureau of Labor Statistics; and data from the 2000–2001 National Survey of Parents sponsored by the Alfred P. Sloan Foundation.

MARCH CURRENT POPULATION SURVEY

The CPS is a nationally representative monthly sample survey of over sixty thousand households from which the monthly employment rate is derived. The annual March survey includes a supplement with extensive information on household structure and income, as well as data on couples' employment characteristics and demographics. Here, the compressed file of the CPS Utilities, released by the Unicon Research Corporation, is used.

AMERICAN TIME USE SURVEY

The ATUS is the first federally administered survey on time use in the United States; data collection for the ATUS began in January 2003. The sample of ATUS respondents is randomly selected from among individuals, age fifteen or older, who reside in households completing their eighth and final month of the Current Population Survey (CPS). Of those selected to participate in the ATUS, about twenty-one thousand individuals completed interviews in 2003 for a 57 percent response rate. There was a sample reduction resulting in about fourteen thousand interviews in 2004, again with a 57 percent response rate. The 2005 and 2006 collections each included about thirteen thousand interviews with a response rate of 56 percent and 55 percent, respectively. The data collection is continuous, but data files are released for each calendar year. This study combines data from 2003–06 to increase the sample of parents.

Using computer-assisted telephone interviews, ATUS respondents provide a detailed account of what they were doing between 4 a.m. the previous day and 4 a.m. the interview day. For each activity reported, respondents are asked how long the activity lasted, where they were, and who was with them. In order to ensure reliable measures on weekends and weekdays, ATUS samples are split evenly between weekdays and weekends. Thus, about 10 percent of the sample is allocated to each weekday and 25 percent is allocated to each of the weekend days. Application of the ATUS final weight compensates for the unequal distribution of days across the week. Because the ATUS is composed of a subset of CPS participants, the data also include extensive information on the labor force characteristics of households, usual hours worked, earnings, and weeks employed over the year. One can think of the ATUS as providing representative samples of person days for subgroups of respondents such as married employed mothers, fathers married to nonemployed wives, and so forth.

NATIONAL SURVEY OF PARENTS

In 2000–2001, twelve hundred parents living with children under age eighteen were interviewed for a national probability sample. Parents were asked an array of attitudinal questions about their activities with children and their feelings about the time they spent with their children, their spouses, and on themselves. Embedded in the study was a one-day diary of time spent the previous day. The data were collected in computer-assisted telephone interviews, with a 64 percent response rate. The diary data from this study are analyzed extensively in a recently published book, *Changing Rhythms of American Family Life* (Bianchi, Robinson, and Milkie 2006). A comparison of the time diary estimates of primary activities from the NSP and the ATUS shows them to be comparable (Allard et al. 2007; Bianchi, Wight, and Raley 2005). The larger ATUS samples are used in this chapter for the diary time-use estimates, but the subjective data collected in the NSP are used for estimates of time pressures.

The three data sets described above were chosen for the unique perspective they offer on the contours of work and nonwork time. The Current Population Survey is the "gold standard" for capturing employment characteristics and assessing work patterns and trends over time. The ATUS data provide the most recent, large-scale time-use data collection, and provide a picture of time spent in activities other than work. The NSP asked respondents whether they felt they spent too little, about the right amount, or too much time with their youngest child, their spouse, and on themselves. In addition, the NSP asked respondents whether they always or sometimes felt rushed and whether they felt as if they were multitasking most of the time. These data can be used to investigate reports of subjective time pressure, something that cannot be done with the ATUS.[1]

Sample and Definition of Work Hours

This analysis is restricted to married individuals, age twenty-five to fifty-four, who live with their own children under eighteen years of age. The sample is further restricted to families where the father is employed full-time, which is based on the Bureau of Labor Statistics definition of full-time employment as working at least thirty-five hours per week. The vast majority of married fathers of children under age eighteen work full-time hours; only about 5 percent of fathers are not employed, and about 4 percent are employed but do not work full-time hours.

The time-use samples are of individuals, not couples, but all data sets include information about the respondent's spouse and children. This allows one to identify fathers by the employment status of their wives and the combined number of work hours of the respondent and his or her spouse. Information on usual hours of work per week (of both the respondent and his or her spouse) collected outside of the time diary is used to identify individuals in couples where the wife works part-time (averages less than thirty-five hours per week) and where both the respondent and spouse work full-time (at least thirty-five hours per week). The work hours of the respondent and spouse are also used to identify individuals who are in a couple with extremely long work hours. That is, using Jacobs and Gerson's (2004) threshold of fifty hours per week, couples where both the husband and the wife each work at least fifty hours per week as reported in response to this "usual hours" question are identified as working exceptionally long hours. These couples likely face great difficulty in reconciling the demands of family with those of paid employment but have not chosen a solution where the wife works a lot less than the husband. This makes them an interesting group, likely more gender egalitarian in time allocation than other couples.

The usual hours estimates captured outside the diary tend to be somewhat higher than estimates of paid work that can be calculated from the time diaries. The "usual weekly hours" question is used to classify couples, because this is the estimate for both members of a couple, as the time diary is collected from only one person per household. For couples where both spouses in the ATUS have usual weekly hours of fifty or more, the average time diary estimate of mothers' paid hours of employment averages 47.5 hours compared with 55.1 "usual hours." For fathers, the time diary estimate of weekly hours is 55.5, compared with 58.9 in response to the "usual hours" question.

The total day of activities is organized into seven main categories: paid work, childcare, housework, shopping/services, sleep, eating and grooming, and free time.[2] Paid work is defined as the total minutes per day spent working at a main or second job, looking for work, traveling during work, taking breaks at work, and commuting. Childcare time equals the total minutes per day spent on direct childcare such as basic care, helping and teaching, talking and reading, playing indoors, providing medical care, and other child-related activities. Housework includes the total minutes per day respondents report engaging in food preparation and cleanup, cleaning house (both indoors and outdoors), doing laundry, repairing or maintaining an automobile, and providing plant or animal care. Shopping and services equals the total minutes per day respondents report shopping for food, clothes, household items, personal care services, government and financial services, car repair, and other services. Sleep is the total minutes per day respondents report sleeping on their diary day. Eating and grooming equals the daily minutes spent eating (including meals at work), showering or bathing, engaging in hygiene and other grooming activities, dressing, resting, receiving medical care, and travel related to personal care. Free time is estimated by adding up the minutes per day spent on education and computer use, religion, organizations, events, visiting, fitness, hobby, TV and radio, listening to music, and communication activities.

Information about who the respondent was with while doing activities is used to develop measures of the time that respondents spent with their children and with a spouse on the diary day. Time with children equals the total minutes per day parents report doing any activity, with the exception of sleeping and grooming, in which a child was present (the ATUS does not collect information on who was present if the main activity reported is sleeping, grooming, or personal activities). For example, if parents are doing housework or watching television, and report a child present during such activities, this time is included in the estimate of time with children. Time with a spouse is constructed by adding up the minutes per day that respondents report doing any waking activity with a spouse present. Time diary estimates are converted from daily minutes to weekly hours by dividing by sixty and multiplying by seven. This provides a metric compatible with the CPS estimates of "usual hours worked per week."

Results

CPS trend data show that the average weekly labor market hours of fathers in two-parent families were fairly constant over the period from 1965 to 2005 (see table 1.1). However, as mothers increased their labor force participation, the combined hours of market work in these families rose from an average of fifty-two to sixty-two hours per week. At the same time, the proportion of all two-parent families where both spouses worked at least thirty-five hours per week—the equivalent of two full-time jobs—expanded from 17 percent to 34 percent. The percentage of couples with very long work hours (i.e., both worked at least fifty hours per week) more than doubled (from 1% to 3%), but remained a very small segment of couples with children.

The bottom panel restricts analyses to dual-earner families, families that increased from 28 percent to 57 percent of all two-parent families over this period. Married mothers' hours averaged between thirty-two and thirty-five hours per week throughout the period, and fathers' hours were around forty-five per week at each time point, with the combined hours of mothers and fathers close to eighty hours per week at each point in time. The percentage of dual-earner couples with both spouses working fifty or more hours increased slightly from 4 percent to 5 percent, but the percentage with both spouses working full-time (about 60% in 2005) was similar to 1965, though higher than during the intermediate time points.

Table 1.1. Joint Labor Market Hours in Two-Parent Families with Children under the Age of 18

	1965	1970	1975	1980	1985	1990	1995	2000	2005
ALL TWO-PARENT FAMILIES									
Mean joint hours	52.1	53.3	51.3	56.0	58.4	61.1	62.4	64.4	62.0
Father's hours	41.7	41.1	38.2	39.0	39.4	39.8	39.9	41.0	39.4
Mother's hours	10.4	12.2	13.1	17.0	19.0	21.4	22.5	23.4	22.7
Both employed 35 or more hours/week (%)	16.6	18.8	18.5	25.3	28.7	32.3	33.0	37.0	34.2
Both employed 50 or more hours/week (%)	1.1	1.0	1.2	1.7	2.1	2.7	3.0	2.7	2.7
DUAL-EARNER TWO-PARENT FAMILIES									
Percent of all two-parent families	28.0	34.3	35.3	46.1	50.7	55.8	58.6	60.8	57.4
Mean joint hours	80.0	78.3	77.2	77.7	78.8	79.6	80.0	80.5	79.5
Father's hours	46.2	45.8	44.8	44.9	45.2	45.6	45.7	45.5	44.5
Mother's hours	33.7	32.5	32.4	32.8	33.6	34.1	34.2	35.1	35.0
Both employed 35 or more hours/week (%)	59.2	54.7	52.2	54.8	56.6	57.9	56.4	60.7	59.5
Both employed 50 or more hours/week (%)	3.9	3.1	3.5	3.7	4.1	4.8	5.1	4.4	4.7

Source: Authors' calculations from the March Current Population Survey.

Note: Universe restricted to all parents who are householders/spouses and the woman is age 25–54.

Prevalence of Couples by Their Work Hours

Table 1.2 presents ATUS data on the distribution of married mothers and married fathers by the joint employment status of husbands and wives. Only a small proportion (about 2%) of all married mothers and fathers are in couples where neither spouse works for pay. Similarly, only about 5 percent of mothers and fathers are in a couple where the wife is the sole earner, and about 3–4 percent of couples (3.2% of mothers and 4.1% of fathers) report that the husband is employed less than full-time. Thus, about 89 percent of married parents aged twenty-five to fifty-four are in couples where the husband is employed full-time. It is this group that is the focus of the remainder of the chapter. In other words, the remainder of the analysis eliminates couples where neither spouse is employed, where only the mother is employed, or where the father is employed but working less than full-time hours (all of which are relatively small groups).

In couples with a father employed full-time (columns 2 and 5), about one-third of the wives are not employed, about 22 percent are employed part-time, and 43 percent to 46 percent are employed full-time. In about 3 percent of these couples, both spouses work fifty or more hours per week. Among couples where both spouses are employed (columns 3 and 6), about 67 percent (65% for mothers and 69% of fathers) have both spouses employed full-time in the ATUS. This estimate is somewhat higher than that of the CPS, where about 60 percent of dual-earner couples are estimated to be full-time working couples. About 5 percent of both mothers and fathers in these couples work long hours (i.e., 50+ weekly hours).

Selected Characteristics of Couples by Their Work Hours

Couples where both spouses work long hours are a highly select group (table 1.3). Mothers who work long hours are much less likely to have preschoolers than mothers who work fewer hours. About 33 percent of the mothers who work fifty or more hours per week have children under age six, compared with around 40 percent of all employed mothers in dual-earner couples, 43 percent of dual-earner couples with a wife employed part-time, and about 56 percent of those mothers who are not in the labor force at the time of the survey. This just reinforces the point made at the outset: married mothers of young children either cannot or will not work in jobs that require excessively long hours. Their paid work "gives" to create time for childrearing.

Not only do mothers and fathers who work long hours have older children, they themselves are older than couples where the wife's hours are shorter or where she is not employed. Thirty percent of mothers in couples where both spouses work fifty or more hours per week are over age forty-five, compared with about 20 percent of mothers employed either part- or full-time and about 15 percent of nonemployed mothers. Similarly, 42 percent of fathers are over age forty-five in couples where

Table 1.2. Couple-Level Employment Status of Married Mothers and Fathers, 2003–2006 (%)

	MOTHERS			FATHERS		
	TOTAL	IN COUPLES WITH A FULL-TIME EMPLOYED FATHER	IN COUPLES WITH AN EMPLOYED MOTHER AND A FULL-TIME EMPLOYED FATHER	TOTAL	IN COUPLES WITH A FULL-TIME EMPLOYED FATHER	IN COUPLES WITH AN EMPLOYED MOTHER AND A FULL-TIME EMPLOYED FATHER
Total	100.0			100.0		
Neither employed	2.5			2.0		
Wife sole earner	5.1			4.9		
Husband employed part time (<35 hours/week)	3.2			4.1		
Husband employed full time (35+ hours/week)	89.2	100.0		89.0	100.0	
Wife not employed	29.4	33.0		30.3	34.1	
Wife employed	59.8	67.0	100.0	58.7	65.9	100.0
Wife employed part time (<35 hours/week)	21.3	23.8	35.6	18.2	20.5	31.0
Both work 35+ hours/week	38.5	43.2	64.4	40.5	45.5	69.0
Both work 50+ hours/week	2.7	3.1	4.6	2.9	3.2	4.9
N	9,013	8,087	5,492	7,842	7,053	4,682

Source: Authors' calculations from the 2003–2006 American Time Use Survey.

Note: Universe is married mothers and married fathers aged 25–54. Percentage distributions are weighted; sample sizes are not.

Table 1.3. Selected Characteristics of Mothers and Fathers in Couples with an Employed Father by Joint Paid Work Hours of the Couple, 2003–2006 (%)

COUPLE STATUS	WITH CHILD <6		AGE 45-54		COLLEGE EDUCATED		IN PROFESSIONAL/ MANAGERIAL OCCUPATIONS	
	MOTHERS	FATHERS	MOTHERS	FATHERS	MOTHERS	FATHERS	MOTHERS	FATHERS
Mother not employed	56.1	61.4	14.8	20.8	32.1	38.6	–	39.6
Dual-earner couples	39.2	41.8	20.3	27.5	39.7	36.3	47.5	39.9
Mother employed <35 hours/week	42.7	45.0	19.6	28.0	39.2	43.5	43.7	46.1
Both employed 35+ hours/week	37.3	40.3	20.7	27.3	40.0	33.1	49.6	37.1
Both employed 50+ hours/week	33.2	38.3	29.7	41.7	61.3	52.2	62.5	52.5

Source: Authors' calculations from the 2003–2006 American Time Use Survey.

Note: Universe is married mothers with a full-time employed spouse and full-time employed married fathers aged 25–54. Percentage distributions are weighted; sample sizes are not.

both spouses work fifty or more hours per week compared with about 28 percent of those with a wife employed part- or full-time and a little over 20 percent where the wife is not employed.

Mothers and fathers who work extremely long hours also tend to be highly educated. About 61 percent of mothers in couples where both spouses work at least fifty hours per week have a college education (or more), compared with 40 percent of all employed mothers (39% of mothers who work part-time and 40% of mothers who work full-time), and only 32 percent of nonemployed mothers.

The educational attainment of fathers varies less by their wife's employment status but follows a similar pattern: a little more than half of fathers in couples where both spouses work fifty or more hours per week are college-educated, compared with lower percentages when mothers are not employed (39%) or work part-time (43%). The group of fathers with the lowest percentage who are college educated (33%) is the group where both spouses work thirty-five or more hours per week, which includes the small segment of couples where both work 50+ hours per week. This finding suggests considerable educational variation among fathers in couples where both spouses work full-time. Some of these couples are very well-educated, upper-income couples, while others are much more likely to be working-class couples with a great need for two full-time incomes. The differences in the percentage employed in professional or managerial occupations by work hours are similar to the educational differences. Couples in which both parents work long work hours (50+ hours per week) are more likely to be employed in professional/managerial occupations compared to their counterparts, where the mother works fewer hours or is not employed.

In sum, extremely long work hours characterize a relatively small segment of couples who have older children, are older themselves, are highly educated, and are probably at a more advanced stage of their career. These differences are important considerations when examining the overall workloads, time allocation, and time stresses of these different groups of workers.

Total Workloads: The First and Second Shift

Time diary data allow assessment of not only hours of paid work but also the hours individuals spend in the unpaid activities of childcare, housework, and other activities, such as shopping for household goods and services—the "second shift" of great interest to feminist scholars (Hochschild 1989). One can argue that both types of labor—market and nonmarket—are essential components of family well-being. If the time parents spend in both the "first shift" of paid labor and the "second shift" of unpaid family work is combined, what does the overall workload look like for mothers and fathers in the different groups of couples identified?

Figure 1.1 shows estimates of total workloads; panel A displays estimates for mothers, and panel B presents estimates for fathers. Mothers are divided into those

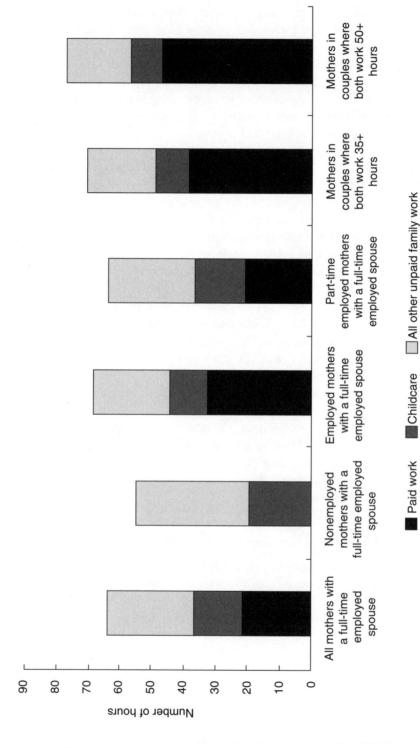

FIGURE 1.1A. Total workloads (paid and unpaid work) of mothers in married couples with a full-time employed father, 2003–2006

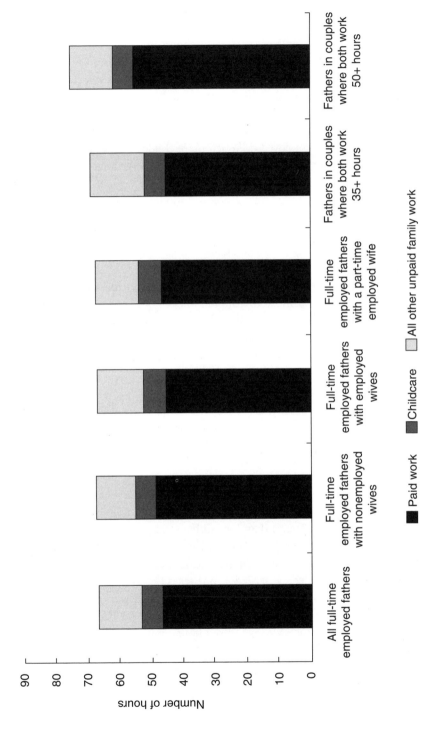

FIGURE 1.1B. Total workloads (paid and unpaid work) of full-time employed fathers in married couples, 2003–2006

who are employed and those who are not. (Fathers are divided into those married to an employed or nonemployed wife.) The other three groups shown in Figure 1.1 are subgroups of employed mothers (or wives, in the case of fathers): those in couples where the wife is employed part-time (less than thirty-five hours a week); couples where both spouses are employed full-time (thirty-five or more hours per week); and couples where both husband and wife report that they usually work fifty or more hours per week.[3] This last group is a subset of the group of couples where both are employed full-time.

Mothers who are not employed do much more childcare and housework than employed mothers, but their overall workload is nevertheless much smaller than that of employed mothers: they average fifty-five hours per week in (unpaid) work. The total workload among part-time employed mothers is sixty-four hours per week, and increases to seventy-one hours per week in couples where both spouses work full-time (35+ hours per week). Weekly workloads are extremely high for mothers in couples with long (50+) paid work hours, rising to seventy-seven hours a week.

Turning to fathers, arrayed by their wives' employment, the fathers with the highest workloads are also those in couples where both spouses work fifty or more hours per week—seventy-four hours per week in paid plus unpaid work (a three-hour lower average workload than for mothers in this kind of couple). Fathers' total workloads are also shorter (four hours shorter on average) than mothers' total workloads when both spouses work full-time (sixty-seven hours for fathers compared with seventy-one hours for mothers). Interestingly, fathers with spouses who are not employed or wives who work part-time have the same overall workloads as fathers in families where both spouses are employed full-time (sixty-seven hours). What this means is that fathers work less than wives when her hours are full-time (a four-hour difference), but they work more (three hours more) than their wives when her hours are part-time, and twelve hours more when mothers are not employed outside the home. Consequently, the average workload of fathers, averaged over all couples with a full-time employed father, is a little higher (by three hours) than for mothers: sixty-seven hours for fathers, compared to sixty-four for mothers. This gender gap disappears if couples where fathers work less than full-time are added to the group.[4]

Workloads remain gender specialized. If one takes the composite for all fathers and all mothers, mothers average twenty-two hours of paid work, compared with forty-seven hours for fathers. That is, mothers average about half the paid work hours that fathers do. Mothers average fifteen hours in direct childcare compared with seven hours for fathers, and twenty-eight hours in other unpaid family work compared with fourteen hours for fathers. Thus, fathers contribute about half as much unpaid work in the home as their wives do. This gender specialization lessens somewhat (though it does not disappear) in couples where both work fifty or more hours per week. Yet even in these couples, fathers average eight more paid work hours than their wives (fifty-five vs. forty-seven) and eleven fewer unpaid hours (nineteen hours of unpaid work compared to her thirty hours), and wives end up with a weekly workload that is three hours longer, on average.

How Do Daily Activities Change in Association with Employment?

Employed mothers average almost thirty hours per week of market work. What activities do they give up or do less of to accommodate hours of market work? Table 1.4 compares the time allocation of employed to nonemployed mothers to provide insight into how activity time changes in association with employment. Column 3 shows estimates of the reduced hours per week that employed mothers spend in other activities, compared with nonemployed mothers. Employed mothers do less childcare (eight hours less), less housework (ten hours less), a little bit less shopping (one hour less), get a little less sleep (three hours less), and have substantially less free time (nine hours less). In percentage terms (column 4),

Table 1.4. Average Hours per Week Mothers Engage in Selected Activities by Employment Status and the Percentage Change in Daily Activities Associated with Maternal Employment, 2003–2006

| | NONEMPLOYED MOTHERS WITH A FULL-TIME EMPLOYED SPOUSE[a] (SINGLE-EARNER COUPLE) | EMPLOYED MOTHERS WITH A FULL-TIME EMPLOYED SPOUSE (DUAL-EARNER COUPLE) | EMPLOYED VS. NONEMPLOYED MOTHERS | |
			DIFFERENCE	CHANGE IN DAILY ACTIVITIES ASSOCIATED WITH MATERNAL EMPLOYMENT (%)
Paid work	0.8	32.7	31.9	100.0
Childcare	20.1	12.0	−8.0	25.1
Housework	26.5	16.4	−10.1	31.6
Shopping/ services	8.7	7.4	−1.3	4.1
Sleep	60.6	57.3	−3.2	10.2
Eating and grooming	15.4	15.5	0.1	−0.3
Free time	35.9	26.6	−9.3	29.3
N	2,595	5,292		

Source: Authors' calculations from the 2003–2006 American Time Use Survey (ATUS).

Note: Universe is married mothers with a full-time employed spouse and full-time employed married fathers aged 25–54. Percentage distributions are weighted; sample sizes are not.

[a] Includes seventy-six mothers who are nonemployed at the time of the ATUS but who report doing work activities on their diary day, such as looking for work, interviewing, and engaging in other income-generating activities that are not considered part of a main job.

32 percent of the difference is attributable to less housework, 29 percent to less free time, 25 percent to less childcare, 10 percent to less sleep, and 4 percent to less shopping.

Table 1.5 compares mothers and fathers in dual-earning couples where the mother works part-time to dual-earning couples where both spouses work full-time (35+ hours per week). Further, the subgroup of mothers and fathers in couples with long work hours (50+) are compared to the overall group of parents in couples where both work full-time hours. Mothers who work full-time average about eighteen hours more per week in paid work than mothers who work part-time (see column 4 in the upper panel of table 1.5). Compared with part-time employed mothers, full-time employed mothers do less childcare (five hours less), less housework (five hours less), slightly less shopping (one hour less), get a little less sleep (almost one hour less), and have less free time (about six hours less). In terms of percentages (column 5), 29 percent of the difference is attributable to less childcare, 26 percent to less housework, 7 percent to less shopping, 4 percent to less sleep, and 32 percent to less free time.

The difference in fathers' paid work hours across these two types of couples is much less pronounced. Fathers in couples where both spouses work thirty-five or more hours per week average about two hours *less* of paid work than their counterparts in couples with a part-time employed wife (see column 4 in the lower panel of table 1.5). Fathers' time allocations are actually quite similar in households where wives work full-time or part-time.

In the 3 percent of couples with very long work hours, mothers average about nine hours more paid work and fathers average about ten hours more paid work than in the overall group of dual-earning couples where both spouses work at least full-time hours (35+ hours per week; note the 50+ hours group is a subset of the total). Employed mothers in couples with long work hours make up this difference primarily by getting less sleep and having less free time. They also do less shopping. For fathers, the difference also comes primarily through less sleep and free time, and third, by doing less housework.

Time with Children

Time diary data allow estimates of parents' total time with their children, not only time when they are doing direct childcare activities (i.e., the estimates shown in tables 1.4 and 1.5). Nonemployed mothers spend much more time with children, averaging sixty hours per week, compared with a much lower amount of time for employed mothers, who overall average thirty-eight hours per week—twenty-two fewer hours with their children.[5] Mothers who work part-time average forty-six hours per week with their children, while mothers who work full-time average thirty-four hours. Long work-hours mothers average the fewest hours with children, yet still spend thirty-one hours per week with them. Recall, however, that the age of

Table 1.5. Average Hours per Week Married Mothers and Fathers Engage in Selected Activities by Employment Hours and Percentage Change in Daily Activities Associated with Long Work Hours, 2003–2006

| | DUAL-EARNER COUPLE WITH PART-TIME EMPLOYED MOTHER | DUAL-EARNER COUPLE WHERE BOTH WORK 35+ HOURS | DUAL-EARNER COUPLE WHERE BOTH WORK 50+ HOURS | BOTH WORK 35+ HOURS VS. COUPLE WITH PART-TIME EMPLOYED MOTHER | | BOTH WORK 50+ HOURS VS. COUPLE WHERE BOTH WORK 35+ HOURS | |
				DIFFERENCE	CHANGE IN ACTIVITIES ASSOCIATED WITH BOTH WORKING 35+ HOURS (%)	DIFFERENCE	CHANGE IN ACTIVITIES ASSOCIATED WITH BOTH WORKING 50+ HOURS (%)
MOTHERS							
Paid work	21.3	39.0	47.5	17.7	100.0	8.5	100.0
Childcare	15.4	10.2	9.8	-5.1	29.1	-0.4	5.1
Housework	19.5	14.7	14.2	-4.8	26.8	-0.5	6.2
Shopping/services	8.3	7.0	6.0	-1.3	7.3	-1.0	11.8
Sleep	57.8	57.1	53.9	-0.7	4.1	-3.1	37.1
Eating and grooming	15.7	15.5	15.5	-0.2	1.2	0.1	-1.0
Free time	30.2	24.6	21.1	-5.6	31.5	-3.5	40.9
N	2,012	3,480	251				
FATHERS							
Paid work	46.8	45.2	55.5	-1.7	100.0	10.3	100.0
Childcare	7.1	6.6	6.2	-0.5	-30.9	-0.4	3.8
Housework	8.9	9.9	8.7	1.0	60.7	-1.2	12.0
Shopping/services	4.5	4.9	4.1	0.4	27.1	-0.8	8.2
Sleep	55.3	56.5	52.9	1.2	70.2	-3.5	34.3
Eating and grooming	15.1	14.5	14.7	-0.5	-32.8	0.2	-1.7
Free time	30.4	30.5	26.0	0.1	5.8	-4.5	43.4
N	1,535	3,147	230				

Source: Authors' calculations from the 2003–2006 American Time Use Survey.

Note: Universe is married mothers with a full-time employed spouse and full-time employed married fathers aged 25–54. Percentage distributions are weighted; sample sizes are not.

children differs dramatically across these groups. Those with lower levels of employ-ment more often have preschoolers who demand more parental time and attention.

Turning to the subjective indicators of time-use experiences arrayed in table 1.6, the feeling that one has too little time with one's children is much more preva-lent among employed than nonemployed mothers. Approximately 18 percent of nonemployed mothers report they have too little time with their children, while this sentiment is shared by nearly one-third of part-time employed mothers, over half of full-time employed mothers, and a little more than two-fifths of mothers in long work-hours couples. With the exception of couples where both spouses work 50+ hours per week, fathers are even more likely than mothers to feel they have too little time with their children. The percentage of fathers with this sentiment is fairly consistent across the different work-hours couples, ranging from 58 percent to 59 percent. Gender differences in a perceived time shortage with children disappear once the longer work hours of fathers are controlled, suggesting that this subjective measure may be picking up something about the "subjective cost" of spending more time away from home and family among the employed (Milkie et al. 2004).

The number of nights the family has dinner together also differs between couples with a nonemployed versus an employed mother/wife, which suggests that this fam-ily activity is also a little more difficult for dual-earner couples than for families where the mother/wife is not employed (table 1.6). Couples with a nonemployed wife eat together approximately five nights a week (5.1 for mothers and 5.2 for fathers). Among part- and full-time employed mothers, this number drops to about 4.4 nights per week, and is even lower among mothers who work long hours (4.2 nights per week). Fathers' estimates across groups are similar to mothers', although a bit higher (4.5 or 4.6 nights per week).

Time with Spouse

Couples who work long hours spend a little less time together (approximately twenty-five hours per week) than couples with a wife employed either full-time or part-time (twenty-seven to twenty-eight hours), who in turn spend less total time together than couples where the wife is not employed (about twenty-nine to thirty-two hours; data not shown). Couples with long work hours are also the most likely to express concern that they have too little time with a spouse: 80 percent of mothers and 84 percent of fathers in couples where both spouses work fifty or more hours per week say they have "too little" time with their spouse (table 1.6).[6] In cou-ples where both spouses work full-time, a little more than two-thirds of husbands and wives say they spend too little time together.

Sleep, Leisure, Rest, Relaxation, and Time Pressure

Employed mothers get less sleep and have fewer hours of leisure per week than nonemployed mothers (see table 1.4). These differences in sleep and free time tend

Table 1.6. Married Mothers' and Fathers' Subjective Time-Use Experiences by Employment, 2000

	ALL PARENTS	NONEMPLOYED MOTHERS/WIVES WITH A FULL-TIME EMPLOYED SPOUSE	EMPLOYED MOTHERS WITH A FULL-TIME EMPLOYED SPOUSE	DUAL-EARNER COUPLE WITH PART-TIME EMPLOYED MOTHER	DUAL-EARNER COUPLE WHERE BOTH WORK FULL TIME (35+ HOURS)	DUAL-EARNER COUPLE WHERE BOTH WORK 50+ HOURS
MOTHERS						
Percent who have "too little time" for						
Youngest (only) child	36.3	17.8	44.0	30.9	52.3	43.7
Spouse	69.7	61.9	72.9	79.2	68.8	79.5
Oneself	72.2	67.0	74.3	71.5	76.0	82.0
Days per week family eats main meal together	4.6	5.2	4.4	4.4	4.4	4.2
Percent who "always" feel rushed	42.5	30.5	47.4	39.5	52.5	52.1
Percent who multitask "most of the time"	65.6	57.2	69.1	63.5	72.8	85.9
N	420	113	307	130	177	18
FATHERS						
Percent who have "too little time" for						
Youngest (only) child	58.5	59.5	58.1	57.9	58.2	40.3
Spouse	60.1	55.9	61.8	49.1	67.9	84.1
Oneself	61.3	69.1	57.9	57.6	58.1	55.1
Days per week family eats main meal together	4.7	5.1	4.6	4.6	4.5	4.5
Percent who "always" feel rushed	34.4	33.1	35.0	31.3	36.7	47.7
Percent who multitask "most of the time"	39.3	41.9	38.3	32.2	41.1	59.1
N	346	93	253	78	175	21

Source: Authors' calculations from the 2000 National Survey of Parents.

Note: Universe is married mothers with a full-time employed spouse and full-time employed married fathers aged 25–54.

to increase as mothers increase their hours of employment. Perhaps the deficits in nonwork activities experienced by employed mothers account, in part, for their feelings of being rushed and multitasking "most of the time." According to the subjective indicators of time pressure in table 1.6, employed mothers more often "always" feel rushed than nonemployed mothers. Thirty-one percent of nonemployed mothers always feel rushed, compared with about 40 percent of mothers who work part-time and 52 percent of both mothers who work 35+ and 50+ hours per week. For fathers, those in couples with long work hours most often feel rushed (47%), but otherwise fathers' reports vary relatively little across groups, with around one-third of fathers "always" feeling rushed.

The feeling that one is multitasking "most of the time" is pervasive among mothers—characterizing 57 percent of non-employed mothers but a much higher 70 percent of all employed mothers, 64 percent of mothers who work part-time, 73 percent of mothers who work full-time or 35+ hours per week, and a remarkable 86 percent of mothers in long work-hours couples who work 50+ hours per week (see table 1.6). A much lower 40 percent of fathers characterize themselves as multitasking "most of the time," though this rises to 60 percent among fathers in couples where both spouses work 50+ hours per week. Nevertheless, the feeling that one is always multitasking is far more common among mothers than fathers. So too is the feeling of having too little time for oneself. About two-thirds of nonemployed mothers report having too little time for themselves compared with about three-quarters of employed mothers. As the hours of paid employment increase, so does the percentage of mothers reporting too little time for oneself, with four out of five mothers in long work hours couples sharing this sentiment.

The group of fathers that reports the least time for oneself is married to a nonemployed wife (70%). These are the fathers who have the highest likelihood of having a preschool-age child in the home. It may be that these fathers come home after work only to begin a second shift of childcare for very young children. The percentage of fathers with an employed wife who reports having too little time for himself does not vary dramatically by the employment hours of his wife—ranging from 55 percent to 58 percent.

Assessing Tradeoffs: Work Hours and Family Life

Over time, there has been a dramatic growth in the percentage of couples with children where both spouses experience the stresses and strains—and rewards—of combining market work with family caregiving. In two-parent families, an overwhelming majority has an employed father, and well over half have an employed mother. Although dual-earning has grown more prevalent over the last four decades and a large portion of these couples now work full-time hours, it is still relatively uncommon for couples to work extremely long hours for pay. Only about 3 percent of all parents in the prime "work and family" ages (age twenty-five to fifty-four) are in couples where both spouses work fifty or more hours per week—and these tend to be older couples without preschool-age children who are highly educated and presumably occupying some of the best jobs in the economy.

How big a problem long work hours is depends on the larger context and whether those working these long hours are doing so by choice. Results from the time-diary data suggest that time with children and with a spouse, as well as leisure and sleep, "give" way to finance market work hours, and that total workloads and expressions of time pressures—too little time for children, spouse, and self, and always feeling rushed—increase with long work hours, especially for mothers.

Yet few mothers work extremely long hours, particularly when their children are young. A sizable percentage of married mothers (more than one-third) are employed no hours, and an additional 20 percent of mothers work part-time hours. Without knowledge of parents' preferences, it is not entirely clear how to interpret these facts. On the one hand, mothers who are *not* putting in long hours may be doing so because they feel they must preserve sufficient time for the family. Full-time hours may be difficult to reconcile with family caregiving, let alone with more than full-time hours. As a result, however, these mothers may be foregoing the best jobs in the economy. On the other hand, mothers who are working no hours may or may not be doing so out of choice. A sizable fraction of these mothers have only a high school education or less, and the costs of employment (e.g., childcare) may outweigh the economic benefit. Another issue for all mothers (and fathers) is whether they can afford to "outsource" tasks such as housework, and whether they are able and comfortable with "outsourcing" the care of their children and the other tasks of family caregiving. Recent findings reported by the Pew Research Center suggest that at least among mothers, fewer hours may be better. That is, working mothers are less likely to find full-time employment ideal and are more likely to find part-time employment ideal today than ten years ago. Furthermore, the percentage of nonemployed mothers who prefer not to work outside the home has increased over the last ten years from 39 percent to 48 percent (Taylor, Funk, and Clark 2007).

Fathers are an important part of this picture. Fathers, who are more likely to work long hours than mothers, may or may not feel they have a choice about working those hours. At the same time, fathers' long paid work hours may be part of the reason why mothers in some families feel they must curtail their hours of employment. Someone must focus on family caregiving—and that someone remains, more often than not, the mother.

This analysis is limited by the cross-sectional nature of the data available to gauge parents' time allocations. One can examine the association between (long) work hours and other uses of time (e.g., how many hours parents work and how they spend their time in other activities during their diary day), but it is less clear what motivates parents to work the hours they do. While a pattern of gains and losses is present in certain time use activities, it cannot be assumed with absolute certainty that "sacrifices" in some activities are done with the expressed interest of "financing" the pursuit of others.

As documented here, a high percentage of mothers, regardless of employment status or hours, feel they are multitasking most of the time, and many employed mothers and fathers feel they have too little time with their children and with each other. However, solving time conflicts and pressures requires assessing the alternatives. The data suggest that families may be weighing the alternatives: parents appear to give up some sleep, some time with children, some time with each other, and a fair amount of leisure in order to increase their paid employment. Yet one of the big factors to give way to time pressures in busy two-parent families with children still seems to be the mother's hours of employment. Full-time employment is still not modal for mothers with children under age eighteen: only 45 percent of all married mothers work full-time hours. Hence, gender specialization in the family continues. Any solution to the "long hours" problem will have to be cognizant of the "short hours" response—jobs with long hours requirements and husbands in jobs with long hours induce a response, and the response is for mothers to shorten their hours, presumably because they decide this is best for the family. However, shortening fathers' hours or curbing long hours in good jobs may just pressure mothers to increase their paid work hours. This may be good for gender equality in the family, but it may not do much to ensure adequate time for family caregiving or the other activities of daily life that contribute to balance, health, and well-being.

2

MULTITASKING AMONG WORKING FAMILIES

A Strategy for Dealing with the Time Squeeze

Shira Offer and Barbara Schneider

Multitasking, or doing more than one activity at a given moment, has become a way of life for most U.S. working families. Considering the complexity of contemporary everyday life, it often seems that there is no other way to get things done but to do many things at once. Among working parents, for whom time is a particularly scarce resource, multitasking has become a strategy for juggling the growing demands of work and family. Talking on the phone while driving, fixing dinner while assisting children with their homework, and preparing for a meeting with a client while scheduling a doctor appointment may be the way to be more efficient and squeeze in more tasks within a limited twenty-four-hour day. But is it really the case? Does multitasking, the simultaneous performance of several tasks or the rapid alternation between them, really help working parents better manage their hectic lives? And what are the emotional benefits and costs of engaging in multiple tasks at the same time?

This issue has been the subject of extensive debate in the popular media over the last few years. Some argue that the development of new technologies, especially the Internet and mobile communication devices, has made it easier for people to carry on multiple tasks simultaneously. Particular attention has been dedicated to the impact of multitasking on productivity as well as its costs (e.g., Healy 2004; Javid and Varney 2007; Wallis 2006). Neuroscientists emphasize the cognitive limits of the human brain, and argue that rather than enhancing efficiency, multitasking slows us down and increases our probability of committing errors (Rubinstein, Meyer, and Evans 2001). Multitasking may also take its toll at the psychological level, by increasing stress and role overload (Bianchi, Robinson, and Milkie 2006).

This study seeks to promote our understanding of the patterns, characteristics, and emotional correlates of multitasking among working parents. Although recent research suggests that multitasking is highly prevalent among working families and that it has increased in the last couple of decades (Bianchi, Robinson, and Milkie 2006), this important issue has been largely neglected in sociological research. But serious questions remain as to how working parents make use of their time in their attempt to better balance work and family responsibilities, and the extent to which multitasking constitutes a strategy for dealing with this challenge. This study uses the Experience Sampling Method (ESM), a form of time diary that provides information about primary and secondary activities, from the 500 Family Study. Findings from the ESM and survey data are combined to address the following questions: (a) How frequently do working parents multitask? (b) Where, when, and what do parents typically do when they multitask? (c) How do they feel when they multitask?

The availability of data about subjective emotional experiences is a major advantage of the ESM. These data allow us not only to examine more carefully simultaneously performed tasks in their everyday context, but they also provide the means to assess the relationship between multitasking, emotional affect, and the social and psychological well-being of parents. Finally, by looking at the multitasking experiences of mothers and fathers separately, the 500 Family Study contributes to our understanding of gender inequalities in contemporary working families.

Background

Working Families and the Time Squeeze

Increased global competition, the move towards a 24/7 economy, and an organizational culture that increasingly rewards long work hours have all substantially altered the occupational conditions and work experiences of many contemporary workers. Growing job demands, together with the decline in job security and stability, have created new challenges for workers and their families, most notably a severe time squeeze. The experience of time pressure has been a major problem for working parents, who typically spend long hours in market work. Jacobs and Gerson (2004) indicate that although the overall combined weekly work hours of husbands and wives has slightly increased since the 1970s, the percentage of families in which both husbands and wives work very long hours has substantially grown, primarily as a result of women's increased involvement in paid work (see also Bond et al. 2003; Gornick and Meyers 2003). The experience of a time crunch is even more severe when nonmarket work is taken into account. Bianchi and her associates (2006) show that the total workload—time spent on both paid and unpaid work—of parents has risen substantially since the mid-1960s.

Demanding jobs and the need to coordinate between two work schedules have made juggling work and family obligations in dual-earner families particularly challenging. More time spent at work typically means less time available for other pursuits, as heavy workloads are perceived to interfere with family life and other nonwork-related activities (Nock and Kingston 1984; Pleck and Staines 1985). They are also associated with potential conflicts over time allocation and time usage (Moen and Howery 1988). Thus the need to fulfill multiple roles and to address their diverse needs and those of their families has required working parents to set new priorities and develop strategies that will allow them to make improved use of their time and better manage their busy lives.

For example, as women's participation in the labor force has increased, the amount of time they have devoted to housework has significantly declined. Although women spend significantly more hours than men doing weekly household chores and are more likely to perform the more difficult and less flexible domestic tasks (Hochschild 1989; Lee 2006; Milkie and Peltola 1999), they spend less time on housework than their counterparts in the 1960s (Bianchi et al. 2000; Robinson and Godbey 1999). The decline in time allocated to housework may have resulted from the growing tendency of many families, particularly those of higher socioeconomic status, to outsource housekeeping chores, such as cleaning services and take-out meals, or to increase their use of technological devices that have made housework more efficient. This decline may also reflect a normative change regarding the importance of housework, implying that homes today are less tidy than they used to be in the past.

Similarly, research suggests that unlike what many have feared, the amount of time that parents, particularly mothers, spend with their children has not significantly decreased following their growing involvement in market work (Bianchi 2000; Bond, Galinsky, and Swanberg 1998; Sandberg and Hofferth 2001). On the contrary, it seems that mothers have developed strategies to maximize their time with children, such as cutting back on housework and including children in their leisure and other activities (Bianchi, Robinson, and Milkie 2006).

Work and family demands, on the other hand, seem to have curtailed free time. Over the years, free time, as well as time with one's spouse, has declined. Recent research suggests that in this domain too there is a noteworthy gender differential. Women report having less time available for leisure and being more likely to have their free time contaminated by less enjoyable activities done simultaneously (Bittman and Wajcman 2000; Mattingly and Bianchi 2003).

Multitasking as a Strategy for Dealing with the Time Squeeze

In light of the growing complexity of everyday life and the persistent experience of a time shortage, multitasking can be a strategy for busy working families to orchestrate their lives and discharge simultaneous work and family obligations. Carrying on several duties at once can help parents gain time by getting more things done in less time. Bianchi et al. (2006) report that multitasking almost doubled for working parents between 1975 and 2000. Using time diary data, they find that the number of multitasking hours per week increased from forty-two to eighty-one for married mothers and from forty to seventy-eight for married fathers.

The question is whether multitasking has allowed parents to accomplish more. Recent research suggests that multitasking at home is highly prevalent. Housework today is typically done in parallel with other tasks (Lee 2006). Similarly, as noted above, parents are more likely to be engaged in childcare while simultaneously doing other activities. According to Zick and Bryant's (1996) estimate, as much as 34 percent of the total time spent on childcare is carried out as a secondary activity (see also Craig 2006).

Multitasking, however, is a typically gendered issue. According to many scholars, women are more likely to multitask than men. Melody Hessing (1994), who interviewed women employed in clerical jobs, indicates that working mothers often manipulate time by performing several chores at once, both at work and at home, in order to save time and run their household more smoothly. The formal and more rigid requirements of the workplace make time at work less flexible and less prone to manipulations compared to time at home. According to Hessing, the synchronization of tasks and events represents a management strategy used by women in response to the double burden they typically shoulder (see also Hochschild 1989, 1997). Hence, accounting for secondary activities can provide more accurate estimates of differentials in time use and help reveal sources of gender inequality in contemporary families. Craig (2006), for example, shows that even when they work full-time, mothers spend significantly more time than fathers in childcare. They assume a larger share of the physical care of children, and are more likely to engage in pleasurable activities with their children while performing other tasks, rather than as a sole activity, as fathers do. Multitasking in this context allows mothers to increase their time with children.

In sum, multitasking is an important part of the adaptation process that working families, specifically working mothers, have undergone as the balancing of work and family demands has become more challenging. Viewed in this way, multitasking can help assess the extent to which working parents have sped up their daily lives (Bianchi, Robinson, and Milkie 2006). But what are the costs that these families pay for running such hectic lives, and what are the implications of multitasking for parents' well-being and family functioning?

Consequences for Emotional Well-Being

The experience of time pressures has serious repercussions for working parents' well-being. Feeling rushed and the frustration of not having enough time for oneself and one's family are very common (Bianchi, Robinson, and Milkie 2006;

Robinson and Godbey 1999). Galinsky et al. (2005) found that more than a quarter of all workers in their study felt overworked and overwhelmed by how much work they had to do. Job-related time constraints are also associated with feelings of guilt about neglecting one's family (Voydanoff 1988). It is therefore not surprising that many parents report a discrepancy between their actual and ideal number of weekly work hours. Particularly among parents of young children, the number of parents who wish to work less (i.e., have shorter workweeks or fewer workweeks a year) is high (Galinsky, Kim, and Bond 2001; Jacobs and Gerson 2004; Reynolds 2005).

The negative spillover effects of work are also more pronounced among those who work long hours. Duxbury, Lyons, and Higgins (2008) argue that the move toward an organizational culture that rewards long hours and more time-demanding jobs has heightened the struggle of workers to combine work and family demands. Using data from a large nationally representative sample of working Canadians, they find an association between extended work hours and role overload. Consistent with their finding, other studies show that levels of work-family conflict are higher in this segment of the working population (Golden and Wiens-Tuers 2006; Jacobs and Gerson 2004; Moen and Yu 2000), among whom the desire to work fewer hours is particularly acute (Gray et al. 2004; Jacobs and Gerson 2004; Moen and Dempster-McClain 1987).

The negative implications of working long hours raise the question of the impact of multitasking on parents' well-being. While multitasking may be a strategy for working parents to get more things done in less time, it can significantly increase their level of stress and take a toll on their emotional well-being and level of functioning. Cognitive research suggests that multitasking is not a very efficient way to accomplish tasks. On the contrary, it has been associated with a reduction in efficiency and lower levels of productivity.

There are limits to the amount of information that our brains can process at once. People can easily perform automatic actions that do not draw on mental resources, such as eating, together with other more complicated tasks. In this case, performance is not likely to be impaired. But when the tasks in question are not done automatically but rather require conscious thought, attention, and planning, efficiency significantly decreases. In their famous study, Rubinstein, Meyer, and Evans (2001) demonstrate that the amount of time lost while switching repeatedly between two tasks increased as a function of the tasks' complexity. But multitasking may impinge on other aspects of human functioning and well-being. For example, employed mothers, who reported multitasking more frequently than their nonemployed counterparts, were also more likely to report feeling rushed and time squeezed (Bianchi, Robinson, and Milkie 2006). One major goal of the present study is to examine the effects of multitasking on working parents' well-being.

The 500 Family Study

Data and Sample

This study is based on data from the 500 Family Study. The 500 Family Study, conducted by the Alfred P. Sloan Center on Parents, Children, and Work, was designed to collect comprehensive information about the experiences of middle-class dual-earner parents and their children at work and at home (Schneider and Waite 2005). The 500 Family Study is a predominantly non-Hispanic white middle-class sample of dual-earner families and their children. The parents in the 500 Family Study are highly educated; most of the fathers and mothers have at least a college degree. The vast majority of the parents hold professional occupations, with almost one-third of all mothers and fathers being employed as executives or managers. The parents in the study work long hours on average; more than 50 percent of fathers and more than 20 percent of mothers report working forty-six hours a week or more. These numbers are higher than the averages reported in a nationally representative sample of middle-class families (Hoogstra 2005). As can be expected from their educational and occupational status, the families in the study earn relatively high incomes; more than 50 percent of fathers and 14 percent of mothers earn more than $75,000 per year.

A major advantage of the 500 Family Study is that, in addition to survey data, it also provides high-quality information about family members' use of time. It employs the Experience Sampling Method (ESM), a form of time diary, to collect information about activities and emotional experiences in the course of a typical day. The ESM used preprogrammed wristwatches to randomly beep participants several times a day during their waking hours. When signaled, respondents were asked to fill out a questionnaire in which they described their primary and secondary activities and feelings, and provided additional information about their surroundings. The ESM thus provides an invaluable opportunity for studying real-time activities and emotional experiences as they occur in natural settings. It is considered a valid and reliable instrument for examining time uses, subjective experiences, and emotional states (Csikszentmihalyi and Larson 1987; Robinson 1999; Warner 1986).

Analyses in this study are based on a subsample of parents drawn from the 500 Family Study, which includes 719 respondents (417 mothers and 302 fathers) in dual-earner families who filled out both the ESM and the survey questionnaires.

Measures

In the ESM, respondents were asked about their primary activity ("What was the main thing you were doing?") as well as secondary activity, if they had any ("What else were you doing at the same time?"). These two items were used to construct a multitasking measure, indicating whether the respondent was engaged in two simultaneous activities when beeped. The *proportion of multitasking beeps* (out of respondent's total number of beeps) for each respondent was then calculated. Respondents were also asked where they were and who was present with them.

In the next stage, all reported primary and secondary activities were classified into the six following broad categories: *work* (refers to work activities done at work, work activities done at home, and nonwork activities done at work such as socializing with co-workers); *housework* (includes child care and shopping); *free time* (leisure activities, hobbies, watching TV, reading, listening to radio, participating in religious events, volunteering, visiting others, doing sports, and using computer for nonwork purposes); *personal care* (includes sleeping, resting, relaxing, and eating meals); *interacting with others* (includes talking with, playing with, kissing, hugging, and fighting with others); and *transport* (includes driving, chauffeuring, and walking). This categorization was used to examine the types of activities that get combined together.

Using a list of emotional states, respondents to the ESM were also asked to indicate how they were feeling when beeped. Three emotional indexes were computed: positive affect, negative affect, and productivity. *Positive affect* is based on three items asking the extent to which respondent was feeling cheerful, relaxed, and good about herself or himself when signaled. *Negative affect* is based on the items of feeling irritated, frustrated, and stressed. *Productivity* is based on three items asking the extent to which respondent felt hardworking, productive, and succeeding in what he or she was doing. Each of these composite measures ranges from 0 to 3.

Finally, to assess the relationship between multitasking and parents' emotional well-being and social functioning, information provided in the survey in combination with the ESM was analyzed. *Work-family balance* refers to parents' assessment of how well they handle family and work responsibilities. It was computed as the mean of the following three survey items: "I feel confident about my ability to handle personal or family matters," "I feel confident about my ability to handle work-related matters," and "I feel I can't cope with everything I have to do." Responses range from 0 to 4 with higher scores indicating a higher degree of balance of family and work lives. *Negative feeling about work and family* is a two-item index, with a 0–4 range, indicating the extent to which the respondent feels bad and guilty about his or her family when working. *Depression* is measured with the Center for Epidemiologic Studies Depression scale (CES-D). The CES-D scale is a twenty-item self-report scale designed to measure the frequency of depressive symptoms in the general population. It is a valid and reliable scale widely used to measure depressive symptoms (Radloff 1991).

Marital quality is measured with an abbreviated version of the ENRICH inventory that includes fifteen items (Olson, Fournier, and Druckman 1987). Scores on this index, which has been normalized, range on a 0–100 scale. *Parent-child relationship* is based on six items that asked respondents to indicate the extent to which the following statements were true: (I am a parent who) "makes my children feel better when they talk over their worries with me," "likes to talk with my children and be with them much of the time," "enjoys talking things over with my children," "enjoys doing things with my children," "cheers my children up when they are sad," and "has a good time at home with my children." A mean across these six items was computed with scores ranging from 1 to 5 (higher scores indicating a better parent-child relationship).

Findings

Patterns of Multitasking

How often do working parents multitask? The results shown in table 2.1 indicate that overall working parents multitask slightly more than half of their waking time, which is the equivalent of approximately eight additional hours a day (.55 × fifteen hours a day). When free time activities (either as a primary activity, secondary activity, or both) are excluded, multitasking is performed in a little less than a third of parents' waking time. Mothers, however, multitask more often than fathers, although the difference is relatively small in size. The mean percentage of multitasking beeps is 58.3 and 51.7 for mothers and fathers respectively; 33.2 and 26.6 when free time activities are excluded.

However, figure 2.1 shows that some variation by gender exists regarding where working parents multitask. Although both mothers and fathers multitask more often at home than in other settings, the percentage of multitasking beeps at home is significantly higher for mothers (56.6) than for fathers (48.3). Fathers, on the other hand, are more likely than mothers to multitask at work (the percentage of multitasking beeps at work is 25.2 and 18.2, respectively). Both mothers and fathers, however, spend about a quarter of the time they multitask in transport or leisure.

Not surprisingly, working parents tend to be with their children when they multitask (see figure 2.2). More than 35 percent of all multitasking beeps are in the presence of children. But this result is mainly derived from the high percentage obtained for mothers. When they multitask, mothers are substantially more likely than fathers to be with their children (39.7% and 28.4% of all multitasking beeps, respectively). Working parents, particularly fathers, also tend to multitask when they are

Table 2.1.   Mean Proportion of Multitasking Beeps

	ALL SAMPLE	MOTHERS	FATHERS
All multitasking beeps	55.52 (17.59)	58.31 (16.93)	51.68 (17.71)***
Multitasking beeps excluding free time	30.57 (13.16)	33.42 (13.26)	26.61 (11.97)***

Source: 500 Family Study.
* p ≤ .05; ** p ≤ .01; *** p ≤ .001 (two-tailed tests).
N = 719; standard deviations in parentheses.

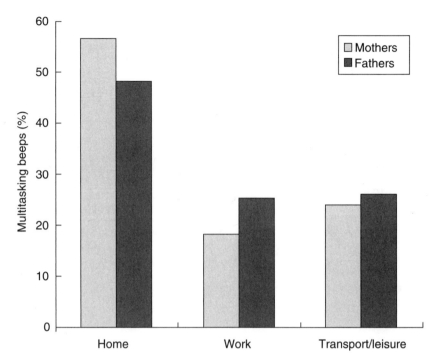

FIGURE 2.1.   Sites of multitasking

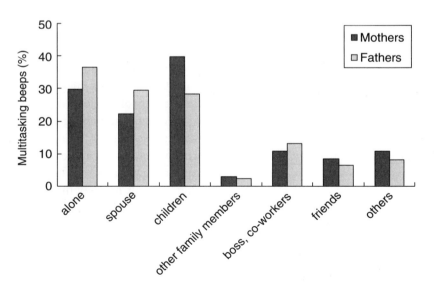

FIGURE 2.2.   Multitasking while alone and in the presence of others

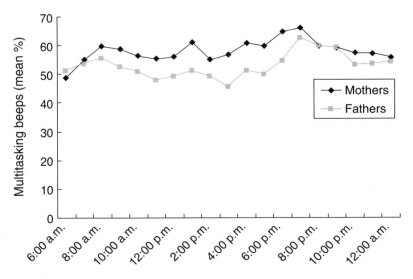

FIGURE 2.3.   Multitasking throughout the day

with their spouse (22.2% for mothers and 29.6% for fathers) or alone (29.8% for mothers and 36.6% for fathers). For both parents, multitasking in the presence of other people, such as co-workers, friends, and relatives, is much less common.

Consistent with these results, figure 2.3 shows that multitasking typically takes place at times when parents are with their children. Multitasking reaches its peak during the early evening hours (around 6 or 7 p.m.), which corresponds to dinnertime and children's bedtime routine. More than 60 percent of all the activities carried on during these hours involve multitasking. Multitasking also increases in the morning (around 8 a.m.), when family members typically prepare and depart for work and school, and in the late afternoon (around 4 p.m.), when children get back home and often need to be chauffeured to their after-school activities. These results are also consistent with the previous finding indicating that working parents are less likely to multitask at work. Figure 2.3 demonstrates that multitasking decreases during the morning work hours. A slight increase is observed around lunchtime. During every hour of the day, except in the early morning (6 a.m.) and late evening, mothers are more likely to multitask than fathers. Overall, however, the pattern of multitasking throughout the day is similar for mothers and fathers.

Combinations of Activities

What do working parents typically do when they multitask? First, a 6×6 table (not shown) based on the classification of primary and secondary activities into broader categories was used (work, housework, free time, personal care, interacting with others, and transport) to identify the most common multitasking combinations. Then, for ease of interpretation, only those combinations that are analytically meaningful for this study were recategorized and analyzed. Work activities were further decomposed into work activity at work, nonwork related activity at work, and work activity at home. The results are presented in figure 2.4. The most frequent combination for mothers is doing housework as a primary activity and something else as a secondary activity, such as talking to children (28.5% of the time), talking to spouse (9.9%), watching TV (9.4%), listening to the radio (7.9%), and snacking, eating, or drinking (7.8%). Doing two housework-related activities is also relatively common, but significantly more so for mothers than fathers (7.9% of all multitasking beeps among mothers compared to 4% among fathers).

The most frequent multitasking combination for fathers is simultaneously doing two work-related activities at work (more than 14% of all multitasking beeps). This combination is also relatively common for mothers, but to a lesser extent (10.7%). For both mothers and fathers, combining work as a primary activity with something else (i.e., a nonwork related activity) as a secondary activity, such as socializing with co-workers, taking a break, and talking to family members, is relatively rare (less than 2% of all multitasking beeps). It is also unusual to combine working at home as a primary activity with doing something else; only 2% of all multitasking (MT) beeps correspond to this combination. On the other hand, multitasking is frequently done during transportation by both mothers and fathers (8.9%

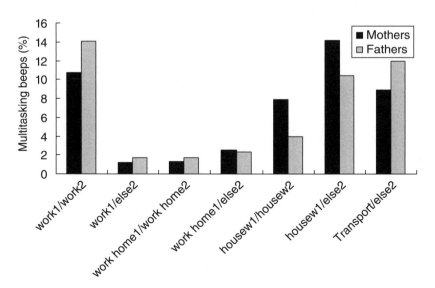

FIGURE 2.4. Combined activities of mothers and fathers by percent of multitasking beeps. "Work" = work-related activity at work; "work home" = work-related activity performed at home; "housew" = housework activity including childcare; "transport" = activities such as driving and chauffeuring; "else" = all activities performed in the other domains.

and 11.9%, respectively). Parents often drive while they listen to the radio or music (31.6%) and talk to their children (12.6%) or spouse (10.5%).

Multitasking and Parents' Well-Being

How do working parents feel when they multitask, and how is multitasking related to their sense of social and psychological well-being? If multitasking is a strategy for negotiating multiple demands and serves as a proxy for life speedup among working parents, then it is likely to be associated with productivity, but also with increased stress and other negative experiences. To examine these hypotheses, multitasking was restricted by excluding MT beeps in which either the primary activity, the secondary activity, or both activities were in the category of free time. The associations between the proportion of MT beeps and the composite ESM emotional measures are summarized in table 2.2. As expected, multitasking was associated with higher productivity for both mothers and fathers. But for mothers, multitasking was also associated with negative emotional affect. As multitasking increased, mothers reported feeling more frustrated, irritated, and stressed. No significant association was found between multitasking and positive affect.

Table 2.2 further displays the correlations between the proportion of MT beeps and several indicators of well-being and social and psychological functioning drawn from the survey. None of the correlations was statistically significant for fathers. For mothers, increased multitasking was associated with higher scores on the index of negative feeling about work and family (i.e., these mothers were more likely to have guilt feelings about their family when they work). Multitasking,

Table 2.2. Correlations with Proportion of Multitasking Beeps

	MOTHERS	FATHERS
EMOTIONAL EXPERIENCES (ESM)		
Positive affect	.026	.087
Negative affect	.139**	.073
Productivity	.149**	.121*
SOCIAL AND PSYCHOLOGICAL WELL-BEING (SURVEY)		
Work-family balance	−.045	.051
Negative feelings about work and family	.173**	.101
Depression	.044	−.021
Marital quality	−.089	−.083
Parent-child relationship	.116*	.037

Source: 500 Family Study.
* p ≤ .05; ** p ≤ .01; *** p ≤ .001 (two-tailed tests).
N = 719.

however, was not associated with negative views of work-family balance. With respect to family relations and social functioning, more positive scores on the parent-child relationship index were obtained for increased multitasking. This result is consistent with past studies showing that working mothers often engage with their children while doing other things, including having them take part in leisure activities, as a way to expand their time with them (Bianchi, Robinson, and Milkie 2006). It is therefore not surprising to find that multitasking is associated with a positive parent-child relationship. The correlation between proportion of multitasking beeps and marital quality, although negative in sign, was very small and not statistically significant.

Conclusion: Multitasking as a Source of Gender Inequality

Working parents frequently multitask, and they do so in every context: at home, at work, and during their free time. The results of this study indicate that, on average, parents multitask about half of their waking time, the equivalent of eight additional hours of activities a day. Although this number is slightly smaller than the one reported by Bianchi and her associates (2006), it clearly indicates that multitasking is the way things are done in contemporary working families.

Both mothers and fathers multitask most often at home rather than in other settings, including their workplace. This finding implies that there is more time elasticity and flexibility at home, which, consistent with Hessing's (1994) observations, allows parents to more easily manipulate time and strategize in this context. Home is the main arena of multitasking; it is where parents attempt to squeeze in more tasks. Multitasking at work is less prevalent and different in nature. When parents are involved in market work, they tend to focus on it and are less "distracted" by nonwork-related matters. The results indicate that when parents do multitask at work, they usually engage in two work-related activities.

Although neuroscientists have shown that multitasking is a rather inefficient way to perform tasks and bears significant cognitive costs, this study finds that for both mothers and fathers, multitasking is associated with feeling productive. If much of parents' multitasking is done as part of household-related tasks that have become highly routinized and can be accomplished relatively easily in conjunction with other tasks, such as cooking, cleaning, and supervising children as they play, then this finding is not surprising.

Following this logic, the finding that parents multitask less at work is not surprising either. One can plausibly argue that in this particular sample of predominantly professional dual-earner couples, work-related tasks are likely to require thought, concentration, and planning, and will therefore be less subject to multitasking. Another explanation could be that parents feel productive and in control of the situation at the very moment of multitasking, but the toll of engaging in two activities simultaneously comes up later. It is possible that parents need to "recover" from particularly intensive episodes of having done many things at once. These effects will not be captured by examining multitasking beeps only.

But most important, the results of this study underscore the gendered nature of multitasking, and contribute to our understanding of gender inequalities in contemporary working families. Multitasking is clearly a strategy used by women to get things done. Although mothers were found to multitask only a little more often than fathers, the meaning and implications of multitasking substantially differs by gender. Mothers were less likely than fathers to multitask at work but substantially more likely to multitask while doing housework, either engaging in two housework-related activities or doing housework and something else at the same time. They were also significantly more likely to multitask in the presence of children and during hours of the day that correspond to intensive childcare activities, such as the morning and late afternoon. This finding is consistent with Craig's (2006) results regarding the gendered nature of childcare. It suggests not only that mothers' share of childcare is larger than that of fathers' but that mothers are more likely to include children in their other activities. However, unlike Bittman and Wajcman's (2000) findings regarding mothers' contaminated free time, this study finds that multitasking is beneficial for mothers' relationships with children.

Finally, although a positive association was found between multitasking and feeling productive among both mothers and fathers, multitasking was also related to negative affect (i.e., feeling irritated, frustrated, and stressed)—but only among mothers. This finding provides further empirical support to the hypothesis that working mothers pay a heavy emotional toll for multitasking (Bianchi, Robinson, and Milkie 2006). This could be explained by the type of activities that mothers typically combine. Doing two household chores at the same time is not very pleasurable. But it could also reflect mothers' perception of being the "household manager." In addition to providing for the basic needs of the family, mothers are perceived to be the main person responsible for organizing and synchronizing the schedules of their family members, planning events and activities, and creating social ties.

Multitasking may help mothers manage the demands of work and home by getting more things done in less time, but it does not relieve them of the physical and psychological stress associated with this double burden. Many of these tasks tend to be taken for granted by mothers and therefore underreported as secondary activities (Lee 2006; Schneider 2006; Zick and Bryant 1996). This implies that the heavy workload and the negative implications of multitasking for mothers' well-being may be even more pronounced than this study indicates.

3

COMING TOGETHER AT DINNER

A Study of Working Families

Elinor Ochs, Merav Shohet,
Belinda Campos, and Margaret Beck

Family mealtimes have received considerable attention in the popular media as a barometer of family well-being. Dinnertime, they report, is an endangered or defunct family ritual that has given way to the demands of parents' work and children's extracurricular activities (RMC Research Corporation 2005). In the United States, as in other societies, the family dinner is viewed as an icon of the family and an ideal toward which contemporary families should strive. Cultural expectations that the family should eat a healthy home-cooked meal together present a challenge to working parents, whose finite time and energies are too often expended on workplace demands.

This study examines the extent to which, and how, working parents and their children manage to come together to share an evening meal. Eating together is a primordial form of sociality, often defining boundaries for a social group (Dumont 1980; Lévi-Strauss 1963, 1969; Malinowski 1935). Across communities and historical time, sharing a meal has constituted an important locus for reifying and structuring social order and for social sense-making. Beyond fulfilling the body's biological need for nourishment, mealtimes are vital cultural sites that are "historically durable, yet transformable, socially organized and organizing, and tempospatially situated arenas, which are laden with symbolic meanings and mediated by material artifacts" (Ochs and Shohet 2006, 35). Distinctions in food types and manner of preparation, along with meal duration, locale, participation, communication, and demeanor are historically rooted, conventionalized, and morally evaluated. Indeed, as Norbert Elias (2000 [1939]) observes, table manners have been viewed as critical to good breeding and "the civilizing process" since at least the Middle Ages. For this reason, mealtime practices are deeply intertwined with social hierarchies (Bourdieu

1979), and mealtimes themselves are cultural sites of socialization into standards of comportment and taste (Ochs, Pontecorvo, and Fasulo 1996).

Yet the structure of mealtimes is also dynamic and subject to shifting social and economic exigencies and preferences. Eating together under the same roof was a singularly defining feature of peasant family communities in the late Middle Ages (Segalen 1986). Yet shared family mealtimes at home as a routine, bounded formal activity in Europe and the United States have been strongly associated with industrialization, which separated the worlds of work and home, and deemed the home a private sphere for cultivating family (Cinotto 2006; Davidoff and Hall 2002; DeVault 1991; Draznin 2001; Gillis 1989; Jordan 1987). The construction of dining rooms, the centrality of the dining table, and the act of dining together on a regular basis became markers of status for the middle class and beyond. Judith Flanders (2003) notes the social importance of dinnertime in Victorian England:

> Dinner had, earlier, been a meal eaten at midday....By midcentury, when most middle-class men were no longer working at home, dinner moved to the later hour of five or six, after the office workers returned home. From this hour, those who did not have to get up for work the next morning pushed dinner ever later, as a sign of leisure. The upper middle classes copied them, in order to indicate their own gentility, and the middle classes, in turn, followed their lead, in order to separate themselves from those beneath them. (266)

In the United States, the Victorian standard of families eating dinner around the table during evenings at home has waxed and waned over time. For example, in their study of Middletown in the 1920s, Lynd and Lynd (1929) report that families bemoaned the decline of the family dinner ritual in their community. Decades later, the 1950s middle class family apparently insisted on dinnertime as a centerpiece of the "Leave It to Beaver" American way of life. However, it is difficult to gauge the extent to which the family dinner meal historically and currently constitutes an ideal toward which families strive rather than a quotidian practice in American households (Cinotto 2006).

The concern with the status of the family meal and, more particularly, family dinnertime in the United States, is highly palpable in public health, social science, literature, film, television, and the popular press. Family dinners are potent cultural sites for generating wistful longings for an arguably imagined past or a possible future family way of life (Sutton 2001). In addition, family meals are charged with exceptional predictive powers for children's well-being and, as a corollary, for sustaining the family as a stable unit. Surveys of family food consumption in the United States link children's reported nutritional habits to their reported participation in family dinners (Neumark-Sztainer et al. 2004; RMC Research Corporation 2005). Recent publications with titles such as *The Surprising Power of Family Meals: How Eating Together Makes Us Smarter, Stronger, Healthier and Happier* (Weinstein 2005) and a plethora of fact-sheet-type websites attest to a public yearning to see family mealtimes as a resource for curing many ills of contemporary life such as family dissolution, childhood eating disorders, cigarette, alcohol and drug use, depression, and low educational achievement.

In addition to frequency of family mealtimes, the composition of family meals, especially the fate of the home-cooked family dinner, and the gendering of food preparation have been a source of considerable attention. Social and cultural studies of food practices have emerged as a lively area of research, relating food preferences and taboos to social status, social relationships, and esthetic, moral, and religious frameworks (De Matos Viegas 2003; Grieshaber 1997; Murcott 1982, 1995; Ochs, Pontecorvo, and Fasulo 1996; Sobal, Bove, and Rauschenbach 2002; Thompson 1994). These studies document the importance of creating, solidifying, and structuring human relationships through daily meals across the world's societies, and examine ideologies surrounding the intake of foods and folk models of what constitutes a meal.

In the United States, popular media describe a trend toward cooking less or not at all (e.g., Scattergood 2006; Scrivani 2005; Visser 1989), one that some individuals make a self-conscious and deliberate attempt to reverse (Calta 2005; Jones et al. 2003; Pisano 2006; Severson and Moskin 2006). Despite their fascination with cooking shows, books, and equipment, modern Americans "eat breakfast in their cars, lunch at their desks and chicken from a bucket" (Scrivani 2005, 15). Some authors suggest that all of the information and resources for cooking in the modern United States may actually overwhelm potential cooks, producing "a terrible anxiety-ridden limbo. There are the empty Calphalon pots. The waiting stove. The drawers full of enticing magazine recipes…but what to serve for dinner three hours from now?" (Scattergood 2006, F1). The failure to plan meals ahead of time may be increasingly common, complicating at-home meal preparation and increasing the expense involved (Chatzky 2006). The *New York Times* reports a "50-year slide away from home cooking," and quotes one parent frustrated with the entire task: "We're always hearing that eating dinner together is the cure for obesity, learning disorders, drugs, divorce, and every kind of problem we have in society…but what no one tells you is how to do all that cooking" (Severson and Moskin 2006).

Although in some contexts, cooking may be a form of religious expression (Sered 1988) and a source of domestic influence (Counihan 1988), scholarship on dinner preparation in industrialized countries generally presents this task as a burden placed unequally on women. Women still report that food preparation is primarily their responsibility, although they spend less time cooking than women in earlier historical periods (Bittman 1995; DeVault 1991; Lupton 2000). It becomes increasingly difficult to find time for this and other household tasks with increased female participation in the workforce, producing significant identity conflicts for some women (Counihan 1988).

Several surveys indicate that children and parents in the United States frequently eat dinner together, but results vary with the age of the child and the ethnicity of the family. The Child Trends Data Bank survey (2003) found that 56 percent of American children ages six to eleven and 42 percent of adolescents ate a meal with their family six or seven days a week. The frequencies were higher for foreign-born than native-born, and higher for Hispanic than non-Hispanic adolescents and young children. The 2004 Healthy Youth Survey in Washington State (RMC Research Corporation 2005) also found that the frequency of eating together declines in American families as children grow older: approximately 78 percent of sixth-grade children and 60 percent of tenth-grade children, for example, reported that they ate dinner with their families always or most of the time. Culling their biennial assessments of the home environment of children from 1986 to 1994, the National Longitudinal Survey of Youth (Bradley et al. 2001) found that nonpoor children ate together with both parents more often than poor children, and that frequencies varied across ethnicities. For example, 69 percent of nonpoor Euro-American and Hispanic children 6–9 years old reported eating a meal with both parents once a day or more, while 60 percent of nonpoor Asian American and 50 percent of nonpoor African American children reported eating a meal with both parents once a day or more.

Most of what is known about the patterning of family mealtimes in the United States is based on reported behavior, rather than direct observation of how, when, where, and how often family members eat dinner. When children report that they eat dinner with their families, it is not clear whether all family members are present, and whether all the family members are eating together at the same time and in the same place. Family members may eat in different rooms, for example, with one child eating in front of the television in a bedroom while other family members eat elsewhere. Or some family members may begin eating long before another family member comes to eat, whereupon the earlier diners may leave the latecomer to finish eating alone. Moreover, reports of which family member is preparing dinner, what he or she is preparing for dinner, and how long it takes to prepare a family dinner generally do not discern the different kinds of involvement in food preparation assumed by family members, and the extent to which a "home-cooked" meal consists of fresh ingredients, convenience foods (e.g., frozen pizza), or a combination of both.

The present anthropological study addresses these lacunae by presenting results of ethnographic observations of family dinnertime preparation and eating patterns across thirty U.S. dual-earner families, whose activities were videotaped during the workweek and on the weekend. This analysis articulates (a) a typology of dinnertime arrangements, (b) the frequencies with which these arrangements characterize the families in this study across the days they were observed, and (c) the status of particular family dinnertime arrangements as sociocultural *practices,* that is, as the outcome of a familial disposition or *habitus* that structures how they routinely participate in their everyday lifeworlds (Bourdieu 1977, 1990). Observations are then related to two popular idioms regarding the fate of family dinnertime in the American cultural imagination, namely the optimistic "Apple Pie" view that regular family dinners continue to characterize American family life, and the pessimistic "Gloom and Doom" view that regular family dinners are no longer viable in the busy lifestyle of contemporary American families.

Method

Participants

Families were recruited from the greater Los Angeles area as part of an Alfred P. Sloan Foundation–funded interdisciplinary investigation of the everyday lives of middle-class, dual-income families with young children. In the present study, thirty families from the UCLA Sloan Center on Everyday Lives of Families (CELF) data set were assessed. These thirty families were heterosexual, dual-income, middle-class households consisting of a married couple with two to three children, one of whom was required to be between the ages of eight and ten. As a marker of middle-class socioeconomic status, families were required to be homeowners with a monthly mortgage. Fliers and newspaper advertisements were used to recruit participants, and emphasis was placed on recruiting an ethnically and occupationally diverse sample. Families were compensated $1,000 in exchange for their participation in the study.

Procedure

CELF families participated in a study that used a combination of naturalistic observation and self-report methods, including ethnographic video-recordings and timed observations of daily activities, semistructured interviews, questionnaires, and salivary cortisol, to document daily family life. As part of this research project, each family was recorded by two videographers during the course of a week for two weekday mornings, late afternoons, and evenings; one Saturday morning; and one Sunday morning and evening. These video recordings yielded approximately fifty hours of video footage per family. To capture family and home life, video recording began as the family members rose to begin their morning routine, stopped during the school and workday, resumed once the children left school and parents left work, and continued throughout the evening until the children retired to bed for the night. Thus, family dinner practices were captured in the course of the standard videotaping procedure across three evenings. Researchers then used these video data to examine families' dinner-related behaviors.[1]

DEMOGRAPHICS

Participants self-reported their ethnic backgrounds, income, education levels, jobs, and number of hours worked per week. The sample was ethnically diverse, but the majority of parents were of white and non-Hispanic descent born outside the greater Los Angeles area, who lived in households with double the median Los Angeles County household income (median = $46,000; U.S. Census Bureau 2006b), and had at least a college degree. In terms of working hours, 63 percent of fathers and 50 percent of mothers reported working between forty and forty-nine hours per week, and 30 percent of fathers and 13 percent of mothers reported working over fifty hours per week.

FAMILY DINNER PARTICIPATION

A family dinner was defined as the main household meal of the evening, and the participation of each family member was documented. To understand the extent to which dinners were characterized by the full participation of the family members, dinners were organized as either having *no family member missing* or *family member(s) missing*. Dinners were then subcategorized into one of the following four patterns: (a) in *unison*, where all family members ate in the same location and at the same time; (b) in *partial unison*, where at least one member was missing but the remaining family members ate in the same location and at the same time; (c) *fragmented*, where family members ate dinner in different locations and/or at nonoverlapping times (i.e., with at least a 10-minute interval between start times); or (d) *part-fragmented*, where at least one member was missing and the remaining family members ate in different locations and/or at nonoverlapping times.

MEAL LENGTH

Meal length was calculated at individual and family levels. At the individual level, each family member's approximate start and stop time for eating was recorded. At the family level, family meal length was calculated as the time elapsed from the start time of the first family member who began eating, until the stop time of the last family member who finished eating. Individual and family meal lengths are both reported in minutes.

It was speculated that that concurrent engagement with noneating activities (e.g., watching television) during dinner may increase meal length. Therefore, family members' engagement in any concurrent activities during dinner was documented. Concurrent activities were defined as those occurring when one or more family members were observed engaging in a noneating activity during dinner (e.g., phone, television, homework).

MEAL PREPARATION

To assess labor distribution during meal preparation, the extent to which family members participated in making dinners cooked at home was documented. Dinners were characterized as being prepared by (a) Mom exclusively, (b) Dad exclusively, (c) Mom and Dad equally, (d) Mom and Dad, with Mom leading, (e) Mom and Dad, with Dad leading, (f) Mom and kids, or (g) other relatives/nanny.

To assess the labor involved in meal preparation, the extent to which meals were prepared *from scratch* (using basic/raw ingredients) or assembled *from commercial foods* was documented. Basic/raw ingredients include fresh vegetables, raw meat or fish, as well as dairy products, oils, dried pasta, and grains, among other items. A *commercial dish* was either purchased in finished form or finished by the home cook entirely according to package directions. Examples include pre-prepared frozen dishes such as pizza or pot pies. A *modified commercial dish* incorporates commercial items but is finished independently by the cook in a way not dictated by package directions. Examples include fish tacos made with frozen fish sticks, a baked pasta dish including commercial tomato sauce and pepperoni, or pigs-in-a-blanket (hot dogs wrapped in biscuit dough and baked). Meals cooked "from scratch" contained less than 20 percent commercial dishes and up to 50 percent modified commercial dishes.

Results

To assess whether the contemporary family dinner practices of this sample fit the idealized or pessimistic models of family dinnertime, it was important to first examine how often families were coming together for dinner. At the family level, the analysis revealed a mixed pattern. Although 77 percent of families had at least one dinner in unison during the three days, 63 percent of families had one or more fragmented dinners during the three days, and 50 percent of families had one or more family members not home at least one day during the three days filmed. Across the sample, only five families (17%) consistently ate dinner in unison across all three days, and seven families (23%) never ate dinner in unison across the three days. To better understand these initial patterns, the individual participation and preparation practices of family dinners were then examined.

Participating in Dinner

In terms of individual participation in family dinnertime, all family members were present for dinner at least 83 percent of the time. As table 3.1 shows, however, Dads were more likely to be missing at weekday dinners than Moms, but Moms and Dads showed more similar levels of dinner participation on the weekends. Since Dads were more likely to be missing on weekdays, it raised the question of whether these men reported working more hours per week than Dads who never missed a dinner. This did not turn out to be the case. Of the eight Dads who missed a weekday dinner, 50 percent reported working forty to forty-nine hours per week and the other 50 percent reported working more than fifty hours per week. Interestingly, of the five families who ate dinner in unison all three days, two fathers reported working more than fifty hours per week. Notably, both were self-employed and more likely to have a flexible schedule than their counterparts who were not self-employed.

Although Dads were more likely to be missing at weekday dinners than Moms, the majority of weekday and weekend dinners were still largely consistent with the idealized perception of families eating together in the same space and location. As

Table 3.1. Family Dinner by Meal Level: Participation on Weekdays and Weekends

PRESENCE AT DINNERS	WEEKDAYS (N = 58)		WEEKENDS (N = 26)	
	FREQUENCY	%	FREQUENCY	%
Mom	54	93	25	96
Dad	48	83	22	88
Child 1	56	97	25	96
Child 2	55	95	22	85
Child 3	16	89	6	100
Guests	7	12	4	13

Note: N = 60 possible meals on two weekdays for 30 families (2 meals were missing);
30 possible meals on one weekend day for 30 families (4 meals were missing).

table 3.2 shows, whether all members were present or not, families ate the majority of dinners in *unison* or *partial unison.* Of the forty-six weekday dinners when no family member was missing, 59 percent were eaten in unison. Similarly, of the twelve weekday dinners where one or more family members were missing, 67 percent were eaten in *partial unison.* A similar pattern was observed on the weekends. As table 3.2 shows, fewer than half of family dinners on weekdays and weekends were characterized as *fragmented* or *part-fragmented,* whether all members were present or not.

In these limited data, there appears to be no clear link between the number of hours worked and family participation in dinner. For example, the percentage of families that had dinner in unison every night during the study is actually slightly higher among families with one parent working 50+ hours a week (18%) than those with both parents working less than fifty hours a week (16%). However, there was some indication that the scheduling of work hours may be a greater impediment to family dinners than the number of hours worked. Thus, the discussion shifts to fathers, as they were significantly more likely than mothers to miss family meals. Eight fathers in eight different families self-reported weekly work schedules that regularly involve working until 7 p.m. or later. In two additional families, the fathers reported working long shifts ranging from twenty-four hours to three days. None of these ten families, which make up 33 percent of the sample, had dinner in unison every night during the study. In the eight families in which the father completely missed dinner at least once, four fathers reported that their workdays ended between 7 p.m. and 10:30 p.m. A fifth father, an airline pilot, works away from home in three-day shifts. A sixth father did not report his usual working hours but held multiple jobs, including an evening job as a sports instructor.

In contrast, of the five families that ate dinner in unison every night, only two families have one parent working as late as 6 p.m. or 6:15 p.m. and the other three

Table 3.2. Family Dinners by Meal Level: How Often Family Members Are Present on Weekdays and Weekends

	WEEKDAYS (N = 58)		WEEKENDS (N = 26)	
	FREQUENCY	%	FREQUENCY	%
NO FAMILY MEMBER MISSING				
Family in unison	27	59	15	75
Family fragmented	19	41	5	25
FAMILY MEMBER MISSING				
Family in part-unison	8	67	6	100
Family part-fragmented	4	33	0	0
IF NOT ALL AT HOME, WHO MISSING?				
Mom	1		1	
Dad	8		3	
Child 1	1		1	
Child 2	1		3	
Child 3	1		0	

Note: N = 60 possible meals on two weekdays for 30 families (2 meals were missing); 30 possible meals on one weekend day for 30 families (4 meals were missing). Percentages presented were calculated from total dinners characterized as *no family member missing* (46 weekday; 20 weekend) and *family member missing* (12 weekday; 6 weekend).

families reported one parent whose return times ranged from 3 p.m. to 5:15 p.m. Three of the five fathers reported being self-employed or small-business owners, with presumably more flexible schedules than others, and one of them worked from an office at home. A fourth father, a lawyer who ends work at 6 p.m., works forty-eight hours per week but comments that his government position provides "more time at home" (perhaps relative to other employers he considered) while his children are young.

Meal Length and Concurrent Activities

On average, family dinners lasted for an average of 29.50 minutes on the weekdays and 33.23 minutes on the weekends. The average eating times of individual family members and guests ranged from 16.25 to 24.67 minutes on weekdays to 20 to 39.50 minutes on the weekends, with young children showing the shortest dinner times and parents and weekend guests showing the longest dinner times. Previous research has suggested that engaging in nondinner activities during dinner is an increasingly common practice. This analysis, however, suggests that dinners without concurrent activities are still the norm. The majority of weekday dinners (n = 39, 69%) occurred without concurrent activities, and only 33 percent (n = 19) of weekday dinners had concurrent activities where one or more family members was doing homework, watching TV, or talking on the phone. This pattern also held true for the weekends. The majority of weekend dinners did not contain concurrent activities (n = 15, 58%) although 42 percent (n = 11) of weekend dinners did contain concurrent activities. When concurrent activities occurred during dinner, however, dinners were likely to be longer. Dinners with concurrent activities lasted forty minutes on average, whereas dinners without activities lasted twenty-five minutes on average.

MEAL PREPARATION

Idealized family dinners are perceived to be characterized by home-cooked meals, whereas pessimistic perceptions suggest that contemporary family dinners are characterized by convenience or take-out food. This study found that CELF families ate home-cooked meals 75 percent of the time on weeknights and 85 percent of the time on weekends. Many of these meals rely on commercial food, however, even though they are prepared (or at least heated up) at home. On weeknights, for example, only one-third of the forty-five home-cooked meals are prepared by a parent from scratch. Of all fifty-eight weeknight dinners, only 25 percent of the weeknight dinners were cooked by a parent from scratch (figure 3.1). A recent nationwide study reports that 32 percent of all dinners were prepared at home from scratch (Sloan 2006). This slightly lower figure may result from the use of direct observations rather than self-reported data, a stricter definition of "from scratch," or a focus on working parents or on weeknights, among other factors.

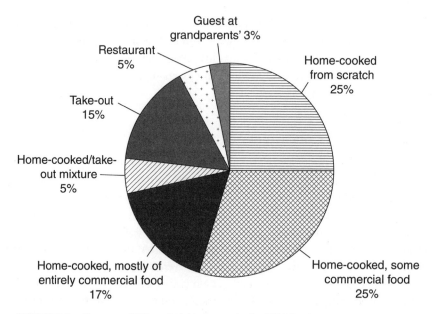

FIGURE 3.1. Sources of 58 weeknight dinners in the CELF Study

Consistent with previous research on the double shifts of working mothers, 60 percent of home-cooked meals were prepared exclusively by Mom, while only 7 percent of home-cooked meals were prepared exclusively by Dad. The study examined dinners in which Mom participated in the preparation, either by herself or with other members of her family, and found that Mom was involved in 91 percent of weekday dinners and 81 percent of weekend dinners, whereas Dad was involved in dinner preparation only 31 to 33 percent of the time. Thus, the labor of meal preparation appears to be disproportionately carried out by women.

Discussion: Reasons for Tempered Optimism

What do these observations indicate about the viability of dinnertime as a cultural site of family unity and healthy meals in the United States? Do the observations support the previously cited, relatively optimistic surveys that report roughly 50 to 70 percent of elementary school-age children eating a meal at home with their parents almost every day? Is the media avalanche bemoaning the demise of the family dinner warranted? Is the home-cooked meal still a family culinary tradition, or has it given way to take-out, restaurant, or other pre-prepared food alternatives? Have gender roles regarding meal preparation and participation remained unchanged since prefeminist times, or has there been a radical shift in response to the exigencies of two parents working outside the home?

The response to all but the last of these questions is a hedged positive, "yes, *but...*" Regarding children and their parents coming together for family dinner, the finding that most of the families ate at least one dinner all together across the week suggests that dinnertime continues to be a culturally important gathering for the families in this study, and supports an optimistic outlook for the robustness of this ritual. *But,* few families ate dinner all together consistently across the week, suggesting that bringing the whole family to the dinner table is not a quotidian practice among the families who were video-recorded.

On the optimistic side, when some or all family members come home for dinner during the week, they tend to eat together at one time and in one location, such as around a table. *But,* it is important to note that between 33 and 40 percent of the weekday dinnertimes involve some or all of the family members eating at different times or in different rooms of the house. During these fragmented meals, one or more family members begin eating ten minutes or more before another family member comes to eat. Upon his or her arrival, one or more of the other family members may already be leaving the dinner area. Another fragmented meal scenario involves one or more family members eating in one room, while another eats somewhere else in the house, such as in the bedroom watching television. Although it is heartening to observe that family members generally congregate for dinner, the fragmented family dinners observed here temper and nuance the more optimistic survey reports of kids and parents frequently eating dinner at home.

Can the busy work lives of parents account for the centripetal and centrifugal patterns of participation in family dinners? The finding that working Dads are missing from the dinner table significantly more often than working Moms might seem to make sense in light of the fact that Dads in this study worked longer hours than did Moms. *But,* a deeper look reveals that a simplistic correlation between work hours and family life is misleading: the Dads who missed family dinners did not work longer than those who came home to eat together with their families. Indeed, as noted, eating all together consistently across the week was more characteristic of families with a parent who worked more than fifty hours a week than of those with parents who worked fewer hours. Moreover, while relative flexibility in workplace schedules freed a few of the working parents to have dinner together with their families, flexible work hours did not account for which families ate in unison and which did not. Of five self-employed fathers, only two always had dinner together with their families, and two missed dinner at least once. Of the three fathers who own small businesses, only one always had dinner in unison with their families. Parents in this study who made it home for dinner left the workplace by about 6 p.m. Some of the work after 6 p.m. may have been voluntary, because it was undertaken by the self-employed or small business owners.

Three conclusions can be drawn from these findings: first, being self-employed or a small business owner with flexible hours does not ensure that a parent will always eat together with his or her family. Second, eating all together at dinner may be primarily a lifestyle decision to return home to engage in this family practice, at least among middle-class families. Third, leaving the workplace before dinnertime (in this sample, by roughly 6 p.m.) may be linked to families having dinner together, and so pursuing this option may help working parents who want to eat with their families. These results are consistent with other studies that found that work schedule, not number of work hours, has a significant effect on quality of life (Barnett 2006).

What about the fate of the home-cooked dinner? Defying the pessimistic position that spending time in the kitchen preparing a meal is a relic of the past, this study found that the vast majority of family dinners were cooked at home. *But* "home-cooked" requires greater scrutiny, in that a home-cooked dinner usually entailed heating up or otherwise preparing packaged foods rather than raw ingredients. The American home cook's reliance on convenience foods, however, may go back decades, as indicated by tuna casserole and other comfort food recipes in *The Joy of Cooking* (Rombauer 1931), which rely on canned or frozen items. Indeed, the editor of newer editions of the cookbook recently confessed that "In '97 we kind of lost our way…you had to make your own béchamel sauce to get the perfect tuna-fish casserole. But that is not what tuna casserole is about. It is about getting home and realizing that there's nothing in the fridge for dinner and that there is nothing wrong with tuna casserole from a can" (Steinhauer 2006, 82).

Preparing tuna casserole from a can is not the only dinner practice that has withstood the test of time and social upheavals in the United States. The gender asymmetry observed in working Dads' and Moms' presence at family dinners is matched in their asymmetrical roles in dinner preparation. As in other studies, the video-recordings, overwhelmingly and without caveat, affirm that Moms are still in the kitchen making dinner for the family most of the time. Even on the weekends, when Dads are present for 88 percent of the dinners, Dads rarely are the main chefs of the family dinner meal. Sociologist Luce Giard (1994) wrote "Manger sert...à concrétiser un des modes de relation entre la personne et le monde" (Eating serves...to concretize one of the modalities of relating the person and the world; 259). This study indicates that the practice of family dinnertime has a certain amount of resonance in the United States for concretizing the family as a social unit. After all, Moms in the study made an effort to prepare home-cooked meals and most families shared at least one dinner together. Yet, the inability of most families in the study to regularly eat together, the many families who ate dinner at home apart, and the quarter of the families who *never* ate together reveal the diminished status of dinnertime as an occasion for gathering the family in the sociocultural ecology of events that compose a family member's day.

As attested in health and well-being interviews conducted with parents in the study, and in side conversations during filming, the vast majority considered "eating well" to be an integral part of attaining and maintaining health, and most couples further related having home-cooked meals to "eating well" and "being healthy." Many parents likewise discussed their efforts to bring the family together for at least one meal a week, a practice borne out in our findings. Yet, parents also bemoaned their and their children's busy schedules, suggesting that today's "fast pace of life" often prevents them from all eating together at the same time. For some families, going out to eat as a family was a viable or preferred solution, while others relied on a combination of convenience foods and/or take-out meals at home, and enjoyed dinners that involve some, if not all, family members. In the opposition between centripetal forces bringing family members to the dinner table and centrifugal forces pulling them apart, the centrifugal forces appear to dominate during the workweek, while centripetal forces gain force only during the weekend. For many U.S. families, dinnertime is what might be called a "sometimes" practice, and as such it is only an intermittent cultural site for the primary socialization of children and the collective consideration of events that affect the lives of family members.

What are the practical implications of this study to policymakers and working families? Although the small sample of families that we studied limited generalizability and our ability to conduct multivariate statistical analyses, our observations resonate with the existing literature and public perceptions of family dinners. Many families want to have dinner together because of the perceived and documented links between family dinners and child well-being (Fulkerson et al. 2006). The "yes, *but...*" conclusion of the family dinner study suggests that policymakers can help families achieve schedules that enable them to fulfill their "yes" intentions of having dinner together. Naturalistic observations suggest that the problem is not the number of hours that parents work, but the time of day when the hours are worked. Both employers and employees should encourage and use flexible schedules to improve work-life balance and preserve this important ritual that promotes family cohesion and child well-being.

Part 2

THE MISFIT BETWEEN OLD WORKPLACES AND A NEW WORKFORCE

4

CUSTOMIZING CAREERS BY OPTING OUT OR SHIFTING JOBS

Dual-Earners Seeking Life-Course "Fit"

Phyllis Moen and Qinlei Huang

Two-career couples are nothing new in American society, but dual-earning has by no means been institutionalized within families or the workforce. Dual-earners reflect a new workforce demography, an increasing percentage of households in which all adults are in the workforce. Still, most working couples struggle under both government laws and regulations and private-sector policies and practices that adhere to the stereotypical (male) lockstep adult course. The expectations surrounding paid work and its rewards are constructed around the "career mystique" belief that a lifetime of full-time continuous employment is the only path to success and fulfillment (Moen and Roehling 2005). However, the career mystique template makes no allowance for family care responsibilities or an insecure labor market. Dual-earners thus confront a fundamental mismatch between the exigencies of two jobs plus family care work and outdated career path expectations, policies, and practices. A second mismatch is created by the global risk economy together with economic downturns that are unraveling established conventions associated with seniority, job security, and retirement.

This chapter focuses on the implications of these two mismatches: the *work-family mismatch,* which renders one or both spouses in dual-earner households vulnerable to the tensions between the new workforce demography and the conventional occupational paths designed for workers without family responsibilities; and the *job security mismatch* resulting from economic downturns, new information technologies, offshoring, and increased competition within a global workforce (Altobelli and Moen 2007; Meiksins and Whalley 2002; Moen and Roehling 2005; Rubin and Smith 2001; Sweet, Moen, and Meiksins 2007; Williams 2000).

We propose that dual-earner couples respond to these mismatches through *ad-hoc career customizations,* that is, adaptive strategies on the part of one or both partners in the form of job turnover, job shifts, or job stability. In today's economy, career customization is not necessarily the result of long-term goals and plans; rather, it is an effort to respond to the mismatches that constrain workers' options, including actual job layoffs of one's self or one's spouse. This study tests the theorized adaptation by examining a sample of dual-earners from the most advantaged segment of the American workforce (married workers with at least some college education, employed in professional or managerial jobs). This is the most likely group to appear in the primary sector of the workforce, holding what have historically been the most stable "good" jobs offering benefits, pensions, access to internal labor markets, and the greatest job security (Kalleberg, Reskin, and Hudson 2000). Arguably, even this privileged sector finds itself in double jeopardy, obliged to customize one or both spouses' career paths in a cultural and policy "career mystique" climate that does not support, and may even penalize, such ad hoc customization (Moen, Sweet, and Hill 2009; Sweet, Moen, and Meiksins 2007).

Dual-earner households may use job shifts or exits of one or both spouses as a strategic adaptation to the time pressures built in to their multiple goals and obligations at work and home. "Opting out" is the phrase many journalists use to depict the informal career customization of dual-career women who exit the workforce because they and their husbands cannot "do it all" (Moen 2008; Moen, Kelly, and Magennis 2009; Stone 2007). Conventional gender norms, together with the future income prospects of each spouse's job, mean that typically wives, not husbands, are the ones doing the opting out. We draw on data from the *Ecology of Careers Study* (Moen 2003) to investigate the conditions under which one or both members of dual-earner couples customize their careers by selecting (or by being selected into) job shifts or exits, whether these are the result of corporate restructuring, work-family conflicts, or simply job or family pressures, overloads, and strains.

Is Customization the Solution?

Prior studies document a widespread desire for more voluntary career-customization options among many sectors of the workforce who do not wish to or cannot follow the lockstep career mystique (Moen and Chesley 2008; Moen and Kelly 2009). These include dual-earner and single parents, child-free couples, singles, empty nesters, care providers for infirm relatives, and couples nearing retirement (e.g., Clarkberg and Moen 2001; Moen 2003; Moen et al. 2000; Moen and Roehling 2005). Several measures could create a wider pool of work-life options in society, including legitimizing a range of career pathways, alternatives to the current linear lockstep. There could be concrete benefits of doing so. Policies and practices institutionalizing alternative career patterns (including opting back in as well as opting out) would eliminate the long-term costs now imposed on employees and couples whose experiences do not fit the lockstep norm (Budig and England 2001; Folbre 2001; Waldfogel 1995, 2001): part-timers, those who interrupt their work lives to care for children or infirm relatives, young workers trying out several occupations, workers wanting or needing to return to school, workers of all ages laid off, older employees who seek encore jobs later in life.

The challenge is that *employers* want flexibility as well—a flexible workforce they can customize through layoffs in the face of economic downturns, competition, mergers, or restructuring. Thus, the concept of flexible career customization comes with two framings: flexible customization by *employees* to facilitate life-course "fit," and flexible customization by *employers* to reduce their workforce or shift work offshore. Some (e.g., Sennett 1998) see flexible employment customization on the part of employers as yet a further unraveling of existing social conventions and relationships exacerbating the "job security mismatch." Both sides of customization affect the employment paths of contemporary women and men. They must respond to the forced customization of their employers, but they also actively customize their own work arrangements, as individuals and couples. What is missing is recognition by employers, managers, and policymakers that customization is the only way to sustain a competitive workforce in the twenty-first century, given both the work-family and the job security mismatches. But couples cannot customize effectively by themselves. Supportive policies and practices are needed that could legitimize alternative, more flexible career paths in occupations and organizations.

This chapter demonstrates that dual-earners have to create their own *informal career customizations* in efforts to maintain control over their lives. Over the two-year study period, one or both partners in the sample commonly switched jobs, changed employers, left for a time and returned to a different job, or else exited the workforce. Is such customization "voluntary" or "involuntary"? It could be argued that it is a combination of both, that job and employment shifts reflect the adaptive strategies of couples in response to an insecure job market as well as couples' efforts to achieve better *life-course fit* between their occupational paths and their family and personal circumstances (Moen and Chesley 2008; Moen and Kelly 2009). The study draws on panel data from a sample of married, middle-class Americans employed in large industries, healthcare, and educational institutions—those who in the past would be most apt to be in the primary, stable workforce—to offer evidence of dual-earners' efforts to tailor their career paths to meet the pressures of two careers, children, caring for ailing relatives, demanding jobs, corporate restructuring, and economic downturns.

Dual-Earner Work, Family, and Life-Course Fit

This study uses data from the two-wave (two years apart) *Ecology of Careers Study,* consisting of a sample of 983 dual-earner couples (excluding those who were self-employed or running a family business) who stayed together through wave 2. The sample is middle class, in that at least one spouse in each couple has at least some college education. In fact, most respondents and spouses (nearly 65%) are college graduates, and most are employed in managerial or professional occupations. (For descriptions of the measures and descriptive statistics, contact authors.)

On average, the husbands in this sample are forty-five years of age, work almost forty-nine hours per week, and have been working for pay on a continuous basis for their current employer for around seven years. The wives in this sample tend to be younger, on average forty-three years of age, work less (around forty hours per week), and average about six years of tenure with their employer. Almost two-thirds (around 65%) of these couples are raising one or more dependent children.

Most people think of the work-family intersection as having negative consequences, in terms of the demands and stresses of jobs spilling over into their personal lives. Instead, this study finds that many dual-earners love their jobs and derive a sense of mastery, growth, and energy from the work they do. In keeping with other studies (Grzywacz and Bass 2003; Grzywacz et al. 2007; Hanson, Hammer, and Colton 2006), this research shows that both positive and negative aspects of the work-home interface can be true—often simultaneously—depending on the job, the employee, and family circumstances.

Changing Jobs, Leaving Work

The lockstep career mystique pattern of continuous employment reifies the notion of "orderly careers" (Moen and Roehling 2005; Wilensky 1981). But we find a surprising amount of informal customization by middle-class dual-earners through various forms of employment shifts over the two years between interviews. Only about two-thirds (64.0%) of the men and even fewer (58.2%) of the women interviewed stay in their same jobs over the two-year period.

Looking first at wives, nearly half (47.8%) of the women interviewed had some type of shift between interviews, with 8.4% exiting completely. Past evidence has shown women to have a more tenuous tie to the workforce than men, so it is perhaps not surprising that almost one in ten of the dual-earner women in the study exited the workforce completely in the two years between surveys. There is some suggestive evidence that those who left may be responding to the work-family mismatch. One in three exiters is a mother with a preschool child at home, and even more are caring for a parent or other infirm family member. Some women exiters report that they retired, but qualitative data suggest that "retirement" in this sample is often a strategic response to the job security mismatch—taking retirement buy-outs rather than risk being laid off (Moen, Sweet, and Hill 2009).

In addition to exiting the workforce, wives experience two other broad customization pathways: changing jobs or exiting but then returning to a new job. Of the women who make a change, six in ten change jobs (61.2%). Three in ten do so through *intra*-employer job shifts (see figure 4.1a), changing jobs but staying with their same employer. Another three in ten switch to work for a different organization. More common than simply exiting is the exit/return path: 15.3 percent of the job changers leave the workforce for a period but then reenter to work for a different employer. This could be a response to either the work-family mismatch or the job security mismatch, or both.

Over a third of the dual-earner husbands also make some type of shift in the two years between interviews. Fewer men (6.6%) than women (8.4%) leave the workforce altogether. Almost half of the men who exited report they have retired (figure 4.1b). Among men who do not remain in their same jobs, almost two-thirds (62%) move to a different job (more than half of these men change jobs but remain with their same employer). Another one in five (19%) leaves the workforce for a while (only a few as the result of downsizing) and then take on a different job, most often with a different employer.

But these are the experiences of individuals. Looking specifically at *couples,* the customization is even more dramatic. In the majority of cases at least one spouse has some type of job shift over the two years between surveys. In fact, only a minority of couples (41.8%) has *neither* partner changing jobs/employers or exiting the workforce. Husbands' and wives' job stability and changes are statistically ($p < .003$) related to one another, but they do not change in tandem. As hypothesized, couples respond to the job security mismatch and/or the work-family mismatch as a couple, with *either* the wife *or* the husband (but not both) changing employers or leaving the workforce. This does not include those who change jobs but remain with their same employer. In fact, in one-fourth (25.17%) of the couples *either* the husband *or* the wife switch jobs but do not leave. In fewer than one in ten (6.89%) couples do both partners change jobs at their workplace.

Who Leaves or Changes Jobs?

Dual-Earner Middle-Class Wives

Multivariate analysis shows that where women work predicts their turnover. Those employed in the for-profit private sector are 3.3 times more apt to leave the work-force (or to leave and return to a different job for a different employer) than those

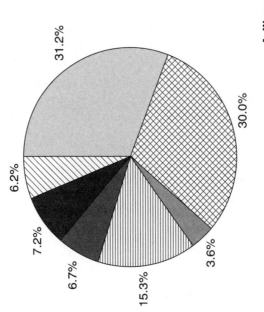

Change job with same employer

Change job with different employer

Left and back with same employer

Left and back with different employer

Left completely, with preschool child at home

Left completely, care for relatives

Left completely, no caring responsibilities, not retired

A. Women

31.2%

30.0%

6.2%

7.2%

6.7%

15.3%

3.6%

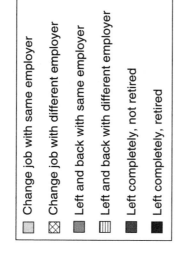

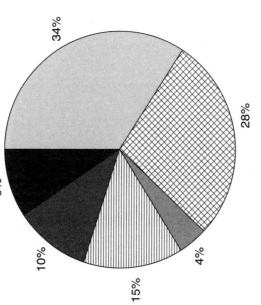

B. Men

FIGURE 4.1. Two-year change in job ties of middle-class men and women in dual-earner households

working in the more secure public (government) sector (see table 4.1). This probably reflects the greater job insecurity and work-family strains in market sector work. But the nonprofit sector is no haven of security or life-course fit. Surprisingly, women in nonprofit jobs (including those working in health care and education) are 4.3 times more likely than government workers to leave the workforce. Thus,

Table 4.1. Logistic Regressions Predicting Dual-Earner Wives' Turnover

	CHANGE WITH SAME EMPLOYER VS. STAY (N = 128) EXP(B)	CHANGE WITH DIFFERENT EMPLOYER VS. STAY (N = 123) EXP(B)	LEFT & RETURN VS. STAY (N = 77) EXP(B)	LEFT VS. STAY (N = 82) EXP(B)
HUSBAND IS AGED 50 AND OVER				
RESPONDENTS' WORK ENVIRONMENT, W1				
Wife in profit org.			3.56†	3.342†
Wife in nonprofit org.				4.315†
Wife in government (reference)				
Wife worked ≤35	0.33*			
Wife worked 45+				
Wife worked 35–45 (reference)				
Wife tenure in primary job	0.996*	0.992**		0.993*
Wife times changed employers	0.708**			
Wife supervise others	1.751†	2.575**	2.069†	
Wife regularly salaried		0.313**		
RESPONDENTS' LIFE-COURSE FIT, W1				
Positive w-f spillover scale				5.823*
Negative w-f spillover scale				8.256**
Positive f-w spillover scale			5.23†	0.091**
Negative f-w spillover scale				0.007**
Interaction of pos. w-f spillover and neg. w-f spillover				0.473*
Interaction of pos. f-w spillover and neg. f-w spillover				3.225**
Negative affect scale	1.856†			
Perceived income adequacy	1.023**		0.983†	
Personal health			1.456*	
RESPONDENTS' EXPECTATION, WORK-HOUR PREFERENCES, W1				
Wife expect to retire with employer		0.308***	0.166***	0.439*
Wife desire work 5+ fewer hours			0.455†	
Wife desire work 5+ more hours			6.518*	
Wife desire work around same hours (reference)				

(Continued)

Table 4.1.   *(Continued)*

	CHANGE WITH SAME EMPLOYER VS. STAY (N = 128) EXP(B)	CHANGE WITH DIFFERENT EMPLOYER VS. STAY (N = 123) EXP(B)	LEFT & RETURN VS. STAY (N = 77) EXP(B)	LEFT VS. STAY (N = 82) EXP(B)
RESPONDENT / SPOUSE CAREGIVING W1–W2				
Have three and more kids			0.418†	
Wife not caregiving W1, caregiving W2				
Wife caregiving W1, not caregiving W2				
Wife caregiving in both waves	0.445†			0.234†
Wife no care giving in both waves (reference)				
Husband not caregiving W1, caregiving W2	2.451*			3.173*
Husband caregiving W1, not caregiving W2				
Husband caregiving both waves		0.258*		
Husband no care giving in both waves (reference)				
SPOUSES' JOB SHIFTS W1–W2				
Husband changed job with same employer	3.461**	2.112†		
Husband changed job with diff. employer				
Husband left and back				
Husband left labor force				
Husband stayed in same job (reference)				

†t ≤ .10, *t ≤ .05, **t ≤ .01, ***t ≤ .001

women working for federal, state, or local government agencies have the most stable arrangements.

Past organizational attachments and future expectations matter as well. Women with longer tenure with their current employer and those expecting to remain with their current employer until they retire are less apt to leave the workforce, suggesting that seniority is still a significant factor reducing turnover. Those with longer tenure (with a history of few job shifts) are also less apt to change jobs within the same organization or shift to work somewhere else. Women managers are about equally likely to (a) change jobs within their current organization (odds = 1.8, almost double the odds of those not supervising others), (b) shift to work for a different employer (odds = 2.6), or (c) exit the workforce for a month or more and then return to a different job (odds = 2.1). Women in good health are more likely to leave their jobs but then go on to the work somewhere else (odds = 1.5).

Since women typically work fewer hours than do men (Jacobs and Gerson 2004; Moen 2003), it is not surprising that women who do put in long hours tend to opt out of the workforce, at least for a time. Earlier models without work-time preferences show that women who regularly put in more than forty-five hours a week on the job are three times more likely to exit and then return to the workforce in some other job, or else to leave the workforce altogether. This suggests that long-hour wives' short- and long-term exits reflect couples' response to the work-family mismatch, in keeping with Stone's findings (2007).

Women's work-hour preferences also matter, in that those few wives who want to work at least five hours more a week than their current schedule are apt to leave the workforce for a time and then return, while those wanting to work fewer hours are less apt to leave and return to work for someone else. These findings reinforce the finding of Clarkberg and Moen (2001) that there are few good options for working less. Dual-earner women who work less than thirty-five hours a week have only a one in three chance of shifting jobs within their same firm (odds = .33).

WOMEN'S LIFE-COURSE FIT: SPILLOVER
FROM WORK TO FAMILY

It seems reasonable to theorize that turnover can be a result of poor life-course fit (as gauged by high negative and low positive spillover in the work-family [W-F] interface as well as little control over working time). However, we find that employees' control over their working time does not predict wives' job shifts or turnover. But there is a statistically significant interaction between positive and negative work [W-F] spillover (table 4.1 and table 4.4) on turnover. As expected, women experiencing poor life-course fit (in the form of low positive work [W-F] spillover in combination with high negative work [W-F] spillover) are 2.46 times more likely to leave the workforce than those with low positive and negative spillover. Women in the optimal arrangement, high positive and low negative work [W-F] spillover (good life-course fit), are also likely to leave (odds = 1.49). And women with a combination of high levels of positive and high negative work [W-F] spillover are less apt to exit the workforce (with the odds of leaving just .72).

This evidence suggests that the spillover-turnover relationship is a complicated one. Positive spillover from work may serve as a "buffer" against the effects of high negative spillover, reducing the odds of women opting out, but women in this circumstance are still 1.49 times as likely to leave as women with low negative and low positive work [W-F] spillover. What is less intuitive is the finding that women with high positive and low negative work [W-F] spillover are also more apt to exit the workforce than those with low scores on both. In other words, even when one's job is very rewarding, it may overwhelm the rest of one's life and/or be insecure or unsustainable for some married women (see similar conclusions in Moen 2008 and Stone 2007).

WOMEN'S LIFE-COURSE FIT: SPILLOVER FROM FAMILY TO WORK

There is also an interaction between positive and negative spillover from family to work (F-W spillover). The expected odds of exiting the workforce for women experiencing a *combination* of both high positive and high negative family [F-W] spillover is 6 percent lower (odds = .94) than women with low positive and low negative family [F-W] spillover scores. As expected, a combination of high positive and low negative family [F-W] spillover (good life-course fit) decreases the odds of leaving the workforce by 47 percent (odds = .53). A combination of low positive and high negative family [F-W] spillover (poor life-course fit) also decreases the expected odds of exiting (odds = .16). This conforms to Hochschild's (1997) thesis that stressors on the home front may make work something of a welcome refuge.

Family care obligations (among adult daughters of aging parents and in-laws, as wives, and/or as mothers) may also push one or both partners to customize their careers. Among this somewhat older sample (average age for women is forty-five), caring for aging parents is a particularly important factor in women's job shifts. This can be seen in the effect of their *husbands'* caregiving on the odds of wives leaving the workforce (table 4.1). Women whose husbands begin providing care for an aging or infirm relative (usually a parent) by the second interview are more apt to exit the workforce themselves, suggesting a possible need to provide support for their care-providing husbands (see Chesley and Moen [2006] for additional findings on couple caregiving dynamics). Wives of caregiving husbands are also more apt to make a job shift within their organization. When their husbands have been engaged in long-term caregiving (doing so at both interviews, two years apart) women have low odds of switching employers. By contrast, wives themselves who have been caring for an older relative (typically a parent) for at least two years (at both interview points) have a low likelihood of shifting to another employer or of leaving the workforce, reinforcing the work-as-haven hypothesis (Hochschild 1997).

There is also evidence of some joint couple-level career customization. In particular, a woman whose husband changes jobs but remains with the same employer is more likely to make a similar within-employer change. She is also more likely to leave to work for a different employer.

Dual-Earner Middle-Class Husbands

Dual-earner men over age fifty are, not surprisingly, the ones most apt to leave the workforce; they are three times more likely to do so than those under age fifty (table 4.2). It is not clear whether this phenomenon reflects conditions at work,

Table 4.2. Logistic Regressions Predicting Dual-Earner Husbands' Turnover

	CHANGE WITH SAME EMPLOYER VS. STAY (N = 128) EXP(B)	CHANGE WITH DIFFERENT EMPLOYER VS. STAY (N = 123) EXP(B)	LEFT & RETURN VS. STAY (N = 77) EXP(B)	LEFT VS. STAY (N = 82) EXP(B)
HUSBAND IS AGED 50 AND OVER				2.820*
RESPONDENTS' WORK ENVIRONMENT, W1				
Husband worked ≤ 35				
Husband worked 45+	2.823*		3.099†	
Husband worked 35–45 (reference)				
Husband tenure in primary job	.996*	.992**		
Husband times changed employers		1.196*		
Husband perceived job security		.981**	.987†	
Number of employees at location for husband			.831*	
RESPONDENTS' LIFE-COURSE FIT, W1				
Positive w-f spillover scale		.292		.664
Negative w-f spillover scale	.610†		.334**	
Positive f-w spillover scale		.453		
Negative f-w spillover scale				.117*
Interaction of pos. w-f spillover and pos. f-w spillover		1.450†		
Interaction of pos. w-f spillover and neg. f-w spillover				2.145*
Mastery scale		3.780**		2.338†
Personal energy			.709*	
Negative affect scale			2.724*	
Perceived income adequacy			.977*	
Personal growth	2.207*			
RESPONDENTS' EXPECTATION, W1				
Husband expect to retire with employer		.351**	.337*	
RESPONDENT / SPOUSE CAREGIVING W1–W2				
Have three and more kids	.490*		.255*	
Wife not caregiving W1, caregiving W2				
Wife caregiving W1, not caregiving W2		.228*		
Wife caregiving both waves			.254†	
Wife not caregiving both waves (reference)				

(Continued)

Table 4.2.   *(Continued)*

	CHANGE WITH SAME EMPLOYER VS. STAY (N = 128) EXP(B)	CHANGE WITH DIFFERENT EMPLOYER VS. STAY (N = 123) EXP(B)	LEFT & RETURN VS. STAY (N = 77) EXP(B)	LEFT VS. STAY (N = 82) EXP(B)
Husband caregiving W1, not caregiving W2		.099*		
Husband caregiving both waves				
Husband not caregiving both waves (reference)				
SPOUSES' JOB SHIFTS W1–W2				
Wife changed job with same employer	2.221*			
Wife changed job with diff. employer				
Wife left and back				
Wife left labor force				
Wife stayed in same job (reference)				

†t ≤ .10, *t ≤ .05, **t ≤ .01, ***t ≤ .001

employer downsizing, or personal choice. Putting in long hours on the job increase the odds of men making a job change within their organization (odds = 2.8) or else exiting the workforce for a brief time and then returning (odds = 3.1).

PERSONAL CHARACTERISTICS REFLECTING LIFE-COURSE FIT

Positive self-assessments are a key component of life-course fit. Men's (but not women's) self-assessments at wave 1 predict their subsequent employment shifts. For example, husbands who score high on the personal growth scale at the first interview have double (2.2) the odds of making a within-employer job shift over the subsequent two years. And dual-earner men with high levels of personal mastery at the first interview have even higher odds of subsequently changing employers (odds = 3.8). They are also twice as likely to leave the workforce (odds = 2.3) than those with lower levels of this personal resource. Men with high mastery and growth may be able and willing to switch jobs and employers, as well as to take advantage of early retirement buyouts. Other psychosocial measures predict husbands' exiting for a time and returning to work for a different employer: these include high negative affect, low levels of energy, and a low sense of income adequacy.

SPILLOVER REFLECTING MEN'S LIFE-COURSE FIT

Both work-family conflicts and enhancements predict husbands' job shifts. There is an interaction between family and work enhancement for men: those with both positive work [W-F] spillover and positive family [F-W] spillover (both indices of high life-course fit) are more apt to switch employers (tables 4.2, 4.4). Specifically, husbands with a combination of high positive family [F-W] spillover and high positive work [W-F] spillover are 1.51 times more likely to move on to work for someone else, compared to husbands who are low in both types of positive spillover. There are low odds (.80) of such employer shifts if husbands have only high positive work [W-F] spillover, or if husbands report only high positive family [F-W] spillover (odd = .74, compared to those low in both).

Husbands who were serving as caregivers at the first wave of interviews but no longer doing so by the second wave are unlikely to have changed employers, as are husbands whose wives stop being a caregiver for infirm relatives (odds = .228). Having a wife engaged in long-term caregiving (over both waves) also reduces a husband's odds of exiting the workforce (odds = .254).

Does Career Customization Reduce the Work-Family Mismatch?

If working conditions contribute to negative work [W-F] spillover, does changing jobs or employers increase life-course fit? Or is it the other demands in one's life that create negative spillover (and poor life-course fit), no matter what the job?

To assess the impacts, if any, of job shifts, we use multivariate regression analysis to examine *changes* between survey waves in two measures: husbands' and wives' control over their work-time and their negative work [W-F] spillover (see Table 4.3). The dependent variable is the wave 2 measure, with the wave 1 measure included in the equation to capture any changes in employees' sense of work-time control and negative work [W-F] spillover over the two years between survey waves.

Looking first at wives, the act of changing jobs (whether with the same or a different employer) but not leaving the workforce increases women's sense of control over their working time, suggesting that they may switch jobs to gain greater temporal flexibility. Mothers of preschoolers also see an increase in their sense of control over their working time and a decrease in their negative work [W-F] spillover, possibly because of their young children growing two years older. Wives' negative work [W-F] spillover increases when they stop caring for an infirm relative, typically when the infirm family member dies. Wives' negative work [W-F] spillover also increases when their *husbands* switch employers, possibly because the demands of a new job reduce husbands' availability and participation on the home front.

For husbands, job shifts are the biggest factor changing their appraisal of life-course fit. One trend indicates that going to work for a different employer increases husbands' control over their work-time even as it simultaneously increases their negative work [W-F] spillover. Another trend suggests that their wives' leaving the workforce between waves increases husbands' work-time control. But having a wife

Table 4.3. Multivariate Regressions Predicting Change in Sense of Life-Course Fit

	WIFE		HUSBAND	
	WORK-TIME CONTROL (N = 840)	NEG. W-F SPILLOVER (N = 831)	WORK-TIME CONTROL (N = 868)	NEG. W-F SPILLOVER (N = 833)
	β	β	β	β
(CONSTANT)	1.108***	.943***	1.361***	.840***
W1 COUPLES' WORK-TIME CONTROL/NEG. W-F SPILLOVER	.646***	.714***	.615***	.645***
Couples' life stages W1–W2				
No change kid aged 0–5	.257*	–.353*		
Respondent no change no child ≤40 *(reference)*				
RESPONDENT CAREGIVING W1–W2				
Respondent not caregiving W1, caregiving W2				
Respondent caregiving W1, not caregiving W2		.176†		
Respondent caregiving both waves				
Respondent not caregiving both waves *(reference)*				
RESPONDENTS' JOB SHIFTS W1–W2				
Respondent changed job with same employer	.253***			
Respondent changed job with different employer	.183*		.229†	.179†
Respondent left and back				
Respondent left labor force[a]				
Respondent stayed (reference)				
SPOUSES' JOB SHIFTS W1–W2				
Spouse changed job with same employer				
Spouse changed job with different employer		.195†		
Spouse left and back				
Spouse left labor force			.132†	.280*
Spouse stayed in same job (reference)				
R^2	.445	.232	.443	.228
(Adjusted R^2)	(.430)	(.212)	(.428)	(.208)

†t ≤ .10, *t ≤ .05, **t ≤ .01, ***t ≤ .001
[a]Those leaving were not asked control or w-f spillover in wave 2.

Table 4.4.   The Impacts of Work-to-Family and Family-to-Work Spillover

ODDS OF WOMEN LEAVING LABOR FORCE[a]

POSITIVE W-F SPILLOVER	NEGATIVE W-F SPILLOVER	OR	POSITIVE F-W SPILLOVER	NEGATIVE F-W SPILLOVER	OR
Low[a] (1.912)	High (3.354)	2.46	Low (3.107)	High (3.053)	0.16
High (3.561)	Low (2.029)	1.49	High (4.595)	Low (1.682)	0.53
High (3.561)	High (3.354)	0.72	High (4.595)	High (3.053)	0.94
Low (1.912)	Low (2.029)	Reference	Low (3.107)	Low (1.682)	Reference

ODDS OF MEN CHANGING EMPLOYERS

POSITIVE W-F SPILLOVER	POSITIVE F-W SPILLOVER	OR
Low (1.622)	High (4.505)	0.74
High (3.227)	Low (2.930)	0.80
High (3.227)	High (4.505)	1.51
Low (1.622)	Low (2.930)	Reference

[a]All work-to-family spillover and family-to-work spillover are continuous variables. Here, low spillover indicates the value of mean minus 1 standard deviation of the variable, and high spillover indicates the value of mean plus 1 standard deviation of the variable.

leave the workforce also increases husbands' negative work [W-F] spillover. Note that having a wife who "opts out" both increases and decreases these two dimensions of life-course fit; husbands' control over their working time increases, but so does their negative work [W-F] spillover, possibly reflecting increasing pressures accompanying their shift to "sole breadwinner" status.

Family Friendliness

There is much discussion about the "family-friendliness" of various employers, but little knowledge of how employees actually assess their workplaces. Accordingly, we asked respondents to rate the friendliness and flexibility of their workplace using several different measures. The first is a single rating, in response to the following question asked at both wave 1 and wave 2 of the survey: "There are some types of things that help working families manage their needs. Using a scale from 0 to

100, with 0 being extremely 'family *un*-friendly' and 100 being extremely 'family friendly,' how 'family friendly' would you rate your workplace?"

The second measure is based on four items (only available in the second interview wave). These items assess the overall workplace culture in terms of providing employees with the flexibility they need to cope with family or personal obligations. Respondents were asked to rate the extent to which the following existed at their workplace based on a five-point agreement scale: (a) "there is an unwritten rule at my place of employment that you can't take care of family needs on company time"; (b) "at my place of employment, employees who put their family or personal needs ahead of their jobs are not looked upon favorably"; (c) "if you have a problem managing your work and family responsibilities, the attitude at my place of employment is: you made your bed now lie in it"; and (d) "at my place of employment, employees have to choose between advancing in their jobs or devoting attention to their family or personal lives." These four questions were condensed into one overall *inflexible culture* scale.

Scholars studying flexible and family-friendly workplaces tend to consider these conditions as more significant for *women than men,* with the absence of family friendliness serving as a trigger for women to move to a different employer or even opt out of the workforce altogether (Stone 2007). However, we find that men's assessments of family-friendliness predicted their subsequent labor market behavior. Men who left the labor force by wave 2 of the survey reported the lowest family-friendliness scores for their workplaces at wave 1 (64.09 on a scale of 0 to 100). Men who changed employers (without leaving the workforce) also rated their previous workplaces low on family friendliness, as did men who exited employment but later returned to a new workplace (ratings were 66.0 and 66.2 on the 0–100 score, respectively). This compares with a wave 1 score of 78.06 on the family-friendliness scale for men remaining in their same jobs with their same employers over the two years between surveys (analyses available from authors upon request).

Shifting Jobs for a Flexible Culture at Work?

There is also a significant association between changes in employment and wave 2 negative workplace culture scores. Specifically, women who change employers between wave 1 and wave 2 rank their new workplaces as more flexible (or less inflexible) than those who remain with their same employer (see figure 4.2). But the difference in inflexibility scores is slight (1.97 and 2.18). Women who stay with their same employer (regardless of whether they take on a different job with that employer) have the most inflexible work culture scores. By contrast, women who leave the labor force and then return to a different job give their new workplaces more positive marks in terms of a culture of flexibility.

One might suspect that women who leave the labor force and then return do so because of a life stage change, such as the birth of a child. But when workplace culture scores are examined in relation to changes in life stage, we find no association

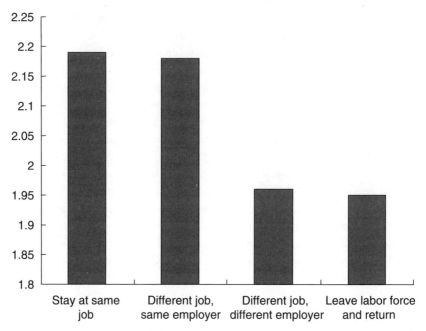

FIGURE 4.2. Women's inflexible workplace culture scores (wave 2) by job stability and shifts (waves 1–2)

between the two: women who have recently had a child do not have significantly different inflexible workplace culture scores from women who are nonparents. Because workers' ratings on this culture score are only available at the time of the second interview, there is no way of knowing if these scores change over time, or whether employees "take on" and adapt to the culture of where they work. However, note that having changed employers predicts better workplace culture scores compared to those who remain with their same employer. This suggests the possibility that inflexible cultures at one workplace may encourage employees to seek new opportunities elsewhere. Men's assessments of inflexible workplace cultures vary less than those of women.

Among the men and women who remain with their same employers through the two years between surveys, it appears that whether they perceive an inflexible workplace culture varies according to their employer, and sometimes men and women working for the same firm have different perceptions. (Recall that the higher the score, the more inflexible employees perceive the workplace culture to be.) Women employed in healthcare organizations and at a large Fortune 500 industry report the most inflexible workplace culture scores (data not shown). However, men employed in these same organizations report far less inflexibility. Men in other large (nonmanufacturing) firms report more inflexible work cultures, as do men (and women) at a large utility company. Women employed in retail or small firms report the most flexible cultures at work.

In some working environments, however, men and women tend to give similar assessments of the degree of flexibility/inflexibility in the workplace culture, with those working in higher education the most similar. Still, men (but not women) employed by government or nonprofit organizations tend to rank them higher in terms of their flexible cultures than men employed in the private sector. Clearly, men's and women's experiences vary in different workplaces.

What then can be said about employees' assessments of life-course fit in terms of the family-friendliness or inflexibility in their workplaces? First, family-friendliness ratings (on a score of 0 to 100) tend to differ more within, rather than across, organizations. Second, assessments of friendliness seem to matter in terms of who stays or leaves jobs in particular organizations. Third, men and women working for the same organization tend to have very different assessments about the nature of its culture, possibly because their *jobs* differ and/or possibly because their *needs and expectations* differ.

Customization as Complex

We have studied informal career customization by dual-earners in an environment where formal customization policies and practices do not exist. In fact, career customization, in terms of exiting the workforce for a time, remains at odds with the rules and regulations based on the assumed lockstep career mystique (Moen and Roehling 2005). Nevertheless, we find that the careers of one or both spouses in most middle-class couples are in considerable flux. This study provides a small window on the dynamics of these processes, showing a surprising amount of turnover and job shifts in middle-class dual-earner households—either as a result of employer layoffs or as a way of seeking better life-course flexibilities and "fit" between the couples' jobs and their family/personal lives.

Accounting for Exits

Exiting the workforce is perhaps the most striking indicator of poor life-course fit. We find that both the job security mismatch and the work-family mismatch precipitate turnover. Meyer (1986, 205) points out that the institutionalized nature of the life course provides individuals with available lists of reasons, motives, and aspirations. Retirement, for example, is an "acceptable" rationale for leaving employment for those of a certain age, even though it may be forced through layoffs or buyout packages. Almost half (46.9%) of the men who left the workforce subsequently called themselves "retired," as did one in five (20%) of the women in this dual-earner workforce sample (see also Moen, Sweet, and Hill 2009).

In contrast to the self-described retirees, three in ten of the men who left say they were either laid off or that their job was eliminated. Over half of the men who left the workforce but do not call it retirement still have children under the age of eighteen at home; the retirement explanation is less acceptable for those still raising children. More men than women say they left for a better or different kind of job (13.4% to 8.6%), but since they were still not employed when interviewed the second time, this could be a more acceptable explanation for being laid off or "downsized."

Women also invoke these explanations, but 14 percent report leaving for family reasons, typically to stay home to care for children, an "acceptable" rationale for women. Almost one in ten (9.4%) say they opted out because they became pregnant or in order to become pregnant. Family demands are rarely the explanation for men's job exits. Only one man in the sample reports dropping out of the workforce for family reasons or to stay home with a child.

Another family reason surfaces for women: 7 percent of dual-earner women exiting work say they left their jobs because they moved out of the area, typically following their spouses' career moves. Only one in twenty (5%) women report that they left because they did not care for their work, their employer, and/or the general work environment (compared to even fewer men: only 2.5% of the men who leave the workforce say it is for these reasons). Given the gendered strategies of adaptation that couples invoke, it is not surprising that people's reasons for exiting differ by gender. Whether these exits are "voluntary" or "involuntary" is open to question, even when employees themselves offer various explanations.

Seeking Life-Course Fit

The absence of fit between dual-earner couples' two jobs and their family needs is what leads to a gendered customization strategy in the form of wives shifting jobs or exiting paid work. Women are more likely to regard themselves as responsible for the family care work, and inflexibility in their jobs sometimes pushes them out of the workforce (Moen 2008; Stone 2007). Husbands' expectations about bread-winning suggest they are less likely to exit the workforce voluntarily, except for the formal exit of retirement (where men are increasingly pushed out early through buyouts).

However, work is also positive for both husbands' and wives' self-esteem, health, and well-being. Recall that a complex relationship (interaction) exists between positive and negative work spillover and the odds of wives exiting the workforce. Almost double (11%) the women with high negative and low positive work [W-F] spillover (poor fit) tend to opt out, compared to only 5.8 percent of women with both high negative and high positive work spillover. This suggests that high positive spillover from one's job serves as a buffer against high negative work [W-F] spill-over. Still, it is clear in both cases that high negative work [W-F] spillover pushes women out of the workforce.

Where one works can also influence career customization. Women at baseline with low negative and low positive work [W-F] spillover and those with high negative but low positive work [W-F] spillover are both more apt to work in the private (for-profit) sector. Those with high positive and high negative work [W-F] spillover are more likely to be working for nonprofits, while government employees are distributed across all spillover categories. Seven in ten part-timers report low negative work [W-F] spillover, with a little over half of those also reporting high positive work [W-F] spillover.

The most "dissonant" cases are those women with high positive and low negative work [W-F] spillover (presumably those experiencing high life-course fit), who nevertheless exit the workforce. Of the twenty-four women who fit this category, three or more each gave the following reasons: "downsized," "no opportunities for advancement," "childcare difficulties," or the "opportunity to return to school," suggesting considerable heterogeneity in why women who enjoy their jobs leave.

Policy Implications

There is to date little in the way of formal, legitimated career customization policies and practices that could permit the successful integration of work and family life within a global risk economy. And yet rules and regulations as well as routine ways of operating predicated on a lockstep career mystique model are undermining the capacities of individuals and families to function effectively and to promote their own well-being. Moreover, outdated rules perpetuate old ways of "one size fits all" thinking and acting in a labor market climate of uncertainty, unpredictability, and change. Although some organizations are paying more attention to "family friendliness," many workers still do not have access to the time off and the flexibility that they need (Clarkberg and Moen 2001; Kelly 2005; Kelly and Kalev 2006; Reynolds and Aletreris 2006; see also Bond, Galinsky, Kim et al. 2005; Bond, Galinsky, Pitt-Catsouphes et al. 2005). Moreover, flexibility policies that have been put in place rarely meet workers' needs (Batt and Valcour 2003; Kelly and Moen 2007).

There is also an absence of safety nets essential for sustaining working families as job loss becomes increasingly commonplace across the life course. This means that women and men in dual-earner households, even those who are white collar and middle class, now have a tenuous tie to particular jobs, employers, or the workforce. We argue that job shifts and exits are simultaneously both voluntary (in terms of decisions made or not made, including whether to accept buyouts) and involuntary (in terms of the inflexible work times, as well as layoffs, "encouraged" early retirement packages, or forced buyouts). Dual-earner career paths are thus *strategic responses* to the work-family mismatch and the job security mismatch—in other words, adaptations to chronic and acute stressors undermining life-course fit.

The challenge to researchers and to policymakers is to identify and foster key ingredients of effective, integrative *flexible career customization*. This means life-course paths that better "fit" the shifting needs of those simultaneously engaged in (a) dual-earning along with childcare or parent-care responsibilities, (b) the contingencies of coordinating husbands' and wives' jobs, and (c) the uncertainties, ambiguities, anxieties, and blurred boundaries of the new global risk and digital economy and the unraveling of retirement as we know it.

The corporate and societal challenge is to recognize the need for (a) formal, le-gitimated customized career path options *with safety nets,* and (b) second chances at reentries and entries into new occupations. Such options would reflect the reality of employers' demands for flexibility and employees' need for flexibility and control over the time and timing of their work. In *Mass Career Customization,* Benko and Weisberg (2007) argue for the development of a range of career-patterning options, creating careers that are more lattice than ladder or lockstep. Heinz (2003) suggests that past lockstep work trajectories are morphing into a contingent life course that requires career negotiations. We have found that dual-earner couples are leading this change, reinventing work and career paths to better fit the risks and realities of their lives. The evidence of Briscoe (2006, 2007) and Becker and Moen (1999) also reinforces this thesis. But current informal customization reinforces gender divi-sions. Research demonstrates the current and long-term costs, especially to women, of such informal customization strategies (Budig and England 2001; Waldfogel 1995, 1998). Whether women and close-to-retirement-age workers are opting out or being pushed out, stereotypes and discriminatory practices reduce their future career—or even employment—possibilities (Correll, Benard, and Paik 2007; Stone 2007). What is required is the rewriting of twentieth-century career scripts to bet-ter fit twenty-first-century realities. Formal customization policies and practices with some safety nets should be the next workforce policy innovation (Moen 2007), increasing employees' career options and thereby offering them and their families greater flexibility and control over the multilayered clockworks and calendars of their lives.

5

KEEPING ENGAGED PARENTS ON THE ROAD TO SUCCESS

Sylvia Ann Hewlett

Ilona Steffen-Cope had been working as a consultant for Booz Allen Hamilton in Germany when, after a short time there, she was transferred to New York. Two years later, she transferred to San Francisco. That was the easy part.

After another two years, Steffen-Cope began commuting to San Francisco from Vancouver, an arrangement prompted by the demands of her partner's career. A year after that, she took a one-month leave of absence to get married in Germany, and ten months later she gave birth to her first child and went on maternity leave. This, however, was not the end of her career. Booz Allen Hamilton supported her throughout these changes (although, she concedes, commuting from Vancouver was particularly challenging).

Since consultants are typically on the road four to five days a week, it could be argued that it does not truly matter where one makes one's home. However, living in Vancouver created a three-pronged existence: client, office, and home base were all widely separated. "During that time, I was spending five days a week in Tennessee with my client, and on the way home I would stop in San Francisco to touch base," Steffen-Cope says. "This made it a ten-hour commute door to door."

So, when Steffen-Cope neared the end of her pregnancy and could no longer travel, it was clear that her priorities and needs were shifting. It was then that she signed on to the new Booz Allen Hamilton program to do special project work from her home. Steffen-Cope was still defined as a full-time employee, but for two months she stopped traveling and worked on a project that had been catalogued as "ideal" for someone in her situation.

Steffen-Cope is thrilled about the projects she has worked on; she claims that everyone she knows who has had a similar arrangement has also had interesting work. "We're too ambitious and too expensive to just be parked for a while," she says.

Steffen-Cope plans to continue with project work in the near term as a way to ease back in: "I plan to return full time, but I'll need to get a nanny up to speed, and I'm breastfeeding, so it will be a while before I could be far away for a week at a time."

Steffen-Cope describes the atmosphere at Booz Allen Hamilton as family-like. Though she has been home with her baby for two months, she still feels part of the team. "My co-workers call me and ask how I am doing," she reports. "They urge me to pace myself. When I asked about a gradual return they said, 'We'll make it happen.'"

When it comes to employer policies, not many are as fortunate as Steffen-Cope. The tugs and pulls of family (whether referring to toddlers, teenagers, or elderly parents) continue to interrupt women's work lives. However, the employment outcome is much less familiar. Few employers reach out with the kind of caring attention Steffen-Cope has received. All too often, a woman in her situation would have been forced to quit.

And many—far too many—do quit. That is why, about two years ago, a noisy debate erupted on both sides of the Atlantic over what Lisa Belkin (2003) of the *New York Times* called "the opt-out revolution." For a number of months, it was rare to turn on the television without encountering various "talking heads" scaremongering about a disturbing trend: a large number of highly qualified women dropping out of mainstream careers. Even the wild success of the television show *Desperate Housewives* was attributed to a supposed glut of "dropout" women—bored silly and looking for trouble on Wisteria Lane.

In the mainstream press, there was a great deal of speculation as to what might be behind this trend. Left-wing commentators tended to blame public policy (shortfalls in childcare and flexible work options), while more conservative analysts simply blamed the victims. Women, it was purported, had a variety of problems, ranging from a failure of ambition to an unwillingness to work long hours. Harvard University president Larry Summers (and now President Obama's top economics adviser), in a startling speech, went so far as to suggest that women were genetically inferior (Hemel 2005, 1).

Despite the heat of this debate, not many new insights or solutions have been offered, in the absence of hard data. Few know the basic facts: How many talented women are opting out? How many years do they stay out? How many want to return to the workplace? And, what policies and practices might help them get back onto that career highway?

In 2004, I founded the Hidden Brain Drain Task Force with Carolyn Buck Luce (Ernst & Young) and Cornel West (Princeton University) to address how to retain and advance highly qualified women and minorities. The fifty global companies and organizations that make up the Task Force are united by an understanding that full utilization of the talent pool is at the heart of competitive advantage and economic success.

The Task Force set out to create a rich data set. In the summer of 2004, three member companies (Ernst & Young, Goldman Sachs, and Lehman Brothers) sponsored a national survey designed to "map" the trajectory of women's work lives. The survey was fielded online by Harris Interactive between June 23, 2004, and July 15, 2004, under the auspices of the Center for Work-Life Policy, a not-for-profit research organization. It comprised a nationally representative sample of 2,443 highly qualified women and 653 highly qualified men in the United States, aged twenty-eight to fifty-five, defined as those with a graduate/professional degree or a high honors undergraduate degree. The survey research was supplemented by focus groups conducted within Task Force companies and companies on the outside (mostly "sister" companies in similar sectors). These focus groups serve to illuminate a much more intimate reality—the feelings and frustrations of the women on the front lines. The resulting study (published in March 2005 by the *Harvard Business Review*) paints a more comprehensive and nuanced portrait of women's careers than has been available to date (Hewlett et al. 2005).

Are Women "Opting Out"?

The answer is a resounding no. Certainly, a sizable number do take some time out. The survey data show that 37 percent of highly qualified women voluntarily leave their careers for a period of time, or, "off-ramp." But the amount of time spent outside the workforce is surprisingly short—an average of 2.2 years. Across sector and occupation, the length of time spent off-ramped varies, ranging from 1.5 years in the banking/finance sector to three years in the legal profession. Further down the road, the vast majority of off-rampers (93%) are attempting to get back onto the career highway. Hype and overblown rhetoric notwithstanding, contemporary women are deeply committed to their careers.

Janice,[1] at last contact, was fighting the frustrating battle of restoring her career path. An executive with twelve years of international experience in the reinsurance industry, an entrepreneur fluent in French, and the holder of a recent master's in business administration from Duke University's Fuqua School, Janice thought that finding a new job would be simple, a thought that buoyed her eagerness to return to her career. Indeed, Janice was welcomed by human resources staffers at the financial services firms she targeted when trying to reenter the workforce after having two children. Yet hiring managers nevertheless found it easy to turn her away. "They'd say, 'Yes, great resume, but she's taken time off. I have an equal number of great managers who haven't taken time off,'" Janice said. Janice sees herself as a highly qualified executive, not as a person who has opted out or ditched her career (personal communication, December 8, 2005).

Off-ramps are conspicuous, creating tension in the workplace, as every empty desk tugs at a company's bottom line. However, there are other ways in which women veer off the professional fast track. Some women choose a "scenic route." They do not step out—instead, they step back, taking a part-time job, a flexible work arrangement, a telecommuting option, or turning down a promotion. For a period of time, these women deliberately choose a less ambitious career path, as a way to be able to enjoy the scenery and "smell the roses," while fulfilling serious responsibilities in the rest of their lives.

This survey shows that 16 percent of highly qualified women currently work part-time. Part-time employment is more prevalent in the legal and medical professions, where 23 percent and 20 percent of female professionals work less than full-time, than in the business sector, where only 8 percent of women work part-time. Another common work-life strategy is telecommuting; 8 percent of highly qualified women work exclusively from home, and 25 percent work partly from home.

Why Do Women Leave?

There is no simple, one-dimensional explanation for why women take time out. For most, career interruptions are a result of a complex interaction between "pull factors" (centered in the family) and "push" factors (centered at work). Prior to conducting this research, it seemed that the tugs and pulls of children would dominate the reasons women leave the workplace. And to an extent, this was true. For 45 percent of the women in this survey, a childcare challenge—specifically, the need to devote more time to children—was the issue that triggered the off-ramping decision. There are other powerful pull factors, as well. For example, 24 percent of women in the survey reported that an eldercare crisis was the trigger issue, the one that forced them out. The pull of eldercare responsibilities is particularly strong for women in the forty-one to fifty-five age group, often called the "sandwich" generation, positioned between growing children and aging parents. One in three women in this age bracket reported leaving the workforce for a period of time to care for a family member who is not a child.

Not to be forgotten lurking behind these pull factors (all of which revolve around family care) is a traditional division of labor between men and women, which remains entrenched and pervasive. Even highly qualified women who are well paid routinely carry the heavier domestic responsibility. Typically, 75 percent of housework and childcare are provided by these women (Coltrane 2000). In fact, a 2001 survey conducted by the Center for Work-Life Policy revealed that fully 40 percent of highly qualified women with spouses felt that their husbands created more work around the house than they performed (Hewlett and Vite-León 2002). So much for the dream of a 50/50 split!

Alongside these "pull" factors are a series of "push" factors, those features of the job or workplace that result in a woman's choice to leave. Twenty-nine percent of women report taking an off-ramp primarily because their jobs are not satisfying or meaningful. The data show that feeling underutilized or underappreciated is a more significant problem than overwork. Not being consulted or being overlooked for a sought-after (and deserved) plum assignment is seemingly more difficult than accepting additional responsibility. Only 6 percent of women off-ramped because the work itself was too demanding. It is also interesting to note that in the business sector, a variety of push factors are more important than pull factors. Fifty-two percent of women in business off-ramped, at least in part because their career was not satisfying (vs. 29% of women overall), while time for children was cited by only 43 percent. The contrast is even more dramatic in law, where 59 percent maintained their career was not satisfying, compared to 26 percent who wanted time for children. These figures perhaps indicate that certain work cultures—specifically large corporations and law firms—have done a particularly poor job developing a supportive environment for talented women.

Of course, neat distinctions between pull and push factors tend to break down when considering the demands of daily life. In the real world, many women deal with an interaction of pull and push factors—one often serving to intensify the other, creating a cascading effect. For example, women are much more likely to respond to the pull of family when they feel hemmed in by a glass ceiling. In the words of one off-ramped television producer, "My two-year-old suddenly appeared needier—and yes, more appealing—the spring I was passed over for promotion. Objectively speaking, I don't think anything changed, but I was newly looking for a reason to take some time off and I wanted to believe that my child needed me at home full-time."

In a strange way, this interactivity between pull and push is good news for companies. It means that a new child or a mother-in-law recently diagnosed with Alzheimer's is not a sure indicator that a woman will quit. Whether or not a woman off-ramps largely depends on whether an employer can conjure up support—and opportunities—in the workplace.

> Jonelle Salter, an offshore installation manager (OIM) for BP (formerly British Petroleum), is inching toward a scenic route, and while BP is not exactly planting rose bushes for her to stop and smell, they are offering arrangements attractive enough to ensure that this thirty-two-year-old Afro-Caribbean woman engineer will not off-ramp.
>
> Salter is extremely valuable to BP. She did a tour of duty on an oil platform off the coast of Aberdeen in the North Sea, and then worked on a gas platform in her native Trinidad, where she married and had a child. As the head person on an oil platform, Salter has been responsible for the health and safety of eighty-plus workers and was trained to deal with physical extremes and the remote possibility of life-threatening emergencies: gas leaks, chemical spills on the platform, and

helicopter crashes. To prepare for her position, Salter went through over a year and a half of physically punishing, highly realistic simulations. "Think of subzero temperatures, ice coating all surfaces, making everything slick, gale force winds— and then a wall of fire, breaking pipes, oil gushing," she says. "It's easy to get rattled and make mistakes of judgment in these situations." As an OIM in the North Sea, Salter was on a four-week rotation: two weeks offshore, two weeks onshore. But her offshore rotations were fraught with loneliness, as she was cut off from friends and family. Later on, rotations were hard on her marriage. "I got irritable and brittle the Monday before leaving—I always seem to pick a fight with my husband. It's the tension of knowing you are about to leave for a while." After her maternity leave, BP created an onshore OIM position for her, more of a human resources role than a conventional OIM position and one that is better suited for someone with a small child.

Looking into the future, Salter sees the possibility of upward mobility at BP. She credits her mentor—a Norwegian woman, married with a son, now a managing director for BP Norway—for her ongoing ambition. Salter says: "When I talk to her, I feel there's nothing I can't do."

Salter also notes that BP also offers a "9/80" schedule option that is promising for parents: under it, an employee fits a full-time schedule into nine days over the course of two weeks, taking the tenth day off. (Personal communication, May 25, 2006)

It is essential to remember that, whether pulled or pushed, only a relatively privileged group of women—those who are married to high-earning men—have the option of off-ramping. Indeed, for a subset of women in the survey, the presence of a high-earning spouse was, in and of itself, an important trigger. Fully 32 percent of the women surveyed cite the fact that their spouses' income "was sufficient for our family to live on one income" as a reason behind their decision to leave the workforce.

As can be expected, men as husbands and fathers factor into and condition their wives' decision to quit a job. This survey uncovers a wide range of men's opinions and attitudes toward their wives' decision to off-ramp. More than half of all husbands (60%) claim they are enthusiastically supportive, but 55 percent also say they are either envious or angry. Money matters loom large. Almost a quarter of the male respondents in the survey (22%) say they are worried about the financial implications of their wife's decision to quit. In one focus group that pulled together husbands of women who had quit, the conversation centered on overload and burden. A surprisingly high percentage of the men in the room felt resentful of the extra load dumped on their shoulders, and were concerned that they might not be able to make up the shortfall in family income. Some saw their wife quitting work as not being part of the "original deal." One focus group participant described his feelings this way: "I feel the rug has been pulled....I thought I was marrying a high-earning professional, not a stay-at-home wife."

Why Do Women Want Back In?

Desperate Housewives notwithstanding, talented women who blithely throw their careers to the winds are the exception rather than the rule. The survey data show that the overwhelming majority of highly qualified women who are currently off-ramped want to return to their careers (93%).

Many of these women have financial reasons for wanting to get back to work. Nearly half (46%) cite "wanting to have their own independent source of income" as an important propelling factor.[2] Women who participated in these focus groups spoke of their discomfort with "dependence." However solid their marriages, many disliked needing to ask for money. Not being able to splurge on some small extravagance or make their own philanthropic choices without the consent of their husbands did not appeal to them. It is also true that a significant proportion of women seeking on-ramps are facing troubling shortfalls in family income: 38 percent cite "household income no longer sufficient for family needs" and 24 percent name "partner's income no longer sufficient for family needs." Given the dramatic rise in the cost of homes (up 55% from 2000 to 2005; Office of Federal Housing Enterprise Oversight 2005, 15), the cost of college education (up 35% from 2001 to 2006; Pope 2006), and the cost of health insurance (up 73% since 2000; Kaiser Family Foundation 2005), it is easy to see why many professional families find that managing a household with one income can prove to be challenging.

Financial pressures do not tell the whole story. Many of these women find deep pleasure in their chosen careers, and want to reconnect with something they love. Forty-three percent cite the "enjoyment and satisfaction" they derive from their careers as an important reason to return. Among teachers, this figure rises to 54 percent, and among doctors, it rises to 70 percent. Sixteen percent want to "regain power and status in their profession." In the focus groups, women spoke eloquently about how work gives shape and structure to their lives, boosts confidence and self-esteem, and confers status and standing in their communities.

Perhaps the most unexpected reason to return to work centers around altruism. Twenty-four percent of women currently looking for on-ramps are motivated by "a desire to give something back to society" and are seeking jobs that allow them to contribute in some way. In the focus groups, off-ramped women talked about how their time at home had changed their aspirations. Whether they were involved in protecting wetlands, supporting the local library, rebuilding a playground, or being a "big sister" to a disadvantaged child, they felt newly connected to the importance of what one woman called "the work of care."

Lost on Reentry

If the overwhelming majority of off-ramped women have every intention of returning to the workforce, few understand how difficult this will be. The survey data show that, while 93 percent of these women want to rejoin the ranks of the employed, only 74 percent manage to do so. And among these, only 40 percent return to full-time, mainstream jobs. Twenty-four percent take part-time jobs, and another 9 percent become self-employed. The implications of these figures suggest that off-ramps are around every curve in the road, but once a woman has taken the turn, opportunities to reenter a career are few and far between—and difficult to find. A great many talented women find the on-ramping struggle a humiliating one: baffling, unfair, and replete with rejection.

The Prevalence of Stigma

Another powerful theme rampant among the focus group discussions was the pervasiveness of stigma. Across a range of sectors—in law firms, media companies, and investment banks—it was found that women (and men) perceive many work-life policies (e.g., telecommuting, job sharing, reduced-hour or part-time jobs) as essentially "off-limits" at their company. Telecommuting is most stigmatized for women—almost four in ten report difficulties taking advantage of this policy. Job-sharing and part-time positions are also severely stigmatized. One new mother described flexible work arrangements (FWAs) as "toxic." At her fast-paced tech company, which has an exemplary set of work-life policies, flexible work arrangements are so tainted, so poisonous, that women routinely quit rather than take up policies that are ostensibly on the books. Paid parenting leave seems to be somewhat less stigmatized than other work-life policies. Since the passage of the Family and Medical Leave Act (1993), parenting leave has become established public policy and this seems to have conferred a measure of legitimacy—at least for women. A higher percentage of men perceive paid parenting leave as a stigmatizing policy.

The Penalties of Time Out

Women off-ramp for surprisingly short periods of time—on average, 2.2 years. However, even these relatively short career interruptions entail heavy financial penalties. The data in this study show that, on average, women lose 18 percent of their earning power when an off-ramp is taken. In the business sector penalties are particularly draconian: in this sector, women's earning power dips 28 percent when they take time out. As one might expect, the longer time spent out, the more severe the penalty. Across sectors, women lose a staggering 37 percent of their earning power when they spend three or more years out of the workforce.

Findings in this area of financial penalties attached to "time out" jibe with the scholarly research. Columbia University economist Jane Waldfogel has analyzed the pattern of female earnings over the lifespan. When women enter the workforce in their early and mid-twenties, they earn nearly as much as men do. And for a few years, they almost keep pace with men in terms of wages. For example, at ages twenty-five to twenty-nine, women earn 87 percent of the male wage. However, when women approach their prime child-raising years (ages thirty to forty), many off-ramp for a short period of time, with disastrous consequences on the financial front. Arguably because of these career interruptions, by the time they reach the forty-to-forty-four age group women earn a mere 71 percent of the male wage (J. Waldfogel, personal communication, June 17, 2001; Harkness and Waldfogel 1999, 22). This suggests the importance of adhering to the "white male career model," a model that evolved to fit the life rhythms of middle-class white males in the 1950s and 1960s. The success of this model relied on a traditional division of labor between men and women, where men were the breadwinners and women were full-time wives, mothers, and homemakers. One feature of this model is that it requires careers to take off in the decade of one's thirties (Hewlett 2007; Hewlett and Luce 2005). In the words of MIT economist Lester Thurow (1984), "The 30s are the prime years for establishing a successful career. These are the years when hard work has the maximum payoff. Women who leave the job market during those years may find that they never catch up."

Downsizing Ambition

Data from this study imply that earning power is not the only cost attached to taking time out. Women also downsize their ambitions, losing sight of their aspirations and losing faith in their dreams. One newly on-ramped woman described her changed attitude: "It took me three years to find this much-less-good job, and during that time I had to accept that I had lost traction in my career. It was a bitter pill. I felt the unfairness of it—I had only been out for twenty months. But it was a fact nonetheless. So I've redefined what I can expect for myself." Another woman who participated in the same focus group, described her old self, before an off-ramp, as this "soaring, thrusting person." That person no longer exists. In her words, "reality bites."

The survey data show that, at young ages, there is not much of a gap between men and women in terms of ambition. However, there is a distinct drop-off in female ambition as women head through their thirties. In the business sector, for example, 53 percent of younger women (age twenty-eight to forty) describe themselves being very ambitious, while only 37 percent of older women (age forty-one to fifty-five) are comfortable with this label.

In her book, *Necessary Dreams*, psychiatrist Anna Fels (2004) argued convincingly that ambition stands on two legs—mastery and recognition. To hold onto their dreams, women must attain the necessary credentials and experience, but they must also have their achievements and potential recognized in the larger world. The latter is often missing in female careers. Particularly in the wake of an off-ramp, employers and bosses tend to be skeptical about a woman's worth. Thus, a downsizing cycle emerges: a woman's confidence and ambition stalls; she is perceived as less committed, and she no longer acquires the good jobs or the plum assignments. This serves to lower her ambition further.

What Do Women Want?

The survey data delves beyond the facts surrounding ambition, to a complex vision of what women really want. Many of their desires center on the quality of the work experience itself. In considering career goals, talented women very much wish to associate with people they respect (82%); to "be themselves" at work (79%); to collaborate with others, to work as part of a team (61%); and to "give back" to the community through the work that they do (both inside their organization and outside in the larger world).[3] They also greatly value recognition from their company or organization (51%). Women tend to emphasize value sets rather than compensation or benefits. In the survey, the only employment benefit to make it onto the "wish list" of the majority of the women was access to a flexible work schedule, which is a priority for 64 percent of the women. Just 42 percent cite a high salary, and only 15 percent want a powerful position.

Women's priorities thus constitute a sharp departure from the traditional male model, and become yet another powerful reason why success within this model is so elusive for women. Thirty-five years after the women's revolution transformed female opportunities, women's work lives remain very different from men's. Grouping together women who take off-ramps with those who take scenic routes, a majority have nonlinear careers. Many women find the need to step out, or step to the side, for a period of time. Looking back at their work lives, almost 60 percent of the highly qualified women in this survey describe their careers as nonlinear: they had not been able to "follow the arc" of a successful career in their sector (Hewlett et al. 2005, exhibit 2.1). An off-ramp or a scenic route has taken them off course.

This suggests that large numbers of talented women fail to fit the traditional white-male model. They are unable to conjure up a continuous, lockstep career path, and are badly positioned to "catch a wave" in their thirties. Besides, their goals and values are profoundly out of sync. Cloning the male competitive model is simply a huge stretch for many women, though some do manage it. Among them are women who sacrifice family life (there is a high degree of childlessness among high-level corporate women) and at least some superwomen who somehow or other "do it all" (Hewlett 2002). Nevertheless, these successful clones are in a minority, and not discussed here. Instead, the focus shifts to the remaining 60 percent: those who struggle with off-ramps and on-ramps and wrestle with claiming or sustaining ambition.

Reversing the "Brain Drain"

Research conducted by the Hidden Brain Drain Task Force has uncovered five essential and cutting-edge policies that work to keep women with nonlinear careers on the road to success: (a) create reduced-hour and flexible jobs, (b) provide flexibility over the arc of a career, (c) remove the stigma attached to nonstandard work arrangements, (d) nurture ambition, and (e) provide outlets for altruism. Member companies of the Hidden Brain Drain Task Force have found ways to set these policies in motion.

BT Group "Achieving the Balance": Flexible Jobs

In the early 1980s, BT Group (British Telecommunications) saw that the future held three big trends: globalization, a rise in available technology, and an increase in the demand and speed at which information would be obtained. In other words, business for communications providers was about to mushroom, and one way to make way for this explosion was to offer employees flexible hours.

In a global economy, this is a logical solution. If an office in London and another in Calcutta are collaborating on a project, it is realistic to assume that a job will run more smoothly if working hours coincide. It also seems sensible for customer relations. Homeowners wish to be at home when cables and phone lines are installed or repaired; these same homeowners are also likely to have jobs themselves. Thus, if consumers would prefer a technician to come at 7 a.m. or 7 p.m., is it not in the company's best interest to consider their customers' concerns first?

Serendipitously, BT determined that many of their workers favored working nontraditional hours. A mom who has to pick up a child at school might need to be free by 3 p.m. However, she might also be able to get to work by 7 a.m. This is an entire working day in terms of hours, but it is a workday disconnected from the traditional model.

Thus BT's "Achieving the Balance" initiative came to be. Employees are encouraged to develop their own attendance patterns whenever and wherever practical. They can balance working from home with long and short days at the office. Workers can also accrue blocks of vacation time to use during school holidays. The flexibility plans provide inclusive opportunities to people with disabilities, those with caretaking responsibilities, and employees returning to work after a career hiatus or maternity break. Jyoti Blew, a BT employee since 1987, is a case in point: "I wouldn't have been able to work; I might have had to look someplace else with more flexibility," she says. After her second child was born, Blew came back without a specific post, but then saw an "advert" for her current job. "I approached my manager with my concerns: that managing a crew of engineers wasn't a woman's job. I sort of thought it was a 'man's job,' but everyone was really supportive," Blew says. Blew maintains an office in a BT complex, but she also has BT broadband at home, so she splits the week up by working from home and going into the office when necessary. As to the men she supervises—"They've been perfect gentlemen" (personal communication, February 6, 2006).

Since implementing its flexible hours plan, BT has seen amazing results. Turnover is only 3 percent, and 99 percent of women return after maternity leave, compared to the U.K. average of 47 percent. BT saves, at a conservative estimate, £5 million a year by not having to replace employees. Women report that they return to BT after a "time out" because of the many variations of flextime available to them. BT is rewarding actual productivity and making the shift to paying salaries based on productivity, not attendance. Business has boomed; productivity was boosted by these arrangements and customer satisfaction has risen by 7 percent.

Lehman Brothers' Encore: Flexibility over the Arc of Career

For years Wall Street has viewed high female attrition rates as an unacceptable but an unalterable fact of life. Lehman Brothers, however, believed there must be a fix for this "truism." Thus, in 2004, Lehman joined the Hidden Brain Drain Task Force and cosponsored a study, *The Hidden Brain Drain: Off-Ramps and On-Ramps in Women's Careers,* to examine this phenomenon. According to the research, only 67 percent of women in banking and finance who off-ramped succeeded in on-ramping. Traditional gender issues become most salient around year five of a woman's career, when female attrition begins to rise relative to men.

Inspired by the Task Force, Lehman launched its Encore initiative in 2005 to help women reengage. Lehman's chief diversity officer, Anne Erni, conceived Encore not just to legitimize women who have off-ramped and want a new road back into the financial services industry but also to give her firm access to a significantly untapped pool of talent. President and Chief Operating Officer Joe Gregory endorsed the idea because it made business sense. Other senior managers at Lehman have also been champions, recognizing that off-ramped women bring personal and professional contacts, in addition to judgment honed by experience.

Invitations for the first Encore event in November 2005 were sent to women who had at least five years' experience in financial services, had been out of the business three years or less, and expressed interest in rejoining the industry. Seventy-one women attended. About half were referred by Lehman employees, and the rest were referred indirectly, some by receiving forwarded invitations. The firm dubbed the event "Encore: Reigniting Your Story." It was structured as a morning of networking, self-reflection, and information sessions. The day kicked off with "Since You've Been Gone," a panel comprised of four Lehman managing directors discussing recent trends on Wall Street. A "storytelling workshop" held later in the morning was designed to help women articulate their nonlinear career story while explaining what they had to offer.

Tellingly, event feedback showed 98 percent of the attendees agreed or agreed strongly that Encore piqued their interest in coming to work at Lehman. An Encore e-mail account was set up to field comments and resumés from participants. Introductory screening sessions were conducted with the majority of women who submitted resumés, resulting in a number of follow-up interviews. Encore has also expanded, beginning with a London event in February 2006. In just a few months' time, Lehman hired over twenty women in New York and London.

Susan Siverson, an Encore participant, credits Encore with her reentry into the workforce. Before Encore, she had thought that the choice was between "working moms" and "nonworking moms." Encore led her to reconsider her observations (of friends and colleagues) that had signaled that part-time work was not a satisfactory option ("the employer would want four days, but you could give only three"). Instead, she saw new potential to position herself to rejoin the working force—on her own terms. Lehman, too, benefited by recognizing the experience and skills in Siverson.

What seemed right for Siverson was to incorporate and work as a consultant one or two days a week. Usually she goes into the office: "To get to know the business and its culture, you have to be there." Siverson has laid out strict boundaries about her available time; how she is best utilized is up to the company" (personal communication, February 23, 2006).

Unilever: Removing Stigma by Walking the Talk at the Top

Fergus Balfour, the managing director for Unilever Ice Cream & Frozen Food in the United Kingdom, works at home most Fridays. It works for him—so much so, that he believes everyone should follow his lead. Flex work was not a concept Balfour had thought much about some five years ago. But at a 2001 Unilever diversity conference, he heard many of his colleagues (mostly women, but some men as well) express a wish to fit their jobs around the rest of their lives. It was not for lack of commitment to work; most loved their jobs. They had practical reasons for wanting to work from their homes on Fridays, to arrange job sharing, or to work compressed hours—that is, to better fit their work around their lives. "When people aren't worrying about what they are not doing elsewhere, they can more easily bring their passion to their work," Balfour explains. By embracing a nontraditional work-life arrangement, Balfour has helped to remove its stigma for others at Unilever.

"I was out of the office a lot anyway on business," Balfour says today. "Why did I have to be *in* the office just because I was in town? What did it matter whether I was talking to people around the world from my desk at home or my desk in the office? All that was standing in the way of my working flexibly was me. My bosses certainly didn't know where I was." Balfour found that he accomplished more work at home than he did in the office. And because he was away from the noise of the office, he was more relaxed on weekends. He also noted that not working in the office on Fridays created a welcome social flexibility. He could meet his wife midday for lunch, then resume work from home until he finished the tasks he set for the day.

Wherever Balfour goes, he brings his advocacy of flextime with him. In March 2004, Unilever sent him to the United States to manage a struggling business unit.

Balfour discovered the unit's employees were doing compressed-week work hours so they could go home on Friday around lunchtime. The practice had its opponents, Balfour recalls, "but I knew how productive people can be when they have flexible hours, so I kept it in place. What does it matter as long as the work gets done?" Balfour turned out to be right. He turned around the division—and it had its best year ever.

"It's an archaic notion that hours at the office reflect output and quality," Balfour argues. He also maintains that flextime is a particularly powerful recruiting and retention lure for talented women. "We can make it easier for women to stay," says Balfour. "We can keep our talent" (personal communication, March 31, 2006).

Booz Allen Hamilton Adjunct Program: Nurturing Ambition

Commercial consulting demands long hours and lots of travel. Assignments can be short and unpredictable. Dr. Ann Bohara, an adjunct professor at the Wharton School of Management who was hired by Booz Allen Hamilton to head its women's diversity and work-life balance initiatives, observes that every year, about 20 percent of each incoming cohort leaves the firm and indeed exits the consulting industry (personal communication, September 22, 2005). Those who progress through the firm's "up or out" assessment process will be in their mid-thirties when they attain vice president or partner—the same years that women are likely to feel the pull of family. Consequently, women are underrepresented in the senior echelons of the commercial consulting profession, including Booz Allen.

These facts resonated with DeAnne Aguirre, leader of her firm's global-organization and change-leadership practice. In her sixteen years at Booz Allen, Aguirre figures she has ramped down and ramped up eight times (personal communication, October 7, 2004). The ways she has remained attached to Booz Allen did not involve a formal program. The company wanted her and made it possible for her to stay; an informal survey of senior women inside Booz Allen indicated that Aguirre's experience was typical.

Thus, after joining the Hidden Brain Drain Task Force, Aguirre began focusing on ways Booz Allen Hamilton could nurture women's ambition by keeping them attached and reconnecting them with firm alumni. Booz Allen launched a pilot program to identify professional staff willing to be part of this test. The firm unbundled consulting work into chunks that could be done by telecommuting or in short stints at the office—or both. A standard employment contract was created that could be activated for chunks of part-time work, whether project-based or research-based. Contract work was defined as a piece of a larger job that demanded either a portion of a workweek or a short but intense assignment for a professional fee and, in most cases, without benefits.

Booz Allen reached out to 148 alumni and secured 99 contracts, 59 among alumni and 40 from among referrals. Intriguingly, half the first contracts went to women—a higher percentage of women than the firm had among its full-time senior partners. DeAnne Aguirre, by now deeply involved in the Hidden Brain Drain Task Force, considered the outcome of this experience and noticed a means of nurturing women's ambition, thus stemming the female exodus from commercial consulting. If one could flex a job, she reasoned, why not flex a career? From that was born the Booz Allen Hamilton "Adjunct" program.

The vision for the Adjunct program is to create a new employee category alongside full-timer, contractor, and flex worker. An adjunct is someone who once worked full-time for Booz Allen and might do so again. In the meantime, an adjunct would enjoy many of the benefits of full-time status, in addition to fees per project completed. An adjunct would be eligible for an appraisal on each project, high-level career planning, mentoring, and benefits, as well as participation in annual conferences and training. Different versions of this program are being discussed around the world as the idea continues to take hold and gather momentum (D. Aguirre, personal communication, October 7, 2004). Women at Booz Allen Hamilton know that when and if their careers have to ramp down, their ambition to rise to the top can stay alive.

Creating On-Ramps and Up-Ramps

This research unveils a harsh reality. A significant proportion of highly qualified women continue to face compromise and sacrifice in their professional lives. There are many dynamics to this process—the complex pull and push factors, ranging from childcare issues to being passed over for a deserved promotion, that lead to the decision to quit for a while. Yet "off-ramps," in and of themselves, further hem women in and limit their professional options. As the data show, the penalties attached to time off can be severe. As women attempt to rejoin the career highway (and the vast majority of off-ramped women do want to get back to work), they face stigma and suspicion from employers who believe that a gap in a resumé means that a person has lost her edge. Most on-ramping women find it impossible to find real, on-track jobs. As a consequence women recalibrate their vocational aspirations. In too many cases dreams get deferred and downsized.

What to do? The thread of hope running through this story is that employers are finally ready to step up to the plate. Booz Allen, General Electric, and Johnson & Johnson, among other companies, are developing programs that create "arc of career" flexibility for women—that allow a working mother or daughter to ramp down and then ramp up with no particular penalty. These new policies stand a chance of being "game changers." Giving a talented woman a second shot at ambition is often all she needs to resurrect her career—and her dreams.

6

ELDERLY LABOR SUPPLY
Work or Play?

Steven J. Haider and David S. Loughran

The aging of the U.S. population, concerns over the long-term solvency of Social Security and Medicare, and recent data have sparked much research on the labor supply of older individuals. The bulk of this research has focused on individuals approaching traditional retirement ages of fifty-five to sixty-four. However, much less research has considered the labor supply of individuals beyond this age, a population referred to here as the "elderly."

Perhaps the most fundamental questions about elderly labor supply address *why* the elderly work and do not work. For example, to what extent do the elderly work because of financial circumstances, such as negative shocks to wealth or unexpected expenditures related to healthcare? Alternatively, to what extent do the elderly work simply because they enjoy work? In other words, might work be considered leisure—or play—for the elderly who continue to work? For those elderly who do not work, are they choosing not to work? Or is it the case that elderly persons who are not employed are having difficulties finding suitable employment?

The apparent reversal of the long-run trend toward earlier retirement and the general aging of the U.S. population make finding answers to such questions increasingly important. The issue has inspired a series of reports arguing that many public and private policies pose serious barriers to work for the elderly, and there should be efforts to eliminate them (Committee for Economic Development 1999; Knapp and Muller 2001; Munnell 2006; Purcell 2003). Concern over this issue has been sufficiently great to warrant hearings in the U.S. Senate calling for action at the federal level to reduce barriers to work among the elderly (Now Hiring 2000).

Understanding what motivates the elderly to continue working is an important ingredient in formulating public and private policies to increase elderly labor supply.

If continuing to work is primarily motivated by financial concerns, then policies that affect elderly wages are likely to be effective. For example, acts such as the Senior Citizens' Freedom to Work Act of 2000, which effectively eliminated a sizeable tax on earnings for Social Security annuitants between the normal retirement age and age seventy, would likely substantially increase the labor supply among the elderly.[1] Alternatively, if the elderly are working primarily to remain engaged in their community or simply because they enjoy their jobs, then policies that affect nonpecuniary aspects of their jobs might be more effective in increasing labor supply. For example, the elderly might be more responsive to policies that allow them greater flexibility in setting their work schedules.

The labor supply decisions of the elderly are driven by a unique set of circumstances. Perhaps most important, the overwhelming majority of elderly people receive or are eligible to receive some level of guaranteed annuity income, whether it is from Social Security, Supplemental Security Income (SSI), or private pensions. Given access to such income, the labor supply of the elderly would likely exhibit different responses to financial incentives and job characteristics than those not receiving such income. The elderly are also much more likely to suffer both acute and chronic episodes of poor health than younger populations.

This chapter directly examines two questions regarding elderly employment: who among the elderly works, and what are their job characteristics? The empirical analysis makes use of two data sets, the annual March demographic supplements to the Current Population Survey (CPS) and the 1998 Health and Retirement Study (HRS98). The first key empirical finding is that employment among the elderly is concentrated among the healthiest, wealthiest, and most educated individuals. The second key finding is that, despite the elderly workforce being comprised of the healthiest, wealthiest, and most educated, they earn very low wages. Nearly 75 percent of individuals ages seventy and above earn wages in the bottom quintile of the overall wage distribution of those ages 50–61. Further analysis reveals that the working elderly report a substantial level of flexibility in their work schedules and a high degree of job satisfaction. One interpretation of these findings is that the elderly may be particularly willing to choose jobs that they desire at the expense of low financial returns.

A Review of Related Literature

The growing importance of the elderly in the U.S. workforce is the product of two well-known trends, the aging of the U.S. population and the leveling off of the long-term decline in male labor force participation at older ages. In 2005, the U.S. Census estimated that individuals age sixty-five and over account for 12.4 percent of the U.S. population. By 2025, this percentage is projected to rise to 18.2 percent (U.S. Census 2006c). Along with general aging, the long-term trend toward earlier retirement in this century slowed considerably in the 1980s and reversed itself in the 1990s, especially for males (Purcell 2000; Quinn 1999). By some estimates, these two trends together imply the elderly will account for more than 5 percent of the total U.S. workforce in 2025 (Fullerton 1999).

The change in male labor force participation at older ages is the subject of an enormous literature. Although there is some consensus that much of the long-run decline must be attributable to increases in real wealth and family income, many also believe that the advent of social programs for the elderly, such as Social Security and Medicare, have played a role.[2] The more recent increases in male labor force participation is the subject of considerable debate, with researchers attributing it to factors such as general economic conditions, changes in Social Security rules, the end of mandatory retirement, the shift away from defined benefit pension plans in the private sector, improving health, and a shift toward a more service-oriented economy (Costa 1999; Quinn 1999). There is no consensus whether these recent increases represent a temporary or more permanent shift in the labor force partici-pation rates of older individuals.

Only a few studies have directly examined the labor force participation of the elderly. Iams (1987) finds that new Social Security beneficiaries in the first wave of the New Beneficiary Survey tend to work fewer hours and for lower wages than they did prior to receiving benefits. Iams also finds that individuals who changed jobs following benefit receipt tend to move into service-oriented jobs. Using the National Longitudinal Survey of Older Men, Parnes and Sommers (1994) find that the prob-ability of work among men ages sixty-eight and older in 1989 is strongly correlated with a strong work ethic, good health, and positive attitudes toward retirement. Pi-enta, Burr, and Mutchler (1994) focus on elderly women and the strong positive cor-relation between their labor force participation early and later in life. A positive correlation between health and employment is also evident among individuals approaching traditional retirement ages (Benitez-Silva 2000; Bound et al. 1999).

Several studies have demonstrated that job characteristics affect the ability of older individuals to remain in the workforce. For example, a number of studies show retirement ages are lower for individuals who work in physically demanding occupations, suggesting that higher physical demands may force some into retire-ment (Gustman and Steinmeier 1986; Hayward and Grady 1990; Holden 1988). There is little evidence to suggest that older workers are less productive in their work activities (Mitchell 1990). A survey of employer attitudes found that employ-ers rate older workers above average in terms of experience, judgment, commitment to quality, and attendance and punctuality (Committee for Economic Development 1999, 29). The same survey found, though, that older workers exhibit less flexibility and adaptability.

A variety of public programs and laws affect the incentive to work at older ages. Social Security is perhaps the most obvious, offering a guaranteed annuity income for the vast majority of Americans beginning as early as age sixty-two. The large spikes in retirement rates at the ages of sixty-two and sixty-five point to a potentially strong role for Social Security in reducing labor supply among older individuals (Lumsdaine, Stock, and Wise 1996). There is mixed evidence that other features of the Social Security system, such as the earnings test, which reduces Social Security benefits for individuals receiving more than a relatively small amount of labor income, reduce elderly labor supply (Friedberg 2000; Gruber and Orszag 2003; Haider and Loughran 2008).

The Employee Retirement Income Security Act (ERISA) and Medicare may affect the demand for elderly workers. ERISA, enacted in 1974, sets minimum standards for pension plans in private industry. The law explicitly requires firms to extend pension benefits to all employees working more than one thousand hours per year. Extending pension coverage to older workers may be quite expensive, and therefore discourage their hiring. ERISA and federal tax codes place some restrictions on employers paying out pension benefits to employees who have qualified for early retirement but are still employed by the firm, although pension benefits may be paid to current employees who have reached the plan's normal retirement age. Some have argued that this may discourage both employees and employers from pursuing a more gradual path to retirement (Purcell 2000). Before 1982, Medicare was the primary health insurance provider for all individuals over the age of sixty-five. Today, employers are required to continue offering private health insurance to individuals over the age of sixty-five for the length of their employment.

The Age Discrimination in Employment Act (ADEA) of 1967 explicitly prohibited age discrimination against individuals between ages forty and sixty-five with only a few exceptions. Since 1967, several amendments have extended the coverage of ADEA. The 1974 amendments extended coverage to government employees. The 1978 amendments prohibited mandatory retirement and extended the upper limit of the protected age class from sixty-five to seventy; the 1986 amendments eliminated the upper age limit of seventy. Amendments in 1982 and 1984 attempted to reconcile ADEA obligations for employee benefits with employer obligations under Medicare and Medicaid. Important amendments in 1990 required age-based differences in benefit plans to be justified by their costs. An exception is that healthcare benefits for employees and their spouses between ages sixty-five and sixty-nine cannot be reduced upon reaching age sixty-five. Neumark (2003) reports that there is considerable evidence of age-based discriminatory hiring practices prior to ADEA. Neumark and Stock (1999), Adams (2000), and Ashenfelter and Card (2002) find evidence that prohibition of explicit age discrimination in hiring and firing boosts the labor force participation of older workers.

The Americans with Disabilities Act (ADA) of 1990 requires firms to accommodate individuals with disabilities. Given that such accommodation can be costly, it is conceivable that firms may be reluctant to hire older workers who are more likely to experience a disability while in their employment. Several studies have found negative employment effects of the ADA for the general population (Acemoglu and Angrist 2001; DeLeire 2000).

Hurd and McGarry (1993) emphasize the likely importance of hours flexibility in determining labor force participation among older workers. In a standard labor supply model, individuals freely choose hours of work given exogenously offered wages, and there are many reasons to believe that older workers would prefer to reduce hours gradually rather than retire all at once. Indeed, transitioning from full-time to part-time employment, often through switching jobs or even employers, is a common pathway to retirement for many older individuals (Blau 1994; Hayward, Crimmins, and Wray 1994; Hayward and Grady 1990; Herz 1995; Ruhm 1990).

There is considerable evidence, however, that hours and wages are offered simultaneously, so workers cannot simply choose hours at a given wage (Dickens and Lundberg 1993; Lundberg 1985). Hurd and McGarry (1993) find that individuals who currently work in jobs where work hours can be reduced, or their responsibilities can be lessened, report a substantially higher subjective probability of working past age sixty-five, even after controlling for a host of demographic, financial, and health characteristics. Thus, the ability of employers to accommodate demands for flexibility may be an important determinant of labor supply among the elderly. Although there is no direct evidence on this point in the case of the elderly, several studies show that accommodation increases the likelihood that individuals suffering from a temporary or permanent disability resume work with earnings comparable to their earnings before becoming disabled (Burkhauser et al. 1999; Daly and Bound 1996).

Data

The empirical analysis uses two data sets, the 1964–99 March demographic supplements to the CPS and the 1998 HRS. The annual March demographic supplement to the CPS surveys a nationally representative sample of households each year. The survey collects information on basic demographic characteristics and labor force participation and income in the preceding year. The CPS provides a long time series on key demographic and employment characteristics of the elderly, and, by pooling multiple years, offers large sample sizes.

HRS98 is comprised of a nationally representative sample of over twenty thousand individuals born before 1948 and their spouses.[3] These data are used to explore the cross-sectional correlates of the labor supply of the elderly and to make comparisons across individuals ages fifty and above. The HRS98 data provide detailed information on health, wealth, labor force participation, and retirement, as well as standard demographic characteristics of individuals.

Because the focus of the chapter is the decision to work, the unit of analysis is the individual. Most analyses pool males and females; separate analyses are presented only when large differences exist. Many of the important determinants of working, such as income and wealth, are measured at the household level. A simple adjustment is made to pool married and single individuals, multiplying household wealth and income by 0.75 for married individuals.[4] Details regarding sample sizes are provided in Center for Retirement Research at Boston College (Haider and Loughran 2001).

The wealth and income data in the HRS98 are of high quality. For example, a series of unfolding brackets are used to solicit responses from individuals unwilling or unable to provide point estimates for many quantities. Wealth and income imputations using these responses are provided by the Institute for Social Research at the University of Michigan (Cao 2000a, 2000b). The measure of wealth is the sum of real estate, business and farm, individual retirement account (IRA), stock, bond, cash, cash deposit, auto, trust, and housing equity wealth, less nonmortgage debt; this measure is referred to as "bequeathable" wealth. This measure of wealth does not account for the value of future nonlabor income from Social Security, pensions, and other annuitized assets.

Who Works among the Elderly?

Figure 6.1 presents the employment rates of males and females ages fifty and above, using data from the March CPS. Male employment (top panel) was relatively constant between 1963 and 1998 for males ages 50–58, declined from 63 to 50 percent for males ages fifty-nine to sixty-four, and declined from 22 to 15 percent for males ages 65+. At the very end of this time series, it appears that male employment may be rising somewhat for males in the fifty-nine to sixty-four and 65+ categories. For women (bottom panel), the decline in employment in the age 65+ category is much less dramatic, although its slight decline stands in marked contrast to the general rise in employment among younger women. Female employment in the age 65+ category generally follows the pattern exhibited in male employment, dipping slightly from 10 percent in 1963 to 8 percent in 1985, and then rising back through the end of the series to 10 percent. As found by previous research, the long-term trend toward earlier retirement has abated.

Table 6.1 examines how employment varies by educational attainment using pooled 1991–99 CPS data. The table shows that employment is higher at higher levels of education at all ages.[5] For example, employment among individuals ages sixty-two to sixty-four ranges from 26 percent for dropouts to 52 percent for those with more than a college-level education. The difference in employment between the more and less educated grows with age. At ages fifty to fifty-eight 53 percent of dropouts work, compared with 83 percent of those with more than a college-level education. By ages seventy-one to seventy-three, these employment rates are 8 percent and 22 percent, respectively. At ages seventy-seven to seventy-nine, the

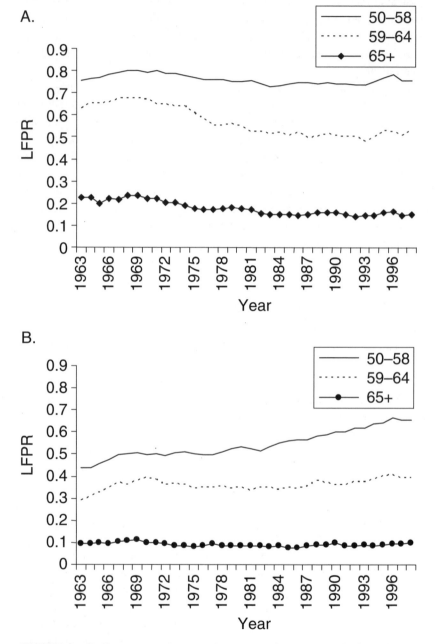

FIGURE 6.1. Employment rates by sex, age, and year. (*Source:* 1964–99 Current Population Survey) A. Males B. Females

Table 6.1. Employment by Age and Education

	EDUCATIONAL ATTAINMENT				
AGE	DROPOUT	HIGH SCHOOL	SOME COLLEGE	COLLEGE	ADVANCED
50–58	0.53	0.68	0.74	0.78	0.83
59–61	0.41	0.52	0.58	0.62	0.68
62–64	0.26	0.34	0.41	0.46	0.52
65–67	0.16	0.22	0.26	0.31	0.42
68–70	0.11	0.15	0.18	0.24	0.28
71–73	0.08	0.10	0.14	0.14	0.22
74–76	0.06	0.08	0.10	0.10	0.17
77–79	0.04	0.05	0.06	0.09	0.14
80–83	0.02	0.03	0.04	0.06	0.08

Source: 1991–99 March Current Population Survey.

Table 6.2. Employment by Age and Bequeathable Wealth Quintile

	BEQUEATHABLE WEALTH QUINTILE				
AGE	LOW	2	3	4	HIGH
50–58	0.57	0.68	0.73	0.74	0.73
59–61	0.44	0.54	0.61	0.62	0.56
62–64	0.28	0.43	0.39	0.42	0.39
65–67	0.19	0.26	0.20	0.26	0.26
68–70	0.14	0.19	0.17	0.15	0.19
71–73	0.09	0.11	0.12	0.10	0.15
74–76	0.08	0.11	0.07	0.07	0.15
77–79	0.05	0.05	0.04	0.08	0.10
≥80	0.01	0.02	0.04	0.03	0.05

Source: 1998 Health and Retirement Study.
Notes: See text for details of wealth measurement. Wealth quintiles calculated within age categories.

difference is even more dramatic: 4 percent of dropouts work, compared with 14 percent of those with more than a college-level education. These statistics show that the workforce becomes increasingly concentrated with age among the most educated individuals.

The relationship between wealth and employment is explored in table 6.2. This table reports employment rates by bequeathable wealth quintile and age, where wealth quintiles are calculated within age categories. As with education, it appears that the wealthiest are more likely to be working than the least wealthy at all ages.

More strikingly, differences in employment rates between the highest and lowest wealth quintiles grow substantially with age. At ages sixty-five to sixty-seven, for example, the employment rate is 19 percent in the lowest quintile and 26 percent in the highest quintile. At ages seventy-seven to seventy-nine, the employment rate in the lowest and highest quintile is 5 percent and 10 percent, respectively. In other words, by ages seventy-seven to seventy-nine, individuals in the highest quintile are twice as likely to work as individuals in the lowest quintile. Thus, employment becomes increasingly concentrated among the wealthiest individuals with age.

Table 6.3 examines how employment varies with health, measuring health as the number of difficulties with Activities of Daily Living (ADLs).[6] Employment is highest among individuals reporting difficulty with the least number of ADLs. This is true at all ages. Unlike with education and wealth, there is not a growing disparity in employment between the healthy and less healthy with age. The healthy are much more likely to be working than the less healthy at all ages.

Because education, wealth, and health are likely to be highly correlated, simple linear regression is used to isolate the partial correlations of these variables with employment. Two dummy variables are incorporated for education (thirteen to sixteen years and 16+ years), four dummy variables for bequeathable wealth quintile, and three dummy variables for having zero, one, and two or more difficulties with ADLs. A dummy variable is also included for whether an individual considers him or herself to be in very good or excellent health.[7] Table 6.4 presents the results of these regressions for five age categories.

Table 6.3.   Employment by Age and Number of Activities of Daily Life Difficulties

	NUMBER OF ADL DIFFICULTIES		
AGE	0–1	2	3+
50–58	0.68	0.63	0.32
59–61	0.56	0.51	0.27
62–64	0.42	0.36	0.20
65–67	0.28	0.21	0.11
68–70	0.21	0.16	0.07
71–73	0.15	0.13	0.07
74–76	0.14	0.09	0.06
77–79	0.09	0.07	0.04
≥80	0.05	0.03	0.01

Source: 1998 Health and Retirement Study.
Notes: Six ADLs are included in this analysis: walking one block, climbing several flights of stairs, stooping, kneeling, or crouching, extending arms above shoulder level, lifting weights over ten pounds, and picking up a dime from a table.

Table 6.4.   The Effect of Education, Health, and Wealth on Employment by Age

	AGE				
	50–59	60–64	65–69	70–74	75+
EDUCATION[a]					
>16 yrs	0.10	0.08	0.06	0.04	0.02
	(0.02)	(0.03)	(0.03)	(0.03)	(0.01)
13–16 yrs	0.07	0.07	0.02	0.01	0.00
	(0.01)	(0.02)	(0.02)	(0.02)	(0.01)
WEALTH QUINTILE[a]					
High	0.00	−0.03	−0.02	0.01	0.02
	(0.02)	(0.03)	(0.03)	(0.03)	(0.01)
2	0.05	0.03	−0.01	−0.05	0.01
	(0.02)	(0.03)	(0.03)	(0.03)	(0.01)
3	0.08	0.06	−0.02	−0.02	0.01
	(0.02)	(0.03)	(0.02)	(0.02)	(0.01)
4	0.06	0.10	0.04	0.00	0.00
	(0.02)	(0.03)	(0.02)	(0.02)	(0.01)
NUMBER OF ADL DIFFICULTIES[a]					
0	0.38	0.27	0.16	0.08	0.04
	(0.02)	(0.02)	(0.02)	(0.02)	(0.01)
1	0.34	0.24	0.11	0.03	0.05
	(0.02)	(0.02)	(0.02)	(0.02)	(0.01)
2	0.33	0.19	0.08	0.03	0.02
	(0.02)	(0.03)	(0.02)	(0.02)	(0.01)
GOOD HEALTH	0.07	0.09	0.06	0.04	0.03
	(0.01)	(0.02)	(0.02)	(0.02)	(0.01)
Dependent variable mean	0.68	0.45	0.21	0.13	0.05
n	5,452	3,623	2,905	2,055	5,054
R^2	0.17	0.13	0.05	0.03	0.04

Source: 1998 Health and Retirement Study.
Notes: Regressions additional include a quadratic in age and dummy variables for male, black, and currently married. Standard errors are in parentheses. [a]Excluded categories are <13 years education, lowest quintile of the bequeathable wealth distribution, and more than two ADL difficulties, respectively.

Looking first at the regression for individuals age fifty to fifty-nine, the coefficients have the expected signs, with the more educated, wealthier, and healthier individuals being more likely to work than the less educated, least wealthy, and less healthy individuals. Consistent with tables 6.1 through 6.3, this is true in the older samples as well, although the effect of being in the highest wealth quintiles is sometimes negative and imprecisely estimated. In the case of education and health, the size of these regression coefficients relative to mean employment generally increases with age, providing further evidence that the working population becomes increasingly concentrated among the educated and healthy. Also notable in table 6.4 is the decline in R^2 with age in these regressions, from 0.17 among individuals ages fifty to fifty-nine to 0.04 among individuals aged 75+. This reduction in R^2 is consistent with other factors, such as job characteristics and preferences, becoming increasingly important in determining employment with age.

What Are the Job Characteristics of the Elderly?

This section examines the jobs that are held by the elderly. Table 6.5 explores mean weeks and hours worked, as calculated from the CPS. A clear pattern emerges,

Table 6.5. Weeks and Hours Worked by Age and Year

	AGE						
YEAR	50–58	59–61	62–64	65–69	70–74	75–79	80+
				WEEKS			
1963–65	46.8	46.2	43.9	38.9	36.8	39.0	36.4
1966–68	47.4	46.6	44.4	39.3	38.3	37.7	39.8
1969–71	47.0	46.1	43.6	37.6	37.8	37.9	37.5
1972–74	47.2	45.8	42.8	37.8	37.8	37.2	38.9
1975–77	46.7	45.3	40.9	35.8	36.6	37.0	34.4
1978–80	46.9	45.7	42.3	37.0	36.0	35.9	35.6
1981–83	46.8	45.3	42.2	37.9	36.8	36.6	37.3
1984–86	46.9	45.4	42.0	37.7	37.4	36.9	36.9
1987–89	47.4	45.2	41.9	39.0	38.3	36.8	36.7
1990–92	47.4	45.2	41.7	39.0	37.9	38.1	36.0
1993–95	47.5	45.1	42.5	39.1	37.6	36.4	39.8
1996–98	48.1	46.0	43.3	40.5	39.2	37.8	38.1
				HOURS			
1975–77	39.8	39.0	36.5	29.7	26.4	25.5	27.6
1978–80	39.8	39.0	36.4	29.8	26.0	26.2	22.9
1981–83	39.3	38.3	35.8	29.7	25.4	23.5	24.0
1984–86	39.6	38.2	35.2	29.2	24.6	24.8	23.4
1987–89	39.8	38.3	34.7	30.1	26.4	26.5	25.0
1990–92	40.2	38.2	34.6	28.8	25.9	25.2	24.5
1993–95	40.6	38.3	35.1	29.9	27.1	24.1	28.9
1996–98	41.0	38.9	35.5	29.9	26.7	26.2	25.2

Source: 1964–99 March Current Population Survey.
Notes: Sample restricted to individuals reporting positive earnings and weeks worked.

indicating that older workers work fewer weeks and hours than younger workers. There is a slight increase between 1963 and 1998 in mean weeks worked among individuals ages 65 and over who are working. No time trend is apparent in hours worked for these individuals. Haider and Lougran (2001) provide further results to distinguish between full-time (defined as working at least thirty-five hours per week and fifty weeks per year, or 1,750 hours per year) and part-time work, showing that older individuals are much more likely to be working part-time than younger workers. Moreover, their supplementary tabulations show that the percent of workers ages sixty-five and over who work full-time has been increasing over time.

Table 6.6 displays the wages of those who work. Median weekly wages, as reported in the HRS98, drop precipitously with age for both men and women. Median weekly wages of males fall from $781 at ages fifty to fifty-eight to $256 at ages seventy-four to seventy-six. This decline is confirmed in the CPS data, which show a decline in the median weekly wages of males from $742 at ages fifty to fifty-eight to $266 at ages seventy-four to seventy-six. Some of this decline is no

Table 6.6. Median Wages ($1998) by Age

AGE	HRS98		CPS (WEEKLY WAGE)		
	HOURLY	WEEKLY	ALL	FULL-TIME	COLLEGE+
MALES					
50–58	17.6	781	742	781	1,099
59–61	15.2	664	635	699	999
62–64	14.1	555	538	712	999
65–67	11.4	372	340	699	700
68–70	10.2	273	280	580	504
71–73	10.2	239	254	547	498
74–76	8.7	256	266	514	481
77–79	10.2	197	298	693	481
≥80	7.6	162	250	740	329
FEMALES					
50–58	11.3	430	411	494	697
59–61	10.2	391	360	453	592
62–64	9.1	308	306	469	508
65–67	8.6	213	220	425	391
68–70	8.1	195	183	387	250
71–73	7.6	201	183	430	267
74–76	6.6	158	156	385	210
77–79	7.3	113	141	330	136
≥80	6.4	112	150	413	272

Sources: 1998 Health and Retirement Study and 1995–99 March Current Population Study.
Notes: Samples include males reporting positive earnings and weeks worked.

doubt attributable to the greater proportion of part-time workers among the elderly, as part-time work typically commands lower wages than full-time work. Even among full-time workers, however, there remains a substantial drop in wages with age. It is notable that wage declines occur across the educational spectrum. In the final column of table 6.6, for example, there is a large decline in the wages of males with a college-level education or more. Thus, even the most educated workers appear willing to work for relatively low wages at older ages. All of these results prove true for women as well.

Whereas Table 6.6 shows that median wages decline with age, table 6.7 examines how wages change at other points in the wage distribution. There appears to be a dramatic shift in the wages of male older workers toward the bottom quintile of the overall wage distribution of males ages fifty to sixty-one. At ages sixty-two to sixty-four, 33 percent of working males in the HRS98 earn wages in the bottom quintile of the age fifty to sixty-one wage distribution. By ages seventy-one to seventy-three, this percentage has increased to 64 percent. At ages eighty and above, 76 percent of workers earn wages in the bottom quintile of the age fifty to sixty-one wage distribution. None of these workers remain in the top of the wage distribution.

Figure 6.2 and Table 6.8 provide strong evidence that older workers are more likely than younger workers to be employed in jobs with flexible work arrangements. Figure 6.2 shows that about 16 percent of the male HRS98 sample ages fifty to fifty-two report being self-employed compared to 30 percent of those ages sixty-five to sixty-seven and 56 percent of those ages seventy-seven to seventy-nine. Females also are more likely to be self-employed at older ages, although this trend is less pronounced.

Table 6.7. Distribution of Working Males by Age and Wage Quintile of Males Age 50–61

AGE	WAGE QUINTILE OF MALES AGE 50–61				
	LOW	2	3	4	HIGH
50–61	0.20	0.20	0.20	0.20	0.20
62–64	0.33	0.19	0.20	0.16	0.12
65–67	0.51	0.15	0.13	0.08	0.13
68–70	0.61	0.17	0.07	0.06	0.09
71–73	0.64	0.12	0.08	0.08	0.08
74–76	0.65	0.14	0.12	0.06	0.03
77–79	0.73	0.06	0.08	0.05	0.09
≥80	0.76	0.11	0.06	0.07	0.00

Source: 1998 Health and Retirement Study.
Notes: Sample includes males reporting positive earnings and weeks worked.

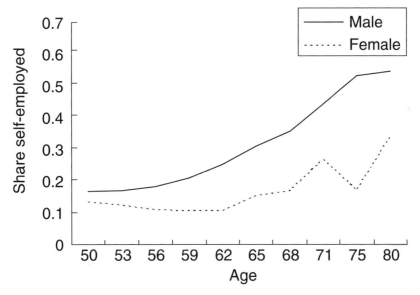

FIGURE 6.2. Self-employment by age. Sample restricted to individuals reporting positive earnings and weeks worked. (*Source:* 1998 Health and Retirement Study)

Job flexibility, as measured by the ability to adjust hours, appears to increase with age among those who are not self-employed as well. In table 6.8, the proportion of working males who report they can reduce hours increases from 0.27 at ages fifty to fifty-eight, to 0.39 at ages sixty-two to sixty-four, to 0.59 at ages seventy-four to seventy-six. A similar increase with age is observed in the proportion that report they can increase hours. For those who cannot reduce hours, there is a decline with age in the proportion who *want* to reduce their hours, which suggests older workers may select jobs with the preferred level of hours. The trend with age is less clear when considering the proportion of workers who cannot, but want to, increase the number of hours they work. This percentage declines through ages sixty-eight to seventy, and then follows no discernable trend. Combining the response to whether individuals can reduce or increase hours worked to determine whether a worker is constrained in their hours in either direction, the estimates show that the proportion of workers reporting being constrained in hours worked falls through ages seventy-one to seventy-three, and then follows no discernable trend. The mean deviation of actual hours worked from desired hours falls from 3.78 at ages fifty to fifty-eight to 0.54 at ages seventy-seven to seventy-nine. These estimates imply that both actual hours and preferred hours decline with age (final column of table 6.8).

A battery of questions in HRS98 asks respondents to categorize the extent to which their job involves physical effort, such as lifting heavy loads or stooping, kneeling, or crouching, as well as good eyesight, intense concentration, and skill in

Table 6.8. Hours Flexibility by Age

AGE	CAN REDUCE HOURS	WANT TO REDUCE HOURS[a]	CAN INCREASE HOURS	WANT TO INCREASE HOURS[a]	CONSTRAINED IN HOURS WORKED	MEAN DEVIATION FROM PREFERRED HOURS	PREFERRED HOURS
50–58	0.27	0.18	0.28	0.20	0.35	3.78	40.0
59–61	0.34	0.18	0.29	0.15	0.31	3.73	37.6
62–64	0.39	0.16	0.33	0.14	0.25	2.80	35.9
65–67	0.48	0.11	0.38	0.14	0.21	2.04	30.6
68–70	0.47	0.14	0.41	0.07	0.17	2.26	29.0
71–73	0.58	0.08	0.52	0.14	0.13	1.47	27.7
74–76	0.59	0.05	0.45	0.21	0.22	2.18	25.0
77–79	0.56	0.04	0.58	0.09	0.08	0.54	22.6
≥80	0.63	0.00	0.47	0.15	0.12	0.46	19.2

Source: 1998 Health and Retirement Study.
Notes: Sample restricted to working individual.
[a]Want to reduce and increase hours conditional on not being able to reduce or increase hours.

Table 6.9. Job Characteristics by Age

AGE	LOTS OF PHYSICAL EFFORT	LIFTING HEAVY LOADS	STOOPING, KNEELING, OR CROUCHING	GOOD EYESIGHT	INTENSE CONCENTRATION	DEALING WITH OTHER PEOPLE	INVOLVES A LOT OF STRESS	REALLY ENJOY GOING TO WORK
50–54	0.34	0.16	0.25	0.69	0.59	0.74	0.67	0.85
55–59	0.36	0.16	0.26	0.60	0.52	0.67	0.61	0.87
60–64	0.39	0.15	0.27	0.59	0.51	0.66	0.53	0.89
65–69	0.33	0.12	0.23	0.58	0.44	0.62	0.41	0.92
70–74	0.27	0.09	0.17	0.61	0.49	0.63	0.38	0.94
75–79	0.30	0.08	0.16	0.67	0.50	0.67	0.22	0.97
≥80	0.32	0.03	0.12	0.59	0.35	0.71	0.28	0.96

Source: 1998 Health and Retirement Study.

dealing with other people. The share of workers reporting that their job involves these activities all or most of the time is reported in table 6.9. Working individuals who state that their job involves physical effort all or most of the time does not change appreciably with age. The proportion that report their job involves lifting heavy loads or stooping, kneeling, or crouching all or most of the time does fall significantly, however, from 0.16 at ages fifty to fifty-four to 0.08 at ages seventy-five to seventy-nine in the case of lifting; and from 0.25 at ages fifty to fifty-four to 0.16 at ages seventy-five to seventy-nine in the case of stooping, kneeling, or crouching.

The need for intense concentration appears to decline somewhat with age, while the need for good eyesight and skill in dealing with other people does not seem to change much with age. These results do not change if males and females are examined separately.

While particular job characteristics do not appear to change markedly with age, the level of stress experienced on the job does fall over time. Whereas 67 percent of respondents ages fifty to fifty-four report that their job involves a lot of stress, only 22 percent of those ages seventy-five to seventy-nine agree with that statement. This could reflect changes in the job characteristics of older individuals, changes in the population of working individuals, or simply that younger people have higher stress levels than older people in general. The final column of table 6.9 shows that the proportion of individuals who report really enjoying going to work increases slightly from 0.85 at ages fifty to fifty-four to 0.97 at ages seventy-five to seventy-nine.

The results of this chapter demonstrate that older workers tend to work fewer hours, are paid lower wages, are more likely to be self-employed and have flexible work arrangements, and work in service-oriented occupations than younger workers. However, it is not known whether these trends reflect a compositional shift in the workforce due to selective retirement or a process in which individuals gravitate toward jobs with particular characteristics as they age. The trend toward a relatively more educated and healthy workforce at older ages is indicative of significant compositional changes in the working population. At the same time, the trend toward lower wages at older ages, even among the most educated, indicates a transition in the types of jobs older workers are willing to hold.

Although this chapter presents much evidence on the characteristics of the jobs for current workers, such evidence does not provide information about those individuals who have already retired. Table 6.10 presents tabulations from the HRS98 on

Table 6.10. Reasons for Retirement by Age

AGE	"FORCED"	POOR HEALTH	WANTED TO DO OTHER THINGS	DIDN'T LIKE WORK	SPEND TIME WITH FAMILY	"FORCED," NOT FAMILY OR HEALTH[a]
50–58	0.38	0.24	0.25	0.04	0.32	0.15
59–61	0.40	0.35	0.30	0.09	0.36	0.09
62–64	0.31	0.18	0.27	0.07	0.34	0.13
65–67	0.28	0.16	0.29	0.05	0.37	0.13
68–70	0.28	0.13	0.25	0.05	0.31	0.18
71–74	0.31	0.13	0.19	0.04	0.26	0.16
75–79	0.40	0.25	0.14	0.04	0.27	0.19
≥80	0.46	0.25	0.10	0.08	0.19	0.25

Source: 1998 Health and Retirement Study.
[a]Percentage of retirees who reported being forced to retire but did not report family or poor health being important.

the reason for retirement by age of actual retirement. The first column of table 6.10 shows that the proportion of retirees who report they were at least partly "forced" to retire from their last job decreases with age at retirement through ages sixty-five to sixty-seven and sixty-eight to seventy, then increases subsequently. However, it is unclear whether respondents interpreted "forced" as their employer forcing them to retire, or some other factor, such as poor health, forcing them to retire. The proportion of retirees who cited a variety of other reasons why they retired is tabulated in columns 2 through 5. Nearly 25 percent of individuals retiring between ages fifty to fifty-eight reported poor health to be a very important reason for retiring, as did 35 percent of those retiring between ages fifty-nine to sixty-one. This percentage then declines to 13 percent at ages sixty-eight to seventy and seventy-one to seventy-four, before increasing to 25 percent at ages seventy-five and above. A substantial proportion of individuals also report "wanting to do other things" and "spending time with family" as very important reasons for retiring. Interestingly, very few individuals claimed they retired because they did not like their work. The final column of table 6.10 records the proportion of retirees who reported that they were forced to retire, but did not report health or spending time with family as important reasons for retirement. This percentage increases from 15 percent at ages fifty to fifty-eight to 25 percent of those retiring at age eighty and above.

Directions for Future Research on Elderly Labor

The empirical analyses of the CPS and HRS98 yield two principal findings. First, it is the most educated, the wealthiest, and the healthiest individuals who tend to work in old age. Prior research suggests there is a causal role for health in determining the ability to work. The labor force patterns, with respect to education and wealth, are likely explained by the more educated and wealthy having stronger preferences for working and access to jobs that allow them to continue working at the hours and level of effort they prefer.

A second principal finding is that the elderly who choose to work do so for comparatively low wages. Given that it is the healthiest, wealthiest, and most educated individuals who continue to work, it does not appear that the low wages among elderly workers are caused by the retirement of high-wage workers; the individuals who continue to work are those who are most likely to have been high-wage workers at younger ages. Rather, it appears that individuals tend to select low-paying jobs as they age. The elderly who are continuing to work almost uniformly report high degrees of flexibility and job satisfaction, consistent with the elderly being willing to trade wages for other favorable job characteristics. Taken together, these findings suggest that nonpecuniary job attributes are important to the labor force decisions of the elderly.

The descriptive analyses presented in this chapter leave a number of important questions about elderly labor supply unanswered. Perhaps most important, the chapter provides only limited evidence on whether individuals who left the labor force did so because they were unable to find employment with the desired bundle of characteristics. That is, were individuals who retired somehow more constrained in their employment opportunities than those who continued to work? The data show that the fraction of workers who claimed that they were "forced" to retire for a reason other than health increases with age and that labor force participation is highest among the most educated older workers—workers who it seems would have the greatest freedom to select jobs that accommodate their needs. It may be that more elderly people would continue working if their employers could accommodate their particular needs, but that such accommodations are least feasible and least profitable for the lower-skilled elderly.

A second important issue rests with the extent to which wages decline for an individual. In view of the high degree of job satisfaction and the change in job characteristics, the relatively low wages for those who continue to work appears to be a choice. However, given the extent to which the elderly work for low wages, it will be worthwhile to document the decline in wages for individuals and more carefully investigate the extent to which declining wages are a choice.

A third important issue is the conceptualization of workplace flexibility itself. For example, what is the implicit price of flexibility? The results are consistent with the elderly choosing to purchase more flexible jobs by accepting lower wages, but little direct evidence has been provided to support this interpretation. In addition, it may be important to distinguish between flexibility on the current job with flexibility in the labor market more broadly. The workplace characteristic questions tabulated in this chapter ask about flexibility on the current job. However, an important source of flexibility might rest with a worker choosing to switch employers in order to obtain the job characteristics that are desired.

Part 3

WORKPLACE FLEXIBILITY

Voluntary Employer Practices
in the United States

7

EMPLOYER-PROVIDED WORKPLACE FLEXIBILITY

Ellen Galinsky, Kelly Sakai, Sheila Eby,
James T. Bond, and Tyler Wigton

In the 1970s, Columbia University scholars Sheila B. Kamerman and Alfred J. Kahn (1978) launched studies documenting family-responsive trends around the globe. They found that, in contrast to almost every other industrialized country, "the United States does not have an explicit national family policy" (428). This statement remains true today (Heymann 2006a). Not only do U.S. employers, rather than the government, provide health insurance, pensions, and other benefits for their own employees, they have largely assumed responsibility for helping their employees' families manage work and family life (Kamerman and Kahn 1987; Kahn and Kamerman 1980, 2002). There has been some national family legislation in the past three decades, most notably the Family and Medical Leave Act of 1993, which provides twelve weeks of unpaid leave for parenting, family, and personal medical care for specified groups of employees. Nevertheless, the American safety net for working families remains primarily voluntary.

Family-responsive employer policies are not new. Every time there was a national need for women to work outside the home, such as during World Wars I and II, employers developed creative initiatives such as childcare, take-home dinners, laundry services, and flexibility (Friedman and Galinsky 1992, 168–207). In the last decades of the twentieth century, the impetus for providing family-responsive initiatives shifted. The influx of working women prompted employers to create a "business case" for providing work and family workplace supports (Galinsky and Johnson 1998).

Flexibility

The Families and Work Institute (FWI) has followed and documented these trends through nationally representative studies of employees, including the National Study of the Changing Workforce (NSCW) in 1992,[1] 1997, and 2002,[2] with comparisons to a nationally representative study conducted for the U.S. Department of Labor in 1977 (Bond, Galinsky, and Swanberg 1998; Bond et al. 2003; Galinsky, Bond, and Friedman 1993; Quinn and Staines 1979). Parallel research includes the Business Work-Life Study in 1998 and the National Study of Employers (NSE) in 2005 (Bond, Galinsky, Kim, and Brownfield 2005; Galinsky and Bond 1998).[3] Their data show employer efforts continuing to expand, first concentrating on female employees, then widening to include men, employees' children, and elderly parents. Employers also recognized that most employees wanted flexibility to deal with their lives outside of work—attending a parent-teacher conference or fixing a leaking pipe. But employees knew that, formal time or leave policies notwithstanding, the broader company culture—or their own individual supervisor—might frown on flexibility, possibly jeopardizing career advancement for people seeking these options (Galinsky 2001; Galinsky and Johnson 1998).

Workplace flexibility directly challenges the assumptions of how work should be done and how employees should be managed (Bailyn 2006; Christensen 2006; Galinsky and Johnson 1998; Rapoport et al. 2002; Williams 2000). These assumptions include (a) the "ideal" employee puts work first; (b) presence at work equals productivity; (c) "face time" (or the time spent at work) equals commitment; (d) all employees want to climb a hierarchical career ladder; (e) family life detracts from work; (f) if you give employees an inch (i.e., flexibility), they will take a mile and will abuse the flexibility they are given; (g) no one will be at the workplace to accomplish needed tasks; (h) it is difficult to manage employees well if supervisors cannot continually monitor them; (i) companies should not interfere in employees' personal lives; (j) competent employees can manage their work and personal lives; if they cannot manage, they should not be working; and (k) there is no need for policies or programs; a supervisor can handle issues with individual employees when they arise.

Even as the demographics of the workforce were rapidly changing in the 1980s and 1990s, employers typically "worked things out with an individual employee," accommodating a single person. As such, flexibility often carried penalties. The 2002 National Study of the Changing Workforce revealed that almost two in five employees (39%) agree that "employees who ask for time off for family reasons or try to arrange different schedules or hours to meet their personal or family needs are LESS likely to get ahead in their jobs and careers." This percentage has remained constant since 1992.

Over this time period, however, *some* employers began to see flexibility as a competitive advantage. In the 2005 National Study of Employers, employers offering eight or more work-life initiatives said they did so for "business" reasons—recruiting and retaining employees (47%), enhancing productivity and job commitment (25%), and reducing absenteeism and lowering costs (6%).

The Status of Workplace Flexibility in the United States and Promising Practices

This study uses data from the Families and Work Institute's 2005 National Study of Employers, which examined employers with fifty or more employees, to depict the status of workplace flexibility in the United States. Trends in employee access to flexibility between 1992 and 2002 are tracked using data from FWI's National Studies of the Changing Workforce. Several employers that received the 2005 and 2006 Alfred P. Sloan Awards for Business Excellence in Workplace Flexibility illustrate the promising practice of flexibility in action.[4] The application process for these awards is quite rigorous, as the scoring is largely based on surveys of employees at the applicant companies. The employers profiled in this chapter were winners of this award and represent diversity in employer size, industries, and geographies (Families and Work Institute 2007).

Traditionally, flexibility has been viewed as benefiting *either* the employer *or* the employee. The organization benefits from last-minute overtime with little or no notice, for example, or by keeping employees on call. Flexibility that primarily benefits employees includes letting employees attend to their personal needs regardless of the impact on employers. The Families and Work Institute's definition of flexibility is an option that benefits *both* the employer *and* the employee. From these studies, six types of flexibility are described: (a) *flextime and flex-place* (periodic and daily flextime, compressed workweeks, and regular or occasional flex-place); (b) *time off and leaves* (time off for family or personal needs without loss of pay, time off for education and training, time off for volunteering, sabbaticals, paid vacation days, and leaves for childbirth, adoption, and sick children); (c) *reduced time* (part-time, job sharing, health insurance for part-time, part-time for supervisory positions, and part-year); (d) *flex careers* (moving off and on the leadership track, sabbaticals, moving between part-time and full-time, gradual return after childbirth or adoption, phased retirement, and defined benefits for employees phasing into retirement); (e) *responsibility, control, and accountability* (control over number of hours and scheduling, control over shifts, control over overtime hours, and control over taking breaks); and (f) *the culture of flexibility* (data from employees on the extent to which they feel supported in using workplace flexibility).

Flextime and Flex-Place: Prevalence according to Employers and Employees

To some, workplace flexibility remains synonymous with flextime: allowing full-time employees to vary their arrival and departure times. In the twenty-first century, there are many additional ways to work flexibly.

PERIODIC AND DAILY FLEXTIME

According to the 2005 National Study of Employers, 3 percent of employers allow all or most of their employees to periodically change their starting and quitting times, what is known as "traditional" flextime. Daily flextime—where employees are allowed to change their arrival and departure times on a daily basis—is embraced by 13 percent of employers. According to the 2002 National Study of the Changing Workforce, employees are much more likely than those in 1992 to be able to periodically change their arrival and departure time (43% in 2002 vs. 29% in 1992), and to change their arrival and departure times on a daily basis (23% in 2002 vs. 18% in 1992).

COMPRESSED WORKWEEKS

A compressed workweek is defined as working longer hours some days in order to work fewer days per week (e.g., a forty-hour workweek is compressed into four ten-hour days rather than five eight-hour days). Ten percent of employers enable all or most of their employees to work compressed workweeks, according to the 2005 NSE. According to employees in the 2002 NSCW, 42 percent have access to compressed workweeks. This form of flexibility was not a subject of inquiry in 1992, so no trend data are available.

REGULAR OR OCCASIONAL FLEX-PLACE

Flex-place is defined as working from home on a regular or occasional basis. Using data from the 2005 NSE, 3 percent of employers allow all or most employees to do so regularly or occasionally. Data from employees in the 2002 NSCW show that only 8.5 percent of employees ever work regular paid hours at home. About 10 percent do paid or unpaid job-related work at home more than once a week. Comparable questions were not asked in 1992.

Flextime and Flex-Place: Promising Practices

The employers selected for profiling flextime and flex-place initiatives include a small employer in the demanding legal profession, a company in the healthcare industry that has a very creative flextime scheme, and a financial service firm that has literally torn down the office walls through its flex-place program.

BAILEY LAW GROUP

Perhaps surprisingly, the 2005 NSE reveals that smaller employers are more likely to allow employees access to daily flextime and compressed workweeks (as well as numerous other forms of flexibility) than larger ones, thus a small company is profiled. Yet within this small business there exists a seemingly improbable situation—flextime and flex-place in a law firm. The legal profession, where billable hours are tantamount to employees' economic worth, is not an industry one would associate with flexibility. However, the Bailey Law Group, a law firm in Washington, D.C., a company of twelve employees on-site and sixteen total, proves that what might seem impossible can not only work but can also make business sense.

Kathy Bailey did not set out to provide workplace flexibility when she founded the Bailey Law Group eight years ago. However, when two of her employees decided to move with their husbands to other states, Bailey moved to retain them both. "They knew our main clients and understood their businesses inside and out," she said. Her focus is on client retention and growth, she explained. She believes flexibility is key to her company's revenues, which have tripled over the last eight years. As proof, she reports that one of her relocated lawyers has brought in a whole new portfolio of clients in her new region.

If Bailey is indifferent as to where her people work, she is equally unconcerned about how their hours are scheduled. Her Washington, D.C., firm specializes in environmental law, commercial real estate leasing, and civil litigation. Staff members are trusted to "work when they need to work," as Bailey is quoted as saying. Although the administrative employees stay close to a regular schedule, others set their own time. "Our hours are 8:30 to 6:00, but no one is judgmental if someone comes in at 10:00," she said. If people want to work at home, it is not a problem. "People just communicate with each other to schedule meetings at convenient times, or we e-mail each other back and forth."

Law firms are notorious for very long hours lasting well into the night. At Bailey Law, however, it is not unusual for parents to leave at 2:00 in the afternoon to pick up their children. One person went on a part-time schedule so she could be home every day with her kids after school. Her compensation has been pro-rated, though her prospects with the firm have not been diminished. As for the costs of flexibility, Bailey sees none. "We've put some equipment in people's homes," she said, "but equipment is cheap. It's replacing people that's expensive."

One might assume that women-run companies are more likely to be flexible, and this is true. According to the 2005 NSE, having more women in the most senior positions is associated with greater workplace flexibility. Companies whose senior ranks include people of color also have a more flexible approach.

ARUP LABORATORIES

Another example of a promising practice in flextime can be found in the health-care industry. Salt Lake City's ARUP Laboratories, an enterprise of the University of

Utah and its Department of Pathology, is a national medical reference laboratory. It is not surprising that the healthcare industry has embraced flexibility, as this industry is feeling the pinch of labor shortages more severely and perhaps sooner than other industries. The demand for healthcare workers is growing twice as fast as the number of professionals entering the workforce, and thus the healthcare industry has a definite need to experiment with new ways to attract and retain employees. ARUP shows the benefits of going beyond the typical forms of flextime to create a unique pattern of working.

ARUP offers some of its 2,025 staff members the option of working a block of seven days at a time, alternating with a block of seven days off. Workdays are ten hours each; employees log seventy hours for a two-week period (complying with the Fair Labor Standard Act). Employees are paid, however, for two forty-hour weeks. Therefore, over the course of the year, they do not accrue additional paid time off, including holidays, as it is built into their schedule. (Interestingly, the idea for a seven-day workweek came from employees who had been asked for suggestions to improve the company's recruitment and retention efforts.)

ARUP is a prime example of this definition of flexibility: it works for both for the employer and the employee. According to ARUP's Anne Ivie, "This is a great alternative for staff and a good deal for ARUP too, which has more than doubled its employee base from seven hundred in 1992 to seventeen hundred employees in 2004, while cutting its turnover rate from as high as 22 percent to 11 percent." For the seven-on/seven-off shift, ARUP ensures smooth operations by pairing each employee with a counterpart handling the opposite schedule. The two employees cover for each other if any scheduling conflicts arise. ARUP also offers staff four-day/ten-hour schedules as well as the conventional five-day-a-week option, and reaches out to attract college students with flexible scheduling for part-time work.

CAPITAL ONE FINANCIAL

In this third example, the profiled company's real estate costs have been cut, productivity has increased, and employee satisfaction has risen. These gains have occurred in response to a pilot program launched by Capital One, a banking company, which gives more than two thousand of its 6,492 employees on-site in Richmond, Virginia (the company has 18,060 total employees) a choice about where they would like to work. It is called the Future of Work (FOW) program because its purpose is to rethink work: it is designed around discovering how each individual works best, not around the conventions regarding buildings or furniture.

The major benefits of FOW for associates are flexibility and choice. Associates determine where they like to work best, and then choose from the following options: (a) an Anchor or Resident, who maintains a dedicated workspace at Capital One, either because they prefer to work out of the same space each day or their roles require them to work from the office; (b) a Mobile Associate, who arrives in the morning, finds a "mobile" workspace, and logs in. They may choose to spend some time working at the office but also choose to spend some time working with their customers, from their home office, the back porch, or at the local coffee shop; or (c) a Teleworker, who work an established amount of their time from home and comes into the office only occasionally. When they do come in, they are able to find a "mobile" workspace, log in, and get to work. These associates receive a budget to help them set up their home office, including all the necessary technology needed to work from home. A home office furniture allowance of $1,000 ensures they have an ergonomic, safe, and effective workspace at home.

"All employees get the tools they need to be successful," said Capital One's Noreen Covino, including cell phones and laptops that can plug in to any of the bank's available workstations. In addition, throughout the FOW space there are "quiet zones," areas that prohibit the use of cell phones and are reserved for associates who require a quiet environment to accomplish their work. Capital One has rolled out tools to support associates, managers, and teams to ensure that each arrangement is the best fit for that associate and his or her business unit. These tools include (a) a Virtual Team Toolkit (VTT), an online learning resource to help associates and their teams successfully navigate the challenges that can arise as a result of working in a virtual team environment; (b) a classroom program for managers who are currently managing associates in a flexible work environment, or for those who wish to learn more about the flexible work arrangement (FWA) program at Capital One; and (c) online FWA conversation guides, to ensure that managers and associates are having effective dialogue about flexible work arrangement requests.

Almost two years after this program's launch, 80 percent of employees say they are satisfied with their workplace, up from 57 percent. These options have allowed the bank to consolidate its real estate portfolio dramatically, gaining the ability to house eight hundred employees in space that previously accommodated three hundred. With those results in hand, Capital One expanded the program to include more workers in 2008 (see table 7.1 for a comparison of the availability of flextime and flex-place nationally and in these companies).

Time Off and Leaves: Prevalence according to Employers and Employees

Time off can be classified in two categories. The first involves time off that is more likely to be *unanticipated and unplanned,* including time during the workday to address personal and family issues, such as waiting for a repair person to fix a broken stove or taking a sick child to the doctor. The second category entails time off that is more likely to be *planned,* such as medical appointments, parent-teacher appointments, vacations, and parental leaves.

Table 7.1. Comparison of Availability of Flextime and Flex-Place

	ALLOWS *ALL OR MOST* EMPLOYEES TO PERIODICALLY CHANGE STARTING AND QUITTING TIMES	ALLOWS *ALL OR MOST* EMPLOYEES TO CHANGE STARTING AND QUITTING TIMES DAILY	ALLOWS *ALL OR MOST* EMPLOYEES TO COMPRESS WORKWEEKS	ALLOWS *ALL OR MOST* EMPLOYEES TO WORK SOME REGULAR PAID HOURS AT HOME OCCASIONALLY	ALLOWS *ALL OR MOST* EMPLOYEES TO WORK SOME REGULAR PAID HOURS AT HOME ON A REGULAR BASIS
2005 National Study of Employers (%) (n = 1,092)	33	13	10	3	3
2006 Sloan award winners (%) (n = 89)	71	46	42	44	22
Bailey Law Group (Washington, D.C.)	*	*	*	*	*
ARUP Laboratories (Salt Lake City)	*				
Capital One Financial (Richmond, VA)	*			*	

* = Allows *all or most* employees.

TIME OFF FOR FAMILY OR PERSONAL NEEDS WITHOUT LOSS OF PAY

This kind of leave tends to be unanticipated and unplanned. According to the 2005 National Study of Employers, 60 percent of employers permit all or most of their employees to take time off for important family or personal needs without a loss of pay. A similar question was posed of wage and salaried employees in the 2002 National Study of the Changing Workforce. The figures roughly parallel the finding from employers: 31 percent say it is "not hard at all" to take time off during the workday for personal or family reasons without a loss of pay and 32 percent say it is "not too hard." On the other hand, 37 percent report that it is "somewhat hard" or "very hard." Data from the 1992 NSCW are not available.

TIME OFF FOR EDUCATION AND TRAINING

Time off for education and training can be anticipated, as can time for volunteering and for vacations. According to the 2005 NSE, 55 percent of employers allow all or most of their employees to take time for education or training to improve their skills. Employees in the 2002 or 1992 NSCW were not asked about time off for education or training programs.

TIME OFF FOR VOLUNTEERING

According to the 2005 NSE, 61 percent of companies with 50 or more employees allow their workers to volunteer in community activities for some period of time during work hours. Among these employers, 11 percent provide no pay during volunteer hours; 40 percent compensate employees for some number of hours up to a maximum of nineteen hours per year; and 49 percent provide twenty or more hours of paid time for volunteer work annually. Employees in the 2002 or 1992 NSCW were not asked about time off for volunteering.

SABBATICALS

According to the 2005 National Study of Employers, 28 percent of employers allow employees to take paid or unpaid sabbaticals of six months or more and return to a comparable job.

PAID VACATION DAYS

The 2005 NSE reveals that 94 percent of companies with fifty or more employees provide paid vacation days to their employees. Employee data from the 2002 NSCW reveal that 78 percent of wage and salaried employees receive paid vacation days. The average amount of paid vacation received by wage and salaried employees is fourteen days per year, ranging from zero to thirty days per year.

THE LAW GOVERNING FAMILY AND MEDICAL LEAVE
AND EMPLOYER COMPLIANCE

Employers responding to the 2005 NSE are mandated to comply with the federal Family and Medical Leave Act (FMLA) of 1993 at some or all sites, unless they meet the legal exemption of having fewer than fifty employees within a seventy-five-mile radius of all worksites. This law requires that at least twelve weeks of unpaid, job-guaranteed leave for childbirth, adoption, foster care placement, a serious personal medical condition, or care of a child or spouse with a serious medical condition be granted to employees who have worked at least 1,250 hours during the preceding year. Data from the 2005 NSE do not allow for a complete analysis of what proportion of companies are out of compliance with the law, but it is possible to determine the number of employers who have only one location and have fifty or more employees. Perhaps surprisingly, it was found that 30 percent of such employers report offering fewer than twelve weeks of family and medical leave. Either these employers are unaware of their responsibilities or they are deliberately violating the law.

MATERNITY LEAVES

According to the 2005 NSE, 22 percent of employers provide fewer than twelve weeks of leave for maternity, 50 percent provide just the twelve weeks required by law, and 29 percent provide more than twelve weeks. Among those employers that offer time off, 46 percent offer at least some replacement pay during the period of maternity-related disability. Of those companies that offer six weeks or more time off after childbirth, only 7 percent provide some pay for the leave *following* maternity-related disability. The 2002 and 1992 NSCW did not ask women questions about childbirth leaves or pay during such leaves.

PATERNITY LEAVES

The 2005 NSE found that 29 percent of employers offer fewer than twelve weeks for fathers, 52 percent offer twelve weeks, and 19 percent offer more than twelve weeks. Among those employers that offer at least some time off for fathers, only 13 percent provide any replacement pay, excluding paid vacation and sick time. The 2002 and 1992 NSCW did not ask men about leave for parenting or about pay during such leaves.

LEAVES FOR ADOPTION

The 2005 NSE found that 22 percent of employers provide fewer than twelve weeks of leave to care for newly adopted children, 58 percent provide twelve weeks, and 19 percent provide more than twelve weeks. Again, employees were not asked about this kind of leave in the 2002 or 1992 NSCW.

LEAVES FOR SICK CHILDREN

Leave for sick children can include leave for everyday illnesses or for serious illnesses. The 2005 NSE asked about leave for the care of seriously ill children, a form of leave mandated in the 1993 Family and Medical Leave Act. It was found that 21 percent of employers offer fewer than twelve weeks for the care of seriously ill children, 59 percent offer twelve weeks, and 19 percent offer more than twelve weeks. The 2002 NSCW posed questions about leave for everyday illnesses, defined as being allowed to take a few days off to care for a sick child without losing pay, without using vacation days, and without having to make up another reason for one's absence. Such leave typically begins without warning, as the onset of a child's illness is usually not predictable. Time off to care for a sick child may consist of being allowed to use one's own sick leave for this purpose, having formal paid family days off, or making informal arrangements with one's supervisor to take time off. Slightly more than half (54%) of the wage and salaried workforce with children say they have *no* time off to care for sick children without losing pay, having to use vacation days, or fabricating an excuse. This group represents a very substantial portion of the workforce. There are no comparable data from 1992.

Time Off and Leaves: Promising Practices

We sought to demonstrate promising practices for time off and leaves by profiling a large company with progressive leave policies for the care of others, for sabbaticals, and for volunteering, and a small company committed to providing time off and to solving problems as they arise.

INTEL

Intel, the semiconductor company in Chandler, Arizona, was founded in 1968 and currently employs about ten thousand workers on-site and fifty thousand nationwide. "Innovation is the way we maintain our competitiveness," said Dawn Jones, a company spokeswoman. "We need employees who are continually recharged, who come to the table with great new ideas. Strong time-off policies support Intel's strategy of innovation by helping people do exactly that."

Intel has the standard forms of time off—allowing all or most employees time off to attend to family or personal needs without losing pay, time off for education and training, time off for volunteer work during regular work hours, and paid vacation days. It also allows twelve weeks of leave for maternity, paternity, adoption, and the care of seriously ill family members. In this instance, however, Intel was selected because of its creative sabbatical program.

All of the 10,100 employees who work in the company's Chandler, Arizona, facility are entitled to a sabbatical of two fully paid consecutive months off every seven years. They can—and do—take the leave, secure that their job will be there when they return. Some people pursue a special interest or change their career path during this leave, while others enjoy a honeymoon or spend time with their children. Overwhelmingly, employees return with a refreshed perspective and increased productivity, Jones reported. Employees can also tap additional time to earn a college diploma or pursue additional training. Factory workers, in particular, take time off for education. Creating microchips requires specialized skills that must be frequently recertified. Intel maintains a favorable tuition reimbursement plan for all qualified employees.

The Chandler facility also promotes volunteering. Its staff recently rounded up more than fifteen hundred holiday gifts for local students and senior citizens. Employees from all parts of the operation later held large gift-wrapping parties. Time off for other community projects can also be arranged with a manager's consent.

What about an unexpected need—such as taking care of a flooded basement or attending a teacher conference? All nonsalaried employees gain six hours off for every month they work. These staff members can dip into the time they have accumulated when a need arises to drive a parent to the doctor, for example. As for salaried workers, they are on the honor system. "We don't punch a time clock," said Jones. "We all just come in and work really hard."

Jones said the cost of these policies is minimal. No one is brought in to substitute for people on sabbatical; colleagues absorb any additional work, which is also a form of job security for the departing employee. "Intel is about technological breakthroughs," Jones said. "To be successful, we need people who are continually recharged, people whose minds can soar. Time off helps us achieve that."

ATLANTIC HVACR SALES, INC.

The second employer profiled, a manufacturers' representative for heating and cooling equipment in Oceanside, New York, is a small employer where it is conceivably more difficult for people to substitute for each other taking time off or leave. Yet, this twelve-employee company makes flexibility work because of the owner's family values. "Flexibility drives an increase in discretionary effort at Atlantic HVACR Sales," said owner David Mann, adding that employees at all levels take on an ownership role in the company—"productivity flourishes, a high level of customer service is attained, and employees are happy to have balance in their work and their personal lives." Mann launched the business twelve years ago with one assistant, who was a single mother of two. He believes that everyone wins when employees are able to work from home, take time off from work for a doctor's appointment, or bring a child to work when childcare falls through.

Reduced Time: Prevalence according to Employers and Employees

If the "ideal worker" is a full-time employee, then working reduced hours can carry a penalty, subtle or not. In fact, employees agree that there are penalties associated with working reduced hours. In the 2002 National Study of the Changing Workforce, employees were asked, "Do people who have part-time jobs receive pay and benefits comparable to what is received by people who work full-time in the same positions, based on the percentage of a full-time job they work? Or do they receive less than a straight percentage of full-time pay and benefits just because they work part-time?" It was reported that 61 percent of the employees working in organizations with part-time employees say that part-time employees receive less overall compensation on a pro-rata basis than full-timers doing the same job, just because they work part-time. For that reason, FWI's definition of reduced hours is constructed so that reduced hours address the most common penalties.

PART-TIME

For the purposes of this study, part-time jobs are defined as those jobs that allow employees to "move from full-time to part-time and back again *while remaining in the same position or level.*" In other words, this definition includes job mobility without demotion. In the 2005 National Study of Employers, 21 percent of employers allow all or most of this kind of mobility to move between full-time and reduced hours. According to the 2002 National Study of the Changing Workforce, 40 percent of employees who are working part-time believe that they could move to full-time hours while remaining in the same position or level. Likewise, 40 percent of those working full-time believe that they could reduce their hours while remaining in the same position or level. Alternately, 24 percent of women and 13 percent of men who are full-timers would prefer to be working reduced hours but do not.

When asked why, 70 percent report that they do not work part-time because they cannot afford to do so, and 44 percent say they would not be allowed to work reduced hours by their employers. Overall, 80 percent of employees who would like to work reduced hours but do not say that they cannot afford to or that they would not be allowed to do so.

JOB SHARING

Job sharing is a form of reduced hours, in which two employees share the responsibilities and divide the compensation and benefits in one job. Overall, 13 percent of employers in the 2005 National Study of Employers reported that they allow all or most employees to share jobs. Employees were not asked about job sharing in the 2002 or 1992 National Study of the Changing Workforce.

HEALTH INSURANCE FOR PART-TIMERS

According to the 2005 NSE, 33 percent of employers provide health insurance for part-time employees, either on a full or a pro-rata basis. According to the 2002 NSCW, only 40 percent of employees in part-time positions are offered health insurance through their jobs, versus 90 percent of full-timers. Sixty-two percent of part-time employees have health insurance from other sources, such as a spouse's job. However, just under one in five part-timers (19%) do not have *any* health insurance coverage, compared with 9 percent of full-timers.

PART-TIME FOR SUPERVISORY POSITIONS

Given the definition of reduced time work, which avoids the most common penalties, it is important to consider whether companies make management positions available to employees who work part-time. Among those employers who offer part-time work in the 2005 NSE, 36 percent do make such positions accessible to part-time workers.

PART-YEAR

The 2005 National Study of Employers asked whether employees are allowed to work part-year, that is, to "work reduced time on an annual basis such as working full-time during the school year and taking a block of time off during the summer." The study found that 16 percent of employers report that they allow most or all of their employees to do so. According to the 2002 National Study of the Changing Workforce, 7 percent of the wage and salaried workforce engages in seasonal work—meaning they work during seasons when their labor is in demand. Among seasonal employees, 42 percent prefer their seasonal jobs, and 58 percent would prefer stable, year-round employment. It is also estimated that another 9 percent or more of employees work only part of the year by their own choosing.[5] Thus, a total of 16 percent of U.S. employees work part-year. In the 2002 NSCW, employees were asked: "If your work allowed it and you could afford to take a cut in pay, would you like to take an extended period of unpaid leave from work each year in addition to any vacation time you take? For example, would you like to be able to take a month off work during the summer to be with children when they are out of school or take an unpaid leave at some other time of the year for whatever personal or family reason?" Among wage and salaried employees not currently engaged in seasonal or part-year work, 52 percent said they would like to work part-year.

Reduced Time: Promising Practices

The employers selected for profiling include one firm of 110 employees that offers job mobility for flexibility and a large firm that has a very creative scheme of part-year work.

KAYE/BASSMAN INTERNATIONAL

Chief executive officer Jeff Kaye has built a successful executive recruiting business of about 110 employees. Kaye/Bassman International in Dallas, Texas, founded in 1981, is now the largest single-site search firm in the country, posting twenty-five consecutive years of growth with a 50 percent revenue increase over the last two years. "Client retention drives our success," Kaye said, and the company maintains that customer loyalty by striving to give employees a great workplace—the very best in the entire state, according to *Texas Monthly*. Kaye said that flexibility is one of the firm's pillars. "We treat our team members beautifully," he explained, "and they treat their clients the same way. In a service business, that's what it's all about."

Recruiters make up 85 percent of Kaye/Bassman's employees, and most can move with no difficulty from part-time to full-time and back again. About 10 percent now have reduced hours, which are an option for people at all levels of the company. "If a senior partner wanted this," he said, "we'd find a way." He would only resist in the case of a new employee who was not doing well. "It just doesn't make sense to down-shift until you've gotten good experience under your belt," he said. If the employee had a family emergency, however, Kaye would surely permit a schedule change.

The company has one job-sharing situation, and Kaye sees more in the offing. Two women with the same clients are hoping to have children, and will share a single position.

In recruiting, commissions are a big part of compensation, so the impact of reduced hours on salary is complicated. If a person were to work half-time instead of full-time, his or her pay would be reduced by half. But if this person was as successful placing candidates while working part-time as he or she was placing them full-time, the end-of-the-year bonus would make up the difference. As for health insurance, employees must log thirty-five hours a week to continue receiving that benefit.

Kaye does not see any expenses tied to flexibility. "Flexibility makes us money," he said. "We look for ways to embrace employees' special needs. One of our employees misses a morning meeting every day because she wants to take her child to school. She also leaves at 3:00 to pick him up, and then makes up the hours at night." There are many ways to define "special needs" at this company. Giving everyone the same special treatment is not necessary, Kaye believes, but everyone should be treated specially.

ACCENTURE

Accenture, the global consulting technology company of 4,060 employees (twenty-four thousand nationwide) in Chicago, Illinois, is piloting an approach that costs the employer nothing—a self-funded sabbatical labeled Future Leave. Individuals identify a time in the future when they choose to be away and continue to work a full-time schedule, choosing to take home a slightly reduced paycheck for as long as twelve months. The rest of their pay is essentially "banked" in a separate account and then cashed out to them when they begin their time away from work. They determine how to spend it, but most employees use it to bridge the compensation gap, although they can use it for travel, a family goal, or to pursue a special interest.

Employees select the exact percentage of "banked" pay and time off with their supervisors, although the time off must be between one and three months. Accenture continues to pay its portion of medical insurance and, when the time off has run its course, employees are assured the same jobs they left at their regular pay. According to Accenture's Sharon Klun, program statistics show employees at all levels of the company use the program, though women are more likely than men to participate. What is the advantage for Accenture? The company believes this part-year program will help retain women, who often have more family responsibilities than men, and lure Generation X and Y men and women recruits who want to work hard, but need balance in their professional and personal lives (see table 7.2 for a comparison of the availability of support for reduced hours nationally and in these companies).

Flex Careers: Prevalence according to Employers and Employees

Flex careers are one of the newer forms of workplace flexibility. During the twentieth century when the United States was primarily an industrial and manufacturing-based economy, before it moved toward a knowledge- and service-based economy, the image of careers that emerged was of climbing a "career ladder," ascending only in a lockstep manner. There was no support for stepping off the ladder—in fact, a step off (a misstep) sent one plunging back to the bottom. The notion of a "one-size-fits-all" career is slowly being replaced in the knowledge and service economy. The images used to describe this new model are of a career lattice, of a highway with off-ramps and on-ramps, or accelerating and then slowing down and accelerating again. Employees are living and working longer, attaching more value to personal

Table 7.2.   Comparison of Availability of Reduced Hours across Employers

	FOR EMPLOYERS WITH PART-TIME EMPLOYEES: SUPERVISORY OR MANAGERIAL POSITIONS ARE AVAILABLE FOR PART-TIME EMPLOYEES	OFFERS HEALTH INSURANCE BENEFITS TO PART-TIME EMPLOYEES	ALLOWS *ALL OR MOST* EMPLOYEES TO WORK PART YEAR	ALLOWS *ALL OR MOST* EMPLOYEES TO SHARE JOBS	PERMITS *ALL OR MOST* EMPLOYEES TO MOVE BETWEEN FULL-TIME AND-PART TIME WORK
2005 National Study of Employers (%) (n = 1,092)	36 (n = 889)	33	16	13	21
2006 Sloan award winners (%) (n = 89)	72	55	10	23	42
Kaye/Bassman International (Dallas)	Yes		*	*	*
Accenture (Chicago)	Yes	Yes	*	*	*

* = Allows *all or most* employees.

and family life, and acquiring personal or family responsibilities that are important to them throughout their work lives. As a result, careers must become more flexible. Moving sideways, down, or off a career track should always include pathways back. Although an employee who follows a flexible career path may not progress at the same speed as if he or she had followed a direct path up, career flexibility needs to contain the promise of moving at fast forward speed (or "putting the pedal to the metal again," as one employee recently described it), if and when employees want to, assuming they have kept up their skills and have talent. In other words, employees do not have to "sacrifice" their careers once and for all for other aspects of life that are important to them.

GRADUAL RETURN AFTER CHILDBIRTH OR ADOPTION

According to the 2005 National Study of Employers, 67 percent of employers permit all or most of their employees to return to work gradually after childbirth or adoption. This issue was not covered by the 2002 or 1992 National Study of the Changing Workforce.

PHASED RETIREMENT

According to the 2005 NSE, 28 percent of employers stated that all or most of their employees can phase in to retirement by working reduced hours over a period of time prior to full retirement; such data are not available from employees on this issue.

DEFINED BENEFITS FOR EMPLOYEES PHASING IN TO RETIREMENT

In the 2005 National Study of Employers, only 16 percent of employers offered both phased retirement and defined benefit plans. Among this 16 percent, 80 percent allow employees to phase in to retirement without reducing their pension payouts.

Flex Career: Promising Practices

Flex careers, by definition, span the working life cycle. Profiled here is a company that provides one form of flexibility when employees have children and another when employees begin to wind down their careers.

ERNST & YOUNG

Ernst & Young (E&Y), one of the world's largest professional service firms in Chicago, Illinois, reported revenues of more than $18 billion in 2006—a figure earned by delivering auditing, tax, and transaction services to companies large and small. Its 1,450 employees (twenty-five thousand nationwide) log a lot of hours driving up those revenues, says Inclusion and Flexibility Leader Deanna Bassett, "and E&Y is fiercely committed to retaining them." But how can people with numerous other options be persuaded to stay in a highly demanding work environment, especially when a new baby is born? The company has developed a strategy to create more flexible careers. E&Y's family and medical leave practices are strong examples of reasons employees remain with the firm. Consider the options for new parents: new mothers and fathers can take three months of fully paid leave. They can add their vacation time, too, and negotiate for whatever additional leave they would like on an unpaid basis.

When parents choose to stop working after childbirth, the company stays connected. Employees are asked if they would like to be called if an opportunity arises, if they would like a computer at home, or if periodic phone calls from Ernst & Young would be welcome. "Sometimes mothers want to come back sooner than expected, and we are open to a lot of possibilities," Bassett said. Indeed, research reveals that 95 percent of these women come back after 2.2 years.

Adoptive parents also have favorable leave practices. They are guaranteed sixteen weeks away from the office, and six of those weeks are paid if the parent is the primary caregiver. If the E&Y employee is not the one providing most of the care, he or she gets two weeks paid leave—and that is just the beginning. Four more weeks, fully paid, are available when the primary parent returns to work.

Does trading the office for the baby nursery brand an employee as uncommitted, as someone not quite suited to an important promotion later? Bassett says no. "We see men who are partners at E&Y taking their full paternity leave," she pointed out. "Our most senior women do too, and employees throughout the company notice. It tells them there is no professional penalty for balancing work and family." E&Y's CEO reiterates that message in his own internal communications. The result is that nearly all women and men who are eligible for a parental leave take it, and E&Y has provided authentic career flexibility without jeopardy.

Similar policies allow employees to care for family members who become ill, including mothers and fathers. Employees can have up to sixteen fully paid weeks to help a close relative through a crisis. When asked about the costs incurred by the company's flexibility practices, Bassett replied, "We're accountants. We've thought all that through, and let me assure you, the cost of our flexibility practices is nothing compared to the cost of losing good people and hiring and training new ones."

Other firms are also pioneering the notion of flexible careers during the prime parenting years. Deloitte created Personal Pursuits, providing three years of leave that includes a mentor and ongoing connections to the company. They are also piloting an initiative called Mass-Career Customization to fill the gap between the traditional "one-size-fits-all" and individually negotiated career trajectories. The initiative enables employees to take a life-cycle approach with the systemic ability to involve the four major dimensions of career progression: role, pace, location and schedule, and workload.

BON SECOURS RICHMOND HEALTH SYSTEM

Bon Secours Richmond Health System, employing five thousand employees in Richmond, Virginia and nineteen thousand nationwide, has successfully created a "culture of aging" to attract and retain employees age fifty and older. The components include: (a) employees can move from full- to part-time on-call status and back in most jobs; (b) managers and hourly employees can telecommute and job share as their jobs allow; (c) employees working more than sixteen hours a week receive all benefits; (d) grandparent employees are eligible for dependent care benefits, including use of the Bon Secours Family Center, childcare services provided by the Bon Secours Health System for employees and students; (e) employees are supported in their career transitions and new skill development through training and development opportunities; (f) employees can participate in Employee Wellness Services, where they can learn about health risks for employees age fifty and older and gain information to address these risks; employees also have access to health fairs and health screening; and (g) employees have access to lifestyle planning through the area agency on aging.

Bon Secours has seen many financial advantages to this program. Their retention of employees in this age group increased from 84 percent in 2005 to 87 percent in 2006. In addition, the number of employees who took phased retirement and then returned to work as needed grew 300 percent from 2004 to 2006. Finally, employee engagement increased over this time. Employee engagement is a

Table 7.3. Comparison of Availability of Flex Careers across Employers

	ALLOWS *ALL* OR *MOST* EMPLOYEES TO TAKE SABBATICALS OF SIX MONTHS OR MORE	PERMITS EMPLOYEES TO MOVE ON AND OFF MANAGEMENT/ LEADERSHIP TRACK	PERMITS *ALL* OR *MOST* EMPLOYEES TO MOVE BETWEEN FULL-TIME AND PART-TIME WORK	ALLOWS *ALL* OR *MOST* EMPLOYEES TO RETURN TO WORK GRADUALLY AFTER CHILDBIRTH OR ADOPTION	ALLOWS *ALL* OR *MOST* EMPLOYEES TO PHASE INTO RETIREMENT	OFFERS A DEFINED-BENEFIT PENSION PLAN TO EMPLOYEES WHO PHASE INTO RETIREMENT
2005 National Study of Employers (%) (n = 1,092)	28	38	21	67	28	16
2006 Sloan award winners (%) (n = 89)	27	91	42	82	34	9
Ernst and Young (Chicago)	*	Yes	*	*	*	Yes
Bon Secours Richmond Health System (Richmond, VA)		Yes	*	*	*	Yes

* = Allows *all or most* employees.

multidimensional concept that entails employees working harder than they have to so that their organization succeeds (see table 7.3 for a comparison of the availability of career flexibility options nationally and in these companies).

Responsibility, Control, and Accountability: Prevalence according to Employers and Employees

Ultimately, workplace flexibility, as defined here, is giving employees more control, as well as more responsibility and accountability. When work "works" for both the employer and the employee, employees must be accountable for ensuring that work is done well and that there is coverage at the workplace for key functions when they work flexibly. Likewise, employers must provide employees with flexibility and must create the mechanisms for employees to be responsible and accountable.

CONTROL OVER NUMBER OF HOURS AND SCHEDULING

According to the 2005 National Study of Employers, 39 percent permit all or most high-level salaried employees substantial control over their hours and scheduling. That percentage drops significantly for lower-level hourly employees, with 13 percent of employers permitting them substantial control over hours and scheduling.

CONTROL OVER SHIFTS

According to the 2005 NSE, 20 percent of employers permit all or most of their employees to have control over which shifts they work. The 2002 National Study of the Changing Workforce found that 74 percent of employees work regular daytime shifts. Interestingly, nearly half (49%) of employees would prefer to have a different shift than the one they now have; this percentage includes those who work daytime hours.

CONTROL OVER OVERTIME HOURS

The 2005 NSE found that 14 percent of employers allow all or most of their employees to have control of paid or unpaid overtime hours. The 2002 NSCW found that 58 percent of employees are not required to work extra or overtime hours, with little or no advance notice, more than once a month.

CONTROL OVER TAKING BREAKS

The 2005 NSE also found that 53 percent of employers allow all or most of their employees to have control over when they take breaks. According to the 2002 NSCW, 68 percent of employees strongly or somewhat agree that they decide when they take breaks.

Responsibility, Control, and Accountability: Promising Practices

The employers selected for these profiles demonstrate that control over work and accountability for business success can go hand in hand. For example, while staff at a medical facility chose their own hours, they are expected to resolve any problems that arise in ensuring full coverage.

ARIZONA SPINE AND JOINT HOSPITAL

Anyone signing up for back surgery or a hip replacement wants superlative medical care. Kristin Schmidt, chief executive officer of the 120-employee Arizona Spine and Joint Hospital in Mesa, believes a strategy of flexibility helps her medical facility deliver just that. Its turnover rate among nurses is less than 2 percent, compared with a national turnover rate of more than 15 percent. "We offer nurses and all our other employees great latitude in choosing how much they want to work and when they want to work," she said, "right down to the timing of their breaks."

Roughly 80 percent of the hospital's 120 employees are nurses, and the rest are mainly doctors, technicians, and administrative staff. "All of them can control the shifts they work," said Heather Lorig, who runs case management and social services at the hospital. "Offering this much choice is easy," she said. "Each unit—inpatient and outpatient, for example—just posts a big calendar in the employee lounge, and people fill in the days and hours they want."

Schedule conflicts are resolved among staff, particularly where nurses are concerned, since extensive cross-training allows them to cover the operating or the recovery room, for example, depending on the hours they want. It is also not uncommon for someone who normally works at night to step in for a day-shift person who needs to visit his daughter's classroom. "Even Kristin, the CEO and a registered nurse, will step in to cover a staffing need," said Lorig. Staff likewise can choose the amount of time they want to work, though they need to work a minimum of twenty-four hours a week in order to retain their benefits.

As in surgical facilities everywhere, unpredictability is standard at the Mesa hospital, and multitasking cannot be avoided. "One patient is in pain, another needs his sheets changed, and three more are asking you questions. You need to go in five different directions at once," said Lorig. What makes multitasking easier to handle is a trimmed-down bureaucracy. "In some hospitals, you have to talk to several different nurse managers before you can take action. At the Arizona Spine and Joint Hospital, a single nurse manager oversees each unit. He or she knows what's going on with each patient and can render a quick decision."

Another kind of flexibility—the ability to throw hierarchy aside—helps offset the strains of those struggling with important, but sometimes tedious, work. "Today there was a nurse with three patients who'd just left the recovery room. She'd been doing vital signs for hours, rotating back and forth between patients in three different rooms, watching the patients' reactions. Two of them needed blood. It really takes a lot out of you, and at one point, she just looked up and said, 'I need help.' So the nurse manager put her sterile scrubs on and started an IV." Lorig added that in a medical facility, no one is above patient care. "If someone needs a bedpan emptied, we just pick it up." The Arizona Spine and Joint Hospital is a well-designed facility with top-of-the-line medical equipment, Schmidt points out. But it is flexibility, she adds, that enables the facility to attract and retain the staff needed to ensure superlative patient care.

NORTEL

Nortel, a twenty-six-hundred-employee voice and data communication company in the greater Durham area in North Carolina, also demonstrates a commitment to flexibility. Fully 80 percent of their employees have the equipment they need to work wherever it is convenient, and 10 percent are based at home. They use the technology that is the basis of their business to enable employees to work in a variety of environments—at home, at work, on the road. The goal of this flexibility is to give employees the tools they need to take responsibility for meeting their business and personal goals.

What about the costs? According to a written statement, "We're beautifully equipped to get our work done, and, in a crisis, we're much less affected than conventional workers. Plus, we're proud of our environmental impacts, like reduced GHG [greenhouse gas] emissions and road congestion."

The Culture of Flexibility according to Employees

This status report on workplace flexibility concludes by examining "the culture of flexibility" as experienced by employees, as this is the heart and soul of flexibility. As anyone who has ever delved into organizational change or effectiveness knows, workplace programs and policies are necessary but not sufficient. An employer could decree a flextime or flex-career initiative, which does not necessarily mean that employees can use it without jeopardizing their prestige in the organization, their possibilities for advancement, or even their job security. Likewise, an employer may not have a formal written policy and yet be very flexible. It always "depends"— depends on how supervisors and co-workers at all levels of the organization actually behave when implementing flexibility. Thus, the culture of flexibility is measured by surveying employees (as is also the case regarding access to and use of other forms of flexibility outlined in this chapter). To assess the culture of flexibility, employees are asked a number of questions about the implementation of flexibility, including (a) whether employees at their organization have to choose between advancing in their jobs or devoting attention to their family or personal lives (b) whether employees who ask for time off for family reasons or try to arrange different schedules or hours to meet their personal or family needs are less likely to get ahead in their jobs or careers (c) how their supervisor treats them when they have family or personal business to attend to (d) whether they feel comfortable bringing up personal or family issues with their supervisor (e) whether their supervisor is understanding when they talk about personal or family issues that affect their work (f) whether their supervisor shows favoritism in responding to employees' personal or family needs (g) whether management rewards those within the organization who support effective flexible work arrangements (h) whether management tries to structure work requirements to avoid a negative impact on employees' personal and family lives (i) whether their employer makes a real and ongoing effort to inform employees of available assistance for managing work and family responsibilities, and (j) whether supervisors are encouraged to assess employees' performance by what employees accomplish, and not just by "face time"—that is, the number of hours they spend at the workplace.

In the National Study of the Changing Workforce, 61 percent of the 2,810 employees surveyed strongly or somewhat disagreed that at their place of employment, employees must choose between advancing in their jobs or devoting attention to the family or personal lives. However, a similar amount (60%) also strongly or somewhat disagreed that employees who ask for time off for family reasons, or try to arrange different schedules or hours to meet their personal or family needs are "less likely to get ahead in their jobs or careers."

The level of support for using flexibility varies, according to employees in the 2002 National Study of the Changing Workforce, ranging from very high support when work or personal issues arise (92%) to lower levels when it comes to organizational support, such as how work requirements are structured or how much effort the employer makes to communicate about flexibility.

The Culture of Flexibility: Promising Practices

The employers selected for profiling have established incentives and other strategies to ensure that the culture they want to create *actually* occurs. The first company measures individual supervisors by the culture of flexibility they create with data from employee surveys; these results affect the supervisors' promotions and compensation decisions. A small company is also profiled whose owner is committed to implementing her support for a flexible culture at her place of business.

FIRST TENNESSEE BANK

In the early 1990s, First Tennessee, headquartered in Memphis, Tennessee, conducted a study of its most profitable retail bank branches. This study confirmed that it is the employees who make the difference. The most profitable branches had the highest customer retention rates and the highest employee retention rates. The company then began to focus on strategies for keeping great employees. Employees told the company they wanted more flexibility and control over their work and more support in embracing both their work and family responsibilities.

A rapid payoff in dollars and cents followed the company's shift to retain employees. Earnings per share rose from 70 cents to $1.10 in just three years, and customer retention increased to 95 percent versus an industry norm of 88 percent. President Frank Shriner explained, "We learned that when our employees were delighted, they made our customers happy too."

First Tennessee's "First Power" culture requires managers throughout the bank to take employees' needs for flexibility seriously. For example, a manager on deadline whose staff member had an ailing mother would give that employee the time he needed to be with his mother. To make up for that person's absence, the manager might marshal a junior staff member's absolute commitment to the project by giving her responsibility for a challenging, visible part of the assignment. The manager also might look for someone in another group, perhaps coming off another project, with a little time to spare, or find another solution. Refusing to give a staff member time to take care of a family emergency would be an unacceptable option.

The emphasis on flexibility begins with recruitment. "Our recruiting conversations highlight our values, emphasizing inclusion and flexibility," said Leigh Ann Spurlin, human resources professional at the Chattanooga site (which has 157 of First Horizon National Corporation's thirty thousand employees). The same messages are interwoven into training for incoming managers—one four-hour class gives supervisors ways to help their staff members manage work and personal lives. The company's *Leadership Success Guide* and internal website also include flexibility guidelines. Spurlin believes, however, that experience may be the best teacher of all.

"We walk the talk, so it doesn't take new managers long to see that flexibility is part of our fabric."

Company adherence to these values is measured and tracked through their yearly Employee Value and Leadership survey. Employees fill out questionnaires, rating their supervisors on a number of factors including flexibility and inclusion. "The results make the culture tangible to everyone," said Spurlin. "Managers know where they're strongest and where they can improve." Managers know that they will be evaluated on how they handle flexibility and inclusion. Staff members can see that they have been heard, and that their voices effect change. In 2005, their Employee Value and Leadership survey found that almost half of their employees said they worked some type of flexible schedule. And, almost 90 percent of employees said their leader is supportive of their ability to embrace both work and personal responsibilities.

Virtually all 157 employees in First Tennessee's Chattanooga office have opportunities for flexibility, including: (a) all tellers can reschedule their hours every three weeks, enabling them to take a daughter to a dance class or spend time with a son's teacher (b) many employees can work from home with laptop computers (c) staff members can take time to care for an ailing relative (d) leaves of up to sixteen weeks can be obtained, with the bank holding employees' jobs for them (these leaves are unpaid, though all opportunities for vacation pay, disability income, and so forth, are first exhausted) (e) part-time schedules can be arranged. Inevitably, there are cases where flexible options do not work out. If the business suffers, First Tennessee ends the arrangement. But overwhelmingly, flexible work arrangements prove successful—for customers as well as employees. In fact, according to a 2009 survey by Brand Informatics Inc., a Rockville, Maryland–based national consumer research company, First Tennessee was ranked number one by customers responding to the loyalty statement, "I love my brand."

NRG::SEATTLE

"I want people to bring their passion to work in the morning," states Michelle Rupp, owner of the insurance brokerage company NRG::Seattle. "I can't say, 'check your personal life at the door.'" Rupp took over her father's insurance company in 1994. Today, the Seattle, Washington firm has fourteen employees, five thousand customers, a premium volume of $8 million, and is one of the nation's largest woman-owned brokerage companies.

Day-to-day work practices build flexibility into every staff member's life, the result of a culture that flows straight from its owner's management style. Rupp insists that everyone work at home one day each week. "You can concentrate better when the phones aren't ringing all around you," she said. All staff members take a three-hour break one Friday afternoon each month—time to go to the doctor, visit a friend, or check in with a child's teacher. Moreover, they receive an extra month's vacation every five years. "If they put those weeks together with their regular vacation, they have two consecutive months off," she said. "It's a little sabbatical. It may mean extra work for colleagues, but everyone knows their time will come."

Why does she encourage her employees to step away from the office? To free up their minds and recharge their spirits, she says. "When I inherited this company, it was fun to create a work environment exactly like one I'd want to work in. My father always saw the business as a vehicle for all of us to lead better lives—not just the owners, but all the employees." After he died, a couple of his staff members said he had never forgotten what it was like to be an employee. "I thought that was the coolest thing," said Rupp. "There's something great about being the kind of boss who says on a Friday, 'We've had a great week. Let's all just go home.' As long as the customers are well taken care of, why not?"

Rupp is flexible as to when staff members come in to the office, as long as new business is coming in and longstanding customers are happy. She herself has recently been trying to achieve more balance in her life, and takes most mornings off, working until 9:00 p.m. or later. "I want to attract people who live their lives with passion and energy, and bring that into the office with them each day," said Rupp. "Flexibility helps me do that. We have fun, provide a wonderful service to a great group of clients and have very little turnover, which goes right to the bottom line. Everybody wins!"

Every day around noon, the NRG::Seattle insurance company goes dark. Someone throws the light switch, and everyone must exit the office. Routines like this make it clear that the owner means what she says about flexibility. Rupp believes her people are restored by slowing down for an hour, taking a deep breath and getting out of the building, so she actually removes the option of working through lunch. People are also reminded that working overtime is discouraged; employee are evaluated not by how much time they spend in the office, but by the happiness of their clients.

For privacy reasons, employee data from these two employers is not reported; instead, average measures of absence of jeopardy and support for working flexibly from the employees of 2006 Sloan Award Winners are compared with the 2002 National Study of the Changing Workforce. Overall, employees of the 2006 Alfred P. Sloan Award Winners rate their employers higher in terms of absence of jeopardy (74) and workplace culture (89), on a 100-point scoring scale where higher numbers reflect more positive responses, than employees who responded to the 2002 National Study of the Changing Workforce, 61 and 76 respectively.

Implications for Employers

As this volume has made clear, the workforce and the workplace are in transition. The 2002 National Study of the Changing Workforce found that these changes are taking a toll on employees: 55 percent of employees feel they do not have enough time for themselves, 63 percent feel they lack sufficient time for their spouses or partners, and 67 percent feel there is not enough time for their children.

The repercussions of these changes are being experienced by employers, as well. The 2002 NSCW reveals that 39 percent of employees are not fully engaged in their jobs, 54 percent are less than fully satisfied with their jobs, and 38 percent are somewhat or very likely to make a concerted effort to find a new job in the coming year. In this climate, employers are challenged to recruit talent, engage and retain workers, and maximize productivity.

FWI's research, however, finds that there are new ways to structure work to benefit both employers and employees. It seems that flexibility is, in fact, a critical ingredient of an effective workplace. And when employees work in flexible and effective workplaces, they are more likely to be engaged in their jobs and committed to helping their organizations succeed, plan on staying with their employer, be satisfied with their jobs, and exhibit better mental health.

This chapter has highlighted the prevalence of six different forms of workplace flexibility, as well as some very exciting and promising practices in each of these areas. The employers profiled make it clear that these workplaces are not only possible, they exist in communities throughout this country.

8

WILL THE REAL FAMILY-FRIENDLY EMPLOYER PLEASE STAND UP

Who Permits Work Hour Reductions
for Childcare?

Robert Hutchens and Patrick Nolen

The problem of balancing work and family life is particularly onerous when an employee wants to work fewer hours to deal with a family crisis. This is probably easiest for an acute crisis for which a couple of days off are required. More complicated are long-term problems, such as a sick or injured child who requires several months of care. This chapter examines how employers react to an especially difficult family-work issue: an employee who wants to move from full-time to part-time in order to care for a young child.

One reason to examine movements from full-time to part-time is that they seem to fall outside the purview of the existing literature on family-friendly policies. The focus of this literature is principally on formal policies such as maternity leave, paternity leave, and leave beyond that required by the Family and Medical Leave Act. Empirical work is often based on an index that combines several different "family-friendly" policies, declaring employers with high values of the index "progressive." It is not at all clear how these progressive employers would deal with an employee who wants to move from full-time to part-time in order to care for a child. The situation may be more a matter of informal practice than formal policy. Indeed, organizations with codified formal policies may be precisely the kinds of employers who do not permit such a shift from full-time to part-time.

Of course, both formal and informal policies and practices can play a role in alleviating work-family tensions, and both are thereby good topics for investigation. It is surely not the case that formal policies are always superior. There are, for example, situations where individual circumstances are more easily addressed through informal mechanisms. Formal policies may be adopted, not because they are more effective, but because organizational size renders informal mechanisms unwieldy.

Moreover, it is interesting to examine how ideas that have been tested using data on formal family-friendly policies can be extended to less visible employer practices; that is, practices that, while family-friendly, may not be included in the employer's written description of personnel or fringe benefit policies.

Thus, this chapter analyzes establishment-level data on whether an employer is willing to accommodate an employee who wants to reduce hours in order to care for a child. In this chapter we seek to understand what types of employers permit such a reduction in hours and whether employers who permit such a reduction tend to also offer more formal family-friendly policies, such as paid maternity and paternity leave.

The Literature

The existing literature on employer responsiveness to work-family issues often focuses on employer-financed benefits or services. For example, an organization that provides onsite daycare or pays for daycare away from the workplace is reasonably viewed as responsive to work-family issues (Goodstein 1994; Ingram and Simons 1995; Osterman 1995). Fringe benefits such as paid maternity and paternity leave are also important (Galinsky and Bond 1998; Ingram and Simons 1995). Finally, a responsive employer has formal policies that assure flexibility in hours such as flextime or parental leave for infant care (Galinsky and Bond 1998; Trzcinski 1991). There is no question that such policies identify family-friendly employers. One worries, however, that this emphasis on formal policies and fringe benefits could bias results toward large organizations. Smaller organizations may use informal practices to address similar work-family issues. Indeed, smaller organizations may have the luxury of addressing each employee's situation individually, and thus may not require formal policies.

Such worries are reinforced by the frequent use of indexes of family-friendly policies. For example, as their dependent variable in a multivariate analysis, Ingram and Simons (1995) use an index whereby an organization is ranked as most responsive to work-family issues when it provided a "dependent care service" as well as a "flexible workplace option." To satisfy this criterion, the firm must have a formal policy that pays for a benefit or service. Goodstein (1994) and Osterman (1995) use a similar index in their work. Although the indexes in some of these studies apparently include informal practices, such practices are viewed as inferior to more formal policies. Ingram and Simons (1995), for example, treat unpaid paternity leave as a type of work-family policy, and apparently include informal practices as part of this. Yet, unpaid paternity leave is viewed as a "cheap response" (p. 1472), and not on the same plane as (say) subsidized childcare.

Research that uses such indexes consistently finds that large organizations are more responsive to work-family issues than small organizations. Summarizing the literature, Fredriksen-Goldsen and Scharlach (2001, 194) write, "Companies with fewer than 100 employees are significantly less likely than larger firms with over 100 employees to offer benefits such as retirement, health insurance, life insurance, disability insurance, or paid time off." Along these lines, after arguing that large organizations are more visible and are under more pressure to respond to work-family concerns, Ingram and Simons (1995, 1468) go on to cite a literature indicating that "large organizations have also been found to be more responsive to work-family issues." This result arises in contingency tables (Ingram and Simons 1995, table 1) as well as multivariate analyses (Ingram and Simons 1995, table 3; Osterman 1995, table 3; Wood 1999, table 6). This chapter examines whether a similar result arises for an alternative measure of employer responsiveness to work-family issues.

Theoretical Framework

This section lays out hypotheses regarding what kinds of employers are likely to permit an employee to shift from full-time to part-time in order to care for a young child. There are potential advantages to such flexibility for both the employer and the parent. From the parent's perspective, such part-time work can permit care of a sick or otherwise needy child while providing earnings, maintaining connections to informal networks, and avoiding loss of firm-specific skills. From the employer's perspective, such flexibility can enhance retention of valued employees. Moreover, at least in comparison to paid parental leave, a part-time arrangement may facilitate employer monitoring and thereby mitigate moral hazard problems.

At least two theoretical frameworks provide insights into what kind of employers permit such a reduction in hours. First, economic theory can be used to develop a model of a cost-minimizing firm that decides whether to let an employee work part-time. Such a theory provides an explanation for why different employers offer different opportunities for part-time work.[1] Second, much of the work on employer responsiveness to work-family issues is built upon institutional theory in sociology.[2] According to that theory, organizations differ in their need to maintain organizational legitimacy, and thus differ in their response to pressures to adopt progressive work-family practices.

In part because of the lack of data necessary for a rigorous test of institutional theory,[3] this chapter primarily relies on economic theories of part-time work. Four hypotheses are presented for why employers differ in their propensity to permit employees to shift from full-time to part-time for purposes of childcare: organizational size, minimum hours constraints, employee demands, and long-term contracts. The first hypothesis comes from institutional theory, and the latter three from labor economics.

Hypothesis 1: Industrial Sector and Organization Size

Institutional theory in sociology argues that large organizations are more visible and held to higher standards than small organizations. Both Goodstein (1994, 357) and Ingram and Simons (1995, 1466) state this as follows: "The greater the size of an organization, the greater its level of responsiveness to institutional pressures for employer involvement in work-family issues." For similar reasons, public sector organizations should be particularly responsive to institutional pressures. According to Ingram and Simons (1995, 1469), "Public sector organizations will be more responsive than private sector organizations to institutional pressures for employer involvement in work-family issues." Applied to this chapter's measure of employer responsiveness to work-family issues, we arrive at the following hypothesis.

Establishments that are part of large organizations and/or public sector organizations are more likely to permit employees to shift from full-time to part-time for purposes of childcare, ceteris paribus.

One way that this chapter contributes to the literature is by examining the effects of industrial sector and organization size on a measure of employer responsiveness that includes informal policies. Such a measure may have advantages over measures that are strictly based on formal policies. This is because, as established in an earlier line of sociological research, large and public organizations tend to be bureaucratic and thereby more inclined to adopt formal procedures (see Mintzberg 1979 or Pugh et al. 1969). A measure of responsiveness that is based on formal policies could yield statistically significant results that are influenced by relationships between the explanatory variables and formality. That is less likely to be a problem for the measure used here.

Hypothesis 2: Minimum Hours Constraints

The second hypothesis arises out of the economic literature on minimum hour constraints. Regardless of an employee's reason for wanting to shift from full-time to part-time work, employer restrictions on the number of hours an employee must work may cause employers to prohibit the shift (Gustman and Steinmeier 1983). If employers require their employees to work a minimum number of hours per week, month and/or year, then the employees can only reduce hours by quitting and taking a different job. This can be stated as:

Establishments that impose minimum hours constraints on their employees are less likely to permit employees to shift from full-time to part-time for purposes of childcare, ceteris paribus.

It is usually argued that the driving force behind minimum hours constraints is the firm's technology; the technology is such that part-time work is costly to the firm. This idea takes at least three forms:

1. *Team production.* In some jobs, efficiency requires that a team of workers be present (Nollen, Eddy, and Martin 1978). Although an assembly line and a

football team are classic examples, there are other jobs, such as police services, that require people to work the same hours so that they can interact as members of a team.

2. *Quasi-fixed employment costs.* Quasi-fixed employment costs do not change with hours worked. Examples are hiring and training costs. Economic theory predicts that employers will only bear part of these costs in anticipation of recovering the rest of the cost over the duration of the employment relationship. A minimum hours constraint may be part of this cost recovery; if an employee works less than the minimum hours constraint, then the employer may not fully recover the initial fixed cost. In fact, there is evidence that the proportion of a firm's workforce that is part-time declines with the magnitude of hiring and training costs (Montgomery 1988).

3. *Supervisory costs.* Another reason for minimum hours constraints—a reason quite similar to quasi-fixed costs—is supervisory cost. Nollen, Eddy, and Martin (1977) indicate that the problem is primarily one of scheduling complexities. "Either there is more scheduling of workers to be done because there are more workers, or scheduling is harder because part-time workers are not continuously available or work irregular schedules" (45).

Empirical work requires observable proxies for constraints on the minimum number of hours an employee must work. Obvious proxies are variables that indicate the extent to which an establishment permits less than full-time work. As detailed below, the subsequent empirical work uses the establishment's policy on job sharing, as well as the presence of part-time workers as indicators of workplaces that *do not* impose constraints on the minimum number of hours an employee must work. Similarly, the establishment's policy on flexible starting times is used as an indicator. Michael Hurd (1996, 25) has argued that flexible starting times reveal the absence of team production.

Hypothesis 3: Employee Demand

A third hypothesis views worker needs and demands as the primary determinant of work-family policies. Since different workers have different needs, if a large fraction of an establishment's workforce is interested in certain types of policies or fringe benefits, then it can be in the employer's interest to respond. It follows that an employer's attitude toward shifts from full-time to part-time for purposes of childcare will be a function of establishment demographics. Thus:

Establishments with employee groups that are disproportionately likely to care for young children are more likely to permit employees to shift from full-time to part-time for purposes of childcare, ceteris paribus.

This hypothesis has antecedents in the theory of compensating differentials (e.g., Rosen 1986). Accordingly, employers grant employee demands for costly workplace amenities either because this helps with retention of valued employees or because some other form of compensation (such as money wages) can be reduced. Although evidence for employer responsiveness to worker demands often focuses on the effects of unions (e.g., Buchmueller, DiNardo, and Valletta 2002; Freeman 1981), there are good reasons to expect a similar effect in nonunion workplaces.

Empirical work requires measures of workplace demographics that are associated with demand for family-friendly policies. One such measure—a measure that is standard in the literature on family-friendly policies—is the percentage of workers who are female. Another feasible measure is the age of the establishment's workforce. If a high percentage of the establishment's workforce is over fifty-five years of age, then one would expect less demand for flexibility with regard to childcare.

Hypothesis 4: Long-Term Relationships

A fourth hypothesis arises out of the literature on training and implicit contracts. Employers differ in the extent to which they encourage long-term employment relationships. Some want to retain workers until they reach retirement, while others accept high turnover rates. Employers with a strong interest in retaining workers would seem particularly likely to accommodate those with a young child. To not do so is to risk low morale and valued employees leaving the job. Thus:

Establishments characterized by long-term employment relationships are more likely to permit employees to shift from full-time to part-time for purposes of childcare, ceteris paribus.

There are several explanations why some employers encourage long-term relationships. Perhaps the most prominent explanations posit that some employers provide their workers with firm-specific training, that is, training that only has value in that specific firm. Much as with quasi-fixed costs, the employer will have an interest in recovering the cost of such training. Since that is not possible if the worker quits shortly after receiving the training, the employer has a strong interest in retaining the worker. A second closely related explanation for long-term relationships arises out of the implicit contract literature. The argument here is that for some productive activities, it is difficult for employers to monitor worker performance. These employers use implicit contracts that are structured to discourage workers from cheating or shirking, and such contracts tend to be long-term contracts (Bulow and Summers 1986; Hutchens 1986; Lazear 1979, 1981).[4]

The subsequent empirical work requires proxies for long-term employment relationships. As detailed below, five variables are used for this purpose: a measure of employer-provided formal training;[5] a variable indicating whether workers are likely to remain with the firm until retirement; a variable indicating the extent to which jobs are filled from the inside; and measures of the fraction of workers with long and short job tenures.

Although the first of our four hypotheses is drawn explicitly from institutional theory in sociology, the last three hypotheses are by no means foreign to this literature.[6] Of particular importance is the employee demand hypothesis. After noting that working women face particularly strong work-family pressures because they often bear primary responsibility for childcare, and after citing an extensive list of previous works, Goodstein hypothesizes, "the greater the dependence of an organization on female employees, the greater its level of responsiveness to institutional pressures for employer involvement in work-family issues" (1994, 358). The same idea is found in Ingram and Simons (1995, 1468), Osterman (1995), and Guthrie and Roth (1999).

The Data

The subsequent analysis is based on a nationally representative sample of 947 U.S establishments. An establishment is defined as a single physical location at which business is conducted or services or industrial operations are performed. An establishment may or may not be part of a larger organization. For example, a school may be one of several establishments that belong to a school district. For purposes of studying an employer's actual behavior, establishment-level data are arguably better than data collected from the larger organization. In contrast to (say) a survey of upper-level executives at corporate headquarters, establishment-level respondents are more likely to know how policy is implemented in practice.

The survey was undertaken for the purpose of studying phased retirement among white-collar workers.[7] As such, the sample was restricted to establishments not engaged in either agriculture or mining, with twenty or more employees, and at least two white-collar employees who are age fifty-five or more.[8]

The sample universe was the Dun and Bradstreet Strategic Marketing Record for December 2000. These data come from credit checks, although information is also obtained from the U.S. Postal Service, banks, newspapers, the Yellow Pages, and other public records. To insure sufficient numbers of large establishments, the sample was stratified by establishment size. When appropriate, the subsequent results are weighted to ensure representative samples. The survey was executed by the University of Massachusetts Center for Survey Research between June 2001 and November 2002.

The survey was conducted by telephone. The survey research firm first contacted the establishment and asked for the person who is best able to answer questions about flexible work schedules and employee benefits; for example, a human resource manager or benefits manager. Interviews were conducted with a CATI (Computer Assisted Telephone Interviewing) system, thereby permitting an interview to be completed over several phone calls. The median number of telephone calls to complete an interview was ten, with 10 percent of the interviews requiring thirty or more calls to complete.

The overall response rate was 61 percent. Most of the nonresponse occurred when screening establishments for eligibility (e.g., at least two white-collar employees age 55+), and before respondents knew the purpose of the survey. Interviews were completed in 89 percent of the establishments that were successfully screened. This is on a par with other establishment-level telephone surveys.[9]

Three Indicators of Family-Friendly Policies and Practices

After asking a series of questions about the characteristics of the establishment and its human resource policies, the interviewer posed the following question:

> Suppose a [randomly selected occupation] wanted to shift from a full-time to a part-time work schedule in order to care for a young child. This employee would like to remain part-time for at least a year, and perhaps longer. (Q1) Would that be permitted in your establishment (Yes, No, Depends, Don't Know/Not Sure)?

Prior to this question, the interviewer asked whether any of the establishment's white-collar workers fell into four occupational categories: (a) professionals (including technical workers), (b) managers or administrators, (c) sales personnel, (d) clerical or office workers. The "randomly selected occupation" in Q1 is one of these four occupational categories. If an establishment did not have white-collar employees in an occupational category (e.g., if it did not include sales people), then that category was excluded from the random selection.

Table 8.1 presents the results of this question. Most establishments answer "yes," although there is variation by occupation. In particular, managers have fewer opportunities to shift to part-time in order to care for a child. This is presumably because it is difficult for an establishment to have a part-time manager.

Table 8.1. Responses to Availability of Shift to Part-time for Purposes of Childcare by Occupational Category (weighted percentages)[a]

	OCCUPATIONAL CATEGORY				
	CLERICAL	MANAGER	PROFESSIONAL	SALES	TOTAL
Yes (%)	53	42	55	47	49
Depends (%)	19	18	20	19	19
No (%)	19	29	19	25	23
DK or NA (%)	9	11	6	9	9
Number of cases	300	297	259	91	947
Total (%)	100	100	100	100	100

[a]Responses to the question, "Does establishment permit shift to part-time for purposes of childcare?"

When respondents answered Q1 with "depends," they were asked what it depends on. The vast majority of respondents indicated that it depends on what kind of work a person does, and whether a part-time arrangement is feasible. For example, "[It depends on] conditions that have to do with the ability to share work. Some work, such as accounting, does not share very well"; "Depends on position of the person and readily available shifting of workload"; "[It depends on] if they had someone to job share with"; "In certain positions, but in others it would be impossible. Our field staff comes to mind and several management positions do not lend themselves to part-time work"; or, "Some departments may not be able to accommodate that, but there may be jobs in other departments that would allow that. They may also provide a temp." In some cases, however, the response evidently depends on the employee who was asking for the shift and why they were asking: "It would depend upon longevity and position"; "If he is a good salesman and they didn't want to lose him they would want to work with him"; "We honor 12 weeks of medical leave; beyond that it would be just depend on the circumstances"; or, "The child would have to be very, very, ill."

For purposes of the subsequent analysis, responses to Q1 are coded into a variable called "Sick-Child" that takes three values: 0 = No; 1 = Depends; 2 = Yes. Observations with a response of "Don't Know" or "Not Sure" are excluded from the analysis. Since the question pertains to different occupations in different establishments, the subsequent analysis uses occupation dummy variables to control for the randomly selected occupation.

Recall that the second goal of this chapter is to examine the extent to which Sick-Child is related to other policies that the literature treats as "family-friendly"; thus, we examine paid maternity and paternity leave. Previous assessments of employer responsiveness to work family issues use similar variables (e.g., Ingram and Simons 1995; Wood 1999). The variables used here arise out of the following questions:

> We would like to know a little about some of your establishment's personnel policies. First, in order to make these questions more concrete, please think of a secure, full-time, white-collar position in your establishment that is occupied by an employee in good standing. Either as a matter of formal or informal policy, would your establishment allow this employee: (Q2) paid maternity leave (Yes = 2, In Some Cases = 1, No = 0, Don't Know/Not Sure); (Q3) paid paternity leave (Yes = 2, In Some Cases = 1, No = 0, Don't Know/Not Sure).

As with Q1, these variables are coded 0, 1, and 2. Cases with "Don't Know/Not Sure" responses are excluded from the analysis.

Although results on both Q2 and Q3 are presented below, for purposes of assessing an employer's family-friendliness, we have a preference for paid paternity leave. This is because paid maternity leave is often provided through paid sick leave policies, and that may not reveal family-friendliness. In contrast, when paid paternity leave is provided, the firm must also provide paid maternity leave.[10]

Descriptive Statistics

Table 8.2 not only provides an overview of the data, but also permits initial steps toward the chapter's two goals. The first row of the table presents overall means for the three indicators of family-friendly policy. Since the mean of 1.34 for Sick-Child lies between one and two, these results indicate that, on average, establishments allow workers to switch from full-time to part-time work to care for a young child. The maternity leave and paternity leave variables have averages of 1.22 and .76 respectively, implying that paid maternity leave is more common than paid paternity leave. The subsequent rows in table 8.2 give corresponding means for these indicators of family-friendly policy when the sample is restricted to the left-hand side categorical variable. For example, for establishments in the construction industry, the average value of Sick-Child is 1.44, while that for maternity and paternity leave are .78 and .22 respectively. Note that the asterisk next to the paternity leave average indicates that this average is statistically different from the overall mean, at a .05 confidence level. Most of the variables in table 8.2 are self-explanatory.

For purposes of this chapter's first goal, understanding what types of establishments permit parents to shift to part-time work for purposes of childcare, the important information is in the "Sick-Child" column of table 8.2. Most of the statistically significant results in this column occur among the proxies for the absence of minimum hours constraints. Establishments with job sharing, a flexible starting time, and part-time work are particularly likely to permit this shift from full-time to part-time work. This is, of course, consistent with the second hypothesis.

In contrast, table 8.2 provides little support for the other hypotheses. With regard to the first hypothesis, establishments in public administration do not have significantly higher averages for "Sick-Child," nor is there evidence that the variable rises with organization size. Although there is some indication that larger *establishments* tend to be more open to a shift to part-time for purposes of childcare, the first hypothesis pertains to organization size, not establishment size. Moreover, table 8.2 provides no real support for the third and fourth hypothesis, since none of the Sick-Child results for proxies of demographics or long-term employment relationships are statistically significant. Of course, there remains the question of whether similar results are obtained in multivariate models.

The chapter's second goal is to ascertain whether an employer's willingness to permit parents to shift to part-time work for purposes of childcare is related to other "family-friendly" policies. The "Maternity Leave" and "Paternity Leave" columns of table 8.2 are particularly relevant to this end. Note that the results on paternity leave are thoroughly consistent with the first hypothesis, a hypothesis that arises out of institutional theory. Specifically, public sector establishments and large organizations tend to provide paid paternity leave. Results on maternity leave are similar, at least with regard to size of organization. In contrast, as noted above, there is no support for the first hypothesis in the Sick-Child column. Looking at the other sections

Table 8.2. Descriptive Statistics for Three Family-Friendly Variables (weighted)

VARIABLE	SICK-CHILD MEAN	SICK-CHILD STANDARD ERROR	MATERNITY LEAVE MEAN	MATERNITY LEAVE STANDARD ERROR	PATERNITY LEAVE MEAN	PATERNITY LEAVE STANDARD ERROR
ALL OBSERVATIONS	1.34	(0.03)	1.22	(0.04)	0.76	(0.04)
INDUSTRY OF ESTABLISHMENT						
Construction	1.44	(0.24)	0.78	(0.34)	0.22*	(0.22)
Manufacturing	1.23	(0.08)	1.31	(0.09)	0.51*	(0.08)
Transport, comm., and utilities	1.14	(0.15)	1.08	(0.17)	0.37*	(0.13)
Wholesale and retail trade	1.34	(0.10)	0.96*	(0.12)	0.57	(0.11)
Finance, insur., and real estate	1.51	(0.15)	1.41	(0.18)	1.03	(0.20)
Services	1.42	(0.08)	1.18	(0.10)	0.65	(0.09)
Health, ed., and social services	1.36	(0.06)	1.28	(0.06)	0.92*	(0.07)
Public administration	1.30	(0.11)	1.33	(0.12)	1.19*	(0.13)
REGION OF ESTABLISHMENT						
Central	1.38	(0.06)	1.21	(0.07)	0.78	(0.07)
South	1.23*	(0.06)	1.21	(0.07)	0.71	(0.07)
East	1.36	(0.07)	1.22	(0.09)	0.60*	(0.09)
West	1.43	(0.07)	1.24	(0.08)	0.92*	(0.09)
SIZE OF ESTABLISHMENT						
Less than 50 employees	1.32	(0.07)	1.29	(0.07)	0.76	(0.08)
50 to 99 employees	1.39	(0.08)	1.16	(0.09)	0.83	(0.09)
100 to 249 employees	1.29	(0.06)	1.12	(0.07)	0.58*	(0.06)
250 to 999 employees	1.30	(0.08)	1.21	(0.09)	0.80	(0.09)
1,000 or more employees	1.58*	(0.12)	1.30	(0.17)	1.12*	(0.17)

(Continued)

Table 8.2. *(Continued)*

VARIABLE	SICK-CHILD MEAN	SICK-CHILD STANDARD ERROR	MATERNITY LEAVE MEAN	MATERNITY LEAVE STANDARD ERROR	PATERNITY LEAVE MEAN	PATERNITY LEAVE STANDARD ERROR
SIZE OF ORGANIZATION						
Less than 50 employees	1.42	(0.07)	1.17	(0.10)	0.63	(0.09)
50 to 99 employees	1.48	(0.09)	1.02	(0.12)	0.76	(0.12)
100 to 249 employees	1.31	(0.07)	0.95*	(0.09)	0.52*	(0.07)
250 to 999 employees	1.22	(0.08)	1.37*	(0.08)	0.94*	(0.09)
1,000 or more employees	1.24	(0.06)	1.52*	(0.06)	0.97*	(0.07)
ESTABLISHMENT IS PART OF LARGER ORG.	1.13*	(0.06)	1.50*	(0.06)	0.94*	(0.07)
DEMOGRAPHICS OF THE ESTABLISHMENT						
Percent white collar (WC)						
Less than 75%	1.37	(0.04)	1.09*	(0.05)	0.64*	(0.05)
75% or more	1.31	(0.05)	1.37*	(0.05)	0.89*	(0.06)
Percent of WC that are unionized						
None (0%)	1.35	(0.04)	1.17*	(0.04)	0.67*	(0.04)
Some (More than 0%)	1.30	(0.07)	1.40*	(0.07)	1.07*	(0.08)
Percent of WC that are female						
50% or less	1.33	(0.05)	1.19	(0.06)	0.66*	(0.05)
More than 50%	1.35	(0.04)	1.24	(0.05)	0.84*	(0.05)
Percent of WC under 35 yrs of age						
30% or less	1.38	(0.04)	1.15*	(0.05)	0.78	(0.05)
More than 30%	1.28	(0.05)	1.32*	(0.06)	0.73	(0.06)

	Mean	(SE)	Mean	(SE)	Mean	(SE)
Percent of WC over 54 yrs of age						
10% or less	1.29	(0.06)	1.34 *	(0.06)	0.86	(0.06)
More than 10%	1.37	(0.04)	1.15 *	(0.05)	0.70	(0.05)
PROXIES FOR ABSENCE OF MINIMUM HOURS CONSTRAINTS						
Establishment has job sharing	1.61*	(0.04)	1.32*	(0.06)	0.90*	(0.06)
Establishment has flexible starting time	1.48*	(0.04)	1.24	(0.05)	0.82*	(0.05)
Percent of work force that is part-time						
None (0%)	1.11*	(0.06)	1.23	(0.06)	0.83	(0.06)
Some (More than 0%)	1.48*	(0.04)	1.21	(0.05)	0.71	(0.05)
PROXIES FOR LONG-TERM EMPLOYMENT RELATIONSHIPS						
Establishment provides formal training	1.35	(0.03)	1.26*	(0.04)	0.79*	(0.04)
How likely 45 yr old to stay to retirement?						
Unlikely	1.36	(0.06)	1.08*	(0.08)	0.54*	(0.07)
Likely	1.34	(0.04)	1.27*	(0.04)	0.84*	(0.05)
How important to fill jobs from within?						
Not important	1.30	(0.08)	1.27	(0.08)	0.69	(0.08)
Important	1.35	(0.04)	1.20	(0.04)	0.77	(0.04)
Percent of WC with 3 yrs or less tenure						
20% or less	1.31	(0.05)	1.34*	(0.05)	0.90*	(0.05)
More than 20%	1.37	(0.05)	1.10*	(0.06)	0.62*	(0.05)
Percent of WC with 15 yrs or more tenure						
15% or less	1.34	(0.05)	1.16	(0.05)	0.65*	(0.05)
More than 15%	1.35	(0.05)	1.28	(0.05)	0.88*	(0.06)

*The mean to the left of the asterisk is statistically different from the overall mean at a .05 confidence level.

of the table, variables that are statistically significant for "Sick-Child" are frequently not statistically significant for paid maternity or paternity leave. These results then strongly suggest that the forces underlying "Sick-Child" differ from those underlying the other two family-friendly policies.

That conclusion is reinforced by the correlations between the three variables. While paid paternity and maternity leave are positively correlated with each other (the correlation coefficient is +.60), Sick-Child is effectively uncorrelated with the other two; the correlation coefficient for Sick-Child and maternity leave is −.04, while that for paternity leave is .05. Thus, at least in terms of these simple correlations, there is no evidence that Sick-Child is related to the other family-friendly variables.

Establishment Characteristics and Sick-Child: Ordered Probit Results

Multivariate models provide another path to this chapter's two goals. In line with these goals, table 8.3 presents ordered probit models of Sick-Child, the employer's response to Q1, and one ordered probit model of paternity leave, the employer's response to Q3. Ordered probits are used because the dependent variable takes three values: 0 if the employee *cannot* shift to part-time to care for a sick child or the employer *does not* offer paternity leave, 2 if an employee *can* shift to part-time or *can* take paternity leave, and 1 if the employer's response is "depends." As is the case with any survey based on voluntary participation in interviews, some respondents did not answer all of the questions. In the subsequent multivariate work we address that factor through listwise deletion, whereby any observation with missing data is excluded. As a result, the analysis is based on 631 observations.[11]

The first model in table 8.3 includes variables that determine the economic and organizational environment within which the establishment operates. Included here are measures of industry, establishment, and organization size; whether the establishment is part of a larger organization; the percentage of the establishment's workforce that is white collar; and dummy variables indicating the randomly selected occupation that was used when asking Q1. Although most of these variables are simply controls, the first hypothesis predicts that both the industry dummies and the measures of organizational size will follow a specific pattern. In accordance with the first hypothesis, establishments that are in public administration and that are part of a large organization are expected to permit employees to shift from full-time to part-time for purposes of childcare. In fact, the coefficient on public administration is neither particularly large nor statistically significant, and the organization size dummy variables do not increase with organizational size. Indeed, establishments that belong to larger organizations have significantly *lower* values of Sick-Child. There is no evidence here in support of the first hypothesis.

Table 8.3. Employer's Response Regarding Shifting to Part-Time to Care for a Sick Child and Paid Paternity Leave

	DEPENDENT VARIABLE											
	SICK-CHILD RESPONSE (=0, 1, OR 2)										PAID PATERNITY LEAVE RESPONSE (=0, 1, OR 2)	
	MODEL 1		MODEL 2		MODEL 3		MODEL 4		MODEL 5			
VARIABLES	COEFF.	SD	COEFF.	SD	COEFF.	SD	COEFF.	SD	COEFF.	SD	COEFF.	SD
INDUSTRY OF ESTABLISHMENT[a]												
Manufacturing	0.2017	(0.406)	0.0631	(0.424)	0.2115	(0.410)	0.2194	(0.408)	0.1586	(0.428)	0.4170	(0.527)
Transport, Comm., and Utilities	-0.2515	(0.438)	-0.4311	(0.457)	-0.1986	(0.442)	-0.2362	(0.443)	-0.2803	(0.465)	0.1204	(0.569)
Wholesale and Retail trade	0.1391	(0.409)	-0.0333	(0.427)	0.1574	(0.414)	0.1710	(0.414)	0.0880	(0.435)	0.2642	(0.536)
Finance, Insurance, and Real Estate	0.4721	(0.464)	0.0771	(0.484)	0.5103	(0.476)	0.4871	(0.467)	0.2612	(0.496)	0.8405	(0.586)
Services	0.3278	(0.406)	0.0175	(0.425)	0.3739	(0.413)	0.3076	(0.410)	0.1444	(0.433)	0.7018	(0.531)
Health, Education, and Social Services	0.3623	(0.401)	0.0154	(0.422)	0.4930	(0.421)	0.3927	(0.404)	0.2647	(0.443)	0.8591	(0.539)
Public Administration	-0.0058	(0.423)	-0.1811	(0.441)	0.0765	(0.431)	0.0586	(0.425)	0.0006	(0.451)	1.1300*	(0.548)
REGION OF ESTABLISHMENT[a]												
Central	0.1597	(0.142)	0.1307	(0.147)	0.1612	(0.143)	0.1407	(0.143)	0.1376	(0.149)	0.1573	(0.158)
South	-0.0365	(0.141)	0.0989	(0.146)	-0.0843	(0.146)	-0.0640	(0.142)	0.0662	(0.152)	0.1091	(0.165)
West	0.1818	(0.152)	0.1124	(0.157)	0.1945	(0.153)	0.1434	(0.154)	0.1029	(0.158)	0.3460*	(0.169)
SIZE OF ESTABLISHMENT[a]												
50 to 99 employees	0.0797	(0.210)	-0.0222	(0.216)	0.1085	(0.212)	0.0817	(0.211)	0.0074	(0.220)	-0.1947	(0.229)
100 to 249 employees	0.0251	(0.197)	-0.0080	(0.202)	0.0282	(0.199)	0.0231	(0.198)	-0.0093	(0.205)	-0.3935	(0.219)
250 to 999 employees	-0.0093	(0.219)	-0.0724	(0.226)	-0.0110	(0.222)	-0.0183	(0.220)	-0.0821	(0.230)	-0.5078*	(0.249)
1,000 or more employees	0.3054	(0.301)	0.1980	(0.311)	0.3038	(0.302)	0.3000	(0.301)	0.2013	(0.313)	-0.3890	(0.332)
SIZE OF ORGANIZATION[a]												
50 to 99 employees	0.0415	(0.262)	0.0327	(0.270)	0.0859	(0.264)	0.0059	(0.266)	0.0061	(0.276)	0.2635	(0.286)
100 to 249 employees	-0.1067	(0.235)	-0.0665	(0.241)	-0.0703	(0.238)	-0.1396	(0.239)	-0.0653	(0.248)	0.2294	(0.264)
250 to 999 employees	-0.1588	(0.245)	-0.0983	(0.252)	-0.1229	(0.247)	-0.1724	(0.249)	-0.0916	(0.256)	0.6372*	(0.274)
1,000 or more employees	-0.0004	(0.282)	0.0191	(0.289)	0.0316	(0.283)	-0.0007	(0.284)	0.0454	(0.294)	0.8337*	(0.319)

(Continued)

Table 8.3. (Continued)

VARIABLES	MODEL 1		MODEL 2		MODEL 3		MODEL 4		MODEL 5		MODEL 6	
	SICK-CHILD RESPONSE (=0, 1, OR 2)										PAID PATERNITY LEAVE RESPONSE (=0, 1, OR 2)	
	COEFF.	SD	COEFF.	SD	COEFF.	SD	COEFF.	SD	COEFF.	SD	COEFF.	SD
ESTABLISHMENT IS PART OF LARGER ORGANIZATION	-0.4123*	(0.152)	-0.3671*	(0.155)	-0.3646*	(0.155)	-0.4154*	(0.153)	-0.3637*	(0.160)	-0.1297	(0.173)
OCCUPATION												
Percent of all that are White Collar	0.0002	(0.002)	-0.0004	(0.002)	0.0008	(0.002)	-0.0002	(0.002)	0.0001	(0.002)	0.0009	(0.002)
Target Occupation for Q1:a												
Clerical	0.2448	(0.181)	0.3748*	(0.186)	0.2457	(0.182)	0.2400	(0.182)	0.3477	(0.188)	0.1392	(0.209)
Professional	0.2706	(0.182)	0.3738*	(0.187)	0.2727	(0.183)	0.2762	(0.184)	0.3563	(0.189)	0.1268	(0.210)
Manager	-0.0808	(0.179)	0.0396	(0.183)	-0.0796	(0.179)	-0.0792	(0.180)	0.0278	(0.185)	0.0763	(0.208)
PROXIES FOR MINIMUM HOURS CONSTRAINTS												
Permit Job Sharing			0.6075*	(0.109)					0.6300*	(0.110)	0.1522	(0.115)
Flexible Starting Times			0.4661*	(0.110)					0.4189*	(0.113)	0.2702*	(0.125)
Percent Part-Time			0.0171*	(0.008)					0.0176*	(0.009)	-0.0050	(0.009)
Square of Percent Part-Time			-0.0001	(0.000)					-0.0001	(0.000)	0.0001	(0.000)
DEMOGRAPHICS OF THE ESTABLISHMENT												
White Collar (WC) that are female					-0.0013	(0.002)			-0.0033	(0.002)	-0.0041	(0.003)
WC that are unionized					-0.0028	(0.002)			-0.0014	(0.002)	-0.0005	(0.002)
WC under 35 Yrs of Age					0.0005	(0.003)			0.0002	(0.003)	-0.0009	(0.003)
WC over 54 Yrs of Age					0.0044	(0.003)			0.0046	(0.003)	-0.0042	(0.004)

DEPENDENT VARIABLE

PROXIES FOR LONG-TERM EMPLOYMENT RELATIONSHIPS

	(1)	(2)	(3)	(4)	(5)	(6)
Establishment Provides Formal Training				-0.0318 (0.039)	-0.0349 (0.040)	-0.0325 (0.045)
45 Yr Old Likely to Stay to Retirement				0.0583 (0.053)	0.0732 (0.054)	0.0514 (0.059)
Important to Fill Jobs from Within				-0.0022 (0.053)	0.0000 (0.054)	0.0580 (0.059)
WC With Job Tenure < 4 Yrs				0.0008 (0.002)	-0.0008 (0.002)	0.0017 (0.002)
WC With Job Tenure > 15 Yrs				-0.0042 (0.002)	-0.0044 (0.002)	0.0069* (0.002)
CUT POINTS						
Cut 1	-0.4339 (0.432)	0.0277 (0.452)	-0.3048 (0.451)	-0.3707 (0.549)	0.1947 (0.579)	1.8315 (0.686)
Cut 2	0.2019 (0.432)	0.7283 (0.452)	0.3349 (0.451)	0.2693 (0.548)	0.9028 (0.579)	1.8952 (0.686)
PSEUDO R-SQUARE	0.0393	0.1010	0.0429	0.0438	0.1078	0.0844
LOG LIKELIHOOD	-612.53	-573.19	-610.25	-609.67	-568.84	-442.11
N	631	631	631	631	631	631
LR CHI-SQUARE (P-VALUE)	50.11 (0.00)	128.79 (0.00)	54.67 (0.00)	55.82 (0.00)	137.49 (0.00)	81.56 (0.00)

[a]The excluded industry is construction, the excluded region is East, the excluded establishment size is 20–49, and the excluded organization size is 20–49.

*t-statistic > 1.96 implying coefficient is different from zero at a .05 confidence level.

The second model in table 8.3 examines the effects of minimum hours constraints. From the second hypothesis, we expect a positive coefficient on the percentage of white-collar workers who are part-timers, as well as the dummy variables indicating that the establishment permits job sharing and the establishment has flexible starting times. This is exactly what happens. There is then solid support for the hypothesis that when establishments use technologies that involve minimum hours constraints, they tend to limit a parent's opportunities to change working hours in order to care for a child.

The third model in table 8.3 examines the third hypothesis by introducing a set of demographic variables. As noted above, of particular importance is the percentage of the white-collar workforce that is female. We expect a positive coefficient on percent female, that is, establishments with a higher percentage of female employees should have higher values of Sick-Child. In fact, the coefficient is negative and statistically insignificant. Results on the percentage of white-collar workers that are unionized and the age composition of the white-collar workforce are also only weakly related to the Sick-Child variable. There is then no evidence here in support of the third hypothesis.

The fourth model in table 8.3 introduces a set of proxies for testing the fourth hypothesis, whereby establishments characterized by long-term employment relationships are more likely to pursue family-friendly policies. In accordance with that hypothesis, Sick-Child should be positively related to indicators of long-term employment relationships (employer provided formal training, forty-five-year-old workers remaining to retirement, filling jobs from within, percentage of white-collar workers with 15+ years in the establishment). Although some of the coefficients are positive, none are statistically significant. In consequence, there is no support for the fourth hypothesis either.

Model 5 tests for robustness. The results from models 1 through 4 are unaffected by including all of the variables in one model. Thus, the evidence in these multivariate models is similar to that in the table 8.2 cross-tabulations: minimum hours constraints play a major role in influencing opportunities for parents to shift from full-time to part-time in order to care for a child. None of the other hypotheses are supported by the data. Indeed, in contrast to the first hypothesis, establishments that are part of a larger organization are *less* likely to pursue this family-friendly policy.

We conclude that establishments that permit workers to move from full-time to part-time for purposes of childcare tend to be characterized by flexibility. They are not usually part of larger organizations, and they have policies such as job sharing and flexible starting times that reveal openness to alternative work schedules. Not only are they small, but they are probably accustomed to handling family demands and crises through informal arrangements.

That conclusion leads logically to the chapter's second goal: examining the extent to which workplaces that permit a childcare-oriented shift from full-time to part-time also have the kinds of family-friendly policies discussed in the literature, such as paid maternity and paternity leave. Since, as noted above, there is almost a zero correlation between Sick-Child and the measures of paid maternity and paternity leave, it is reasonable to expect that different explanatory variables will be important when each of these measures is used as a dependent variable in a multivariate model.

Indeed, that is the case. Column 6 of table 8.3 presents estimates of model 5 from the "Sick Child" section, but with the establishment's policy on paid paternity leave as the dependent variable. One could do the same with maternity leave or by presenting models 1 through 4; however, model 5 allows us to discuss all hypotheses and suffices to make the point: the results for "Paternity Leave" are quite different from those for "Sick Child." Comparing the model in column 5 and column 6, the signs on eleven of the thirty-six coefficients differ. Moreover, unlike Sick-Child, paid paternity leave is strongly and positively related to being in public administration and size of organization; as the number of employees in the organization increase, the coefficients become increasingly positive, with the coefficient on organizations with more than one thousand employees being positive and statistically significant. This is similar to the findings in Ingram and Simons (1995), Osterman (1995), and Wood (1999). Note that despite the differences between what determines both policies at an establishment, there are some similarities. In particular, there is a positive relationship between flexible starting times and both "Sick-Child" and "Paid Paternity Leave." The larger message of column 6, however, is that the determinants of paid paternity leave are quite different from the determinants of opportunities to move from full-time to part-time in order to care for a young child. Although both are family-friendly policies, they are driven by different forces.

One could argue that this conclusion only applies to observable variables. There may conceivably be unobserved variables that influence both "Sick-Child" and "Paid Paternity Leave." For example, there could be a special employer attitude toward employee needs that permeates the employer's response to a situation involving sick children or the need for paternity leave. By this argument, the explanatory variables in the ordered probits fail to measure an unobserved employer ethos. Had it been measured and included in the model, we would have found strong evidence of a common factor, and concluded that both Sick-Child and Paid Paternity Leave were driven by similar forces.

One way to check for this is to estimate a bivariate model and examine the correlation between the error terms. We thus estimated several bivariate probits that conditioned on the variables in columns 5 and 6. No matter how the bivariate probit was specified, the estimated value of the correlation between the errors ("rho" in the parlance of bivariate probit estimation) was never statistically different from zero and was often negative. Thus, there is no evidence of an important latent factor that is common to the two models. Again, all the evidence indicates that we are dealing with different phenomena here. Both paid paternity leave and permitting shifts to part-time for purposes of childcare can be viewed as family-friendly policies, but different forces drive them.

Implications of the Results

This chapter shows that different types of employers pursue different types of family-friendly policies. In particular, large organizations are much more likely to provide paid maternity and paternity leave, while establishments that are not part of a larger organization are more likely to permit an employee to shift to part-time in order to care for a young child. An explanation for family-friendly policies needs to account for these different patterns of behavior.

Certainly part of the explanation is cost. Large organizations can more easily provide fringe benefits such as paternity leave, pensions, life insurance, and child-care subsidies because they are able to reap the benefits of economies of scale. Other things being equal, the cost of an additional person on paternity leave or an additional pension plan participant is almost certainly lower for a large organization than for a small organization. Moreover, while permitting employees to work different hours on different schedules could create a coordination nightmare in a large organization, a small organization with one or two establishments may be able to handle multiple schedules through informal arrangements. If an organization seeks to be family-friendly, then it is likely to do so in a way that minimizes cost. And that could very well translate into different policies for different types of employers. By implication, the absence of formal policies such as paid paternity leave should not be read, in and of itself, as a failure to address work-family issues. This is especially true for smaller employers.

Another part of the explanation for why different types of employers pursue different types of family-friendly policies may lie in the extent to which a policy is visible to outside parties. Institutional theory in sociology emphasizes how different types of organizations face different pressures for involvement in work-family issues. For example, as noted above, public sector organizations are expected to be more responsive to work-family issues because they are subject to a higher level of scrutiny from external parties (e.g., the media). This hypothesis seems eminently plausible. One implication would seem to be that such an employer is likely to respond with policies that are visible to outside parties. Paid paternity leave is such a policy. It is easy for an outsider to verify that the policy exists and that male employees with children have benefited from it. Permitting parents to shift from full-time to part-time work in order to care for a young child may be a much less visible policy. Outside parties cannot easily determine how the policy is implemented, or whether the arrangement works in a way that is satisfactory to parents. If an employer is responding to outside pressures and must choose between two equally costly policies, one of which is visible to outside parties and the other effectively invisible, the employer is likely to choose the more visible policy. Thus, something similar to conspicuous consumption could be part of the explanation for why different employers pursue different policies.

Viewed from that perspective, the Sick-Child policy considered here may lie outside the set of family-friendly policies explained by institutional theory in sociology. Institutional theory may be effective in explaining policies that are especially visible to outside parties; perhaps a policy of permitting shifts from full-time to part-time for purposes of childcare falls outside a boundary that defines what is "especially visible." By implication, it may be fruitful for future theorists to examine and explain the locus of that boundary.

Finally, our results lead to a point about indexes of family-friendly policies. There is no question that the employer policies considered in this chapter—policies such as paid paternity leave or permitting parents to shift to part-time work for purposes of caring for a child—are family-friendly policies. But the evidence indicates that these policies are determined by different forces. Lumping these and similar policies together in a single index may obscure important relationships that could be more fully understood by looking at the separate components. The point is similar to Christopher Jenck's (1992) comments on the concept of the underclass. Although out-of-wedlock births and criminal behavior may well be elements of a "meta-problem," they are arguably determined by very different social and economic forces. From a social science perspective, the best strategy for enhancing knowledge may be to focus on understanding what determines the separate components.

9

WORKPLACE FLEXIBILITY FOR FEDERAL CIVILIAN EMPLOYEES

Kathleen Christensen,
Matthew Weinshenker, and Blake Sisk

When considering the relationship between the federal government and workplace flexibility, the typical approach is to focus on the government in its policymaking role, rather than on its role as employer. This is an oversight that needs to be rectified. Focusing only on its capacity to pass laws or issue regulations ignores another critical way in which the federal government influences the adoption and implementation of workplace flexibility in the United States, and that is through its role as employer.

The federal government is the nation's single largest employer (Congressional Budget Office [CBO] 2007). While the total civilian workforce in the United States totals 139 million workers, approximately 2.7 million of these workers are employed by the federal government as civilian employees, representing approximately 2 percent of the total U.S. workforce (CBO 2007, 1; Executive Office of the President 2008, table B-46; these numbers do not include the nearly one million Postal Service employees or the nearly 1.5 million military personnel). These federal civilian employees cover a wide range of responsibilities, working in more than eight hundred occupations in more than one hundred federal agencies.

This chapter reviews the availability and utilization of different workplace flexibility policies for employees of federal agencies, because they are by far the largest share of the federal civilian workforce. (Policies and laws governing certain employees of the executive branch, Congress, and the judiciary, as well as military and postal personnel, will not be addressed here.)

Over the last thirty-five years, the federal government, (and, to a lesser extent, state and local governments) has played an important role in approving, piloting, and implementing different forms of flexibility in its many agencies. The federal government was an early adopter of flexibility for its *full-time employees,* through its adoption of flextime, compressed workweeks, leave banks (which allow employees to donate paid leave to co-workers in need), and telecommuting. It also led the way in early initiatives for *reduced hours or leaves.* For example, in the early 1970s the federal government authorized the first federal pilot project on flextime, contemporaneously with efforts in the private sector (Olmsted and Smith 1994; Pierce et al. 1989). Furthermore, through well-designed and implemented pilot programs, the federal government has effectively institutionalized flexibility, by creating, in many federal agencies, workplace cultures in which flexibility is an accepted way of working.

Yet, despite these advances, progress on flexibility within the federal government has been uneven. While leading the way with flextime, compressed workweeks, and telecommuting, the federal government has lagged behind the private sector in offering career-continuous part-time work, as well as other forms of flexibility (including phased retirement), specifically targeted to their aging workforce. Furthermore, it has not been able to ensure consistency in availability or implementation of flexibility across the different federal agencies or departments.

Despite this unevenness, new hires of the federal government expressly value the flexibility offered them. New civilian federal hires rate flexibility as a critical factor in their decisions to pursue careers in this sector. According to a recent report to the president and Congress, new hires of all ages revealed a strong desire for job security and traditional benefits such as health insurance and retirement benefits (U.S. Merit Systems Protection Board 2008). But they also showed a nearly equal desire for more control over the hours and timing of work through time off (via sick days, vacations) and through flexible schedules and telecommuting. The desire for flexibility ranked substantially higher as a consideration in their decision making than did federal provision of childcare subsidies or facilities. Clearly, the provision of flexibility is much less costly than is the provision of dependent care subsidies or on-site childcare centers (U.S. Merit Systems Protection Board 2008).

Federal Government as Early Adopter

The characteristics of federal jobs, and of the individuals who fill them, have created unusually fertile conditions for the implementation of flexibility. The federal workforce is a highly skilled one. More than half of all federal civilian workers work in professional, managerial, and financial occupations compared to only 29 percent in the private sector (Partnership for Public Service [PPS] 2008, 3; see also CBO 2007). There is considerably less inequity between low-paid and high-paid positions in federal employment than in the private sector (Gornick and Jacobs 1998). Federal employees are also less likely to work fifty or more hours per week, or to work at night or on weekends, than private sector employees (authors' calculations based on U.S. Census Bureau 2004). Finally, federal agencies employed a disproportionate share of the female workforce when many forms of flexibility were being introduced (Gerson and Jacobs 1998), even though this is no longer true (CBO 2007).

Although conditions in some parts of the private sector vary widely from those in federal employment, the federal government has been a model employer (Bohen and Viveros-Long 1981; Bruce and Reed 1994) from which some flexible arrangements have diffused. Available data do not permit consistent comparisons between the actions of the federal government and the private sector as employers, regarding access to and utilization of workplace flexibility. However, sufficient evidence has arisen since 1970 to argue that the federal government has been an early adopter in promoting and implementing certain types of workplace flexibility since the early 1970s.

Alternative Work Schedules: Flextime, Credit Hours, and Compressed Workweeks

HISTORY AND POLICY

Alternative work schedules (AWS) include flextime (the ability to choose one's own start and end times at work), compressed workweeks, and the unique credit hours system that will be described below. Although flextime and compressed scheduling are often discussed separately in the broader workplace literature, they are combined here because of their close connection in the regulations governing federal employees and in many government documents. These are the forms of workplace flexibility about which it may be said most unequivocally that the public sector has been a leader among U.S. employers.

The first federal experiment in allowing employees to select their own start and end times was initiated by the Bureau of Indian Affairs in 1972, the same year the first corporate flextime policies in the United States were implemented at Control Data Corporation and Hewlett Packard. In 1974, a second experiment was begun at the Social Security Administration (Bohen and Viveros-Long 1981; Ezra and Dickman 1996). The success of these federal experiments spawned several imitators, such that by 1978, two hundred thousand federal workers, or roughly 10 percent of the federal civilian labor force of the day, were taking advantage of flextime (Bohen and Viveros-Long 1981). Estimates of the fraction of private sector employees using flextime at the same period (all of which were based on nonrepresentative samples of businesses) ranged from about 1 percent to 8 percent (Cohen and Gadon 1978; Nollen and Martin 1978). Regardless of the specific number one accepts as valid, the federal sector was clearly a leader.

Because of the success of the various federal experiments, Congress passed the Federal Employees Flexible and Compressed Work Schedules Act (FEFCWA) of 1978, allowing a three-year trial of alternative scheduling in any interested federal agency beginning in 1979. The trial was renewed through the passage of a revised

Act in 1982, and in 1985 the provisions of the 1982 Act were permanently authorized (Workplace Flexibility 2010 [2006b]).

Before congressional action, all federal scheduling experiments were patterned on the same approach that had first been tried at the Bureau of Indian Affairs: traditional flextime. All employees had to work a day of standard length, and to be present during certain times designated as "core hours." Given those constraints, employees could choose their arrival and departure times anytime within the non-core or "flexible hours" (Bohen and Viveros-Long 1981; U.S. Office of Personnel Management [OPM] 2008).

Although this core hour-flexible hour system remains available, the final version of the Act additionally permits agencies to offer several other options or not to allow alternative scheduling at all. First, agencies are permitted to allow employees to earn "credit hours" for working more than a normal forty-hour week. Credit hours accumulate in employee accounts, and can be used to "purchase" reduced-hour days or days off, with the restriction that only twenty-four hours may be rolled over from one biweekly period to another. Second, agencies can also permit compressed workweeks, where employees work more than the standard eight-hour day, and receive one day off every other week in exchange, sometime referred at as "80/9." Despite the possibility of this additional form of flexibility, employees were limited from combining a compressed workweek with any other scheduling flexibility, including flextime or the use of credit hours (OPM 2008).

Compressed workweeks, it must be noted, are hardly a federal innovation. The Gulf and Mobil oil companies have given their drivers such schedules since 1940, and they grew rapidly in popularity during the 1970s (Pierce et al. 1989). However, the federal government appears to have advanced their utilization by white-collar workers further than had the private sector, just by dint of such workers making up a larger percentage of the federal civilian workforce. Today, flextime is utilized far more than compressed workweeks, in both the federal workforce and the private sector.

In spite of the early popularity of flexible and compressed schedules among the federal workforce, the process leading to their institutionalization in 1985 did not run completely smoothly. Particularly at the beginning, the leadership of the American Federation of Governmental Employees, a union representing significant numbers of federal workers, was hostile toward flextime, a sentiment shared by some union leaders in the private sector. Public and private sector unions have objected that employee-chosen start and end times encourage longer hours without corresponding increases in pay (Pierce et al. 1989).

The strongest public and private sector union opposition, however, has been to the credit hours system. Traditionally, the Fair Labor Standards Act and its analogue, the Federal Employees Pay Act, have mandated that employees who work more than a standard-length day be paid time-and-a-half for overtime, unless they are classified as exempt. Union leaders have feared that the credit hours system, by allowing workers to receive compensatory time off (or "comp time") instead of overtime pay, would eliminate earning opportunities for those who desired them, because budget-conscious managers would give all the extra hours to those who wanted to be "paid" in time instead of money (Bohen and Viveros-Long 1981; Small Business Encyclopedia n.d.).

In the federal case, union objections did not prevent passage of the FEFCWA. Bohen and Viveros-Long (1981), analyzing the committee hearings preceding the law's passage, concluded that liberal members of Congress (congresswomen in particular), were persuaded that the benefits to working mothers outweighed the union's objections. It is likely that mothers in the union rank-and-file agreed, and were able to soften their leaders' stands. However, unions retain considerable control over their members' access. The Act provides that, for the roughly 60 percent of federal employees represented by a union, alternative work schedules may be made available only after collective bargaining.

It is worth noting that, aside from federal service, credit hours are available elsewhere only in the public sector. Even before Congress allowed federal agencies to implement it, the credit hours system was legalized for state and local governments by a 1976 Supreme Court ruling, which was later confirmed by a 1985 federal law (Wood and Sevison 1990). However, a bill to modify the Fair Labor Standards Act in order to permit comp time for nonexempt private employees was defeated in 2003, due in large part to union opposition (Small Business Encyclopedia n.d.).[1] Although similar legislation has been reintroduced in subsequent sessions of Congress, as of this writing a bill has not come close to being passed (U.S. Congress H. R. 6025).

UTILIZATION AND AVAILABILITY

According to nationally representative data from the May 1985 supplement of the Current Population Survey (CPS), 12.4 percent of full-time wage and salary workers had the ability to vary the start and end of their working days. This survey, conducted just as Congress moved to permanently authorize the Flexible and Compressed Work Schedules Act, found that 20 percent of federal employees had the same option (Mellor 1986). The high federal figure was no doubt due in part to the wider availability of traditional flextime in federal agencies than in private corporations, and in part to the credit hours system that was only permitted in public employment. By the time the CPS revisited the same question in 1997, larger fractions enjoyed scheduling flexibility, but the discrepancy between the federal government (35.1%) and the workforce as a whole (27.6%) remained nearly constant. In 2004, the most recent year the CPS asked about flextime, the numbers had barely changed; they were 34.5 percent and 27.9 percent, respectively (authors' calculations based on U.S. Census Bureau 1997, 2004). Flextime may have reached a proverbial saturation point, in the federal government and the larger economy, by the late 1990s.

Although the federal government has been a leader in alternative scheduling, the availability of specific scheduling options varies from agency to agency. As noted above, the law allows a wide variety of options, but does not require agencies to offer any particular one, or any alternative scheduling at all. A 1994 report issued by the U.S. General Accounting Office (GAO) offers a more comprehensive picture of the actual availability of scheduling policies than anything published subsequently. The report, based on a survey of fifty-nine federal agencies that were selected on the basis of variation in size, found that all but two of them offered some kind of flexible or compressed schedule options for some employees. On the other hand, fourteen of these fifty-nine federal agencies only allowed employees to choose start and end times within a fixed, eight-hour day. Fourteen others "limited...participation to certain employee groups." Only twenty permitted employees to earn and spend credit hours. Yet "at the other extreme, seven organizations permitted at least some of their employees to work maxiflex schedules, which basically allowed the employees to create their own work schedules with supervisory approval" (GAO 1994). The authors of the report concluded that the key reason more options were not available in more agencies was supervisor reluctance.

Nevertheless, it is worth remembering that 97 percent of the federal agencies had some policy in place to offer flexible or compressed schedules to some employees in 1994. This is a dramatic contrast to the 40 percent of private sector employers who had adopted flextime policies, and the 21 percent figure for those who had adopted compressed workweeks, as reported in 1993 surveys (Gold 1998; Olmsted and Smith 1994). Although these private sector numbers had improved to 68 percent and 39 percent by 2005, according to figures from the National Survey of Employers, as reported in chapter 7, the federal government remains at the forefront in making these alternatives available.

Telework

HISTORY AND POLICY

Telework is the name the federal government has employed for what is more commonly referred to as telecommuting or working at home. Within the United States, the federal government, as well as selected states, was an early adopter of this spatially distributed work arrangement. Unlike flextime, however, telework was not rapidly taken up by large numbers of federal workers, despite the fact that the federal government has spared little effort over the last fifteen years in encouraging employees to telework (and encouraging supervisors to facilitate this decision). As a result, the utilization of this form of flexibility has lagged behind the private sector.

Although several small work-at-home programs, some of which even predated the age of the personal computer, had previously been tried by federal agencies (Joice 1993), the first large-scale public sector telecommuting pilot was conducted by the California state government. In 1988 and 1989, California conducted a controlled experiment in which two hundred state employees were allowed to telecommute, while a matched group of 150 worked exclusively in the office. The results were highly favorable for telecommuting advocates. Telecommuters reported improved quality of life compared to the nontelecommuting control group, and supervisors were satisfied with telecommuting employees' productivity and with their own ability to manage remote employees (Fleming 2003).

Inspired, perhaps, by the success of the California experiment, seven states and the federal government began telework pilots of their own immediately afterward. Launched in early 1990, the federal pilot got off to a very slow start; it took more than six months after the official start date for the first three agencies to participate. In hindsight, this was the first instance of telework's slow and painful growth in federal employment. By January 1993, however, thirteen hundred employees in thirteen agencies were working from home some of the time (Joice 2000). Only employees with excellent performance ratings were allowed to participate, a policy that largely continues today. A 1993 report by the U.S. Office of Personnel Management (OPM), the central federal human resource agency, concluded that telework was successful "in areas such as job performance, motivation, quality of life, and costs... using employees with proven performance." On the issue of worker satisfaction, the report elaborated that "participating employees were very positive about their [telework] experience. Their indications of improved motivation toward work, quality of life, health and stress levels were impressive" (Joice 1993).

Since 1993, elected officials' support for federal telework has been strong and bipartisan. Telework is viewed as a way to reduce the costs of office space, to reduce absenteeism, to improve workers' ability to respond to family needs and their quality of life, to attract new employees (including individuals with disabilities), to reduce the expense, frustration, and pollution associated with commuting, and to ensure the continuity of federal operations in the event of an emergency (Joice 1993; OPM 2004). High-level support has been expressed in a series of executive and legislative directives and initiatives, culminating in a 2000 law that mandated all agencies to establish telework policies. This support has also been expressed through the opening of telecenters—in effect, satellite offices across the Washington, D.C. metro area that permit interested employees to work outside of their own homes, but closer to home than their regular offices. There are fourteen federally supported telecenters today, while virtually no private sector counterparts exist.

UTILIZATION AND AVAILABILITY

Despite this political support, telework utilization has lagged behind policymakers' hopes and expectations. In January 1996, the President's Management Council launched the National Telecommuting Initiative (NTI) with the aim of promoting telecommuting in the labor force as a whole, but especially in federal employment. NTI assessed the number of federal teleworkers at that time to be nine thousand, and set a goal of increasing the figure to sixty thousand by October 1998. With the direct support of President Clinton, federal agencies did expand the number of telecommuters. However, the twenty-five thousand telecommuters in October 1998 fell far short of the initial goal (Joice 2000; OPM 2004). At 1.4 percent of the federal workforce, the federal rate of utilization compared poorly to contemporaneous estimates of private sector telecommuting, which ranged from 8 to 11 percent of the workforce (Joice 2000).

Why did the government telework utilization lag behind the private sector? Wendell Joice (2001), a U.S. General Services Administration official involved in the implementation of telework, argued that the most important factor was management resistance: "Despite a wide array of specific concerns expressed by managers, the basic issue is that the world is transitioning into new ways to work and new work cultures. Most current managers were trained and excelled in operating in an industrial-era workplace, and now they are being asked to change ingrained attitudes and behaviors. It's not easy and, for the most part, it's not happening" (6). Results from a survey of federal managers released in 2007 indicated that, a few years later, reluctance was still widespread. Three-quarters of these managers feared lost productivity and difficulty managing teleworking employees (Barr 2008). Joice believed that managerial attitudes, however, were not the only impediment. He maintained that employees were reluctant to depart from familiar ways of working, that staff members providing support for information technology were uncomfortable with supporting remote employees, and that certain outdated legal requirements placed barriers in front of telework utilization.

Telework opportunities have been widely available to federal employees in spite of the barriers in recent years, but far from universally so. In 2006, 56 percent of the federal workforce was eligible. The main reasons the other 44 percent was not was that their job duties were deemed to require their presence on-site, or that their job performance did not meet agency-defined minimum criteria (OPM 2007). For example, the U.S. General Accounting Office (GAO) required, according to a 2001 report, that employees have good performance appraisals, "have proven to be dependable, independent, and highly motivated," and "have demonstrated an adequate understanding of the operations of the organization" (U.S. General Accounting Office 2001b).

Since 1998, the fraction of the federal workforce that has taken advantage of telework has grown, albeit without catching up to the private sector. In 2006, over 110,000 federal civilian employees teleworked at least once per month. This was 6.12 percent of the total federal workforce, and about 9 percent of the eligible workforce, substantially lower than the 15 percent of the total U.S. workforce who telecommuted a few years earlier, according to the 2001 Current Population Survey. The absolute number of federal telecommuters in 2006 was actually down from 119,248 in 2005, mainly due to callbacks, or new limits on employees' ability to telecommute, by the Interior, Treasury, and Commerce Departments (OPM 2007). An Interior Department official stated that the callbacks were motivated by "some managers' security worries about the potential theft of laptops with sensitive data, or hackers intruding on remote users' wireless networks" (Shellenbarger 2008, D1). It is worth noting that the federal callbacks have been mirrored by restrictions on tele-commuting at large corporations such as AT&T, Intel, and Hewlett Packard (ibid.).

Despite the more limited growth than hoped for, high-level support for federal telework continues. As of this writing, several bills to further promote teleworking in federal agencies were under consideration in Congress.[2] Whether further congressional action can finally achieve teleworking parity between the federal and private sectors will be an important subject for future research.

Part-Time Employment and Job Sharing

The story of part-time employment in the federal government is an even starker example of repeated high-level policy initiatives having minimal impact on the number of participating employees. Available evidence suggests that the primary barrier, as with telework, has been one of a workplace culture that has been unable to fully integrate part-time employees. On the other hand, policy efforts led to the federal government becoming a very early adopter of job sharing, defined as an arrangement where two part-time employees share one full-time position, and these efforts have also helped to improve the quality of part-time federal employment in some significant ways.

The history of part-time federal employment stretches far back into the past. Before 1978, part-time arrangements were ad hoc, few in number, and tended to exist only in the lowest employment grades, meaning they were held by clerical and low-skilled blue-collar employees. In 1977, 2.3 percent of the federal workforce had permanent part-time jobs, as defined by their employing agencies (U.S. Merit Systems Protection Board 1991). The next year, Congress passed the Federal Employees Part-Time Career Employment Act of 1978. As described in a subsequent report by the U.S. Merit Systems Protection Board (1991), "this piece of legislation was particularly noteworthy in its forward-thinking intent, as 13 years ago, it foreshadowed many of the work and family 'values' which are considered state-of-the-art today" (39). The text of the act specifically stated the hope that it would allow the federal government to tap the productive potential of older workers, parents, students, and others whose needs precluded working a full-time schedule.

The Part-Time Career Employment Act standardized the rules for part-time employment for federal civilian employees. According to this Act, part-time employment was defined as sixteen to thirty-two hours per week (or thirty-two to sixty-four hours per pay period),[3] and agencies were required to give part-time employees prorated health benefits. These changes benefited the small number of employees whose supervisors had abused the lack of part-time standards by employing them involuntarily for thirty-nine hours instead of forty, to avoid treating them as full-time (U.S. Merit Systems Protection Board 1991). The act also encouraged the expansion of part-time work, and job sharing in particular, by replacing the rigid "head count" system that had counted all workers as one "head" against each agency's employment "ceiling," with a full-time equivalency (FTE) system. With this FTE system, two part-time workers, including job sharers, now counted as the equivalent of just one head, thereby eliminating a significant disincentive for supervisors to approve part-time schedules (Olmsted and Smith 1994). Congress also considered mandating agencies to set aside 2 percent of all positions for part-time employment, but ultimately decided against this (U.S. Merit Systems Protection Board 1991).

Although the fraction of the federal workforce on permanent part-time schedules rose for the first couple of years following the act's passage, it began to decline again in 1981. By 1989, it was back down to 2.3 percent—ironically, the same percentage that existed just prior to the act's passage. As a point of comparison, 18.1 percent of all employed persons held part-time jobs that year, according to the Bureau of Labor Statistics' definition of part-time employment as less than 35 hours per week (Tilly 1991).

As the authors of the U.S. Merit Systems Protection Board (1991) report note, however, the part-time jobs that did exist were of higher quality than they were before the 1978 law. Not only was it now impermissible to treat those working thirty-nine hours per week as part-time, but a far larger share of the part-time workers were employed at high service grades, meaning they were better paid and more likely to be skilled professionals. In a related development, a larger fraction of the part-time employees were sharing full-time positions with another worker. Although trustworthy estimates of job sharing in the private sector are not available that far back, Olmsted and Smith (1994), in their history of the practice, assert that the federal government was one of the earliest users in the United States. In summary, the evidence strongly suggests that more federal part-time jobs were "voluntary" (chosen at the employee's preference) and part of a career track in 1989 than in 1978, and that fewer were "involuntary" (chosen for economic reasons, only because full-time work was unavailable) and economic dead ends. In contrast, Tilly (1991) has estimated that the percentage of the part-time private workforce who would have preferred to have full-time positions had been on the rise in the 1980s.

Recognizing that their efforts had improved the quality of part-time positions, but had not increased the quantity, Congress and the OPM renewed their efforts to promote part-time employment, and especially job sharing, in 1990. OPM was required to establish a formal job-sharing program; all agencies were asked to publicize part-time work and job sharing as options for their full-time workforces, and an electronic system called the OPM Connection was established to enable would-be job sharers to learn about one another (Olmsted and Smith 1994). Since then, modest gains have been posted. By 1999, 3.44 percent of the federal workforce worked reduced hours (OPM n.d.c). By September of 2007, this had risen further to 3.65 percent, a miniscule number (466) of whom were permanent employees classified as job sharers (OPM n.d.a). By comparison, the part-time fraction of the entire U.S. workforce in February 2008 was 16.59 percent. Keeping the distinction between voluntary and involuntary part-time work in mind, the data indicate that just under 80 percent of the part-timers (or about 13.25% of the nation's workforce) had taken part-time schedules for noneconomic reasons—a key indicator that their schedules were voluntary (U.S. Bureau of Labor Statistics 2008, table A-5).

Why has the proportion of federal workforce with part-time arrangements remained low? Little evidence is available to directly address this question. For example, although it is plausible to suppose that the federal workforce contains a lower fraction of positions that are commonly part-time (such as food service) than the private sector, a definitive analysis is lacking. However, available reports demonstrate that part of the answer is resistance to part-time scheduling, on the part of both supervisors and workers who are grounded in a work culture that stigmatizes those who work fewer than full-time hours. In a recent interview-based study of female federal employees who had utilized various forms of workplace flexibility, Walker (2007) found most current and former part-timers were dissatisfied with the experience, largely due to its effect on their treatment by supervisors and others in the organization. They reported being expected to shoulder a full-time workload for less pay, being "mommy-tracked" and overlooked for promotions, and being unable to transfer to other positions while on a part-time schedule. In sharp contrast, few women who had experience with telecommuting perceived any of these negative consequences. Furthermore, aside from their treatment by others, many current and former part-timers felt that reduced-hours work was less personally fulfilling, because the tasks and assignments that could feasibly be done on their schedules were not as challenging or interesting as the ones they had tackled before.

The report on the usage of scheduling flexibilities at the General Accounting Office (2001b) provided a similar picture. Although the GAO had employed a relatively large number of part-timers during the 1994 to 1998 period, the part-timers felt their chances for promotion had been hurt. In fact, only 4.2 percent of the part-timers had been promoted during those five years. In contrast, while nearly one-fifth of teleworkers also believed their usage of flexibility had harmed their careers, 27.5 percent had been promoted. Moreover, 60 percent of surveyed GAO employees reported that they did not know how to request a part-time schedule. This suggests that, in spite of the congressional mandates to do so, agency officials had not zealously educated workers about their options. Taken together, the evidence suggests that while the legal and formal institutional requirements are in place to accommodate part-time work and job sharing, the federal government has a long way to go in overcoming the cultural hurdles to their acceptance.

Paid Family and Parental Leave

In 2000, legislation proposing that the federal government offer six weeks of paid parental leave to all employees was introduced in Congress. Congress solicited an analysis of the proposed benefit from the OPM. In its report, OPM recommended that the federal government *not* offer a new paid leave benefit to parents after the birth or adoption of a child. Although this seems surprising at first glance, given the traditional use of benefits to attract employees to the federal service, the OPM's report asserted that paid parental leave was not needed to maintain the federal edge over other employers in generosity of benefits. The agency argued that "the federal government's leave policies and programs compare favorably with benefits offered by most private sector companies" (OPM 2001), and that consequently human resource directors in the federal executive departments did not see expansion of parental leave benefits as a major factor in enhancing recruitment and retention of well-qualified workers.

Ever since OPM propounded a uniform leave policy in 1986 (Bruce and Reed 1994), the federal government has been generous in allowing paid annual leave (the federal term for vacation leave), paid sick leave, the use of donated time off via leave banks, and leave without pay to be used as family leave. Under the current guidelines (OPM 2008; OPM n.d.b), most full-time employees earn thirteen days of sick leave and thirteen to twenty-six days of annual leave each year. What makes the federal policy particularly generous is the fact that unlimited unused sick leave and thirty days of unused annual leave may be carried over from year to year, and subsequently used for family purposes. Twelve weeks of accumulated paid sick leave may be used annually by either parent to care for a child or other family member with a "serious health condition." Up to thirteen days may be used to care for family members with a "minor illness" or to accompany family members to routine medical appointments, although these reduce the leave available in case of a more serious condition. In addition, sick leave may be used by mothers and fathers during pregnancy, after childbirth, and for purposes related to adopting a child. Annual leave is even more flexible, as it may be used for any family care purpose, including bonding with a healthy child. However, supervisory approval is required in advance, rendering annual leave potentially less available than sick leave.

For workers who have not accumulated sufficient paid leave to satisfy their needs, several options are available. In 1988, the Federal Employees Leave-Sharing Act permitted agencies to establish leave transfer programs, through which employees with excess paid leave could donate it to co-workers in need. Although not all agencies allow leave transfer, the programs caught on quickly and are widely available (Olmsted and Smith 1994). Employees may also request an advance of up to thirty days of annual and sick leave not yet earned. Finally, unpaid leave is also available. Federal employees are covered under the provisions of the Family and Medical Leave Act of 1993, which grants up to twelve weeks of unpaid leave for childbirth, adoption, or family care.

How do these policies compare to the private sector? A special category of corporate-sponsored paid leave for new parents, particularly for new mothers, is no longer unusual, particularly in large firms. As reported in chapter 7 of this book, 46 percent of employers provided short-term paid maternity leave in 2005. Only 13 percent allowed new fathers to enjoy this benefit. The fraction of Fortune 100 corporations offering paid maternity leave was 75 percent, according to a 2008 report by Joint Economic Committee of Congress (2008). Unlike federal employees utilizing paid leave for a birth, however, corporate employees on maternity leave often earn a fraction of their normal pay, according to results from the National Survey of Employers (Bond, Galinsky, Kim, and Brownfield 2005). According to the same source, about half of companies with fifty or more employees allow parents a few days off to care for a sick child without using vacation time, taking unpaid days off, or lying about their reasons for absence. In summary, although the federal government lags behind the majority of large corporate employers in offering distinct parental leave, its employees, unlike many of their counterparts in the private sector, enjoy the ability to use sick as well as annual leave for family needs, at full pay and regardless of gender.

Recently, a few state and local governments have begun to step in to widen access to paid sick leave in the private sector and mandate its availability for family purposes. A 2003 law passed in Connecticut requires employers in the state who offer paid sick days to let employees use them to care for ill family members (Aspen Publishers 2007). Going one step further, San Francisco enacted a law in 2007 requiring all private employers to award sick leave usable for the employee's own illness or that of a family member (DeBare 2007).

California has been the leader in requiring employers to offer paid family leave. Beginning in 2004, most workers in the state became eligible to take six weeks of leave per year, at partial pay, to bond with a newborn or care for a seriously ill family member (Sherriff 2007). Washington and New Jersey have enacted similar measures more recently.

Motivated by the increasing availability of parental leave as a distinct category, several new paid-family-leave bills were introduced in Congress in 2007 and 2008. The supporters of one of these bills, the Paid Parental Leave Act of 2007, said that it was designed to correct a flaw in current policy, namely that many new parents in federal service are recent hires without the accumulated leave to take paid family leave or the economic means to take unpaid leave (Ballenstedt 2008). The Bush Administration, however, opposed the new benefit, proposing instead to let employees purchase optional short-term disability insurance that would provide income replacement in case of childbirth or another disabling condition (Barr 2008). The bill did not pass the Republican-controlled Senate in 2008, but it had been reintroduced in 2009 (U.S. Congress H.R. 626), and its fate was pending as of this writing. Adding parental leave to the existing federal leave policies would certainly help maintain the government's position as a generous provider of flexibilities to its workforce.

Flexibility for an Aging Workforce: Federal Government as Laggard

Although the federal government has made concerted efforts, with varying degrees of success, to implement some forms of alternative work schedules, it has been slow to pilot or implement flexibility that specifically targets its aging and retired workforces. Twenty years ago, the private sector was unlikely to offer much in the way of phased retirement, that is, the gradual reduction in work hours over a finite period, ending in retirement (Christensen 1989), but private sector employers have significantly increased this program's availability over the intervening years (Bond, Galinsky, Kim, and Brownfield 2005). In contrast, until recently the federal government did not have phased retirement on its radar screen, much less on its books, and its only real effort, until very recently, involved an "unretiree program," whereby postretirement federal employees could be reinstated.

Today, that is changing. The federal government is rapidly coming to terms with the aging of its own workforce, and in recent years has begun to implement a number of innovative policies and practices by which it can retain its own older workers, as well as recruit older workers outside of government onto the civil service payroll. Some of these programs are being pursued as public-private partnerships in specific departments or agencies, such as in the Department of Treasury or the Environmental Protection Agency. Demographic realities are driving the current efforts. The federal civil service workforce is markedly older, on average, than the workforce in general. Nearly six out of ten federal employees (58%) are over the age of forty-five, as compared to four out of ten in the general workforce, according to the Partnership for Public Service (PPS 2008, 1). As a result of this aging workforce, the federal government estimates that over a half a million full-time permanent federal workers will leave the federal government over the next five years, primarily through retirement. This represents, according to a recent report, nearly one-third of the federal government's full-time permanent workforce (PPS 2008, 1).

It is generally recognized that the federal government needs to pursue a three-pronged approach to stave off a significant labor shortage within its own workforce. It needs to: (a) step up its efforts to *attract young and mid-career workers;* (b) to pursue policies that will *increase the retention of its own aging* workforce; (c) and to *recruit older workers whose careers have been outside government.* Workplace flexibility is an attractive means to achieve both retention and recruitment across this three-pronged approach.

History

Thirty to forty years ago, as members of the baby-boom generation were entering the workforce and building their careers, minimal attention was paid to older workers. The aging of the workforce, both in the private and public sectors, was understandably of little concern. In that climate the federal government did little to encourage its own older workers to stay on the federal payrolls. However, the federal government did provide allowances for federal retirees to be reinstated in federal jobs under certain circumstances.

Although federal law allows its own retirees to return to work, postretirement, for the federal government, on reinstatement these retirees have their retirement annuities reduced by the amount of their salaries or wages when they are reemployed, unless an exception is approved. The law limits waivers to "positions for which there is exceptional difficulty recruiting or retaining a qualified employee" and to temporary employment while "the authority is necessary due to an emergency involving a direct threat to life or property or other unusual circumstances. Generally, when other retirees become a Federal employee there is NO reduction in their Federal pay or in their retirement pay or annuity" (USA Jobs n.d.). Furthermore, federal retirees under the age of seventy, like all workers, may have their Social Security check reduced if their annual earnings exceed the established limit (Senior Executive Service n.d.).

As a result of these financial penalties, many experienced older workers are more apt to return to the government as self-employed independent contractors, rather than as employees, which may end up being more costly to the government (PPS 2008, 16). Yet before this is taken as fact, it will be important for researchers to examine the degree to which these workers have taken on projects as independent contractors because such work provides more flexibility than would be available to them as employees.

Recently, the federal government has begun to explore what it will take to recruit and hire older workers from outside the federal government. In a recent survey, hiring managers and human resource personnel in federal agencies were asked to identify work conditions that would be attractive in recruiting older workers into federal employment. Topping their lists were workplace flexibilities, including "part time and alternative work schedules; job sharing; short-term assignments; telecommuting and medical leave programs; [and] increased vacation time for experienced new hires" (PPS 2008, 7). Clearly, control over the time and timing of work is viewed as a major recruiting tool for the federal government as it faces large-scale retirements over the next ten years. Yet a parallel survey of older Americans reveals that, although they value flexibility, they do not believe the federal government provides it. In a national survey of older Americans (who do not work for the federal government, but could be appropriate targets for its recruitment), Peter Hart Associates, a national polling firm, found that "only 10% of respondents believe government offers 'flexible work schedules,' compared to 47% of mature workers who say flexibility is something they desire" (PPS 2008, 11). Therefore, a significant mismatch exists between what those in government view as an effective recruiting tool and what those who are recruitment targets believe is available.

This flexibility gap—between workers' demand and perceived supply—is probably both a gap in public relations and in practice. As noted earlier in the chapter, the Merit Systems Protection Board found that among new federal government hires, 71 percent were seeking a position where flexible or alternative work schedules were available, and 39 percent were seeking the option to telecommute (U.S. Merit Systems Protection Board 2008). But there is also likely to be a gap in practice between older workers' demands for flexibility and its supply. As workers in the federal government, they will have access to all existing forms of flexibility, including flextime, part-time, compressed workweeks, and telecommuting. Yet phased retirement still is not on the federal books, nor is there, in most agencies, a culture in which part-time opportunities are pursued by more than a handful of employees. And part-year, an arrangement that might be particularly attractive, is not an option except in particularly seasonal types of jobs.

Current Initiatives

One innovative direction that the government is undertaking is through private-public partnerships. For example, the Environmental Protection Agency has joined forces with the National Association for Hispanic Elderly, National Asian Pacific Center on Aging, National Caucus and Center on Black Aged, National Council on the Aging, National Older Worker Career Center, and Senior Service America. These groups have forged an innovative partnership, the Senior Environmental Employment Program (SEE), whereby experienced workers fill government positions without taking the civil service examinations. As such, SEE participants are not government employees, nor are they employees of the nonprofit partner. Rather, they are SEE participants whose work is supervised by one or more federal employees, and whose human resources procedures are administered by the nonprofit partners. Currently, SEE funds fifteen hundred full- and part-time workers (Moos 2008). In addition to SEE, IBM is working with the Treasury Department to rotate older workers out of IBM and into federal employment.

In summary, the federal government has a mandate from its own workforce to face the fact that it is aging and to begin to provide the flexibility that this aging workforce needs and wants. To effectively retain its own older workforce and recruit from the outside, the federal government has to adopt more aggressive approaches to flexibility. The Partnership for Public Service (2008) proposes that Congress should pass legislation to allow for phased retirement and that it should enable agencies to hire federal retirees on temporary assignments without the penalty of reducing their retirement annuities (17).

In so doing, many feel that the federal government could set an important example for the rest of the country. As Helen Dennis, a consultant on older worker issues, states, "This matter of an aging workforce cuts across the entire economy. The government should lead by example and serve as a role model for how employers engage and keep older workers" (as cited in Moos 2008).

To its credit, the federal government has begun to set in motion efforts to create more flexible opportunities for older workers in federal agencies. It has created an Interagency Task Force on Older Workers to coordinate the efforts of the federal agencies that have regulatory jurisdiction over, or a clear policy interest in, issues relating to older workers. And the OPM has also developed a Career Patterns Initiative, a new approach that requires federal agencies to rethink the traditional 9-to-5, office-based career as a way to bring the next generation of employees into federal government positions. According to this Initiative, different types of workplace flexibility, including telecommuting, flexible work schedules, and part-time and part-year must be seen as "natural and regular ways of getting work done and not as aberrations" (OPM 2006).

Federal Flexibility Past, Present, and Future

The purpose of this chapter has been to use existing literature and data to review the availability and utilization of flexible workplace policies in federal employment. The federal government has been an early adopter of innovative policies, particularly when it comes to flextime, compressed schedules, the ability to utilize accumulated sick leave for family reasons, and (at the level of workplace policy) telework and part-time schedules. The federal government has had a more familiar role in creating a legal environment that mandates or supports flexibility in private employment (as in the case of the Family and Medical Leave Act) or, correspondingly, discourages or forbids it (as in the Fair Labor Standards Act provision that forbids credit hours). Many have argued, however, that the federal government also influences other organizations as a model employer when it comes to flexibility (Bohen and Viveros-Long 1981; Bruce and Reed 1994). Although the government's level of influence on the private sector's human resources policies is difficult to assess, it is clear that federal flexible workplace policies have a direct impact on the lives of many of the 2 percent of civilian American workers in federal employment. This, we believe, is reason enough to review them.

It has been demonstrated, however, that the federal sector has not led the way in every conceivable form of flexibility. Forward-thinking policies on permanent part-time employment have consistently produced very low utilization numbers relative to the rest of the workforce. To a lesser extent, the same disjunction between policy and utilization has existed for telework. When it comes to flexibility for aging workers, the policies have not even been in place. Research into the dynamics behind the facts, understandably, has been less common than the facts themselves. Existing reports suggest that the barriers to increased implementation and utilization of flexibility are mainly cultural; they stem from resistance, by supervisors and eligible employees, to policies that shake up accepted ways of working. It would certainly be valuable for scholars to investigate further the factors affecting uptake of federal flexibility policies.

It is a commonplace belief that the federal government cannot compete for employees, particularly those with specialized knowledge or skills, on the basis of salary alone (U.S. Merit Systems Protection Board 2008). To offset this competitive disadvantage, it has traditionally offered nonpecuniary rewards such as reasonable hours, job security, and the opportunity for public service. Flexible scheduling and career pathways appear to be similar incentives to choose federal employment; indeed, they are increasingly being considered that way by the Office of Personnel Management itself (OPM 2006). Therefore, despite cultural resistance, there is reason to believe that the federal government will continue to be a generous provider of flexibilities in the future. The only real question is whether it will once again become a leader in introducing new ones to the American workforce.

10

THE ODD DISCONNECT
Our Family-Hostile Public Policy

Joan C. Williams

Imagine two families, one in the United States and one in Sweden, both of which experience the birth of a child.[1] In the first family, a working couple in Sweden has a newborn son in January. Both parents stay home during the first two weeks of the child's life, because, since the 1970s, fathers have been granted ten days of paid leave after childbirth (Crittenden 2001). After that, the mother continues her paid leave and the father returns to work at 80 percent of his former schedule, taking advantage of the government's policy that both parents can return to work on a reduced schedule until their youngest child is eight years old (ibid.). In August, the father takes a full month off at 80 percent of his pay—Sweden has guaranteed fathers an extra month off at 80 percent pay during the first year of their children's lives since 1984 (ibid.). Swedish law also provides that new parents have fifteen months of paid leave to share as they choose (in addition to the "daddy days" described above) (Clearinghouse on International Developments in Child, Youth, and Family Politics at Columbia University [Clearinghouse] 2002; Crittenden 2001; European Union Online n.d.). The following January, the parents switch roles: The mother returns to work at 80 percent of her former schedule, while the father stays home to care for the child for six more months. The parents decide not to use the additional leave available to them: three months at a flat rate and three months unpaid leave (Clearinghouse 2002). Beginning in June, when the child turns one and a half, both parents stagger their schedules so each gets some one-on-one time with their son; for the remaining time they enroll their son in a government-subsidized childcare center. Although Sweden has not yet reached its goal of making quality childcare available to every child, it does ensure that lower-income families receive financial assistance for childcare (Crittenden 2001; Skolverket n.d.).

In the second family, a working couple in the United States has a daughter. The father takes no leave, since he has no right to paid leave and they cannot afford to lose any of his salary. They are fortunate: the mother's employer is covered by the Family and Medical Leave Act, and, meeting the act's requirements, they can afford to be without her salary for her twelve weeks of unpaid leave. During her pregnancy, the mother continues to hunt for quality childcare at an affordable price, with little success. Finally, shortly before the mother's leave is up, they find a suitable daycare that takes infants and has an opening. It is not convenient to their home or either parent's workplace, and knowing that over half of all infant care in the United States is fair to poor in quality (Gornick and Meyers 2003) makes them nervous. The mother returns to work, which given her hour-long daily commute, means she is away for fifty hours a week. Since she does the daycare drop-off and pick-up, the father has very little time with the child. Every time the mother asks for time off to take her daughter to the pediatrician, she feels the backlash: her employer sees her as less committed, and her co-workers feel that she is not pulling her own weight.

After a year of this, feeling that her career is not advancing as she had hoped and worried about the scarcity of time with her child, the mother decides to work part-time. She finds that she is given mommy-track work: the stigma increases, her hourly pay decreases, and she loses most of her benefits and any chance for promotion (Glass 2004). Like many parents, she cannot find part-time childcare; accordingly, she continues to pay for expensive full-time care while working only part-time.

After another year, this mother joins the one in four U.S. mothers who are out of the labor force. She and her husband have decided that, given her low salary, lack of career prospects, and high childcare costs, she does not earn enough to justify having her child "raised by strangers." Once her salary is gone, her husband feels under increased pressure to work longer hours, and becomes one of the one-third of fathers who works forty-nine or more hours a week (Williams 2000). Eight years later, after the birth of a second child, both children are in school all day, and the mother attempts to return to work despite her now-stale job skills.

While the families sketched here are fictional, many real families face similar situations. This chapter is written from the perspective of a theorist pondering the landscape from the height of ten thousand feet, using data developed by the Center for WorkLife Law. It begins by highlighting how work-family conflict—which places families at all income levels in impossible situations—differs in different class contexts. This discussion is vital to forging a legislative coalition to address work-family conflict in the United States. The chapter then considers the role of the press in creating an environment in which the high levels of work-family conflict are discussed chiefly in terms of professional women's personal choice to "opt out." Next, the chapter examines why it may be more challenging to build a coalition for successful work-family policy in the United States than in other countries. It concludes by discussing how, true to habit, the United States is once again engaging in public policy through the courts, with a recent spike in cases involving family responsibilities discrimination.

Work-Family Conflict across Class Lines: The Odd Disconnect in American Politics

Work-family conflict is felt by all American families, yet how families experience it differs by their class context: whether they belong to the professional-managerial class, form part of the "missing middle," or are among those earning the lowest wages. Understanding these differences is an essential precursor to public policy efforts designed to reduce work-family conflict.

Professional-Managerial Class (PMC) Families

Claudia Goldin (2004) examined five cohorts of college graduate women, and concluded that few successfully combined family with careers, even defining "career" very modestly. Only 13 to 18 percent of baby boomers attained both their career and family goals, as did only 21 to 28 percent of Gen-Xers (those graduating from college between 1980 and 1990; Goldin 2004). A key problem faced by professional-managerial class (PMC) families is the 24/7 schedule that defines commitment among high-level professionals. More than one-third of PMC men (37.2%) work fifty or more hours a week (Jacobs and Gerson 2004, 37). Twice as many men (40%) as women (20%) with college degrees work such hours (ibid., 35).

The gender effect of long hours is greatly exacerbated by motherhood. Nationwide, 95 percent of mothers aged twenty-five to forty-four work less than fifty hours per week, year-round (U.S. Census Bureau 2006a), which is less than "full-time" in most high-level jobs in business, academia, and the professions. "The best jobs have become more demanding over time. Long hours on the job are expected in many professional and managerial settings, far in excess of the forty-hour workweek that was established as the national standard more than sixty years ago" (Jacobs and Winslow 2004, 106). Given that college-educated women tend to be married to college-educated men who are often working long hours, the demand for part-time work among PMC women is intense. A survey of highly educated women found, of those in business, 89 percent wanted access to reduced-hour jobs (Hewlett et al. 2005, 62). In a national survey of five hundred dual-career families, 65 percent of women working full-time said they would prefer to work part-time (Grossman 2001).

If women feel this way, why do they not work part-time? The penalties associated with part-time work are very harsh. Women working part-time in the United States earn 21 percent less per hour than full-timers, a part-time penalty that is seven times higher than in Sweden and over twice as high as in the United Kingdom (Gornick and Meyers 2003, 63, figure 3.4). "Ultimately, choosing a part-time job is almost always synonymous with choosing a lower-paying job" (Wenger 2001, 2). Not only do workers have to take "scut work at low pay to get a part-time schedule" (Lewis 2005), they also often sacrifice benefits such as pensions and health insurance. What the United States lacks is thirty- to forty-hour-a-week jobs accompanied by benefits (Gornick and Meyers 2003, 152).

The ideal worker in high-level jobs not only works long workweeks but also works for forty years straight, taking no time off for childbearing, childrearing, or eldercare. High-level managers and professionals "are expected to make work the central focus of their lives" (Blair-Loy and Wharton 2004, 151), a norm of "work devotion" that does not mesh with the social roles of women. Eighty-one percent (81%) of American women become mothers by age 44 (Dye 2008, 2), who typically need time off for childbearing. American mothers also do a disproportionate share of family work: 75 percent of routine housework such as laundry and cleaning, and 61 percent of the childcare (Gornick and Meyers 2003, 71). Women also provide three-fourths of the care for elderly parents (Wachovia n.d.).

The norm of work devotion is a particularly poor fit for American women, who are expected to show their devotion to family in ways that strike many people in other countries, primarily European ones, as excessive and bizarre. Sociologists have documented the "ideology of intensive mothering" that now pervades families in the professional-managerial class (Hays 1996; Lareau 2002). Judith Warner (2005) both documents and critiques this new model of motherhood from the perspective of her experience of almost six years in France. In France, Warner writes, "work was considered a normal part, even a desirable part, of a modern mother's life. It was considered something that broadened her horizons and enhanced her self-esteem—healthy and good things for herself and her children. Taking time for herself was equally considered to be a mother's right—indeed, a mother's responsibility—as was taking time for romance and a social life" (10).

Upon her return to the United States, Warner "was surprised to see laudatory stories [in the local press] of 'dedicated' mothers who spent their evenings and weekends driving to and from soccer, attending Girl Scout cookie meetings, uber-momming, generally, twenty-four hours a day. I had never once, in almost six years, met a woman in France living her life at this level of stress" (13).

As I have noted elsewhere, this is quite a new phenomenon:

A sharp shift occurred between the generations of my mother (b. 1918) and mother-in-law (b. 1923) and my own (b. 1952). Both my mothers—one affluent, one working-class—think my generation is truly odd because we focus so much attention on our children. If one rereads the Mrs. Piggle-Wiggle books, published in the late 1940s and early 1950s, one finds their attitude fleshed out. These charming children's books tell the story of Mrs. Piggle-Wiggle, an expert at curing children of misbehavior. In the books, mothers focus on getting invited to Mrs. Workbasket's Earnest Workers Club and having the boss to dinner in order to help their husband's careers; serving meals to husbands who are cross if they are late; appeasing husbands to avoid having them spank some sense into the children. No mother is ever shown playing with her children. Nor do children expect to be entertained. They do an endless stream of errands and chores for the adults and they entertain themselves.... The notion that mothers' role was to "entertain" children (as they would describe it) would have seemed as bizarre as the contemporary notion of "floor time." (Williams 2000, 36)

"Floor time," suggested by Dr. Stanley Greenspan, a renowned child psychiatrist who teaches at George Washington Medical School, epitomizes the ideology of intensive mothering:

> Spend at least thirty minutes a day focusing exclusively on your child, and let her take the lead. Tune in to her interests and feelings, and march to her drummer. If she wants you to get down on all fours and bark like a dog, do it. Participate in the action, but don't control it—she's the director, and you're the assistant director.... Floor time, writes Greenspan, "creates the whole basis for security, trust, and self-worth that a child will need from here on." (Cited in Williams 2000, 36)

Greenspan admits that floor time played no part of his own childhood. "In fact, Greenspan's mother used to tell him that he was such an easy, independent baby that she would leave him outside the house in a crib while she was inside doing chores" (Williams 2000, 37).

Work-family conflict of PMC families stems chiefly from the expectation that committed workers will devote fifty-plus hours per week to their jobs for forty years straight, in a society with both harsh penalties for part-time work and hyped-up ideals of motherhood.

The Missing Middle

In talking about families in the middle, one immediately runs into terminological problems. Families whom PMC academics call "working class" often refer to themselves as "middle class." As is the academic tradition, this chapter refers to these families as "working class," but also (following Theda Skocpol) as the "missing middle" (Skocpol and Leone 2001). Missing middle families are a vital, but often forgotten, element of any social change coalition.

Missing middle workers have been much less studied than managers and professionals. Indeed, the erasure of class in the United States has also meant that they are studied less than low-income families. The Center for WorkLife Law's report, *One Sick Child Away from Being Fired: When Opting Out Is Not an Option* (Williams 2006), uses the Center's database of union arbitrations to explore work-family conflict in these families. One striking difference that emerges immediately between these and more affluent families is many working-class employees' lack of flexibility

(Heymann 2000, 116; Williams 2006). Whereas PMC families typically can take off time at will to go to a school play, attend a parent-teacher conference, or take a child to the doctor, many working-class employees cannot. Indeed, nearly three-quarters of working adults in the United States say they have no control over their work schedules (American Federation of Labor–Congress of Industrial Unions [AFL-CIO] n.d.). Higher-income workers are much more likely to exercise control than are those with lower incomes: two-thirds of working parents earning $71,000 or more have access to flexible scheduling, as compared to less than one-third of those earning less than $28,000 (ibid.). Only 30 percent of Americans with incomes in the top quartile—but over half (54%) of those in the bottom quartile—cannot choose when they begin and end their workdays (Heymann 2000, 116).

In addition to their lack of flexibility, many American workers have a striking lack of leave. More than a third of all working parents in the United States lack *both* sick leave *and* vacation time (Kornbluh 2003), and, of course, many more have sick leave but no vacation time, or vice versa. The result is that many workers are one sick child away from being fired. Examples from union arbitrations are eye-opening. A single mother who worked as a packer was fired when she left work in response to a call from her brother, telling her that her four-year-old had fallen in a playground accident, resulting in a head injury (*Knauf Fiber Glass* 1983). A bus driver was fired when she arrived three minutes late because her severely asthmatic son had suffered an asthma attack (*Chicago Transit Authority* 1999). A single mother was fired for tardiness stemming from the fact that her son had Crohn's disease, which required her to unhook him from his IV, bandage him, administer medication, and get him to school, then take two buses to bring her baby to childcare, before taking a third bus to reach her job (*Chicago Transit Authority* 1997). She often worked through lunch to make up the time she missed when she was late, but she was fired nevertheless (ibid.).

Illness is not the only exigency that causes conflicts between work and family for divorced parents, single moms, and tag-team couples (those who work opposite shifts to cover their childcare needs). A mother in the midst of a divorce was fired from her job at a factory that produced night vision goggles when she refused a shift change that (she felt) would cause her to lose custody of her children (*ITT Industries, NightVision Roanoke Plant* 2003). A material handler, who was a divorced father of an asthmatic son, was fired when he needed to stay home with his sick child (*Interlake Material Handling Div., Interlake Conveyors Inc.* 2000). A single mother working as a Social Security Administration contact representative was treated as absent without leave (AWOL) when she refused to report for work because her regular babysitter had car trouble and her back-up babysitter was in the hospital with her own husband, who had suffered a heart attack (*Social Security Administration, Westminster Teleservice Ctr.* 1990). A tag-team father, a factory worker, was fired when his regular babysitter was sick; he had taken the day off instead of his wife, because her employer's absenteeism policy was stricter than his employer's (*U.S. Steel*

Corp. 1990). These real-life illustrations show a face of work-family conflict that is virtually unknown. The press rarely, if ever, writes about it (Marcus 2006), and even the unions that represent such workers are often unaware of the prevalence of these types of problems.

Another equally unknown problem is mandatory overtime. Although it is difficult to quantify the prevalence of mandatory overtime in the United States, in one recent study over one-quarter (28%) of full-time workers surveyed faced mandatory overtime requirements, and over one in five (21%) actually worked overtime hours because it was mandated by their employers (Golden and Wiens-Tuers 2005). Whether required or not, Americans are working increasingly longer hours, with nearly one-third of U.S. workers regularly putting in more than forty hours per week, and one-fifth over fifty hours per week (Golden and Jorgensen 2002). Often, the assumption is that overtime is desirable, on the grounds that union members earn time-and-a-half for each overtime hour worked, as non-exempt workers under the Fair Labor Standards Act (1938). However, the Center for WorkLife Law's arbitration database shows that many workers often face discipline or discharge due to work-family conflicts stemming from the requirement to work overtime. American workers work among the longest hours in the world, even longer than workers in Japan (International Labour Organization 2003; Jacobs and Gerson 2004, 126–27). Mandatory overtime requirements place many tag-team families in the situation of having to choose between the job of the mother and the job of the father. To quote the general counsel of the American Transit Union:

> Our members were being fired because they refused to stay for mandatory drug and alcohol tests, which last up to three hours. They had no problem taking the tests; the problem was that they were triggered at or near the end of their shifts. And with little or no advance notice, they could not stay even as paid overtime, because they had to get home to take care of their kids. (Cited in Williams 2006, 15)

Single mothers face equally harsh "choices." For example, a single mother who worked as a telephone installer was fired when she left work in defiance of a new company policy requiring that installers respond to every customer who called before 3 p.m. The policy made it impossible for workers to know when they would get off work. The installer was fired for insubordination when she refused to work overtime for fear of losing her childcare (*GTE California, Inc.* 1992).

Unlike professionals, whose work often can be done anywhere or during flexible hours, union workers often have jobs in factories, hospitals, or emergency services, such as the police or the fire service. For these on-site jobs in which specific hours must be covered, the professional model of individually negotiated flexible work arrangements is not particularly suitable. Job shares, however, may be: although factory workers typically work a standard eight- or ten-hour day, not everyone should be required to work all five days—one person working three days a week could share a job with another working the remaining two days (Appelbaum et al. 2001).

The ability to use personal time in two-hour increments is also an important consideration, to enable a worker to take unpaid time off for parent-teacher conferences or to take an ailing elder to a doctor's appointment. State laws also are relevant here—for example, California statutes allow workers forty hours a year of unpaid leave to participate in activities at their children's school (California Labor Code §§ 230.7, 230.8); allow workers to use up to half of their accrued annual sick leave to care for a sick child, parent, spouse, or domestic partner (Cal. Labor Code § 233); and, in certain circumstances, allow employees to take time off on one day and make it up on another day, without requiring overtime pay (Cal. Labor Code § 513).

Low-Wage Workers

Low-wage workers face particularly harsh work-family conflicts, which thankfully have been better documented than those of the missing middle. Low-wage workers are much more likely than are others to be single mothers: women who have spent at least five years as a single mother have half the income of women who have never been a single parent (Rose and Hartmann 2004). These women are also much more likely than other workers to depend on family members or friends for childcare, given the lack of government subsidies for all but a small percentage of those in need, the high cost of childcare, and the low minimum wage they typically are paid (Albelda and Cosenza 2000; Heymann 2000). Such informal childcare arrangements are more likely to break down than the kind of formal childcare most PMC families can afford (Heymann 2000). In addition, many low-wage single mothers have little choice but to leave their children home alone in dangerous neighborhoods, often at shockingly young ages. As a result, low-income parents are more likely than others to have to interrupt work because of problems with childcare (ibid.).

Low-wage workers also are far more likely than others to be providing more than thirty hours a week of unpaid assistance to parents or in-laws (ibid., 118). Additionally, the lack of sufficient public transportation in many U.S. cities leaves many parents to take slow, cumbersome, and undependable public transportation, such as the single mother, discussed above, who lost her job because she was late to work: she had to take three buses to deliver her kids to school and to childcare and to reach her job (*Chicago Transit Authority* 1997). Furthermore, low-income families are more likely than other U.S. families to be dealing with issues of ill health and lack of health insurance, where access to medical care, if available, is received only by waiting long and unpredictable periods of time (Heymann 2000). Finally, low-wage workers are more likely than other workers to lack paid sick and/or vacation leave and to face inflexible schedules at work (ibid., 115–16). Mothers with a high school education or less are more likely than other mothers to work rotating schedules or "unsocial hours" (the European term for evening and weekend work), and single mothers within this group are the most likely to do so (Presser 2003, 202–3).

Arbitrations dramatize the kinds of brutal conflicts that low-wage employees often face (Williams 2006). In *Tenneco Packaging Burlington Container Plant* (1999), the arbitrator reinstated with full back pay the grievant, a single parent of a mentally handicapped son, who was terminated after twenty-seven years for failing to report to work when her son's caregiver could not work. In *State of New York, Rochester Psychiatric Center* (1986), a healthcare center fired a mental health aide who had worked for her employer for nine years. She had a history of attendance problems, almost all of which stemmed from her status as a single parent. The arbitrator overturned her discharge, stating that the situation was "shocking to one's sense of fairness."

The Odd Disconnect

Fully 95 percent of American women and 90 percent of American men say they wish they had more time to devote to family (Gornick and Meyers 2003, 53). In Europe, the national debate tends to be not whether to implement policies to help reconcile work and family, but how best to do so (Kamerman 2005). In the United States, in contrast, work-family issues have been barely a blip on the radar screen of American politics. Why has the widespread experience of work-family conflict failed to spur action in the United States to date?

This description of work-family conflict in different social locations can help answer the question of why, given the acute levels of work-family conflict, this issue has not gained political purchase. One clue emerged in a Capitol Hill conversation. A staffer for a member of Congress who represents an urban area was puzzling over how to connect with the voters on work-family issues. The staff had developed a work-family bill, and the congressional district was an urban area, full of professional women who clearly cared about work-family issues. Yet there remained a strange disconnect, an inability to engage and inspire these voters. The problem, it seems, was that the bill in question focused on short-term leaves and subsidized childcare, neither of which is of much help to PMC women—most of whom already have short-term leave, and none of whom would be eligible for subsidized childcare.

One policy alternative with the potential to help women—and men—in all three groups (PMC, working class, and low-income) is part-time equity: proportional pay, benefits, training, and advancement for part-time work. Part-time equity would help PMC workers because they could opt for thirty-five- to forty-hour workweeks, in return for proportional pay and advancement, thereby avoiding the outlandish hours often required of fast-track professionals. It would help working-class single mothers and tag-team families struggling with long hours of mandatory overtime, and also help low-income workers by discouraging employers from keeping them in part-time work as a way of depressing wages and eliminating benefits.

Part-time equity presents significant and, for now, somewhat insuperable challenges in terms of coalition building. Yet it will be important to begin to create the kind of cross-class academic literature that will provide the basis for assessing the potential of various policy alternatives. The challenge is in designing policy initiatives that yoke three forces: (a) the political power of professional women; (b) support from a union movement apprized of the important role work-family conflict in the lives of its members; and (c) the moral clout and political capital of poverty advocates. Although this approach is not the only answer, it does help formulate the right question.

"My boss is not interested in the problems of professional women": The Media's Role in Creating the Public Policy Environment

When a second congressional staffer was questioned about work-family issues, she was discouraging. "My boss," she maintained, "is not interested in the problems of professional women" (anonymous staffer to author, personal communication, 2001). The news media play an important role in affirming this widespread misconception. In a content study of 119 newspaper articles, the Center for WorkLife Law's report *Opt Out or Pushed Out? How the Press Covers Work-Family Conflict* (Williams, Manvell, and Bornstein 2006) found a very consistent storyline. Featured prominently in the *New York Times*, but also pervasive throughout U.S. newspapers, the "Opt Out" storyline (so named because of Lisa Belkin's germinal 2003 cover story in the *New York Times Magazine*, "The Opt Out Revolution") has four basic elements: (a) a disproportionate focus on professional-managerial class women; (b) depictions of women as "pulled" into traditional roles by their own biology or psychology, glossing over the external "pushes" such as workplace inflexibility, the lack of public policy supports for working families, or discrimination against mothers; (c) coverage of work-family conflict as a "soft" human interest story rather than as the (microeconomic) story of workplace/workforce mismatch or the (macroeconomic) story of the systematic deskilling of women once they become mothers; and (d) a focus on women in one particular situation: *after* they drop out of the paid workforce and *before* they divorce.

Focus on Professional-Managerial Class Women

In the Center for WorkLife Law's study, over half (58%) of the women discussed in stories on work-family issues in the *New York Times* were in high-status or other traditional masculine white-collar jobs (Williams, Manvell, and Bornstein 2006)—although only about 8 percent of American women hold those jobs (Rose and Hartmann 2004). Newspapers' persistent focus on professional-managerial class women is ironic, given that more affluent mothers are *less* likely to be out of the labor force than are less affluent ones (England 2006; Williams, Manvell, and Bornstein 2006, 22–23).

Pulls without Pushes

In nearly three-quarters of the stories the Center for WorkLife Law examined, the overall tone was one of pulls rather than pushes (Williams, Manvell, and Bornstein 2006). The classic storyline depicts women pulled into traditionalism by biology or psychology. This picture is not supported by the available evidence. A 2004 study found that only 16 percent of the highly qualified women surveyed exhibited a stable preference to be stay-at-home moms. In sharp contrast, fully 86 percent cited workplace pushes as a key reason they quit (Stone and Lovejoy 2004). While only 6 percent of the articles surveyed *refer to* workplace pushes as key reasons for women's departure, the women quoted often tell of leaving the workplace only after they have been denied flexible schedules or part-time work—illustrating the role of workplace inflexibility in *pushing* women (who are depicted as "choosing" to leave) out of the workforce (Williams, Manvell, and Bornstein 2006). The women in the articles also tell of leaving the workforce only after they discover that their salaries will do little more than cover (or will not cover) the high costs of childcare; or that they could not find good childcare; or that the tax system made it uneconomic for them to remain employed—all illustrating how the lack of family supports in the United States fuel the loss of women's human capital (ibid.). Less often, but increasingly, stories are emerging in the press documenting the role of "maternal wall" stereotyping and bias (that is, the motherhood equivalent of the glass ceiling that all women face) in driving mothers out of good jobs (e.g., Attkisson 2004; Belkin 2006; Cummins 2006; Mitchell 2006; Stark 2006; Zahn 2006).

Soft, Often Autobiographical, Human Interest Stories

No major newspaper would cover unemployment by having a reporter interview a handful of well-heeled acquaintances or muse on a personal period of unemployment. The idea is ludicrous; unemployment is a serious economic issue. However, when it comes to reporting on the unemployment of mothers, that is just what some American newspapers have done. One sharply contrasting alternative for how to cover the issue of mothers' employment appeared in the *Economist* magazine in 2006. Entitled "Women and the World Economy: A Guide to Womenomics" (2006), the article treats women's relationship to work as an important economic issue:

> Making better use of women's skills is not just a matter of fairness. Plenty of studies suggest that it is good for business, too…despite their gains, women remain the world's most under-utilized resource. Many are still excluded from paid work; many do not make best use of their skills…greater participation by women in the

labour market could help to offset the effects of an ageing, shrinking population and hence support growth.

In glaring dissimilarity to the Opt Out storyline, which depicts workplace issues in a framework of individual choice and ignores the economic implications of the systematic deskilling of mothers, the *Economist* presents the issue firmly in a macroeconomic frame. The natural next step is to examine how mothers' workforce participation can be supported through public policy: "To make full use of their national pools of female talent, governments need to remove obstacles that make it hard for women to combine work with having children," by providing "parental leave and childcare, allowing more flexible working hours, and reforming tax and social-security systems that creates disincentives for women to work" (ibid.).

The Macroeconomic Deskilling story is an obvious alternative to the Opt Out story, and over one-quarter (25.5%) of the stories in the Center for WorkLife Law's study mention one or more women who have taken a lower-status or lower-wage job because of work-family conflict. Yet only 12 percent discussed the negative impact on the economy of the loss of talent, and only 16 percent of the articles surveyed appeared in the business section; many more were soft, feature-type articles (Williams, Manvell, and Bornstein 2006).

Near-Exclusive Focus on Mothers after They Drop Out and before They Divorce

Stories on work-family conflict in the United States almost invariably focus on mothers after they drop out of the paid workforce and before they divorce. Women in this situation have every motivation to describe the situation as reflecting their free choice. There is little benefit to sacrificing a career for the good of the family, then souring the family by complaining bitterly of one's loss. If reporters spoke with women before they dropped out, while they were still trying—often with little workplace support or downright workplace hostility—to "make it work," quite different stories might well emerge. If reporters consulted Opt-Out women who found themselves divorced, again they would hear quite different stories. Yet these groups virtually never appeared in the articles surveyed. The steady diet of interviews *only* with relatively affluent women, *only* after they opt out, and *only* before any of them divorce, allows Opt Out stories to paint an unrealistically rosy picture of women's "choice" when "opting out."

The myopic focus on this one group of women also allows Opt Out stories to minimize the economic impact on the family of losing one breadwinner. If Opt Out stories discuss the economic impact on the family at all, typically their focus is on the family's short-term inability to buy luxuries (forty-four out of 119 articles; Williams, Manvell, and Bornstein 2006), such as "the baby sitter, the cleaning lady, the dry cleaner, summer camp for the 6-year-old, expensive vacations, the chi-chi hairdresser, the shopping sprees...vacations, eating out, nightclubs in South Beach and buying clothes whenever they wanted" (Veciana-Suarez 1994). This is an inaccurate picture of the economics of dropping out for most working families, given that working women in the United States, on average, bring home 28 percent of the family income (Gornick and Meyers 2003, 68–69, figure 3.8).

Nor is opt-out women's long-term economic vulnerability discussed in most of the stories: only 16 percent of the articles surveyed even mentioned it (Williams, Manvell, and Bornstein 2006). Of the 119 articles, none linked women's "opting" out to the fact that 69 percent of elderly poor are women (U.S. Census Bureau 2005); or that women, over their lifetimes, earn only 38 percent of the wages of men (Rose and Hartmann 2004); or that mothers earn only sixty-seven cents for every dollar earned by fathers (Gornick and Meyers 2003, 68, figure 3.7). Only seven out 119 of the articles reviewed mentioned the possibility of divorce (Williams, Manvell, and Bornstein 2006).

The Opt Out storyline has critical effects on public policy. Most important, it perpetuates the inaccurate view that work-family conflict is a problem of only privileged professional women. This view is held not only among politicians; it also resounds in some union circles. Unions differ widely in their attitudes toward this issue. Some unions view work-family issues as core union issues, whereas others continue to view work-family conflict as just a professional women's issue. This is vitally important, given that no work-family bill can be expected to gain support—much less pass—without union backing.

The first step in changing the Opt Out storyline is to disseminate the growing literature, discussed above, documenting that work-family conflict affects men as well as women, and low- and middle-income workers as well as the professional-managerial class. The second step—a much more difficult one—is to use this knowledge to forge a coalition capable of passing new legislation.

The Challenge of Building a Work-Family Coalition

The coalition that produced the Family and Medical Leave Act (FMLA) consisted of a solid base of inside-the-Beltway feminist groups, antipoverty advocates, and unions. These groups seem important to any coalition designed to take the next steps on work-family issues. In sharp contrast to many European countries, which have a broad social consensus that the state should provide a baseline of resources to every citizen, antipoverty advocates in the United States have a difficult trail to forge. The purchasing power of the minimum wage has fallen 20 percent since 1997 and is 30 percent lower than it was in 1979 (Economic Policy Institute n.d.). A raise in the minimum wage is finally a reality (the first in ten years), but it has been a long time in coming and has been linked with a further decrease in the estate tax. Given the difficulty in raising the minimum wage at a national level, those involved in the living wage campaign have moved the battle to the local level (Living Wage Resource Center n.d.).

If the prospects for a living wage at a national level are bleak, the prospects for social subsidies are even less promising. Since President Clinton's "welfare reform" of 1996 (the Personal Responsibility and Work Opportunity Reconciliation Act), indigent mothers are limited to five years of benefits and are required to look for work (Committee on Ways and Means 2006), often with little or no subsidy to pay for adequate childcare. Facing an ocean of need and public demand for tax cuts, antipoverty advocates often argue, understandably, that any funds for social programs should be preserved for those most in need. This may well be a short-term strategy. As the adage goes, "Programs for the poor are poor programs"—they lack the kind of solid political constituency that supports universal programs such as Social Security.

Inside-the-Beltway feminism has its own political mandates. In many European countries as well as in Japan, falling birthrates, combined with ambivalent (or racist) attitudes toward immigration, create political will for family supports in order to draw women into paid work. In the Nordic countries, policies have aimed to effect fluidity in gender roles, notably through "daddy days" of parental leave that can be taken only by the fathers. In France and other Continental countries, the focus is more on socializing mothers' burdens, without a sustained focus on bringing fathers into family care (Gornick 2001). Under either model, European feminists share the characteristically European assumption that all citizens should enjoy a baseline of benefits from the state. This assumption was codified into the European Union requirements, such as the requirement for paid maternity leave, four weeks of vacation, paid or unpaid parental leave, and paid leave to care for family members who are ill.

The United States, of course, is very different. The birthrate is higher, and massive immigration erases worries about the need for women's labor (although it should not). Neoliberalism predominates, insisting on the need to unleash the wealth-creating power of the market, with government's role limited to ensuring a level playing field that guarantees equal opportunity. The political will for social subsidies in the United States seems to have evaporated for the time being. Yet Americans take discrimination very seriously—much more seriously than most Europeans.

And, just as European feminists hold European views, American feminists remain Americans. The major feminist groups inside the Beltway—the National Women's Law Center, the Women's Legal Defense Fund (now the National Partnership for Women and Families), the Institute for Women's Policy Research, and (a later entry) the NOW Legal Defense Fund (now Legal Momentum)—were founded by lawyers and economists.

These East Coast feminists tended to be "equality" feminists opposed to "special treatment" for women, whereas on the West Coast the center of gravity was closer to "maternalism" (empowering women in their traditional roles). This split erupted into an intense internal battle in the 1980s over the case of *California Federal Savings and Loan Association v. Guerra* ([*Cal Fed*] 1987). In that case, West Coast feminists defended California's maternity leave statute, while the major feminist groups in Washington opposed it, arguing that it was precisely the kind of protective labor legislation that always redounded to women's detriment (Krieger and Cooney 1983; Williams 1989).

The West Coast contingent won the *Cal Fed* case, but equality feminism won inside the Beltway. Thus, the national leave legislation rejected a maternity leave for women only—despite the fact that such legislation could have passed long before the FMLA—in favor of a statute that avoided "special treatment" for women by lumping maternity leave in with paternity leave, personal medical leave, and leave to care for ill family members.

Equality feminism has a profound effect on how the work-family agenda is defined within Washington. Under its influence, the work-family agenda traditionally has focused on short-term leaves and subsidized childcare. The leaves-and-childcare agenda reflected the equality feminist assumption that women will take a short three-month leave and then return to full-time work, delegating childcare to others. (A maternalist feminist would critique this assumption on the grounds that it requires women to conform to what Arlie Hochschild [1994] calls "the clockwork of male careers.") Equality feminism made part-time work controversial among Washington feminists, although Heidi Hartmann, the influential head of the Institute for Women's Policy Research, has recently said that she no longer opposes measures that encourage women to work part-time. Her prior fear was that part-time work would serve only to further marginalize women, but in fall 2003 she wrote,

> Personally, I'm less worried than I used to be that [reduced hour] accommodations will reify a "mommy track" and more convinced that they will increase women's lifetime labor force participation and their earnings. I also believe that men will increasingly use such accommodations, the less stigmatized they become, and the more that reduced time jobs have good pay and fringe benefits and advancement potential. (Hartmann 2003)

Of the major feminist lobbying organizations, the National Partnership for Women and Families has traditionally focused on paid leave (and led the coalition to pass the FMLA; National Partnership for Women and Families n.d.), while the National Women's Law Center (n.d.) has concentrated on tax breaks and subsidies for childcare. Legal Momentum (formerly NOW Legal Defense Fund), a more recent entrant into the work-family policy arena, has followed suit: when, in 2003, it launched its Family Initiative, its focus was exclusively on childcare (Legal Momentum n.d.).

American feminists' focus on leaves and childcare is understandable. With respect to leave, it *is* a bit strange for the United States to rank with Lesotho, Papua

New Guinea, and Swaziland as one of the only four countries in which parents lack access to paid parental leave (Heymann 2006b). Yet the focus on leaves has costs. For employers, short-term leaves arguably are more disruptive that long-term, well-planned flexible schedules, particularly in a country where employers (not the government) cover the costs of leave. Requiring individual employers to finance leaves means that U.S. employers have to pay an absent worker, then either pay again to hire a temporary worker, or overwork the remaining employees—often not a desirable situation for anyone. In a society that lacks government subsidies for paid leave, employers' assumption that work-family public policy equals more paid leaves has definite political costs.

Childcare, too, is fraught with political liabilities. In Europe, childcare is understood to be an expression of social solidarity, and is provided in neighborhood-based centers often staffed by personnel paid on the same scale as public school teachers. But in the United States, childcare typically entails consigning one's child to the market. At best, it triggers the commodification anxiety that arises when social relationships traditionally handled within the family are allocated to the market (Williams and Zelizer 2006). At worst, the idea of government-subsidized childcare calls up imagery not of social solidarity, but of an institution that is embattled in the same fashion as many public institutions in the United States. Childcare advocates have recognized that the poisonous political dynamic triggered by demands for "childcare" are best handled by characterizing the need as one for "early childhood education"—although, given the sorry shape of many public schools, that hardly seems to be a silver bullet. (It should be noted, however, that universal pre-kindergarten has been passed in some states, including "red states" such as Georgia, Florida, and Oklahoma; Pre-K Now n.d.). Finally, to the extent that both nationally subsidized paid leave and subsidized childcare require large new social programs, this era of the "Great Recession" hardly seems the historical moment to identify work-family public policy with large new spending programs.

All of these are essential concerns because, at a national level, one cannot expect even Democratic sponsors to support work-family legislation that is not actively supported by the major women's groups in Washington, D.C., nor can one expect sponsors to support labor legislation that is not supported by unions. Unions have supported paid leave, both because it sets a higher baseline that allows them to focus their bargaining on other issues, and because of their ideological commitment to helping all workers, not just union members. Thus, unions played a crucial role both in the passage of the FMLA and in the enactment of a paid family leave insurance program in California.

In many European countries, unions have played a major role in work-family policy. For example, British legislation granting workers the right to request flexible hours was developed in conjunction with unions, and the Trades Union Council recently called for its expansion (Fagan, Hegewisch, and Pillinger 2006). American unions vary greatly in terms of their awareness and receptiveness to work-family issues, but many union activists still see wages and benefits—but not work-family conflict—as core union issues. Work-family conflict may still be written off as "just a professional woman's issue" (which is understandable, given the Opt Out story prevalent in the press) or as a luxury issue that inevitably takes a second seat in bargaining to the core issues of wages and benefits.

Union support for working-time legislation differs in the United States and Europe for several reasons. First, falling real wages in the United States in recent decades have led some working-class families to depend on overtime work (typically by the father) in order to preserve their standard of living (Zweig 2000). Europeans have not seen the sharp rise in disparities of income that Americans have in the past few decades, nor the concomitant dependence of some working families in the United States on overtime to supplement the family income.

Nor have European unions been forced to deal with the distortions of economic incentives created by the idiosyncratic system in the United States of delivering health benefits through employers.[2] One effect of this odd system is that, as the cost of health insurance has spiraled, some employers have responded by changing good full-time jobs with benefits into poor-quality part-time jobs without benefits to drive down effective wage rates by eliminating workers' benefits packages. This practice has shaped unions' negative perception of part-time work—"radioactive" was the word used in one conversation.

* The delivery of healthcare through a job link also creates a different public policy environment in the United States and Europe with respect to part-time equity— that is, the guarantee of proportional pay and benefits for part-time workers (guaranteed in Europe by the 1997 Part-Time Directive; Gornick and Meyers 2003, 163). Because employers are responsible for health insurance in the United States, unions justifiably fear that a mandate for part-time equity would cause employers to shift benefit dollars away from the unions' (full-time worker) members, to share the ever-shrinking benefits pot between full- and part-time workers.

Unions in both the United States and Europe are suspicious of "flexibility." Given the power differential between workers and management, unions' strategy is to minimize employers' discretion; "flexibility" is feared as a return to managerial discretion. Yet many Europeans work within the "social contract" tradition that allows unions and employers to come together to broker the kind of hard trade-offs that cultivated Germany's system of work time accounts—in which workers give employers the right to vary hours on a weekly basis in return for a shorter workweek (Bispinck 2005). Because the United States lacks this tradition, American unions are more likely to simply oppose flexibility. As one labor leader explained (paraphrased here), "You have to understand that when an employer gives something to one worker, we make it our business to demand it for all other workers. So in my union, if someone comes to me and says they need to leave early to take a child to an appointment, I say no" (anonymous labor leader to author, personal communication, 2006).

It is obvious that Europe and the United States have sweeping cultural differences that translate into quite varied policy environments. Due to the Obama Administration's stated interest in work-family balance, these dynamics and the relevant political landscape may begin to change. Nevertheless, in view of these challenges—and because most public policy at the national level *on any subject* is incremental—it seems likely that new legislation on working hours and workplace flexibility will be incremental. In this context, it is important to assess the interaction between the ongoing efforts to pass new legislation and the current boom in litigation over work-family issues.

Public Policy through the Courts: The Trend

The United States has a tradition of using the courts to advance public policy. While the legislative majorities needed to regulate U.S. businesses remain elusive, juries spur corporate self-regulation by imposing large judgments on those whose products injure consumers. Civil rights advocates such as Charles Hamilton Houston began the civil rights revolution in the federal courts in the 1930s and '40s, long before the passage of the 1964 Civil Rights Act. Anti-smoking advocates have relied in significant part on litigation, not legislation, to educate the public about the perils of tobacco smoke and change the behavior of tobacco companies. Feminists relied on the courts, not new legislation, to transform sexual harassment from "something any woman worth her salt could handle" to a socially condemned—and potentially very expensive—behavior.

A similar phenomenon is occurring in the work-family arena. Although much remains to be done in the legislative arena to help working families balance competing demands of work and family, mothers and other family caregivers are suing to advance their rights at work (Williams and Bornstein 2008). To date, the Center for WorkLife Law has documented over 1,900 court cases alleging discrimination based on family responsibilities using seventeen theories under existing state and federal law. The number of lawsuits filed alleging family responsibilities discrimination (FRD, or "Fred," as Lisa Belkin [2006] dubbed it in a *New York Times* article) has ballooned dramatically: a 2006 WorkLife Law study reported a nearly 400 percent increase in the number of FRD lawsuits filed between 1996 and 2005 as compared to the prior decade, 1986 to 1995 (Still 2006, 2).

Moreover, plaintiffs have a high, 50 percent success rate in FRD cases, and when they win, the potential for liability is substantial (ibid., 13). Of the cases the Center for WorkLife Law has collected to date, the largest individual FRD verdict was $11.65 million; the largest class action judgment was $49 million; and, in over 125 cases, verdicts or settlements topped $100,000.

Most FRD cases are filed by women; but the data run contrary to the conventional wisdom that litigation can only help professional-managerial class (PMC) women: in the 2006 study, 62 percent of those cases collected as of 2005 were filed by nonprofessionals (Still 2006, 8–9). Cases have been filed by low-wage workers such as grocery clerks, nurses' aides, and waitresses; by blue-collar workers such as truck drivers, police, and firefighters; by pink-collar workers such as secretaries, teachers, and retail managers; by middle-wage workers such as computer sales staff, customer service supervisors, and account managers; and by PMC workers such as executives, lawyers, and accountants. Regardless of where they fall in the socioeconomic spectrum or social hierarchy, after bearing children, women hit the "maternal wall."

This boom in FRD litigation comes as a surprise to many legal commentators. Until recently, the accepted wisdom among law professors was that work-family conflict was not litigable (Williams and Bornstein 2008, 1316–20). Mary Becker has argued that conservative courts made federal employment statutes virtually useless (as cited in Williams and Segal 2003, 103). Kathryn Abrams has argued that employment statutes could not help women because work-family conflict reflected not discrimination, but mothers' choice (as cited in Williams and Segal 2003, 78). Others have argued that litigation could not help most mothers, who really do need shorter hours and other accommodations: the only women federal employment law could be expected to help were ideal-worker women who, like men, could work full-time and full force for forty years straight (Williams and Segal 2003, 107–8). Still others have argued that discrimination statutes could not help the three-quarters of women who work in sex-segregated jobs (Williams 2000, 66), given those plaintiffs' inability to point to "comparators"—similarly situated men who were treated differently (Chamallas 1999).

None of these entirely reasonable predictions has proven true (Williams and Bornstein 2008). One early case, *Trezza v. The Hartford, Inc.* (1998), broke new ground when a court rejected the defendant employer's argument that it had not engaged in gender discrimination by failing to promote a woman lawyer, because in her stead it promoted a woman without children. The relevant comparison, the court asserted, was between the treatment of men with school-age children and women with school-age children (*Trezza v. The Hartford, Inc.* 1998). This lens showed that, of the forty-six occupants of the job in question, not one was the mother of a school-age child (ibid.). *Trezza* taught plaintiffs alleging maternal wall discrimination not to compare *women* to *men* but *mothers* to *others*.

Perhaps the landmark FRD case is the 2004 case of *Back v. Hastings on Hudson Union Free School District*, decided by the Second Circuit federal court of appeals. In *Back* (2004), the plaintiff was a school psychologist who (according to the facts as presented at summary judgment, where the court adopts the plaintiffs' version of the facts) received excellent performance reviews until she neared the end of her three-year probationary period. As Back approached tenure, her principal and the head of personnel began to express doubts, commenting that Back's position was not the job for someone with "little ones," that it was "not possible for [her] to be a good mother and have [the] job," and that her good performance was just "an act" that would end once she got tenure (*Back v. Hastings on Hudson Union Free School District* 2004, 115).

Back lost on a summary judgment motion in the district court, but prevailed when her case was appealed to the Second Circuit, in an opinion written by Judge Guido Calibresi, the liberal-leaning former dean of Yale Law School (and citing the Center for WorkLife Law's law review article [Williams and Segal 2003] published a year before). Calibresi's opinion held that Back did not need to point to a similarly situated male comparator to make a claim for gender discrimination under Title VII—something she could not do, because so few school psychologists are men (*Back v. Hastings on Hudson Union Free Sch. Dist.* 2004). Instead, the Court held that Back could prove discrimination without a comparator because she had evidence of maternal wall stereotyping. "It takes no special training to discern stereotyping in the view that a woman cannot 'be a good mother' and have a job that requires long hours," the Court wrote (ibid., 120). "Where stereotypes are considered, the notions that mothers are insufficiently devoted to work, and that work and motherhood are incompatible, are properly considered to be, themselves, gender-based" (ibid., 121).

Thanks in part to *Back*, today's plaintiffs' attorneys know to litigate this type of case as a stereotyping case. For example, when CNN's *Paula Zahn Now* did a piece on FRD, it quoted the plaintiff's employment lawyer saying, "What's at the heart of a lot of these cases is a stereotype, the assumption that you can't do both, you can't be a parent and you can't be a good employee" (Zahn 2006). The stereotyping approach has the potential to help ideal-worker women whom employers assume will cease to be ideal workers once they have children, on the assumption that mothers are committed to their children but not their jobs.

But the stereotyping theory also has the potential to help women who, true to stereotype, *do* want fewer hours or less travel after they have children. These women, too, may encounter bias because the schema (stereotype) of mothers links motherhood with negative assumptions about competence and commitment. For example, one study showed that, while businesswomen are considered highly competent, similar to businessmen, housewives are lumped alongside stigmatized groups such as the elderly, blind, "retarded," and disabled, to use the words tested by the researchers (Eckes 2002; Fiske et al. 2002). A more recent study showed that, when compared to nonmothers with the same qualifications, mothers were 79 percent less likely to be recommended for hire, viewed as less competent and committed, offered $11,000 less in suggested salary for the same job, and held to higher performance and punctuality standards (Correll, Benard, and Paik 2007). Even if a mother is not an ideal worker—for example, because she can no longer be available all hours of every day—this does not mean that she is less competent when she works, or that she can legally be held to higher standards for promotion than fathers. Now that psychologists have begun to understand and document the maternal wall (Biernat, Crosby, and Williams 2004), even women living traditionally feminine biographies can challenge family responsibilities discrimination in the courts.

The fact that litigation has helped not only ideal-worker women but also mothers playing traditional roles was dramatized by a case decided by one of the more conservative circuits in the country, the Seventh Circuit, in the 2005 case of *Washington v. Illinois Department of Revenue*. The case involved a mother who filed a race discrimination complaint against her employer. Allegedly in retaliation for filing her complaint, her supervisor took away the flex (7 a.m. to 3 p.m.) schedule she had worked for years in order to be home in time to care for her son, who had Down Syndrome (*Washington v. Illinois Dept. of Revenue* 2005). At the trial level, a magistrate court granted summary judgment in favor of the employer, holding that changing Washington's flex schedule did not amount to retaliation (ibid.). The Seventh Circuit disagreed, reversing the decision and finding for Washington in an opinion written by conservative Judge Frank Easterbrook (ibid.). Forcing Washington to work 9-to-5 instead of 7-to-3 "was a materially adverse change *for her,* even though it would not have been for 99% of the staff," the Court held, with the "practical effect…[of] cut[ting] her wages by 25%, because it induced her to use leave for two hours per day" (ibid., 662).

When the conservative U.S. Supreme Court agreed to review a different retaliation case, *Burlington Northern and Santa Fe Railway v. White* (2006), most knowledgeable advocates assumed that the standard set by the Seventh Circuit in *Washington v. Illinois* would be overturned. It was not; in fact, the Supreme Court ruled unanimously in favor of adopting the test for retaliation set out in *Washington v. Illinois* as the nationwide standard for what type of conduct amounts to retaliation in all Title VII cases (*Burlington Northern and Santa Fe Ry. v. White* 2006). Moreover, although the Supreme Court case did not involve FRD, allowing the Court to easily gloss over caregiving issues entirely, it chose not to do so. Instead, it addressed FRD explicitly, noting that "context matters": "A schedule change in an employee's work schedule may make little difference to many workers, but may matter enormously to a young mother with school age children" (ibid., 2415). Setting an objective "reasonable person" standard, yet circumscribed within the context of the employee, the Supreme Court sent the message that, when it comes to retaliation, courts need to meet mothers in their current social roles, without holding them to the standard of constant availability traditionally expected of ideal workers.

The Supreme Court's *Burlington Northern* decision may have astonished most legal commentators, yet it was the second decision in three years in which the conservative U.S. Supreme Court made a surprising decision that favored plaintiffs where family responsibilities discrimination was involved. In the 2003 case *Nevada Department of Human Resources v. Hibbs,* conservative Supreme Court Justice William Rehnquist wrote a majority opinion that limited the very federalism doctrine he had created. Rehnquist ruled that the federal Family and Medical Leave Act (FMLA) applied to state governments, in the case of a man seeking FMLA leave to care for his wife injured in a car accident. The Supreme Court, adopting the words of feminist law professor Nina Pillard, signaled that it takes maternal wall stereotyping very seriously, stating that "the fault line between work and family [is] precisely where sex-based overgeneralization has been and remains strongest" (*Nevada Dept. of Human Resources v. Hibbs* 2003, 738).

Why have conservative as well as liberal courts found in favor of plaintiffs in FRD cases and helped to develop FRD case law? FRD cases are family values cases (Williams 2000). As political commentators have begun to recognize, Americans in red states, blue states, and everywhere in between believe that family caregiving is an important family value. Courts have been the first to find their way to this insight; the challenge that remains is to reach legislators, to use progress in the courts as a way to build a legislative coalition.

Progress in courts of law has also had an impact in the court of public opinion, as media coverage of FRD lawsuits has begun to provide an alternative to the Opt Out storyline that blames mothers' marginalization on their own "choices" to leave the paid workforce. One telling example is the CNN story that focused on a new maternal wall study, and profiled a case filed by plaintiff Julia Panley-Pacetti (Zahn 2006). Panley-Pacetti told a very receptive Paula Zahn that she had waited to have a child until she was thirty-four years old, "until my career was on track, until my income was in place so that I had the resources to support a child." She was called her boss's favorite, received three promotions and four raises in four years, and spoke with her boss "on the phone sometimes ten different [times] a day, working on things of the highest priority." Then Panley-Pacetti got pregnant. Suddenly, she found that she could not even get her boss on the phone; she had the distinct impression that "they didn't know how to deal with my pregnancy." Once she gave birth, however, she received up to a dozen or more phone calls and e-mails a day, as late as 11 o'clock at night. "What did you think [was] the message your bosses were sending you, to flood you with that kind of work while you're out on maternity leave?" asked a clearly outraged Paula Zahn. Panley-Pacetti said that her boss was very explicit, telling her, "You need to tell us whether you're willing to give 100%, because if you're not, we need to figure out a way to do it without you." She was "among a handful of people" laid off shortly thereafter while still on maternity leave. She and her husband lost their house, and, with their daughter, were still living with her grandfather at the time of the CNN story (ibid.).

CNN's coverage of Panley-Pacetti's story is a dramatic departure from the Opt Out storyline. First and most important, it sends the message that often mothers do not opt out—they are pushed out by illegal discrimination. Second, while the Opt Out stories typically send the message that wives' salaries are "pin money" that go for luxuries, Panley-Pacetti's situation—that of losing the family home—dramatizes that mothers work, as do fathers, to support the family and provide the necessary material resources for middle-class life. Paula Zahn's outraged tone communicates that the issue has moved from the arena of personal choice into the realm of social entitlement: as presented, it is clear that this mother found herself unemployed because of the inappropriate behavior of the *employer,* not because of the free choice of the *mother.*

Litigation is an important piece of the puzzle for resolving work-family conflict, not because an individual wins an individual case, but because the law "affects us primarily through communication of symbols, by providing threats, promises, models, persuasion, legitimacy, stigma" (Albiston 2008). In 2003 the Center for WorkLife Law published its first article on FRD surveying only about twenty cases (Williams and Segal); one management-side employment law website recommended that companies should avoid stereotyping and judge employees on their work, rather than on unsupported assumptions—things that were clearly required by the law at the time—adding that they should also offer part-time equity, allow telecommuting and flextime, and establish employee leave banks—none of which was required under the case law of the time (HRHero.com 2002). Sociologists have explained that the way the law effects social change is through intermediaries, such as employment lawyers, who often give a cautiously wide berth to the law—in part as a risk management strategy, and in part because shifting a set of social interactions into a legal framework changes the general sense of who is entitled to what. Another example of this phenomenon is the feedback given by a management consultant in response to a Center for WorkLife Law presentation on FRD:

> Your presentation last Friday…provided [two] important things: I will be able to talk about flexibility using new terms (maternal wall bias, prescriptive stereotyping[,]…family responsibilities discrimination) and to cite court cases like the ones you mentioned and bring credible data to the table.…I know companies spend a lot of money trying to avoid risk. By showing the significant potential for liability that these cases may have[,] it gives me another point of entry for the business case. (C. Pagani-Tousignant, personal communication, May 1, 2006)

In short, the sharp increase in litigation over work-family issues hold the potential for two kinds of change. The first is to shift the national understanding of work-family conflict from being a problem of personal priorities and of individual women "opting out" of the paid workforce toward being an issue of hostile and inappropriate workplace conditions that public policy has failed to address. The second change is to shift employers' understanding of work-family conflict from being an issue they can voluntarily choose to address by offering employees benefits toward being a risk-management issue with the potential for significant legal liability. The boom in FRD litigation and the success rate of FRD plaintiffs taps into the prestige of science and the language of capitalism to send the message that employers who mishandle work-family conflict face serious legal risks; *Business Insurance* has already written on the topic of FRD (Gonzalez 2006).

Although litigation is not the "holy grail" for resolving work-family conflict, it is a key piece of the puzzle. It resonates in the native tongue of entitlement. It sends the message that many mothers want to work, they need to work, and that their rights are often violated when they do work. This is very different language for insisting on family-responsive policies than the twenty-five-year reliance on the argument that employers might choose to give workers family-friendly benefits to enhance their bottom lines. Instead, the message is not simply that employers *should* change conditions for mothers but that they need to change them now, or risk facing expensive lawsuits. In the absence of public policy, FRD lawsuits help to harness the institutions of capitalism to effect social change.

A Bird's-Eye View

Taking a bird's-eye view from ten thousand feet, this chapter has explored several themes related to work-family policy in the United States. A look at existing research provided a snapshot of work-family conflict in three different social locations: low-wage families, professional-managerial class families, and the missing middle. A discussion of media coverage illustrated the role of the press in perpetuating the misconception that workplace flexibility is just a professional woman's issue. An exploration of contrasts between unions, feminist groups, and poverty advocates in the United States and Europe offered a way to begin to understand why the United States has lagged so far behind in its public policy supports for working families. The chapter concluded by contrasting this lack of family supports with the recent rise in family responsibilities discrimination litigation, leading to the observation that, once again, the United States is creating public policy through its courts.

Much as it has always been, relying on the courts is the worst possible way to create public policy. Courts cannot finance paid leave, require high-quality childcare, or meet the needs of America's working families; they address large-scale social problems case by case, driven by individual narratives rather than by broad-scale data. Yet court decisions are leading business insurers to send the message that, according to experts,[3] "employers need to take steps to address the exposure, including properly training their employees to ensure that they do not engage in work-life discrimination and developing policies that mitigate the risk to the greatest extent possible," and that "employers need to build a workplace that acknowledges that employees have family responsibilities and does not penalize them for addressing those responsibilities" (Gonzalez 2006). When business insurers start to report this message, businesses themselves take notice—and may begin to change.

Litigation is only one strategy for achieving social change, a strategy that has serious limitations. Yet until there is the political will to institute paid family leave or subsidize high-quality childcare, until there is an effective political coalition to establish part-time equity or the right to ask for flexible working hours, it is, at least, a start.

Part 4

WORKPLACE FLEXIBILITY

Practices from Abroad

11

LIMITING WORKING TIME AND SUPPORTING FLEXIBILITY FOR EMPLOYEES

Public Policy Lessons from Europe

Janet C. Gornick

Two facts vividly capture the situation of American employees compared to their counterparts in a number of other Western countries. The first fact is that American employees, on average, spend many more hours per year at their workplaces (see figure 11.1). In 2002, workers in the United States—men and women combined—averaged over 1,800 hours per year spent in paid work, compared to, for example, just over 1,700 in the United Kingdom, fewer than 1,600 in Belgium and Sweden, and fewer than 1,500 in France, Germany, and the Netherlands (Mishel, Bernstein, and Allegretto 2005).

The second fact is that American workplaces are much less regulated than workplaces in most European countries. As a result, employees in the United States lack multiple legal rights that are in place elsewhere, including the right to be subject to a maximum number of hours worked per week, the right to a minimum number of paid days off, the right to be protected from pay discrimination if they work part-time, the right to formally request a change in their work hours, and the right to take paid family leave to temporarily care for dependents.

This chapter provides an overview of selected public policies that shape working time as of approximately 2002 in six European countries: Belgium, France, Germany, the Netherlands, Sweden, and the United Kingdom, compared to those in place in the United States. The six comparison countries were selected to ensure a degree of cross-national diversity. Although these countries have much in common—they are all high-income countries and all members of the European Union—they also represent diverse welfare state models. Comparative social policy scholars have long classified the Belgian, French, and German systems as exemplars of the conservative model, in which public provisions generally replicate market outcomes (see, e.g., Esping-Andersen 1990). The Swedish system is viewed

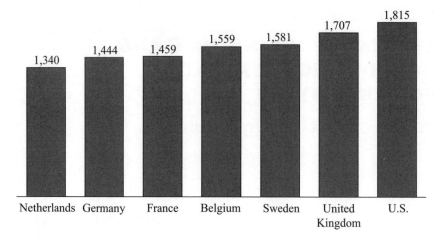

FIGURE 11.1. Workers' average annual hours in paid work, 2002 (Mishel, Bernstein, and Allegretto 2005)

as typifying the social democratic, or social rights, model in conjunction with a sustained emphasis on gender equality. The Dutch social protection system blends conservative and social democratic elements, while the British system, with some marked similarities to the United States, represents the residual (minimally regulated) social protection model. It is useful to assess diverse countries with varying degrees of similarity to the American case, as it serves as a reminder that protective working time regulations are not "one size fits all." They vary, as do the national economic and political systems in which they are embedded.

Throughout the European Union (EU) countries, the regulation of working time has been prominent on policy agendas for decades, at both the supranational and national level. The EU enacted two working-time directives in the 1990s, the 1993 Directive on Working Time and the 1997 Directive on Part-Time Work. These were binding for EU member countries, requiring national-level policy implementation by 1996 and 2000, respectively. The former addresses both maximum weekly hours and entitlements to annual paid days off; the latter addresses compensation parity for part-time workers.

In recent years, one of the core emphases of European policy reforms has been the reduction of employees' work hours. Working time reductions in Europe have been advocated for reasons that have varied both across countries and over time. In the 1980s, the emphasis was most often on combating unemployment by spreading available work; later the rationale shifted to health and safety concerns. But, more recently, public discourse in a number of countries has evoked the need for "work-family"—or "work-life"—balance (Organisation for Economic Cooperation and Development [OECD] 1998, 2004). In a telling example, politicians in France arguing for working time cuts adopted the slogan "*travailler moins pour vivre mieux*" (work less, live better). In several countries, the stated rationale for reducing work hours includes supporting a more gender-egalitarian distribution of paid and unpaid work (see Fagnani and Letablier 2004).

In many European countries, policy reforms aimed at reducing working time appear to have had an effect. In the last twenty years, average annual hours decreased in most EU countries, and, in several, some portion of that decrease is attributed to declining full-timers' hours. In some countries, average hours also declined due to a rising percentage of workers (mostly women) working part-time (Lehndorff 2000).

The United States could hardly be more different. Average annual work hours in the United States actually *increased* during the last two decades (ibid.). Why have work hours in the United States not decreased, as they have in Europe? Some portion of the explanation is clearly the American legal context. Remarkably, the normal workweek in the United States, set by national legislation enacted in 1938, has not been reduced in nearly seventy years. Perhaps even more remarkably, efforts to reduce working time are virtually absent from contemporary American policy agendas. Working time scholar Jon Messenger (2004) recently noted that "from an American perspective, until very recently working time never seemed to be more than an afterthought in discussions of labor issues and labor market policies. Even now, with changes to United States overtime in the news, the focus is not on the *number of hours* that people work, but rather *how much they will be paid* for working those hours" (xviii). As Messenger observes, Americans typically view long hours in a positive light—as evidence of American industriousness and the cause of America's comparatively high per capita GDP.

This chapter looks abroad to consider some crucial policy mechanisms that shape employees' working time, in particular by limiting both weekly and annual work hours and by supporting some forms of flexibility—which, in this chapter, refers to flexibility from the workers' perspective. A growing literature on workplace flexibility emphasizes that workers can be granted "flexibility" in multiple ways. Feldblum (2005) offers a typology of workplace flexibility with regard to the scheduling of hours (e.g., flextime and compressed workweeks); the number of hours worked (e.g., reduced-hour and part-time work); the opportunity to take career breaks and to return (e.g., sabbaticals, "on and off ramps") and the ability to take short-term breaks (e.g., an afternoon off to take a child to a medical appointment).

This chapter focuses, in particular, on three types of working time measures. It begins by covering two mechanisms that limit working time for employees: the setting of the standard workweek and the establishment of entitlements to paid days off. Together, these exert a strong effect on total hours actually worked per year. The chapter then focuses on policies intended to improve the quality of part-time work and/or to raise the availability of part-time or flexible schedules. This is followed by an analysis of policies that grant workers the right to take temporary paid leave from employment–focusing, in particular, on leaves that enable working parents to care for young children. In each of these three sections, institutional arrangements operating in the six European countries are compared with those in the United States, and the role of the European Union itself in setting working time conditions is addressed. The chapter argues that, in the United States, these protections and benefits are largely left to the market, and the result is that lower-skilled, lower-paid workers have much less access to workplace supports (e.g., paid vacation days, paid family leaves, and flexible schedules) than do their more advantaged counterparts.

The final section of this chapter briefly reviews recent literature on the advantageous effects linked to these policies, and then addresses three important concerns sparked by ongoing efforts to reshape working time. Each raises the possibility that policy efforts aimed at reducing work hours, granting workers flexible scheduling options, and/or offering benefits such as paid leave may have some problematic consequences. One concern is that the reduction in work hours, particularly in Europe, is being achieved at the cost of more nonstandard, and, paradoxically, less controllable or predictable work scheduling. A second is that strengthening reduced-hour work may exacerbate, rather than alleviate, gender inequalities in paid and unpaid work. A third concern, often voiced in the United States, is that labor protections (such as those aimed at reducing work hours or requiring that employers honor scheduling requests) and strong generous social policies (such as paid family leave) are harmful to the macroeconomy. Clearly, these are all potentially worrisome concerns and they deserve consideration. The chapter concludes by exploring the question of why public workplace supports are so lacking in the United States.

Limiting Work Hours

In these six European countries, the shaping of work hours and efforts to reduce them operate in diverse institutional contexts. In all of these countries, labor law plays a key role and, to varying degrees, collective bargaining does as well; the two frameworks generally operate in an integrated fashion. In these six countries, union coverage rates tend to be high—about 70 to 80 percent in Germany and the Netherlands, and 90 percent or higher in Belgium, France, and Sweden. The United Kingdom is distinct, set apart by the limited reach of collective bargaining; the coverage rate is only about 30 percent. In the EU, diversity in policy-setting mechanisms is supported at the supranational level. The EU directives relating to working conditions allow member countries to implement required practices through legislation, formalized agreements among the social partners (groups representing employers and workers), or some combination of the two.

In the United States, in contrast, only about one worker in seven is covered by a collective agreement, and, not surprisingly, the working time conditions that are in place are largely determined by labor law. Although unions influence the working conditions of those American workers who are organized, their reach is limited.

Hours Worked per Week: Regulating the Normal Workweek

On both continents, one of the most direct mechanisms for shaping working time is the establishment of a normal, or standard, full-time workweek. "Normal weekly hours" generally refers to the threshold above which overtime becomes payable. Some EU countries establish normal weekly hours, through various combinations of legislation and collective agreement, while others regulate maximum hours, but leave the setting of normal hours exclusively to the bargaining table.[1]

Currently, in all six of these EU countries, the normal full-time workweek, for at least a substantial majority of workers, is set at below forty hours—thirty-five hours in France, and between thirty-seven and thirty-nine hours in the other countries (see figure 11.2). In the United Kingdom, an outlier among EU countries, there is no statutory normal workweek[2] and, while collective agreements, on average, set the week at about thirty-seven hours, only a third of the British labor force is covered.

The United States sets normal weekly hours, via legislation, at forty hours, which is above the standard typical in most EU countries—and a full five hours per week above the French standard. In the United States, any effects associated with the comparatively long standard week are compounded by the limited reach of the Fair Labor Standards Act (FLSA). The FLSA excludes many workers, including managers and supervisors and those over specified earnings limits, from its requirement that

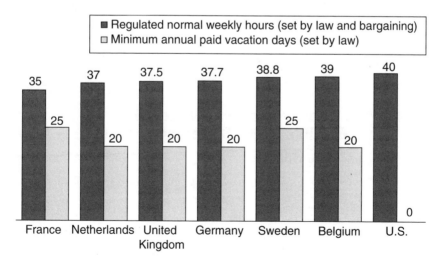

FIGURE 11.2. Working time regulations: Institutionalizing hours worked per week and days worked per year, early 2000s (Gornick and Meyers 2003)

overtime is paid after forty hours of weekly work; approximately 27 percent of full-time workers in the United States are exempt.

Days Worked per Year: Granting Paid Days Off

In addition to setting weekly hours, many countries effectively set the normal number of days worked per year, meaning that working time policies define the meaning of not just full-time work, but full-year work as well. The full year is defined, in practice, by the establishment of entitlements to annual paid days off. As with normal hours, paid days off (often referred to as vacation entitlements) are embedded in diverse institutional frameworks. In these six European countries, a statutory minimum exists and collective agreements typically raise that minimum for many covered workers. In Europe, some homogeneity is again imposed by the 1993 EU Working Time Directive, which requires "that every worker is entitled to paid annual leave of at least four weeks in accordance with the conditions for entitlement to, and granting of, such leave laid down by national legislation and/or practice" (Europa 1993). As reported in figure 11.2, in practice, workers in these six EU countries are typically entitled to between twenty and twenty-five days per year of paid vacation (or, about four or five weeks). That means that full-year work corresponds to approximately forty-seven or forty-eight weeks a year.[3]

Again, workers in the United States work under substantially different rules. In the United States, national legislation is silent with respect to paid days off, and collective bargaining reaches only a small share of workers; vacation benefits are granted voluntarily by employers. Recent research, drawing on the National Compensation Survey, found that American workers with five years of service in enterprises with one hundred workers or more were entitled to, on average, about fifteen vacation days per year; workers with shorter tenures and in smaller enterprises receive substantially fewer (U.S. Department of Labor 2006); many hourly workers have no paid days off.

Raising the Quality and Availability of Part-Time/Flexible Work Schedules

Parity for Part-Time Workers

In these six European countries, other working time measures complement those that directly influence work hours and days. In all six countries, part-time workers are legally granted pay and benefit parity vis-à-vis comparable full-time workers. In addition, in all of these countries employees have some sort of legal right to shift to, or to request to shift to, a part-time and/or "flexible" work schedule.

Policies aimed at improving the quality of part-time work are widespread throughout Europe. A crucial force behind these measures is the 1997 EU Directive on Part-Time Work, which specifically extends the framework of antidiscrimination protections to part-time workers, both women and men. The official purpose of this directive was "to eliminate discrimination against part-time workers and to improve the quality of part-time work" (Europa 2004). Specifically, according to the directive, "In respect of employment conditions, part-time workers shall not be treated in a less favorable manner than comparable full-time workers solely because they work part-time unless different treatment is justified on objective grounds," and "where appropriate, the principle of *pro rata temporis* shall apply," meaning that compensation for part-time workers should be prorated.

By the early 2000s, all six of the EU countries in this study implemented the directive via some mix of legislation and collective agreements (see table 11.1, first column). The national measures address—for part-time workers—various combinations of pay equity, occupational benefits, training and promotion opportunities, and bargaining rights.

In contrast, with the exception of coverage under the national minimum wage law, the U.S. Fair Labor Standards Act is silent on part-time workers' remuneration, and other elements of American policy that affect part-time workers offer few protections. Although not generally viewed as "working time policy," regulations that govern employer benefits have important consequences for the relative quality of part-time work in the United States. Both the Employee Retirement Income Security Act (ERISA) of 1974 and the federal Internal Revenue Code set rules that give employers the right to offer different benefits to part-time and full-time workers.[4]

In the United States, this is especially consequential with regard to health insurance. Because the United States has no national health insurance program, the overwhelming majority of working-age Americans rely on employers for coverage. Importantly, a disproportionate share of part-time employees works for employers who offer no health insurance at all. One reason is that part-time workers are overrepresented among small employers, who are the least likely to offer health plans (U.S. General Accounting Office [GAO] 2001a).

Many part-time workers who work for employers that do provide coverage are excluded due to their part-time status, in accord with federal regulations that govern employee benefits. The Internal Revenue Code regulates "self-insured" health plans, referring to plans where employees and employers pay into a fund that reimburses health claims. The tax code permits self-insured employers to exclude part-time workers from health coverage, with part-time defined as thirty-five hours per week. Furthermore, self-insured employers are not permitted to discriminate on the basis of compensation levels, but they are permitted to exclude categories of workers—such as hourly workers or workers in selected job classifications—that, in practice, contain large numbers of part-time workers. Under the national tax code, employers with "fully insured" health plans (their carriers are external insurance companies) have even more leeway to treat part-time and full-time workers differently, as they face no nondiscrimination requirements at all. In practice,

Table 11.1. Measures that Improve the Quality of Part-Time Work and/or Raise the Availability of Part-Time Work or Flexible Schedules (approximately 2001–2003)

	MEASURES THAT IMPROVE THE QUALITY OF PART-TIME WORK	EXAMPLES OF MEASURES THAT GRANT PARENTS OR ALL WORKERS THE RIGHT TO WORK PART-TIME OR FLEXIBLE SCHEDULES
Belgium	EU Directive on Part-Time Work implemented in 2000.	Since 2002, private sector workers have the right to a time credit (with financial allowances available), to be used at any time throughout their entire working career. They may take time off as career interruptions or convert to half-time work – for up to a total of 1 year – without losing their employment contract or social security rights. This credit may be extended to a maximum of 5 years, by agreement. Employees also have the right for a maximum of 5 years to reduce their working hours by one-fifth; in practice, most adopt a 4-day week. A specific system exists for companies with fewer than 10 workers (which includes a requirement for the employer's consent.)
France	EU Directive on Part-Time Work implemented in 2000.	Since 2000, an employee may seek reduced hours in the form of one or more periods of leave of at least one week in order to meet family needs (e.g., school holidays). This is organized by annualizing the employee's working hours. The employer may refuse this for objective reasons associated with running the enterprise.
Germany	EU Directive on Part-Time Work implemented in 2001.	Since 2001, employers with 15+ employees must allow employees to reduce their hours (after 6 months employment), unless there are justifiable "business reasons," as determined by the courts; employees must give three months' notice. Part-time workers may request increase to full-time and should generally be given preference over other applicants unless there are compelling business reasons otherwise.

Country		
Netherlands	EU Directive on Part-Time Work implemented in 2000.	Since 2000, employers with 10+ employees must allow employees to reduce their hours (after 1 year employment), unless there are "serious business grounds" for refusing. They must have 1 year's tenure, may apply to change hours only once every 2 years, and must give 4 months' notice. Part-time workers should be allowed to increase their hours, unless the change "would create serious problems of a financial or organizational nature for the employer."
Sweden	EU Directive on Part-Time Work implemented in 2002.	Since 1978, employed parents have had the right to work reduced hours initially as a 6-hour day, but currently the up to 25% reduction may also be worked by reducing the number of days per week worked, until their child is 8 years old or has completed first grade, whichever is later. There is a limited employer right to refuse the proposed distribution of hours.
United Kingdom	EU Directive on Part-Time Work implemented in 2000.	Since 2003, employees (in enterprises of any size) have a legal right to request flexible working time, including part-time work. They must have a child under age 6 or a disabled child under age 18, 26 weeks' service, and not have made an application within the previous 12 months; the purpose of change must be to care for the child. The employer has seven different grounds on which to refuse an application and must give reasons for such a refusal. Minimal compensation is available for a refusal but only if the employer has failed to consider the request properly.
United States	The FLSA guarantees part-time workers the minimum wage, but it offers no legal protections with regard to pay equity, benefits, or job conditions.	Some unions have won the right to reduced working time on a temporary basis so that workers can take care of family needs. For example, SEIU Local 715 (service employees) won a policy under which members may reduce working time by 1%, 2%, 5%, 10%, or 20%.

Sources: See Gornick and Meyers (2003); Gornick and Heron (2006); and Hegewisch (2005).

Notes: The 1997 EU Directive on Part-Time Work calls for (a) eliminating discrimination against part-time workers and improving the quality of part-time work and (b) facilitating the development of part-time work on a voluntary basis. Several countries (e.g., France, Sweden) also allow parents to work part-time while on parental leave.

231

these latter plans include two-thirds of all American workers with employer-based insurance (Employee Benefits Research Institute [EBRI] 1998).

A parallel situation exists with respect to the regulation of private pensions. ERISA, in combination with the Internal Revenue Code, allows employers to exclude from pension plans those workers who work fewer than one thousand hours annually—which translates to about half-time work. As with health insurance, employers are also permitted to exclude entire job classifications from pension coverage, albeit subject to IRS sanctions if they are found to be unfairly sorting workers into categories. To the extent that excluded job classifications are filled by part-time workers, substantial numbers will be de facto ineligible for pension coverage.

Rights to Work Part-Time and/or Flexible Schedules

The EU Part-Time Directive also urged, but did not require, member states to eliminate obstacles that limit opportunities for part-time work and it instructed employers to "give consideration" to workers who request transfers between part-time and full-time work as their personal and family needs change (Europa 2004).

Long before the Part-Time Directive, Sweden had already set the gold standard on the right to part-time work. Since 1978 Swedish parents have had the right to work six hours a day (at prorated pay) until their children turn age eight. After the directive, other European countries added new protections. Some are focused on rights to part-time work in particular, while others address the process of working, or requesting to work, flexible hours more generally.

Within the last decade, each of these six countries has enacted some sort of measure aimed at workers who wish to work part-time or flexible work hours. To cite some examples, Germany now grants the right to work part-time to employees in enterprises with more than fifteen workers; the Netherlands enacted a similar right in enterprises of ten of more workers. A recent United Kingdom law grants employees, in enterprises of any size, the legal right to request flexible working time—including part-time work—in order to care for a child under age six or a disabled child under age eighteen. The employer has seven grounds on which to refuse an application and must give reasons for such a refusal. In addition, Belgium grants employees a number of flexible work-time rights, including the option to work 80 percent time for five years. In most cases, employers have a safety valve; they can refuse a change on business grounds, but those grounds are often subject to official review. (In contrast, U.S. federal law offers no protections aimed at employees who wish to change their work schedules. As noted in table 11.1, there is some union activity along these lines underway in the United States. Of course, the reach of unions remains limited regarding flexible scheduling, as it does with all working time measures.)

Hegewisch (2005) analyzed the British, German, and Dutch "flexible working rights" law in detail. She drew a number of policy lessons based on these three so-called light touch laws. Among them, she concluded that despite worries to the contrary, "the floodgates did not open" (meaning, the volume of requests has been manageable); that most employers received at least one request for a schedule change but very few received more than five; that the large majority of requests were acceptable to employers; that the implementation costs were minimal; and that few requests have ended up in court. Hegewisch closes with a strong recommendation for measures along these lines, concluding that "a legislative framework which recognizes both the individual and the business case can make an important contribution to creating a new organization of work which is both more balanced and more productive" (4).

However, a later review of these laws by Hegewisch and her colleagues highlighted some of the weaknesses of these measures, especially in the United Kingdom. In their 2006 assessment, Fagan, Hegewisch, and Pillinger (2006) are particularly critical of the British approach. First, they fault the United Kingdom law for restricting access to workers with caregiving responsibilities, because that restriction fails to support workers seeking either phased retirement or lifelong learning; the Dutch and German laws cover a broader cross-section of workers. Furthermore, Fagan, Hegewisch, and Pillinger conclude that, in practice, workers in the Netherlands and in Germany have more options for securing flexible working time arrangements, in part because workers in the United Kingdom lack sufficient rights to challenge employers' business reasons for refusing their requests. Clearly, these new "flexible working rights" laws remain works in progress, and future evaluations will be invaluable for identifying their full impact.

Finally, in addition to the laws reported in table 11.1, which apply to either all workers or to caregivers, some European countries have enacted measures specifically for older workers. These measures are part of a larger effort in Europe that aims to encourage older persons to remain in the labor force later in life. This policy shift, an explicit reversal of previous early-retirement policies, has been motivated largely by the looming demographic crisis and its anticipated effect on social insurance financing. To that end, a number of countries have enacted laws that encourage older workers' access to part-time work and/or to flexible scheduling. Some have implemented explicit rights allowing older workers to reduce their hours (or to request to do so) so that they can retire in phases; partial-pension policies generally accompany these rights to work part-time. McCann (2004) reviews these policies, offering Austria, Finland, and Spain as examples, and reports that eligible older workers typically receive an income that consists of wages for the hours that they work, in combination with some pension income. Permissible hours reductions usually fall in the range of 25 to 75 percent.

McCann (2004) also reflects on this "worker choice legislation" more generally, and concludes that "although the outcomes of the enactment of this kind of legislation are not yet clear, it may have the potential to advance gender equality by allowing for shorter hours to become more widely available" (23). She observes that, in the past, women who wished to work part-time have typically been forced to change jobs, often incurring substantial penalties with respect to their wages and career opportunities. These laws, if successful, will enable more women to shift their hours while remaining in their current jobs, thereby making part-time work available across a wider range of jobs and occupations and, in general, reducing the penalties associated with working part-time. Extending these measures to men, she argues, challenges traditional assumptions about gender differences in working patterns; as such, these measures raise the likelihood that men will engage in various forms of reduced-hour or flexible scheduling.

Providing Paid Family Leave

Although limited work hours, part-time parity, and the laws that govern requests for work-hour changes could clearly benefit many workers—including workers at various ages and with diverse caregiving needs—some employees need to take temporary but sustained breaks from employment. This is often the case following the birth or the adoption of a child. The opportunity to take a temporary leave, with both job protection and at least some wage replacement, is a key element in the landscape of working-time-related policies in Europe. Although there are other types of paid family leaves in place in various countries (e.g., to care for older sick children or for elderly dependents), this section focuses on leaves designed specifically for new parents.

Paid family leaves schemes are complicated, as there is enormous variation in eligibility and benefit structures—even the boundaries of what constitutes paid family leave are contested—and thus it is a challenge to compare them meaningfully. In order to maximize comparability across countries, the generosity of paid family leave is measured here in a particular way: as the maximum number of "fully paid" weeks of leave available to new mothers, should they choose to take all of the leave that is available to them.[5] That includes maternity leave as well as portions of parental leave that they can draw.[6]

Across these six countries, the generosity of family leave policies varies markedly. As reported in figure 11.3, there is substantial variation in the total number of weeks of full-time wage replacement available to new mothers. The most generous paid family leave policies are found in Sweden, where mothers have access to about forty-two weeks of full-time wage replacement. The continental countries included here (the Netherlands, France, Germany, and Belgium) provide twelve to sixteen weeks of fully paid leave.[7] Provisions in the United Kingdom are less generous,[8] and the United States stands out as the exceptional case, as it is alone among these seven countries (and one of only five countries in the world) with no national policy of paid maternity leave.

It is important to note that, in addition to benefit generosity, there is much cross-national diversity in the extent to which paid leave policy features are gender

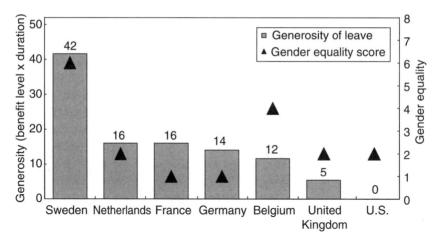

FIGURE 11.3. Paid family leave: Fully paid weeks available to mothers and scores on gender equality scale, early 2000s (Gornick and Meyers 2003)

egalitarian. Countries vary vis-à-vis the generosity of provisions extended to fathers and the extent to which policy designs encourage fathers to take the leave to which they are entitled. In figure 11.3 (see the triangles), these seven systems are compared on this second dimension. Note that each country is scored on a six-point "gender equality scale." The logic of this scale derives from empirical research findings that indicate that male take-up is encouraged by nontransferable rights (meaning rights that cannot be transferred to female partners), combined with high wage replacement. Countries are assigned one point on this gender-equality scale if they offer any paid paternity leave, two points if fathers have parental leave rights that are nontransferable, and up to three additional points capturing the level of wage replacement (three points if benefits are wage-related and at 80 percent or higher, two points if benefits are wage-related but at less than 80 percent, and one point if benefits are paid but at a flat rate).[9]

Figure 11.3 reveals that these are, indeed, two distinct dimensions. That said, Sweden clearly stands out as having both the most generous and the most gender-egalitarian design. The four continental European countries, with less extensive benefits, offer incentives for fathers that are comparatively weak. Belgium and the Netherlands are partial exceptions, in that they alone (at the time point of this comparison) offer fathers a short period of paid paternity leave, as well some leave rights that cannot be transferred to their partners.[10]

In the United States, in addition to the absence of national-level paid family leave benefits, gender-egalitarian provisions in the laws are also weak. Fathers in the United States have some incentives to use the unpaid leave granted to them through national law (the Family and Medical Leave Act), in that their entitlements, if not used, are lost to their families. At the same time, the absence of wage replacement constitutes a serious disincentive to male take-up.

"Double Whammy": The Regressive Distribution of Employer Provisions

As reported in the previous sections, a number of worker supports that are publicly provided in Europe are, for the most, absent from the law in the United States. U.S. federal law provides workers with no minimum number of paid vacation days each year, no paid family leave, and no right to change (or to request to change) their work schedules.

Many of these provisions, of course, are granted to American workers through their employers. They may be offered as part of a standard employee benefit package, and/or they may be negotiated on a case-by-case basis. Leaving these provisions to the marketplace means that, on average, fewer American workers have access to them. But there is another crucial repercussion of leaving these benefits to the marketplace: their distribution is highly regressive, in that higher-skilled, higher-income workers are much more likely to have access to these kinds of benefits and protections than are less advantaged workers. There are multiple reasons underlying that distributional result. One is that more highly skilled workers are more expensive to replace, so employers offer various types of leave and flexibility in order to retain them. In general, more highly skilled workers also have more bargaining power vis-à-vis their employers.

Several recent studies have revealed the extremely regressive distribution of workplace benefits. For starters, after a one-year length of service, private sector workers earning less than $15 an hour are granted, on average, 7.7 paid vacation days per year, compared to 10.3 for higher earners. Similarly, workers in blue-collar occupations are entitled to 7.1 days per year on average, compared to 10.2 days for those in white-collar occupations (U.S. Department of Labor 2006).

Paid leave is also unevenly available. The share of working parents with access to *any* paid leave is less than 46 percent for those with poverty-level income but over 83 percent for those with incomes at or above 200 percent of the poverty threshold (Ross Phillips 2004). Similarly, Waldfogel (2006) reports that only 36 percent of service workers have any paid sick leave, compared to three-quarters of white-collar workers. Low-income workers are also much less likely than their higher-earning counterparts to have access to flexible job schedules, and/or to have control over their starting and quitting times (Williams 2006; see Levin-Epstein 2006 for a review of recent research).

Clearly, the absence of government provision of these crucial supports for working families leads to lower levels of support for workers, on average. But perhaps the more worrisome outcome is not the lower level, on average, but the regressive nature of the distribution of these benefits. Lack of access to annual paid days off and, even more so, to periods of paid leave and to scheduling flexibility leaves many low-income workers in a time crunch. It also renders them unable to respond to family emergencies and other unexpected needs; the inevitable conflicts that arise make low-income workers especially vulnerable to loss of job quality and to job loss altogether.

Intended and Unintended Consequences

Many of the advantageous effects that these policies could offer workers, their families, and their employers, have been well documented. This package of supportive policies would be likely to reduce actual work hours, narrow the compensation gap between part-time and full-time workers, raise the likelihood that workers would apply for schedule changes that better match their needs, reduce employee turnover, raise women's employment rates, and increase the amount of time that parents have to spend with their young children.

Several empirical studies assess the effects of normal-hour thresholds, and find evidence that lowering institutionally established thresholds reduces actual working time among employees (see Gornick and Meyers 2003; OECD 1998 for reviews). A number of studies have estimated the magnitude of the effect of reducing regulated standard hours on actual hours worked. Estimates of the magnitude of this effect range from about 75 percent to nearly 100 percent of the change in standard work hours. Researchers have reported the effect on actual hours to be about 77 percent in the United Kingdom; 85 to 100 percent in Germany; and close to 100 percent in France (see Gornick and Meyers 2003 for a review of this research). Although maximum hours have received less attention in empirical research, they too seem to have a strong effect on actual hours worked. Grubb and Wells (1993), for example, assessed the effects of restrictions on overtime hours. They found that, across Europe, maximum limits on annual overtime hours, which ranged from under one hundred to over five hundred hours per year, were a strong negative predictor of the observed frequency of overtime work. For an overview of the effects of working time regulations, see Rubery, Smith, and Fagan (1998). Drawing on variation in statutory and bargained normal hours across Europe, they concluded that "national working time regulations can be seen to have a major impact on usual working time" (75).

In addition, the limited evidence that exists also indicates that the generosity of vacation entitlements has a strong effect on the days per year actually worked. Like European workers, American workers take up their rights at relatively high levels; one study found that about 70 percent of employed Americans take all of their allocated vacation days (Expedia 2004). A recent cross-national study (Altonji and Oldham 2003) found that one additional week of legislated paid vacation translates to about thirty-five fewer hours worked per year.

The effects of part-time legislation on part-time work rates and/or part-time workers' remuneration are not well known, in part because the EU Part-Time Directive and the national measures that followed were implemented only recently; several outcome evaluations are under way. There are correlational findings that link regulation to the availability or quality of part-time work: for example, more protective regulations are seen in countries with larger part-time labor markets and smaller pay penalties. One recent study finds that part-time/full-time wage differentials in Germany, the United Kingdom, and especially in Sweden are substantially smaller than those reported in the United States, where part-time workers' compensation is not protected by law (Bardasi and Gornick 2003).

Like the new part-time parity laws, most of the European "flexible working rights" laws have been enacted too recently for comprehensive evaluation. However, a growing body of empirical research has evaluated the effects of flexible work arrangements more generally. Studies have found that having access to flexible work options can increase workers' well-being, by increasing their job satisfaction, reducing stress, and decreasing commuting time (Casey 2006; Levin-Epstein 2006).[11] Accumulating evidence also points to beneficial effects for employers, in the form of employee retention and reduced turnover costs (Levin-Epstein 2006); increased employee satisfaction, engagement, and commitment; and expanded opportunities for recruitment (Corporate Voices 2005).

Finally, a large body of empirical research assesses the impact of family leave policy, primarily on mothers' employment patterns. The evidence indicates that access to leave has the potential to reduce labor market inequalities between men and women by facilitating continuous employment and reducing wage penalties associated with motherhood (Glass and Riley 1998; Hofferth 1996; Joesch 1997; OECD 2001; Smith, Downs, and O'Cornell 2001). Other research suggests that access to family leave may have health benefits for children, especially in the form of reduced infant mortality (Ruhm 2000; Winegarden and Bracy 1995). Evidence that very young children do better on other dimensions when a parent is at home is less consistent, although the most recent research suggests that high levels of parental employment during the first year of life are associated with worse outcomes for at least some groups of children, and that these effects persist well into grade school (see, e.g., Meyers et al. 2004).

What about Unintended Consequences?

At the same time, a number of concerns have been raised, in academic literatures and in the popular media, about the possibility of unintended consequences. One concern is that the reduction in work hours is being achieved at the cost of more nonstandard and less controllable and/or predictable work scheduling. Second, some argue that efforts to strengthen reduced-hour work inevitably create new forms of gender inequality, because it is women, overwhelmingly, who will choose shorter-hour work. A third concern, frequently voiced in the United States, is that labor protections (regarding working hours) and strong generous social policies (such as paid family leave) may damage the macroeconomy.[12]

INCREASING NONSTANDARD SCHEDULES

Many scholars of working time policies have raised the possibility that efforts to reduce work hours may have some problematic consequences, especially for workers and their families. In recent years, while several European countries have implemented reductions in total work hours, a number of these countries have ushered in new practices that increase *employers'* options to schedule workers "flexibly"—which, in practice, often means during nonstandard hours. These new practices are on the rise largely because an increasing number of European employers are operating under various "annualized hours" (AH) schemes. AH schemes allow employers to average workers' hours over periods of time ("reference periods") longer than a week—and, in some cases, up to a year (hence the terminology). AH schemes, of course, enable employers to fit workers' schedules to production or commercial needs, and the result is that more workers are scheduled during nonstandard hours (including during evenings, nights, and weekends) and/or assigned hours that rise and fall weekly, monthly, or seasonally. AH schemes also allow employers to pay less (or no) overtime, as overtime thresholds may not be set weekly, but for the reference period as a whole.

Some of the momentum underlying AH schemes, which expanded in the 1990s, came from the EU itself. The 1993 Working Time Directive explicitly allows working hours up to the forty-eight-hour weekly maximum to be calculated over a four-month period, which can be extended up to twelve months by collective agreement. Furthermore, the directive implicitly allows member countries to establish reference periods of longer than a week for normal and/or overtime hours as well. In most countries, AH schemes are mainly designed at the bargaining table, and they vary widely across and within countries. Although AH arrangements are usually favored by employers, employees' representatives typically agree to them—or even initiate them—in exchange for some compensatory benefit, most often, a reduction in total work hours (Kouzis and Kretsos 2003). Thus, in practice, legions of European workers may have gained shorter hours at the cost of more nonstandard work scheduling and, in many cases, reduced control and predictability.[13]

For workers with family care responsibilities, even with reduced total hours, having a nonstandard, uncontrollable, and/or unpredictable schedule can make reconciling work and family responsibilities difficult. In a groundbreaking study, Fagnani and Letablier (2004) report findings from a survey that queried French parents with young children about the impact of the thirty-five-hour law on their ability to balance work and family. The French case is a significant one—with implications for other countries—because annualization schemes, set at the sectoral or company level, are widespread and reference periods of twelve months are not uncommon.

Fully 58 percent of French parents report that the thirty-five-hour law has made family care easier for them, a finding that underscores the importance of working time reductions for employed parents. However, that figure is substantially lower among workers who have nonstandard-hour schedules (i.e., evenings, nights, weekends), those whose hours are imposed on them (rather than chosen by the worker or negotiated with the employer), and those whose employers do not respect notification periods in relation to working patterns (Fagnani and Letablier 2004). A recent OECD study concurs. OECD researchers used data from the Third European Working Conditions Survey, pooled across nineteen countries, to assess factors that affect workers' ratings of their "degree of conflict between working life and family life." Not surprisingly, work-family conflict is higher among those with longer total work hours. However, controlling for total hours worked, conflict is also significantly higher when daily hours vary, workdays per week vary, starting and finishing times vary, schedules change with no notice or with only a day of notice, or when workers have little control over their working hours (OECD 2004).[14] Fagnani and Letablier (2004) sum up: "Taking into account the extreme heterogeneity of workplaces, it is not sufficient to mechanically reduce working time for there to be an improvement in the daily lives of working parents" (568). The scheduling of hours, as well as the processes governing that scheduling, matter a great deal.

Annualization schemes are widespread in several European countries and further extensions are proposed at the EU level and in a number of member countries as well. If annualization schemes gain strength in Europe and elsewhere, the potential gains for workers of winning shorter hours are likely to be seriously compromised. Protective mechanisms for workers (such as enforceable minimum notification periods and/or time-bank agreements that divide control over scheduling between employers and workers) will be crucial, or the advantages of shorter work hours may be more than offset by increasingly problematic scheduling practices. Where consumers' or employers' demand for "24/7" operation is especially strong, it may be impossible to control the growth of nonstandard-hour work, in which case other policy responses may be needed to help workers cope. The "flexible working rights" laws themselves may be one important ingredient in a protective policy package.

GENDER INEQUALITY

Strengthening reduced-hour work also raises thorny questions about gender equality. If shorter full-time hours and more available part-time hours are taken up disproportionately by women, more parental caregiving time may become available, but gender equality in time spent in paid work will worsen. It remains an open question, with respect to shorter-hour work (and parental leave as well), as to whether men will eventually take advantage of these options as often as women.[15]

Part of the logic of improving the quality of part-time work, of course, is to draw more men into it. And, in fact, men's engagement in part-time work increased in the 1990s in a number of European countries, including Belgium, France, Germany, and the Netherlands (European Foundation 2004). Recent survey results indicate that the substantial majority of male part-time workers, like their female counter-parts, are voluntarily working part-time, which suggests that the new rights-to-part-time-work may be a factor underlying this increase. Nevertheless, part-time work remains overwhelmingly feminized in most industrialized countries. A coun-tervailing view argues that even if part-time work remains feminized, it still has some gender-equalizing potential, in that establishing viable part-time work op-tions also draws some women into paid work who would otherwise refrain from employment altogether (Bardasi and Gornick 2003). It is possible that improving the availability of quality part-time work may, in general, have the effect of reducing gender gaps in employment rates, while increasing gender gaps in hours worked among the employed. In the end, this is an empirical question and one that calls for continuing study.

From a gender equality perspective, some working time scholars have concluded that reducing full-time weekly hours may be a more promising strategy than shor-ing up part-time work; see, for example, Jacobs and Gerson (2004). Mutari and Figart (2001) make this argument persuasively: "The alternative to policies that ac-commodate work hours to the gendered division of labor are policies that change the male model of full-time employment. Reductions in the standard workweek are a long-term solution for achieving gender equity in the labor market and the re-distribution of domestic labor.... A shorter work can enable both men and women to participate in the labor market on an equal basis" (40–41). In fact, this view—that shortening the full-time week is a gender parity strategy—seems to be gaining ground in a number of European countries. Fagnani and Letablier (2004) observe that in France, where part-time work has always been viewed with skepticism, the French thirty-five-hour law "had the [explicit] objective... of improving equality between men and women." The effects of reducing normal weekly hours on gen-dered distributions of labor also call for further study.

EFFECTS ON MACROECONOMIC OUTCOMES

It is also widely argued, especially in the United States, that generous social policies are harmful to the macroeconomy. Is that a reasonable worry? Is there a larger price to be paid for the benefits that families are likely to reap? Throughout the 1980s and much of the 1990s, unemployment rates across Europe were much higher than those in the United States; some European countries experienced persistent double-digit unemployment rates. Many American scholars, political actors, and journalists make the argument that policy ideas should not be imported from Eu-rope because these social policies and labor market regulations have actually *caused* Europe's unemployment woes. As the argument goes, high social insurance taxes raise labor costs, which lower the demand for labor; demand is further depressed by labor market regulations that, for example, restrict employers' options with regard to employee schedules.

The claim that generous social welfare provisions weaken the economy has been aimed broadly at everything from old-age pensions to unemployment insurance to work-family programs. A sober read of the evidence provides little support, however, for the conclusion that Europe's unemployment problems are explained by social policy. In a *Journal of Economic Perspectives* literature review, Nickell (1997) concluded that some welfare state features do seem to drive up unemployment rates—in particular, unemployment benefits with extremely long durations, coupled with weak active labor market policies. But other welfare state and labor market features—such as high payroll taxes, high overall taxes, high wage replacement rates, high unionization, and strict employment protection legislation—have been no less common in high-employment than in low-employment countries.

More concretely, the argument that European-style social policies and labor market regulations are incompatible with strong economic performance has been dramatically weakened by recent recoveries in most of the European economies. This conclusion is underscored by evidence from these six countries. In 2002, the end of the period to which these policy data pertain, all six of these comparison countries reported single-digit unemployment rates. While the rates in France and Belgium were clearly at worrisome levels (7–9%), the unemployment rate in Sweden was 4 percent (below the U.S. rate at that time). The case for a tight link between labor market regulations (in particular, protections for workers) and high unemployment is simply not persuasive.

It is also crucial to note that the recent economic recoveries in Europe have been achieved without major reversals in public spending on social policy. Labor market deregulation and welfare state restructuring have been prominent issues on political agendas across Europe in recent decades. Several European countries have substantially loosened labor market regulations, and some social programs have been scaled back in some countries. Restructuring has been most common in old-age pensions, due to worries about rapidly rising dependency ratios, and in programs that economists identified as harmful to (male) labor supply, including long-term unemployment compensation and disability benefits. Although important, these adjustments were relatively modest and did little to weaken the basic structures of social provision (Gornick 2007; Gornick and Meyers 2001). Restructuring of the European welfare states has been, contrary to many popular accounts, quite modest in general. And in the midst of these changes, one of the key policies focused on here—paid family leave for both women and men—was singled out for protection and expansion in nearly every European country. Since the mid-1980s, average public spending on cash transfers to families (per child) have increased sharply in nearly every European country. Bolstered by decision making at the EU level, provisions for family leave have been expanded in several countries, and entirely new programs introduced in others. All in all, the European experience provides encouraging evidence that these family leave policies are economically feasible, even in fiscal hard times.

And what about the macroeconomic consequences of reducing working hours? A parallel line of criticism has focused on the shorter work hours that are now standard in these six comparison countries and elsewhere in Europe. Some critics on both sides of the Atlantic, in fact, point to the United States as the superior model. As the argument goes, Americans' long work hours may produce strains for many workers and their families, but Americans, largely as a result of their work hours, enjoy a higher standard of living. Indeed, the United States ranks third among the thirty OECD countries in per capita income (after Luxembourg and Norway), using purchasing-power-adjusted exchange rates. There is no question that all six of these comparison countries lag behind the United States in per capita income.

Does that mean that, on average, Americans, with their longer hours, enjoy a relatively higher standard of living? Some scholars argue that it is misleading to measure "standard of living" solely in monetary terms, without taking into account time investments. As Osberg (2002), a Canadian economist, has argued persuasively: " 'Quality of life' or 'economic well-being' may be hard to define precisely, but most would agree that they depend on both an individual's income level and the discretionary time they have in which to enjoy it" (22).

So, American workers, on average, do take home high incomes compared to workers elsewhere, but for many American workers and their families, that economic payoff is compromised by the family time-poverty that enables it. It is also the case that Americans work such long hours that they may be on the diminishing-returns portion of the productivity curve. Although the United States leads the world in gross domestic product per worker, it is ranked eighth among the OECD countries in GDP per worker hour. And, in fact, per-hour output in the United States is only average, relative to these and other comparison countries with shorter work hours. It may be that American workers could shift some hours from work to family and see a rise in hourly output.

Reflections on the American Context

Americans today are working longer hours, with many fewer institutionalized working time protections, than are their counterparts in a number of European countries. Workers in the United States have access to fewer measures that limit their working time and they work with virtually no protections related to the compensation of part-time work, the right to formally request a change to their work hours, or the right to take temporary paid family leave to care for their family members.

Why is the policy landscape in the United States so different relative to many European countries? The lack of public policy in this area is, of course, consistent with lower levels of social protection in the United States more generally. A large and longstanding academic literature has explored the causes of so-called American social policy exceptionalism. Some scholars locate its roots in institutional factors that have limited the development of labor parties and unions; others stress aspects of American political culture that have long privileged reliance on the market, rather than the state, to distribute resources—and many scholars have identified interactions between the two. Recent lines of scholarship explain the durability of existing social policy configurations through policy feedbacks; that is, policies are understood to shape political outcomes, which in turn can make policy change all the more unlikely.

At the same time, while American social policy overall is relatively more limited, arguably something more specific is operating here. Across some policy arenas, such as retirement, disability, and unemployment benefits, American social policies actually resemble policy provisions in other rich countries. But in the area of work-family reconciliation policies—paid family leave, childcare, the regulation of working time—the United States is extremely exceptional (Gornick and Meyers 2003).

Why is work-family policy so remarkably limited in the United States? Although a full analysis of the causes is outside the scope of this chapter, several factors merit mentioning. First, the so-called mommy wars (the public debates about the consequences of maternal employment) are especially intense and polarized in the United States, fueled further by American religious conservatives who believe that (middle-class and affluent) mothers should largely refrain from employment when their children are young. Divisions on these issues pervade even progressive policy advocacy communities, creating barriers for successful policy movements. Second, it is often observed that American political culture valorizes hard work and devalues leisure, relative to many European societies; policies aimed at shortening paid work hours are often viewed with ambivalence in the United States. Third, in many European countries, concerns about low aggregate fertility have led to work-family policy expansions, both in earlier decades and in the contemporary period; low fertility, overall, has not yet become a prominent issue in the United States, eliminating one powerful contextual factor. Fourth, although business associations in many European countries often protest protections for workers that are required by law, the power of business in policymaking is somewhat blunted, relative to the United States, in part due to limits on the flow of private moneys into the political process. And, finally, it has been widely documented that, unfortunately, Americans lack awareness about the successful operation of diverse work-family policies in so many other high-income countries.

Before American policy actors will move toward implementing substantial working time protections—and other work-family reconciliation supports—Americans will need to build a new social consensus on the need for governmental support for workers. What would enable such a consensus? For starters, many Americans would have to adopt a dramatically altered discourse about the role of government more generally in shaping social and economic outcomes. Second, Americans would need a new interpretation of "family values," one that recognizes the damaging consequences for American workers and their families of time poverty and inflexible employment. Finally, policy advocates would have to alert more Americans to the extreme exceptionalism of current policy offerings in the United States relative to the other high-income countries of the world.

12

PARENTS' EXPERIENCES OF FLEXIBLE WORK ARRANGEMENTS IN CHANGING EUROPEAN WORKPLACES

Suzan Lewis and Laura den Dulk

It is widely acknowledged that parents need flexibility to manage work and family boundaries. However, the impact of flexible working arrangements on employees with family responsibilities depends on many layers of context. Nevertheless, much of the research on flexible work arrangements either focuses on organizational policies and support and relatively neglects wider societal and economic context (S. Lewis 1997; Swody and Powell 2007; Van Dyne, Kossek, and Lobel 2007), or focuses on social policies to support working parents and neglects the workplace context (e.g., den Dulk, Peper, and Van Doorne-Huiskes 2005; Gornick and Meyers 2003).

This chapter will discuss some findings from a cross-national European study that explored the ways in which employed parents with young children experience flexible working arrangements, in a range of national and workplace contexts. The project, *Gender, Parenthood and the Changing European Workplace* (short name *Transitions*),[1] set out to examine how young European men and women negotiate motherhood and fatherhood and work-family boundaries in workplaces that are undergoing substantial changes in the context of different national welfare state regimes and employer supports. The countries included were Norway, Sweden, Portugal, France, the Netherlands, the United Kingdom, and two postcommunist countries, Bulgaria and Slovenia. This wider study examines the ways in which pressures associated with the global economy were played out in diverse contexts. Would certain national policies and workplace policies and practices support and protect working parents more than others? Or would the effects of globalization on working practices override the impact of diverse contexts leading to more homogeneity of experiences? This chapter focuses more specifically on the ways in which flexible work arrangements are experienced by working parents in diverse national contexts and changing organizational settings.

Background

The work-family field of research developed from a realization that the public and private spheres, traditionally considered to be separate and gendered domains, are in fact related and interdependent. This is now widely accepted, although the nature of the interrelationships remains a topic of research and debate. However, while increasingly sophisticated models of work-family connections, work-family conflict, enrichment, and facilitation have been developed (Carlson and Grzywacz 2008; Demerouti and Geurts 2004), less attention has been paid to the complex interrelationships between various aspects of home and work domains, and the multiple layers of context within which they operate. Cross-cultural studies of work-family conflict begin to address this (Aycan 2008), but cultural factors are only a part of wider social contexts. Moreover, the study of cross-national differences in work-family conflict, although important, captures only a limited range of impacts of contextual factors. To advance the understanding of the complexity of work and family systems and the wider systems within which they operate, a shift to systems-level thinking is necessary (Carlson and Grzywacz 2008). Carlson and Grzywacz argue that systems-level thinking is critical to adequately represent the complexity of both the work and family domain and the interrelationship between the domains. It is also crucial to look beyond work and family systems to the interrelationships between work, family, and wider social systems. Change in one layer of context affects and is affected by other layers of context. For example, change in social policy on parental leave requires changes at workplace levels, and lack of related workplace changes can be a barrier to the effectiveness of public policies (Haas, Allard, and Hwang 2002).

Systems thinking, with its emphasis on the interaction between mutual and dynamic influences of multiple social systems, provides a useful framework for examining the implementation and take-up of initiatives on flexible working arrangements and other supports for employees with family or other personal life commitments. It acknowledges that such flexible working initiatives are situated within multiple layers of context (including workplace context) especially the working practices, structures, and cultures of specific organizations as they adapt to changing conditions and demands. Aspects of wider social contexts are also significant, including public policies, economic factors, and national cultures, norms, and expectations. More broadly still, the global context is vital to an understanding of flexible working arrangements and their consequences, through its influence on local workplace change. This chapter also discusses different layers of context relevant to working parents' experiences of flexibility to manage work and family boundaries, to reveal various models of workplace flexibility.

At the cultural or normative layer, parents combine work and family in contexts where there are diverse values and social constructions of motherhood, fatherhood, and parenthood (Gambles, Lewis, and Rapoport 2006; Lewis 1991). Overall, European countries have witnessed the gradual unraveling of the male breadwinner model into dual-earner societies, although the nature and rate of change is uneven both across and within countries (Crompton, Lewis, and Lyonette 2007). For example, there are different models of combining work and family life; in some countries two full-timers are the norm, while in others the one-and-a-half earner model is more common (ibid.; Fagnani, Houriet-Ségard, and Bédouin 2004).

Cultural values feed into or reflect social policy. At the EU level, a number of initiatives have been implemented to ensure a minimal level of support for the reconciliation of paid work and family in member states. These include regulations on working time, parental leaves, and equal rights for full- and part-time workers (den Dulk and Van Doorne-Huiskes 2007). At the national level, diverse gendered norms and values are reflected in different welfare states' regimes in Europe, and particularly in the nature and extent of public work family provisions (den Dulk, van Doorne-Huiskes, and Schippers 1999; J. Lewis 1997; see table 12.1).

As table 12.1 shows, there are substantial supports for working parents in Norway and also in the postcommunist countries, Bulgaria and Slovenia, although provisions in the latter countries are declining in the transition to the market economy. Moreover, the transition has been associated with the demise of the "working mother" contract (Metcalfe and Afanassieva 2005). Public provisions to support working families in the Netherlands, Portugal, and the United Kingdom were introduced more recently, and are less widely developed. Some countries focus on long leaves, and therefore have less need for early childcare. Moreover, level and affordability of childcare provisions vary across states (EU Expert Group 2005).

National governments in Europe have also recently turned their attention to opportunities for flexible working, with policy developments focusing, in some cases, on all employees and in others specifically on working parents (EU Expert Group 2005). However, employers often have much discretionary space concerning whether and how working parents can apply flexible work options (S. Lewis 1997, 2001; Powell and Maneiro 1999). The reduction of working hours is more common in Norway, the United Kingdom, and the Netherlands than in the two postcommunist countries and Portugal. Bulgaria lacks a law on the reduction of working hours, while in Slovenia the provision is restricted to parents with children under three years of age (EU Expert Group 2005). In the Netherlands in particular, part-time work by women is widely accepted and women often view this as a satisfactory solution for managing work and family life, even though they are aware of the career costs, illustrating the crucial interrelationships between cultural

Table 12.1. National Policies on Leave Arrangements, Childcare Provision, and Policies on Flexible Working, 2004

COUNTRY	MATERNITY LEAVE	PATERNITY LEAVE	PARENTAL LEAVE	LEAVE TO CARE FOR SICK CHILD	PERCENTAGE OF CHILDREN IN FORMAL CHILDCARE 0–2YRS	FLEXIBILITY
Norway	6 weeks of parental leave	10 days, unpaid leave	42/52 weeks, paid at 80% or 100% of earnings	10–15 days per year paid	40% (1997 data) or cash for home care	Right for parents of young children to request reduced hours Time account scheme
Slovenia	105 days, fully paid	90 days, 15 days fully paid, 75 days minimum income	260 days, fully paid		Over 40% of 1–3 years old (2002–03)	Right for parents of young children to request reduced hours
Bulgaria	19.3 weeks, paid at 90% of earnings	None	33 months, flat rate payment for 21 months, unpaid for 12 months	60 days at full pay until child is 3 and reduced pay when child is older	Circa 10% of 1–3 years old	None
Portugal	120 days, fully paid	5 days, fully paid	6 months unpaid leave	30 days unpaid	22% (2002)	Right for parents of young children to request reduced hours or to have flexible working hours
United Kingdom	26–52 weeks (depending on employment history) of which 6 weeks paid at 90% of earnings, 20 weeks flat rate	2 weeks, paid at flat rate	13 weeks unpaid leave, in blocks of maximum of 4 weeks	28 days per year (unpaid)	26% (2003)	Right to request flexible work for parents of young children. Flexible work includes a change in working hours, days, or place of work.
Netherlands	16 weeks fully paid	2 days	13 weeks unpaid leave	10 days at 70% pay	17% (1997)	Right to reduce or extend working hours for all workers

Sources: Fagnani et al. (2004); Immervol and Barber (2005); EU Expert Group (2005).

and policy systems (Gambles, Lewis, and Rapoport 2006; Portegijs, Hermans, and Lalta 2006).

Statutory entitlements also interact with voluntary workplace provisions for flexible working, which will be discussed later. However, most research shows that there is an implementation gap between policies (whether state or workplace) and practice. For example, while flexible work options are in place, few may take the opportunities available (Gambles, Lewis, and Rapoport 2006; Haas, Allard, and Hwang 2002; Sutton and Noe 2005). This gap can be at least partly explained by economic and labor market conditions, workplace culture and change, and gendered sense of entitlement.

National policies interact with economic factors and labor market conditions. For example, part-time work would not be an option, even if it were available, in low-wage economies where families need two full-time incomes. In more affluent countries, many families can afford one partner being employed part-time. In post-communist countries, the transition to a market economy has been accompanied by new experiences of job insecurity and unemployment that limit the utilization of work-family provisions (Kovatcheva 2000).

National policy and company policies to support work and family must be implemented at the workplace. There is now much evidence that implementation and experiences of these provisions depend on workplace cultures and supports (Andreassi and Thompson 2008). Despite a growing body of research on the development and implementation of work-family policies, however, there has been much less attention to the impact of other trends and practices in organizations as they change in response to global competition and technological advances, which put growing pressure on working time and effort. Continuous change is a reality in contemporary organizations (Bauman 1998; Gambles, Lewis, and Rapoport 2006; Sennett 1998), and is likely to interact with other layers of context within which parents manage the boundaries between work and family life.

Experiences of flexible working arrangements are also influenced by sense of entitlement, an individual set of beliefs constructed within specific social contexts (Lewis and Smithson 2001). Sense of entitlement, a concept developed from social justice theory, is theorized as influencing the support that people feel is fair and equitable, and therefore feel entitled to expect and entitled to use (S. Lewis 1997; Lewis and Smithson 2001). The phrase, used in this way, is subjective; it is distinct from, although influenced by, formal policy entitlements, and develops on the basis of social comparison and perceptions of what is normative and feasible. For example, parents who see their peers receiving support for reconciling work and family are more likely to expect the same "choice" to take up supports offered, or to feel aggrieved if they are not supported. It is also highly gendered, with mothers more likely to feel entitled to take up work-family supports, though not necessary to career advancement, and men less often feeling entitled to work-family support, even in countries that encourage fathers to be actively involved in fatherhood (Lewis and

Smithson 2001). Most research on experiences of flexible working arrangements tends to neglect the impact of interacting social systems. The objective of this study, therefore, is to examine parents' experiences of flexible working arrangements, taking into account various interrelated layers of context.

The Transitions Study: Methodology

To examine parents' experiences of flexible working arrangements in diverse contexts, this project uses data from case studies of private sector organizations in six European national settings. These studies were carried out as one phase of a larger cross-national research project.[2] The six European states were selected purposively to provide a range of policy, economic, and cultural contexts. A cross-national team carried out the research project with partners in each participating country.[3] This collaborative model of cross-national comparative research has many advantages over single researchers working cross-nationally. Researchers bring their own native knowledge of national contexts and languages to all stages of the research, although they must also question aspects of these contexts and interrogate their own cultures. Working cross-nationally facilitates this process.

Data were collected in Peak,[4] a British insurance company; BIC, a Dutch banking and insurance company; Slofinance, a Slovenian bank; Perelik, a Bulgarian bank; PPC, a Portuguese consultancy firm; and BOC, a multinational company in Norway. All the case study organizations were undergoing substantial changes as they continued to adapt to the changing nature of work and global competition. The Bulgarian and Slovenian organizations were also undergoing massive changes as the countries made the transition to a market economy. The case studies consist of relatively large companies with relatively good working conditions compared to the national average. However, they do not represent "best practice cases" that are known for their flexible working arrangements. On the contrary, some cases, such as Perelik, the Bulgarian case, are not very advanced with respect to formal organizational policies compared to other companies in the same sector.

The case study approach was selected to gather in-depth, contextualized data on organizational processes (Yin 2003). Case studies are useful for understanding complex phenomena and processes within specific contexts and for investigating contemporary phenomena in real life contexts (ibid.; Lewis, das Dores Guerreiro, and Brannen 2006). This approach therefore provided opportunities to explore processes of organizational change; to observe the ways in which public policy and organizational policies interact at the level of everyday practice in the context of these changes; and to study how these various processes impact parents' experiences of flexible working arrangements within wider contexts.

Each case study involved an analysis of relevant organizational documents, focus groups with employed parents with young children (some employees were expecting

Table 12.2. Case Study Characteristics

	COUNTRY	INDUSTRY	NUMBER OF FOCUS GROUPS	NUMBER OF WORKING PARENTS	NUMBER OF MANAGER INTERVIEWS
Peak	U.K.	Insurance	6	24	6
BIC	Netherlands	Banking and insurance	4	32	8
BOC	Norway	Multinational	4	15	6
PPC	Portugal	Consultancy/accountancy	9	24	2
Slofinance	Slovenia	Banking	8	29	7
Perelik	Bulgaria	Banking	5	37	7

their first child), and interviews with managers at different levels. Participants were recruited via human resources managers. The manager interviews were used for context-setting—providing a management perspective on the workplace changes—while the focus group data provides an employee perspective constructed within a group context, a "public" account that provides insight into the organizational and societal culture within which employment and parenthood were experienced (Smithson 2000, 2006). Focus group protocols and interview schedules were developed collaboratively to take account of diverse national perspectives. They were translated into national languages and back-translated to ensure comparability. The focus group schedule covered a range of topics, including parents' perspectives on workplace changes, the implementation of flexible working arrangements and other aspects of workplace support, the role of managers, and critical incidents, such as when a child is ill. In the interviews, managers were also asked about workplace changes, policies and practices relating to employed parents, and how they deal with critical incidents in their own work and family lives, as well as how they manage subordinates with family responsibilities. In total, there were six case studies involving thirty-six focus groups with 161 mothers and fathers of young children (including some single parents), as well as thirty-six manager interviews (see table 12.2).

Analysis of Data

Fieldwork questions were developed to facilitate comparison within and across organizations. Given the complexity of cross-national research using multiple case studies, organizing the data analysis under clearly specified analytic themes was important. Thematic analysis of the data was undertaken by organization, using this framework, and then cross-national comparisons were carried out. One issue that arose at the analytic stage was how to deal with diverse perspectives among managers and employees. One approach is to triangulate data, looking for consistencies, to find the "correct" or "valid" accounts of organizational processes. However, this assumes that there is just one way of accounting for what is going on in organizations. Another view is that there are multiple realities, and that it is important to understand all of these, rather than searching for a single "truth." The latter approach was adopted in this study.

Findings: Organizational Contexts

The findings are presented in two parts: first, the participants' accounts of workplace change and supports, and second, the impact of these conditions on working parents' experiences of flexibility for managing work-family boundaries.

Accounts of Workplace Change

The case study organizations were all undergoing considerable change and turbulence. Mergers and acquisitions as well as restructuring and downsizing contributed to feelings of deep transition and constant change. Employees in all case studies reported an intensification of work; that is, increasing employer expectations in the face of downsizing and "efficiency" drives, as well as changes in work organization that frequently put more stress on individual responsibility to manage demanding tasks and schedules (Burchall, Lapido, and Wilkinson 2002). Work intensification and, often, feelings of job insecurity were by-products of new forms of competition in the global economy, including the transition to a market economy in Slovenia and Bulgaria, where the changes were particularly dramatic.

Organizational Support for Working Parents—Policies and Practices

Since parents have to manage their work and family lives in increasingly demanding contexts, workplace support and flexibility are arguably more important than ever. The source and extent of workplace support for working parents in the case study workplaces varied. At one extreme, in the relatively recently privatized organizations in Bulgaria and Slovenia, parents relied on long-standing government support for reconciling work and family life in the form of childcare, leave for care of sick children, and parental leave entitlements. Yet beyond compliance with regulations, there was little voluntary formal employer support. In fact, parents and their managers in these two countries often did not consider organizational support for work and family life to be operationally feasible within a market economy. The focus was on economic drivers, the survival of the company, and earning enough money to maintain a family. Supporting both work and family was regarded as a cost and a luxury beyond the means of a developing economy. A Bulgarian mother was typical in arguing that "there is no private employer caring for his employees. The state is one thing, the employer is another thing" (employee, Perelik). Nevertheless, there was much informal flexibility support for parents from older managers in the Bulgarian bank (perhaps as a legacy of the communist regime), although this was declining among younger managers schooled in capitalism.

At the other extreme, in the United Kingdom, the Netherlands, and Norway, which offer varying levels of state support for parents, flexible working arrangements are not necessarily considered incompatible with workplace efficiency and competitiveness, and indeed are often viewed as productivity or efficiency initiatives arising from other changes. In the U.K. finance sector organization, for example, managers cited mergers and acquisitions as the catalyst for a drive to create a new culture based on increased flexibility and trust:

> It's a different kind of, the old adage that a happy workforce is a productive workforce, isn't it. . . . If you start challenging, 'Well, why are we working 9 to 5,' because you know customers do ring after 5 o'clock, so why not leave it open 'til 6 when there's people willing to work 'til 6? So, why are we saying no to people? It's just about challenging some of the preconceptions that were there . . . and I think we're changing the culture in a positive way . . . because we do recognize that we're only successful if our people are happy. (British mother, manager, Peak)

In practice, this involved a shift from a formalized flextime system to more informal flexibility based on support and trust. It was presented as a strategic initiative to enhance performance through a focus on people and their needs and well-being, in the context of increasing workplace demands. However, parents reported that this was not always consistently applied in practice, and there remain many barriers to overcome.

The actual formal flexible working arrangements available in these case studies, beyond those covered by state policy, varied across countries and were related to social and cultural contexts. In the Bulgarian and Slovenian banks there is no tradition of formal flexible working arrangements. In the Slovenian case only slight deviations of starting times are allowed, while the Bulgarian case is characterized by fixed working times. In both cases working from home and reduced hours are almost nonexistent. In the Norwegian, British, Dutch, and Portuguese cases, working conditions are good compared to the national average, but only the Dutch insurance and banking company and the Norwegian multinational company stand out as good employers regarding flexible work arrangements. Within BOC's flexible start and finishing hours, incentives for teleworking and reduced hours are available. The Dutch case, BIC, has policies on reduced hours, a compressed workweek, flexible start and finishing hours, and experiments with distance working. For example, compressed working weeks were sometimes used in the Dutch company, where employees worked longer daily hours over four days rather than five. This was facilitated by the reduction in the workweek in the banking sector from forty hours to thirty-six hours that came into force in the 1980s, as part of a collective agreement for the sector. The downside of this, for parents, is that the days worked are very long, leaving little time in the evening for the family, and drop-offs and pick-ups at crèches (daycare) can be complicated. Also, it can only work if a partner can also schedule his or her working week around this, which may explain why it is popular, particularly among men in the Netherlands, where a high proportion of women work part-time. In many of the case study organizations, self-managed teams provided autonomy and flexibility, although as discussed below, this could be problematic in some cases when combined with an intensification of work.

As in other studies (e.g., Gambles, Lewis, and Rapoport 2006), a range of countries displayed a widespread implementation gap between policies (whether government or organizational) and actual practice, although the gap varied across organizations and was less severe in the Norwegian case than elsewhere. Generally, it appeared that employer support (formal or informal) was often forthcoming during crises (sick child, seriously ill family member), but less so in everyday working life with respect to the flexible needs of working parents. Lack of flexibility was particularly striking in Slovenia and Bulgaria.

Despite the organizational change that is going on across all of the case studies, one area of continuity is the prevailing male model of ideal workers who do not need time or energy for family (S. Lewis 1997, 2001; Rapoport et al. 2002).

> We have all the options, parental leave to sabbatical leave, and it is really possible, but in practice your decisions should be taken with care because they can harm your career....It's the same with all these policies; it is possible, but take care—it's at your own risk, it's not as ideal as you might expect. (Dutch father, manager, BIC)

The study also highlights the continuing gendered expectations in all the countries (to varying degrees, least in Norway) that policies for combining paid work and family care are primarily, or only, for women. This assumption is often made by managers at all levels, as well as by many of the parents themselves.

Accounts of Experiences of Flexible Working Arrangements and Employer Support in Diverse Contexts

Although space precludes a full analysis of parents' experiences of flexibility to manage work and family demands within the various layers of contexts, in this section some of the complex relationships between contextual factors and parents' experiences are explored and illustrated. Five major interrelated themes emerged in relation to experiences of flexible working arrangements in diverse contexts. First, the intensification of work was a dominant theme in all the case studies, exacerbated by an intensification of parental responsibilities. Second, the pace of change and job insecurity in many contexts challenges experiences and sense of entitlement to use flexible working arrangements. Third, line manager support is crucial, as reported in many other studies. Fourth, the role of colleagues and feelings of guilt emerged as key factors in the context of work intensification and an increase in teamwork. Finally, experiences of flexibility are influenced by context-related expectations and produce seeds of positive change and related transitional tensions.

Intensification of Work (and Parenting)

The national contexts—particularly lengths of and payment for leaves, childcare options, and opportunities to work part-time or flexibly, as well as economic conditions—make a difference in the ways in which parents experience both paid work and parenting. However, the effectiveness of national regulations in supporting employed parents depends on how these are implemented in the workplace, in the context of ongoing organizational change and wider labor market trends. In particular, the intensification of work can make it difficult for parents and their managers to deal with family-related leaves. The parents in this study were managing work and family in particularly demanding, competitive, and pressured contexts, including intensified workloads alongside rising demands of parenthood. The intensification of work was a major theme:

> It is proved by numbers. The productivity factors indicate there is more money, more profit per employee. But that means there is greater extent of work. We don't increase [the] number of workers in spite of enlarging the market. The absent workers are not replaced, so those that remain have to do their own work, plus the work of an absent person. (Slovenian female manager, Slofinance)

> We demand a lot from people. All the time we think it's temporary, but there is always something new. (Dutch father, employee, BIC)

> That's the way it is. Tasks are more complex and have to be done more quickly. Information technology makes it so that we exchange information very rapidly. People expect to get an answer fast. You can reach people day and night. There is more pressure [because of information technology] and you can see that very clearly. (British male senior manager, Peak)

Intensive work demands also undermine progressive national or workplace policies.

Part-time and reduced hours work schedules provide one example. Reduced-hours schedules, available in many of the case study organizations in Norway, Sweden, the Netherlands, and the United Kingdom, can provide a very satisfactory arrangement for new parents in relatively affluent contexts if it is supported by management:

> I've worked here since [19]85, so this is my everyday life and as far as I've seen it there aren't any negative sides when getting children....When I came back from leave I asked to have 60% work, and there was not a problem. I can continue with that for years if I so wish. (Norwegian mother, employee, BOC)

However, such arrangements were often undermined by intensified workloads in these case studies. Managers and colleagues often supported reduced hours in principle, but workloads and expectations were not reduced proportionally to the reduction in work hours. In other cases, work was redistributed to other team members, resulting in overload for part-time workers and/or their colleagues, such as this Dutch mother, a BIC employee: "I still have to do the same amount of work, only in less hours. My workload is not adjusted."

Parents experienced not only an intensification of work, but also an intensification of the demands of parenthood. The parents in this study in all countries held high expectations of what a "good" parent should do, which typically involved far more care and parental input, as well as more financial resources, than their own parents had been able to provide. Pressure to conform to "intensified" parenting came from parents' expectations, as well as from wider societies, and, in some countries, from national initiatives to encourage more parental involvement of various forms, such as in schools.

Pace of Change and Job Insecurity

Parents' concerns for future job opportunities in rapidly changing job climates can also undermine public and workplace policy to support parents. For example, Bulgarian mothers are entitled to nearly three years' parental leave, but the participants stated that they took only a few months' leave because they feared that they would lose their jobs or be unable to keep up with the fast pace of change if they stayed away for a longer period. This was illustrated by this focus group excerpt:

> [Antonia]: The tendency is to take as short maternity leave as possible, and you hurry up to go back to work. You fight for your position with tooth and nail.
>
> [Kostadina]: Everything is so dynamic now. And things change all the time. Leaving work for two years keeps you far behind the others. The normative documents, the requirements for the employees, change very quickly. In order to provide a better future for your children, you should catch up with the others.
>
> [Rositza]: After two years on a maternity leave they have to train you again. (Bulgarian mothers, employees, Perelik)

Job insecurity and work intensification appear to be becoming normalized across countries, justified by employers by the need to remain competitive in increasingly global markets.

The Importance of Line Managers

As in other research (Bond et al. 2002; S. Lewis 1997, 2001), line manager support or lack thereof was of crucial significance for working parents' options for negotiating their paid work and family responsibilities. Although this is true in all the case studies, it is particularly so in the countries with fewer supportive national regulations and a shorter history of people taking up family supportive initiatives; in organizations where there are limited resources to cover absent personnel; and in contexts where the work-family debates are framed within a discourse of the competing, rather than interrelated, needs of business and employees' work-family needs:

> In fact everything depends upon a manager and how they will respond to the needs of young parents....This informal policy is much worse than the written one. (Slovenian male manager, Slofinance)
>
> Yes, some things depend very much on the manager you have and that is a danger. There are all kinds of rules people have to keep to, but there is much between the lines, what is allowed and agreed on and whatnot. (Dutch mother, employee, BIC)

However, interviews with managers in the case study organizations highlight some of the dilemmas they experience:

> We are in a team with six people; one is on a four months' leave, the other has maternity leave, so you lose a great part of your manpower. And to replace them takes a lot of hassle, or you end up with trainees who finally start to get it after three months. When I oversee this situation as a manager, this is very badly solved by the organization. (Dutch father, team leader, BIC)

Changing conditions, including heavy workloads and high performance targets for managers, can reinforce task- rather than people-centered management styles. Middle and lower level managers, in particular, have to negotiate intensified targets, changing working practices, and parents' expectations of support. In this context, agreeing to requests for reduced working hours but without reducing the workload, or by redistributing the extra work among work team members, was one strategy that managers developed for dealing with perceived conflict between employee and organizational needs.

Role of Colleagues and Feelings of Guilt

One management strategy developed in many of the organizations involves delegating responsibility for flexibility to relatively autonomous work teams. In these contexts, and with intensified workloads and a decreasing likelihood of official replacement for employees taking leave for family reasons, the support or disapproval of colleagues became increasingly significant. On the positive side, in some cases parents displayed considerable solidarity in the context of the intense demands from both paid work and parenting, and helped each other out by covering for each others' absences. However, the combination of work intensification and "high performance" management techniques (White et al. 2003), such as relatively autonomous teams, can also generate feelings of guilt regarding colleagues who have to cover for parents who take leave (e.g., if a child is ill). This can undermine parents' willingness to make use of their entitlements. In these contexts, colleagues often became agents of social control who can be more significant than managers in determining the flexibility experienced by parents:

> I know that legally that's possible, but let's be honest, when there's work that takes eight hours and you say you want to work six hours, another person will have to be hired to do your job or your co-workers will have to work overtime. But the organization doesn't take on new workers or pay out the overtime hours, so nobody wants to work overtime. And that's why they simply won't tolerate it. (Slovenian father, employee, Slofinance)

> You know that if you do not go to work, the others would have to work harder. (Bulgarian mother, employee, Perelik)

> AA: [If a child is sick] it is impossible to be absent an entire week.

> BB: The company doesn't create obstacles to that. It is more our sense of responsibility, of mutual support. Obstacles to that are the deadlines, nobody obliges us to come....We work in teams. (Portuguese working parents, employees, PPC)

> I feel guilty sometimes because of, not so much my boss, but my colleagues and some colleagues who don't understand what I go through, what I have to do. One guy particularly keen about the clock, and has to be there at 9 o'clock and you know, somebody will walk in at 10 past and you can see him look at the clock or his watch [laughter]. *I feel so much more as though I have to justify myself to him then, than my manager.* (British working parent, Peak, emphasis added)

A decade ago, managers' attitudes to flexible working often prevented employees from requesting or being allowed to work flexibly (Bond et al. 2002; S. Lewis 2001). Yet this study demonstrates that parents are now as, or even more, likely to be prevented from working flexibly by heavy workloads. For example, parents are often reluctant to take family-related leaves because work is rarely covered fully while staff is away, and work is often passed to overburdened colleagues, or accumulates, to be dealt with on the return to work. This trend thus undermines the right to ask for flexible work time, which is enshrined in legislation in some countries (Fagnani, Houriet-Ségard, and Bédouin 2004).

Expectations, Seeds of Positive Change, and Transitional Tensions

Parents' satisfaction with and experience of flexible working arrangements were influenced by their expectations of and sense of entitlement to work-family support, which in turn were related to the various layers of context. Some examples of positive changes were found in some social systems, and the subsequent sense of entitlement to support among some parents. However, if changes in one layer of context were not reflected in changes in other social systems, this created transitional tensions. For example, some countries, particularly Norway, are experiencing the growing involvement of fathers in parenting, encouraged by government policies and campaigns. This has raised expectations of shared parenting, but also created tensions when some employers continued to expect that men should not take family leaves. Norwegian parents tended to have high expectations of workplace support and therefore to be more critical than others of the implementation gap:

> [The organization] has many fine words on paper on many things; among others gender equality and consideration for the life situation of employees. Maybe they could get even better at following up what they have on paper? That would make this company even better for everybody. (Norwegian mother, employee, BOC)

At the workplace level, organizational change can raise expectations of support for managing work and family boundaries, and therefore generate a greater willingness to take entitlements and to develop mutual flexibility, with give-and-take by employees and their managers. For example, Peak, in the United Kingdom, launched a company drive for culture change, including more flexibility and trust. This initiative, within the wider context of a high-profile government campaign and national debates on "work-life balance," raised expectations of support among parents, some of whom were able to work very flexibly and effectively. Tensions arose in this context because of management inconsistency in applying the new culture, due partly to intensification of work, but also to the lack of change in the values and skills of many managers:

> I don't think there's consistency across the company anyway, across departments....Our manager's under the impression that the supervisor's position is 9–5—which isn't in our contract–and she has made you feel bad if you ask to go early, which isn't what flexible working's all about. (British expectant mother, employee, Peak)

More generally, the inconstancy of management support and the failure to replace team members in self-managing work groups can also be seen as examples of transitional tensions, as changes in one layer of context lag behind those in other related systems. Simultaneous change is therefore needed at many different levels of contexts to nurture these seeds of positive change and overcome "transitional tensions." Currently, however, there are other forms of change in workplaces associated with globalization, particularly intense workloads, and in some cases, job insecurity, that often undermine seeds of positive change and exacerbate transitional tensions.

Implications: The Importance of Context for Flexible Working Arrangements

Can flexible working arrangements help to manage the growing pressures from work and home? Although parents' experiences of flexible work arrangements varied across the case study organizations and national contexts in this study, a number of common themes emerged. First, the implementation gap between policies (whether government mandated or voluntary) and practice is exacerbated by the changing nature of work—especially intensified workloads, the fast pace of change, and in some contexts, job insecurity—which can challenge flexible work arrangements and weaken positive changes in some social systems. Although flexible working policies and practices can bring opportunities to integrate paid work and family, particularly if this is associated with greater autonomy, the intensification of work flexibility can also be used to support heavier workloads, leading to a blurring of work-family boundaries or long working hours that intrude on family time or energy (see also EU Fifth Framework Programme 2003; Kossek, Lautsch, and Eaton 2005). Managers play an important role in determining parents' latitude to work flexibly, but are constrained by intense workloads and targets. In the changing European contexts that were examined, the roles of colleagues and workloads featured were equal to, and in some cases more important than, those of manager support.

This chapter demonstrates the importance of a systems approach to understanding parents' experiences of work and family support. Parents' experiences are situated within multiple layers of context. For changes in one layer of context—whether social policy, workplace, or family—changes are required in other layers of context in order to be effective. Without such changes, transitional tensions arise and flexible working arrangements are less beneficial for parents. Certainly some national provisions and policies and employer-flexible working practices can provide support for working parents, albeit in complex ways, mediated by the interaction of factors such as economic context, employees' expectations, and sense of entitlement to support.

Is it possible to identify good practices in flexible working arrangements? The findings from the study point to the difficulty in defining what good practices are, as these are so complex and context-dependent. Practices such as devolving responsibility for flexibility to relatively autonomous work teams can enhance feelings of control, and may in some contexts constitute good practices—but they are undermined in the organizations studied, by intensified workloads that made parents reluctant to change working patterns because of the impact on already overburdened colleagues.

Changing times and shifting realities present challenges to conventional wisdom. The male model of continuous, full-time, and inflexible work may have been appropriate at certain times and places, but it is being challenged by increasingly diverse workforces. By the same token, flexible working arrangements that might be effective at one time are sensitive to changes in the nature of work and workplaces in the global economy. Flexible working arrangements continue to be important for the reconciliation of paid work and family responsibilities, but they also need to be monitored regularly to ensure their continuing effectiveness in rapidly changing global and local contexts. For example, intensified workloads make it difficult to take up policies that might otherwise be beneficial.

Nevertheless, it is possible to make some recommendations for policy and practice from this study, although these take the form of general principles rather than clear-cut practices or solutions. Regulation of working time is important, but not sufficient. Attention needs to be paid to workloads and the pace of work, as work intensification underpins many of the barriers to effective flexible working practices. Manager training and support for implementing flexible working arrangements remains crucial, but again it must be recognized that intensified working conditions play an important role in manager behavior. Self-managing work groups can provide autonomy and flexibility to parents, but if they are to be effective there should be renewed attention to reasonable workloads and adequate staffing. Finally, changes in policy practices in one layer of context must be accompanied by strategic efforts to bring about commensurate changes in other social systems, to support parents in reconciling work and family demands.

13

WORK HOURS MISMATCH IN THE UNITED STATES AND AUSTRALIA

Robert Drago and Mark Wooden

Many academics and practitioners are urging employers to provide workplace options that allow their employees to reduce the number of hours they are required to work. For example, Hewlett and Luce's (2005) study of highly educated women concludes that businesses need to create reduced-hours positions for women, and particularly new mothers, if they are to retain their positions as valued employees. For academics, Drago and Williams (2000) promote the notion of a half-time tenure track to permit academics to downshift their academic responsibilities when family demands are high, and return to full-time schedules when family demands lessen. For older workers, Leslie and Janson (2005) highlight the importance of allowing reduced-hours opportunities for those seeking phased retirement.

Calls for reduced hours correspond to evidence of a time problem, in which many employees working long hours prefer but cannot obtain fewer hours, and many employees working short hours (working thirty hours or fewer a week) prefer but cannot obtain longer hours (Jacobs and Gerson 2004). This time argument implies a shortage of medium-hour jobs;[1] this preference of work hours appears in several studies of the United States (Drago 2000; Jacobs and Gerson 2004). In each case, the absolute number of employees who work long hours is larger than the group of employees who work short hours. Additionally, several studies have conducted cross-national analyses that examine the number of hours worked and the preferences of employees (e.g., Jacobs and Gerson 2004; Organisation for Economic Cooperation and Development [OECD] 1998, 2004; Rubery, Smith, and Fagan 1998). This chapter provides a quantitative analysis that compares data from the United States and Australia on both the hours worked and the hours employees prefer.

Australia and the United States exhibit striking similarities: both are part of the developed world, have democratic governments, and are highly integrated into the global economy. Both nations have witnessed an increasing diversity of family forms, a rise in delayed and denied childbearing, and continuing gender inequality (Drago, Scutella, and Pirretti 2007). Jacobs and Gerson (2000) found that among nine developed countries, Australia and the United States have the highest proportions of employees reporting working long hours each week (at least fifty hours per week).[2] This suggests that comparisons of these two nations should yield similar results, but the institutional responses to these issues may be different.

For example, in Australia, there are governmental policies that provide attractive part-time opportunities for mothers, and other policies that are supportive of low-wage employees. However, in the United States, several studies show a more equal division of labor in the household, but higher rates of full-time labor force participation of women, especially among mothers with children under the age of eighteen. This chapter specifically examines which of these two nations faces the most serious issues of time management, and why differences between the two countries may exist.

Time Mismatch

The notion of a shortage of medium-hour jobs—those within the range of thirty to forty hours per week—fits the norm of the forty-hour week in the United States and of the thirty-eight-hour week in Australia. Many employees would choose these hours, but are forced into jobs with either longer or shorter hours jobs than they desire, and consequently they tend to view themselves as either over- or underworked. But why would employers provide fewer medium-hour jobs than employees' desire? Several dynamics may be at work.

In a perfectly competitive labor market, employees who desire shorter or longer work hours should be able to negotiate these desires with their employer, or switch employers if they cannot achieve their goals. Various cost factors might make labor markets less than perfectly competitive, and generate a time disconnect in the process. Fixed costs of employment are relevant here. For example, providing an office or equipment, family health insurance coverage, pensions, or vacations based on years of service all drive up the fixed costs of hiring and retaining employees. Employers have an incentive to spread these fixed costs over a larger number of work hours per employee, and thereby generate the demand for overwork. Fixed costs might also affect employees, as in the case of liability insurance premiums for medical doctors in the United States. Since these premiums can run to tens of thousands of dollars per year, physicians may feel pressured to work long hours to make up for these costs. If some physicians drop out of the market as a result, the demands on remaining doctors will rise, exacerbating the tendency toward longer work hours.

Employee bargaining power may also be relevant. If one set of employees in a workplace is unionized, while another set is not, employers may have an incentive to work union members for long hours to cover the fixed costs of benefits. On the other hand, the union may provide job security to members by demanding that nonunion employees be used to cover fluctuations in product demand, which might in turn generate fewer hours of work for nonunion employees.

Regardless of the causes of mismatch, earlier longitudinal evidence from the same Australian data set employed here identifies both the patterns of overwork and underwork we expect to see (Reynolds and Aletraris 2006). Moreover, that study finds many of these mismatches are not resolved over time. The study did not, however, compare data from Australia and the United States.

The Ideal Worker Norm

The notion of an ideal worker norm developed by Bailyn (1993) and Williams (2000) applies to individuals. These are primarily managers and professionals who feel compelled to work long hours for periods of years or decades without interruption, and whose performance is judged in part by high levels of "face time" in the workplace. Both Drago (2007) and Jacobs and Gerson (2004) use the ideal worker norm as an explanation for time mismatch by arguing that it serves as a socially constructed category within the economy. Those who buy into the concept are willing to work long hours, while those who are unwilling to work long hours are eventually penalized with low pay, job insecurity, and shorter hours of work than one might prefer. It also explains overwork among employees who work long hours. Individuals who hold ideal worker status may not believe that long work hours are appropriate or desirable, but they may nevertheless maintain long hours to avoid the penalties associated with deviance.

Family and Gender Roles

Two different visions of family and gender roles can help to explain divisions between long- and short-hour employees. One is related to norms, and the other to efficiency considerations. Considering norms, Williams (2000) argues that the ideal worker norm is gendered, in the sense that men's sense of self-worth is tied to their income and commitment to career, with men more prone to brag about having to put in long work hours. In addition, norms around motherhood lead women themselves, as well as their friends, family members, colleagues, and employers, to expect that they will bear and rear children and perform other caregiving tasks for family and community (Folbre 2001). Drago (2007) extends this logic by arguing that the motherhood norm leads many women in managerial and professional occupations to minimize or hide caregiving commitments in order to avoid being cast as deviants from the ideal worker norms. As a result, women in managerial and professional positions may often prefer shorter hours but be unwilling to even inquire about, much less demand, reduced hour options.

Within the family, these norms suggest that it is often rational for heterosexual parents to take on either traditional or neotraditional roles. In traditional families, fathers serve as long-hour breadwinners, while mothers function as full-time homemakers. In neotraditional families, the division of labor is slightly blurred, with the man working long hours, the woman working short hours, and the man providing a substantial if unequal amount of household labor (Moen and Roehling 2005). Norms inside of the family can explain why it is the father per se who works long hours. To the extent individuals implicitly challenge these norms, fathers working long hours will report overwork, while short-hours mothers will claim underwork.

Becker (1985) explains the existence of traditional and neotraditional families by appealing to efficiency considerations. In this view, the gains from specialization in couple families make it optimal for one member to focus on paid work, and the other to devote their efforts mainly to unpaid work for the family. However, these considerations should not generate a time mismatch; employees are selecting either long- or short-hour jobs in a rational fashion.

Government and State Policies

Governmental supports for families and the unemployed, as well as labor market regulations, may alter time mismatch by providing incentives to either employers or employees. On the employee side, supports such as universal health insurance, high minimum wages, portable pensions, and prohibitions against unfair dismissal each place employees in a stronger position to demand and obtain their preferred hours. The situation is more complicated on the employer side. As government policies increase the wage, benefit, or dismissal costs of employees, employers have an incentive to avoid hiring employees into short-hour positions. For these reasons, employers may seek to create long-hour positions, but be in a weak bargaining position to demand such hours.

Employers may also have an incentive to create short-hours jobs if legal distinctions affect fixed costs of employment. This is the case with the U.S. Employee Retirement Income Security Act (ERISA) law, which distinguishes full-time from part-time employees for benefits provisions. The law makes fixed costs high for full-time employees, providing an incentive for employers to seek long hours from that group, while the low fixed costs of part-time employees can help to explain underwork within that group, as employers seek to prevent them from incurring the fixed costs associated with full-time employment.

U.S. and Australia Comparisons

Historically, Australian wage determination was largely centralized under the "awards" system, wherein unions and employers negotiated rates to which most other wages were pegged (Davis and Lansbury 1998). As recently as 1986, unions represented over 45 percent of Australian employees. That figure has declined sharply, standing at only 22.4 percent in 2005.[3] Award coverage remains high, and in the late 1990s was still estimated to have been in excess of 80 percent of the civilian workforce (see Joint Governments' Submission 2000, table 5.12). Nevertheless, by 2004 it was estimated that only 20 percent of the workforce were reliant on the award minimum for their wages. Since unions serve to enhance employee bargaining power, the historical strength of Australian unions should lessen the time mismatch there, even if the measured effects of union membership do not differ across the two nations.

Another notable difference is the Australian distinction between "casual" and "permanent" employees. Historically, casual employment was specified in awards to provide employment-at-will for employers of certain types of labor. Permanent employees, on the other hand, enjoyed relative job security. The casual distinction, in tandem with high dismissal costs for permanent employees, provides employers with an incentive to work permanent employees for long hours (to minimize the total number of permanent employees), although the greater bargaining power associated with high dismissal costs may place permanent employees in a strong position to avoid overwork. At the other end of the spectrum, given the ease of replacing such employees, casuals may often be used sporadically and for short-hour tasks. Consistent with this argument, there is a substantial overlap between part-time and casual employment, with an estimated 65 percent of casual employees working part-time hours.[4]

In terms of gender, Australia is arguably more traditional. Although the participation of women in the labor force has increased dramatically in both nations in recent decades, female labor force participation rates in Australia still lag behind those in the United States; 66.3 percent of working-age women in Australia in 2004 were either working or actively looking for work, compared with 69.2 percent in the United States.[5] Not only are Australian women less often employed, but part-time employment is more common among those who do hold jobs. According to OECD data for 2004, just 8.1 percent of male employees in the United States and 18.8 percent of female employees worked on a part-time basis (defined as less than thirty hours per week). By comparison, in Australia 16.1 percent of working men and 40.8 percent of working women were defined as part-time.[6]

One reason for these differences is that income supplements for poor families, and particularly for poor single mothers, are higher in Australia (Drago, Scutella, and Pirretti 2007). It appears that the incentive for mothers to either be non-employed or to work part-time is greater in Australia, while the ability of employers to demand and obtain shorter hours than these women prefer may be weaker.

Other differences in governmental policies in the United States and Australia could help to explain a general divergence in the prevalence of overwork and underwork. Of greatest relevance, Australia has a higher minimum wage, universal health coverage, portable pensions, more substantial income supports for the poor, and guaranteed wage equality for part-time work. Minimum wages, as of 2002, were $5.15 per hour in the United States for up to a forty-hour week, and $11.35 per hour for a thirty-eight-hour week in Australia (or around $9.40 in U.S. terms). According to a study by the UK Low Pay Commission (2005), as of mid-2004 the national minimum as a percentage of median wages for adult wage earners was 58.8 percent in Australia, but only 32.2 percent in the United States.

Health insurance is mainly funded through employer contributions in the United States, whereas a national taxpayer-funded system exists in Australia, effectively raising the fixed costs of full-time employment in the United States for employers who provide health insurance. In addition, ERISA permits employers to discriminate against part-time employees in the provision of health insurance (Kelly 2006), hence the fixed costs of full-time employees are typically higher than they are for part-time employees in the United States. American employers therefore have a stronger incentive to work full-time employees longer hours, and to prevent part-time employees from achieving full-time status, thereby increasing the time mismatch.

Accentuating that dynamic, pension benefits are typically tied to employment in the United States, and are often provided only to full-time employees. In Australia, portable pensions are usually available to all employees.[7] As argued earlier, a higher minimum wage, universal health insurance, and portable pensions should each serve to expand employee bargaining power in Australia. Partly as a result, but also due to the awards system, the part-time hourly wage penalty that is found in studies of the U.S. labor market is nonexistent in Australian studies (see Booth and Wood 2008; Rodgers 2004). As with greater income supports for the poor, these differences in part-time wages should be associated with a reduced incidence of underwork among short-hour employees.

Analyses of the Time Mismatch between Countries

Using data from the National Study of the Changing Workforce (NSCW) for the United States, and the Household, Income and Labour Dynamics in Australia (HILDA) Survey for Australia, both from 2002 survey administration, this study compares employee preferences and mismatches of work time in the United States and Australia. The NSCW was designed to produce a random sample (after weighting) of the population within the forty-eight contiguous states of individuals employed for monetary gain who were at least eighteen years of age and in the civilian labor force. A total of 3,504 persons responded.[8] The sample used here is limited to individuals who answered the "usual and preferred" hour questions, and were employed as wage and salary earners.[9] The sample includes 2,349 respondents. The HILDA Survey is a longitudinal survey of a stratified, random sample of Australian households in 2002, and includes 13,041 individuals in 7,245 households.[10] The sample here (n = 5,480) is limited to civilian employees who were at least eighteen years of age who responded to the questions on "usual and preferred" working hours. Comparability of the two samples is enhanced by limiting the samples to holders of a single job, thereby reducing the number of relevant NSCW questions from three to a maximum of two. About 14.3 percent of the NSCW sample, or 408 respondents, were excluded as multiple jobholders. Around 8.9 percent of the HILDA Survey sample, or 553 respondents, were similarly excluded as multiple jobholders.[11] For both the HILDA and the NSCW, all estimates are weighted to represent the relevant populations.

Both surveys ask about usual weekly hours in all jobs and preferred work hours.[12] The HILDA Survey includes a single item about "usual" total work hours over a four-week period. Obtaining usual hours in the NSCW sample requires summing responses to three questions: (a) paid hours on the main job, excluding unpaid extra time or official overtime; (b) unpaid extra time and official overtime on the main job; and (c) all time on any other job or jobs. It seems likely that these multiple questions are likely to generate an overstatement of usual hours, at least relative to results from a single question (Golden 2006). The mean HILDA Survey response is 37.7 hours, and the mean NSCW response is 43.0 hours, while figures from the International Labour Office for 2001 place average Australian work hours at 35.2, with a U.S. figure of 34.2 (International Labour Organization [ILO] 2003a, table 4A). These differences suggest the HILDA figures are likely to be more reliable, and that measured levels of overwork will be overstated and underwork understated in the NSCW.

Following the usual hours questions, both surveys cover preferred hours. In the NSCW, a single item addresses ideal work hours per week at all jobs, and yields a mean response of 35.0 hours with a standard deviation of 14.3.[13] HILDA Survey respondents were asked whether, taking into account how it would affect income, they would prefer to work fewer, about the same, or more hours than now. Those responding fewer or more were then asked how many hours they would choose to work, again accounting for how that would affect income. Setting responses of "about the same" at the value of usual hours, and combining this with responses on the hours of work respondents would choose, results in a preferred hours variable with a mean of 36.1 hours and a standard deviation of 12.3. The fact that preferred hours figures are quite close across the two surveys—35.0 compared to 36.1 hours—suggests that the income caveat in the HILDA Survey did not substantially affect the results. However, the two-hour difference in the standard deviation of preferred hours suggests that the additional HILDA Survey question on whether preferred hours are about the same as usual hours may have caused more apparent matches in the Australian data. Indeed, over half of HILDA respondents claimed that usual and preferred hours were about the same.

The time mismatch variable can be generated by subtracting usual from preferred hours. A time mismatch of the type addressed here will then exist if long-hour employees typically report negative values on the variable (i.e., usual beyond preferred hours), with short-hours employees reporting positive values (i.e., usual hours less than those preferred). Using the figures just discussed results in a HILDA time variable with a mean of −1.5 and a standard deviation of 9.1 hours, and a NSCW variable with a mean of −8.0 and a standard deviation of 16.3 hours. Note that the much higher absolute NSCW figure could either reflect a higher incidence of overwork in the United States, the overstatement of usual hours, or both phenomena.

Estimates of mismatch, as found in Drago (2000) or Drago, Tseng, and Wooden (2005), are based on ordinary least squares regressions of the time mismatch variable against a constant term and usual work hours, as in equation (1) below. If the estimated intercept (α) is positive and the slope coefficient (β) is negative, and they together generate a zero point ($-\alpha/\beta$) in an intermediate range of hours, such that underwork characterizes short hours and overwork long hours, then there is evidence of mismatch. The strength of the time variable can be approximately gauged by the absolute value of the slope coefficient.

$$\text{Time mismatch} = \alpha + \beta \text{ UsualHours} + \varepsilon \qquad (1)$$

If the equation is estimated separately for the United States and for Australia, and the intercept is larger and the slope coefficient absolutely larger in the United States, then it can be concluded that the time mismatch is more severe in that nation. However, as apparent matches are overstated in the Australian results, the same result could occur. Alternatively, because the NSCW leads to a general overstatement of usual hours, the intercept should be smaller and the slope coefficient absolutely larger in the United States, generating lower measured levels of underwork and higher levels of overwork in that nation.

To disentangle underwork and overwork, responses on the mismatch variable are separated into the three categories of underwork, matching, and overwork. Because so many HILDA Survey respondents claimed that usual and preferred hours were about the same (thereby making the value of the time mismatch zero), the data is made more comparable by categorizing any preferred and usual responses at or within five hours of each other as a match. Using a cutoff of zero hours differences found 56.3 percent of HILDA Survey respondents and 22.7 percent of NSCW respondents reporting a match, while the five hours cutoff raised the HILDA Survey figure to 64.2 percent, but the NSCW figure to 35.9 percent (the latter figures are over 5% closer to each other).[14] Multinomial logit regression is applied to ascertain the effects of various independent variables on the probability of falling into either the underwork or overwork categories, with the matching category being omitted.

Consistent with the theoretical discussion, a variable for union membership (Union) is employed as an indicator of employee bargaining power. Ideal worker status is proxied by employment in a professional or managerial occupation (Prof-Manager).[15] To understand gender dynamics, first the effects of part-time employment for women are isolated by including a dummy for women who are employed part-time and not mothers (NonMomWomenPT). The effects of motherhood and of marriage are then picked up with dummies for single mothers working part-time (SingleMomPT) and for married mothers working part-time (MarriedMomPT). Given that men only rarely work part-time, gender and family variables for this group include only dummies for men per se (Men) and for fathers (Fathers). The omitted category for the gender and family variables then covers women employed full-time.

Given that neotraditional families may either create overwork for men and underwork for women (or instead, in the Becker view, alleviate overwork and underwork), variables for men in neotraditional families (NeotradMen) and for women in these families (NeotradWomen) are constructed. The cutoffs for membership in a neotraditional family are necessarily somewhat arbitrary, and two of these are considered: couple families in which the man reports usual hours at least five hours above those for the woman, and the subsample of those families in which the man reports at least ten more hours. Since neotraditional families are correlated with marriage, children, and part-time employment for women, all part-time or family variables are excluded from relevant regressions, excepting the gender variable (Men) to ascertain the net effects of neotraditional arrangements.

Results

Results for NSCW and HILDA estimates of the time mismatch are reported in table 13.1. In each regression, the constant is positive and significant, while the usual hour coefficients are negative and significant, consistent with the time mismatch logic. Further, the results support the interpretation of a more severe time mismatch

Table 13.1.   Time Divide Estimates

VARIABLE	NSCW COEFFICIENT (S.E.)	HILDA COEFFICIENT (S.E.)
α	22.65 (1.091)**	10.818 (.316)**
UsualHours	−.713 (.024)**	−.327 (.008)**
Adjusted R^2	.271	.241
F-statistic	851.40**	1724.09**
Sample size	2284	5425

Notes: **Statistically significant at the .01 level. Weighted to approximate the relevant population distributions.

in the United States. The constant terms imply that individuals working zero hours would prefer to work over twenty hours in the United States, but just eleven hours in Australia. An individual working fifty hours per week would report thirteen hours of overwork in the United States, but only 5.5 hours of overwork in Australia.

Of course, the overstatement of matches in the HILDA Survey data could also explain the differences in time divide coefficients. As a test, all respondents claiming to prefer about the same hours they currently work were pulled from the HILDA sample, and the regressions were then repeated. Even in this subsample of under-worked and overworked respondents, the time problem is less pronounced in Australia.[16]

Multinomial logistic regressions were then run for the categories of underwork and overwork for the NSCW and HILDA subsamples, as reported in table 13.2. Even after expanding the matching category to include respondents reporting dif-ferences in usual and preferred hours of up to and including five hours per week, the percentage of underworked individuals is still slightly higher in the NSCW (14.6% compared to 12.7%). However, reported overwork is still over twice as prevalent in the United States (49.5% compared to 23.1%).

Considering the Union coefficients, unions reduce reports of underwork in both nations, with particularly strong effects in the United States. In both nations, union attempts to ensure full-time employment for their members may help to explain the lack of underwork among union members. The distinction between union mem-bership and the far broader scope of award coverage may help to explain the rela-tively weaker effect in Australia.

Turning to the ideal worker variable, managers and professionals are found to be less likely to report underwork and more likely to report overwork in both nations. These results fit the notion that ideal workers are expected to work long hours, but that many implicitly reject the norm, and would prefer shorter hours in both na-tions. The underwork effect is almost twice as large in the United States, while the overwork effect is over twice as large in Australia. The larger size of the Australian overwork effect suggests that the ideal worker norm is more often internalized in the United States.

For family and gender coefficients, nonmother women employed part-time fre-quently report underwork, and rarely report overwork, but the underwork effect is over twice as large in Australia. Given that a larger proportion of Australian women who are not mothers are also employed part-time, it seems that much part-time employment in Australia is related to sex discrimination rather than motherhood per se. Single mothers employed part-time are more likely to report underwork, particularly in the United States, and are less likely to report overwork, particu-larly in Australia. These differences fit the notion that governmental supports for single mothers are superior in Australia, therefore making part-time employment more viable for single mothers. In both nations, married mothers employed part-time report frequent underwork and infrequent overwork.

Table 13.2 Underwork and Overwork Estimates: Multinomial Logits for the National Study of the Changing Workforce and the Household, Income, and Labour Dynamics in Australia Samples (five hours difference cutoff)

VARIABLE	NSCW SUBSAMPLE: COEFFICIENT (S.E.)	HILDA SUBSAMPLE: COEFFICIENT (S.E.)
	UNDERWORK	UNDERWORK
Constant	−1.454 (.174)**	−2.931 (.181)**
Union	−1.464 (.274)**	−.465 (.104)**
ProfManager	−1.542 (.215)**	−.722 (.120)**
NonMomWomenPT	.986 (.249)**	2.300 (.204)**
SingleMomPT	3.655 (.624)**	2.661 (.259)**
MarriedMomPT	2.050 (.302)**	1.800 (.213)**
Men	1.171 (.206)**	1.724 (.192)**
Fathers	−.164 (.184)	−.462 (.126)**
Observations (%) in category	334 (14.6)	694 (12.7)
	OVERWORK	OVERWORK
Constant	.495 (.087)**	−.861 (.070)**
Union	.190 (.122)	−.020 (.073)
ProfManager	.272 (.100)**	.717 (.070)**
NonMomWomenPT	−2.082 (.255)**	−2.082 (.223)**
SingleMomPT	−.343 (.223)	−2.845 (.674)**
MarriedMomPT	−1.257 (.285)**	−1.379 (.159)**
Men	−.380 (.114)**	−.479 (.086)**
Fathers	.164 (.131)	.378 (.089)**
Observations (%) in category	1132 (49.5)	1258 (23.1)
Observations in regression	2289	5446
Pseudo-R^2	.178	.141

Notes: * Statistically significant at the .05 level; ** at the .01 level. Weighted to approximate the population distributions. Omitted category is preferred and usual hours at or within five hours.

In contrast, men often report underwork but infrequently report overwork in both nations, even though they work longer hours than women in both nations. Fathers, however, are less likely to report underwork in Australia, and more likely to report overwork in that nation, suggesting that they respond to caregiving commitments by preferring to reduce hours, even if they are not able to do so easily.

Table 13.3 reports the results that arose after excluding many of the gender and family variables, and including the neotraditional family dummies for women and men. The coefficients for union membership, professional and managerial employment, and for men are similar to those found in table 13.2. Among

Table 13.3. Underwork and Overwork Estimates for Neotraditional Families—Multinomial Logits for the National Study of the Changing Workforce and the Household, Income, and Labour Dynamics in Australia Samples (five hours difference cutoff)

VARIABLE	NSCW SUBSAMPLE: COEFFICIENT (S.E.)	HILDA SUBSAMPLE: COEFFICIENT (S.E.)
	UNDERWORK	
Constant	−.722 (.126)**	−1.330 (.080)**
Union	−1.329 (.267)**	−.486 (.103)**
ProfManager	−1.535 (.209)**	−.762 (.119)**
NeoTradWomen	.304 (.207)	.001 (.127)
Men	.499 (.156)**	.231 (.103)*
NeoTradMen	−1.302 (.330)**	−.704 (.126)**
Observations (%) in category	334 (14.6)	694 (12.7)
	OVERWORK	
Constant	.260 (.087)**	−1.259 (.069)**
Union	.235 (.121)	.008 (.072)
ProfManager	.350 (.098)**	.739 (.070)**
NeoTradWomen	−.387 (.145)**	−.443 (.113)**
Men	−.317 (.109)**	−.313 (.093)**
NeoTradMen	.772 (.152)**	.686 (.092)**
Observations (%) in category	1132 (49.5)	1258 (23.1)
Observations in regression	2289	5446
Pseudo-R^2	.112	.070

Notes: * Statistically significant at the .05 level; ** at the .01 level. Weighted to approximate the population distributions. Omitted category is preferred and usual hours at or within five hours.

neotraditional women, overwork is relatively rare in both nations while underwork effects are negative and overwork effects positive for neotraditional men. These results fit Becker's view that neotraditional families resolve time allocation issues for couples where women are concerned, but the effects are adverse for the men in neotraditional families, who report significant levels of overwork in both nations. The latter finding suggests that men with families often wish to, but do not effectively, challenge expectations of long hours associated with the ideal worker norm.

When this analysis is repeated after reclassifying neotraditional families as those where the man works at least ten hours more per week than the woman (not shown), the outcome leaves the overwork result in place for men, but with a positive and significant coefficient for underwork and women in the NSCW. These results are inconsistent with Becker's notion of neotraditional families as a time allocation solution, instead fitting the notion that many men and women feel trapped by the norms generating neotraditional arrangements.

Summary and Implications for the Two Nations

The evidence presented here is consistent with the existence of a time mismatch in both the United States and Australia, in which a shortage of medium-hour jobs is associated with a high incidence of underwork among short-hours employees and a marked prevalence of overwork among long-hour employees. Furthermore, the time management problem is more severe in the United States. Greater bargaining power among Australian employees and stronger governmental supports for the financial and health needs of families can help to explain the lesser time divide in Australia, as predicted. Of course, a relative overstatement of usual hours in the U.S. data could help to explain higher measured levels of overwork there, but does not predict the higher levels of underwork found in the U.S. data, nor does any overstatement of matching caused by the HILDA preferred hours question account for the differences found in the data.

Unions in both nations seem to protect members from both short hours and underwork. Contrary to expectations, however, unions do not seem to prevent the emergence of overwork among their members. The ideal worker norm, as proxied by professional and managerial status, accounts for much of the time mismatch. In both nations, the results suggest that short hours and underwork are mainly relegated to nonideal workers (particularly in the United States), while long hours and overwork are concentrated within the ideal worker group. The concentration of reported overwork among ideal workers is particularly strong in Australia, suggesting the ideal worker norm is more often internalized among managers and professionals in the United States because they are less likely to view long hours as overwork.

Gender effects suggest that women are often forced into part-time positions, as reflected in consistent reports of underwork across the part-time employed groups of single mothers, partnered mothers, and nonmother women. The fact that underwork reports among the nonmother, part-time group are more pronounced in Australia suggests that women there are more often blocked from taking full-time positions, or that pure sex discrimination may be operating in addition to, or instead of, any discriminatory dynamics regarding motherhood.

Relative to women, men more often report underwork and less often claim overwork in both nations. Given that men tend to work longer hours than women, these findings fit the existence of male norms surrounding long hours, with reduced hours or part-time employment functioning to undercut perceived masculinity. In Australia, fatherhood partially reverses these linkages, suggesting that many Australian fathers both accept and would like to achieve reduced hours employment to make time for family commitments. Weaker evidence suggests these effects may also exist in the United States.

Neotraditional family structures are not associated with underwork among Australian women, and are only mildly related to underwork for women in the United States, so the structure often serves the preferences of many women. However, neotraditional arrangements are consistently associated with overwork among men, a finding that fits the possibility that norms, rather than efficiency considerations, often drive families into neotraditional structures.

These findings yield a variety of policy implications. For labor unions, the results suggest that both nations could benefit from attention to the prevention of overwork. The results also fit the notion that governmental supports for employees and for families can help to ameliorate both overwork and particularly underwork, and that the Australian government provides stronger supports at present. American employers might, of course, object to proposals for such supports precisely because their bargaining power would be reduced. Nevertheless, the prospective benefits for employees (and their families) are clear from the analysis.

The Australian government, however, seems to have done a poorer job of serving employees in terms of full-time employment options for women. It appears that sex discrimination in hiring for full-time employment may often occur in Australia, and that either stronger equal opportunity laws or enhanced enforcement of existing laws might be beneficial for many women. Australia may have achieved a greater degree of pay equity, but it lags on gender equity in hiring.

It is also clear that challenges to the ideal worker norm, in the form of corporate flexibility policies and supportive workplace cultures, would be valued by many employees. If employees had access to, and did not expect to be penalized for utilizing, reduced-hours options, the results suggest that the options would be used extensively in both nations, given the prevalence of long hours and overwork.

On balance, if more medium-hour jobs were available, it is likely that work hours would fall in both nations, but particularly in the United States. Given that those who currently experience overwork and long hours tend to fit the ideal worker norm, reduced hours for this group could reduce income inequality. Furthermore, although many long-hour men do not report overwork, those who do tend to be fathers in neotraditional families, where reductions in their work hours would be most likely to translate into increased involvement in childcare and housework. An expansion of medium-hour jobs might therefore improve levels of gender equality.

14

RENEWED ENERGY FOR CHANGE
Government Policies Supporting Workplace Flexibility in Australia

Juliet Bourke

Workplace flexibility is receiving a great deal of attention in Australia, particularly from Labor federal government elected in late 2007, but also from members of the previous conservative federal government, business representatives, and nongovernmental organizations. At first glance, such attention may seem positive, but this assumes that the term "workplace flexibility" has a uniform meaning for each of those stakeholder groups, and that the balance between employer and employee rights is evenly weighted. Although the previous conservative government espoused a commitment to work and family, it was perceived by some commentators (Group of 151 Australian Industrial Relations, Labour Market and Legal Academics 2005) as undermining work-family balance[1] by providing employers with greater industrial control over employees. Hence, the underlying meaning of the term "workplace flexibility" needs to be deconstructed, since it is freely used by both main political parties, as well as the broader community, but it may well mean different things to different sectors and therefore drive different policy approaches and legislative outcomes.

An Australian Snapshot

This chapter analyzes the previous government's approach to workplace flexibility, and in particular the introduction of sweeping industrial reforms known as "WorkChoices," the effects of which are still present in the labor market; the newly elected Labor government's approach through its election commitment to amend WorkChoices, which is currently under way (see the epilogue to this chapter for an update as of July 1, 2009); and state discrimination laws for workers with caring responsibilities. It will also consider whether current legal workplace frameworks and policy initiatives are sufficiently supportive of the work-family agenda.

In terms of flexibility and the work-family agenda, is Australia moving forward, standing still, or going backward? Taken as a whole, Australia's progress on the work-family agenda for the past ten years can be characterized as "two steps forward and one step back." However commitments by the Labor federal government elected in 2007 to improve outcomes for "working families" have the capacity to now drive the workplace flexibility agenda forward with speed.

Framing the Discussion

To help frame the discussion of workplace flexibility, it is important to identify whether the objective of flexibility is to (a) enable employers to have greater control over employees' working conditions; (b) enable employees to have greater control over their working conditions; or (c) provide a framework for employers and employees to balance their mutual work and family responsibilities. Hence, while the same phrase "workplace flexibility" may be used by a range of key stakeholders (e.g., government/Opposition, businesses, and employees), the ultimate objective plays a vital role in defining the policy framework and legal implementation processes. These objectives may not be transparent in an environment of political correctness and political savvy; moreover, they may be blurred for each stakeholder group.

Does workplace flexibility enable, or indeed encourage, employers and workers to balance their mutual work and family responsibilities? The assumption behind this framework is that supporting a work-family agenda is both good for business and good for employees, and correspondingly, that excessive control by either employers or employees is detrimental to the sustainability of employees and/or the workplace. Where should the policy and legislative lines be drawn to achieve this dual agenda, and how does Australia rate? Accepting this definition of (mutual) "work-family flexibility" as a starting point, what might be the indicators of flexibility policies that are supportive of the work-family agenda? Within the Australian context, four key indicators of work-family flexibility can be assigned: access to flexible work practices without disadvantage; reasonable and predictable hours; legal redress for practices that do not honor the work-family balance; and sufficient structural support to provide real choice.

ACCESS TO FLEXIBLE WORK PRACTICES
WITHOUT DISADVANTAGE

"Without disadvantage" means that employees should not be harassed or treated detrimentally because they wish to, or in fact do, use a flexible work practice (e.g., job-share arrangements, leave arrangements, part-time work, working from home, changing the start and finish time of the workday, or taking leave). If this first indicator were fulfilled, one would expect to see flexibility (e.g., part-time work) considered normative, and not productive of workplace disadvantage or stratification, even if it is not mainstream.

ENSURE REASONABLE AND PREDICTABLE HOURS

There have been two significant changes in working arrangements in Australia over time regarding the "reasonableness" of working hours. The first is an increase in the average weekly hours for both full-time and part-time workers, and the second is the reduction in the proportion of employees working a standard week (defined as 35–40 hours), arising from the increase in part-time work. If this second indicator were fulfilled, employees would have greater control over, and satisfaction with, the number, spread, and predictability of their working hours in order to balance their family responsibilities, while still ensuring that business needs are met.

A LEGAL SAFETY NET FOR NONCOMPLIANT CONDUCT

The third indicator is legal support for workplace flexibility, and in particular, legal redress for conduct that discriminates against, neglects, or marginalizes the work-family agenda. Without a legal safety net, supportive policy statements become less compelling. There is evidence for the importance of legal drivers in relation to equality of opportunity (including work-family) in Australia, based on the 2008 National Diversity and Equality Survey.[2] The survey reported that 76 percent of best practice organizations indicated that a key driver for implementing a diversity/equality strategy is legal pressure (Equal Employment Opportunity Network of Australasia 2008). If this third indicator were fulfilled, legal processes would be in place to protect employees from workplace decisions that prioritize work over family and fail to find a balance between the two.

ENSURE SUFFICIENT STRUCTURAL SUPPORT
TO PROVIDE REAL CHOICE

Finally, while workplace policies and legal processes may support workplace flexibility, practical access to flexible work arrangements occurs within a broader context, namely structural supports for work-family balance. For example, access to quality and affordable care is a key determinant of workforce participation levels, and in particular the use of workplace flexibility. If this fourth and final indicator were fulfilled, choices about flexible work arrangements would be "real" choices, and not made in the absence of broader structural supports that generate a predetermined outcome (namely withdrawal from, or reduced participation in, the labor market).

In summary, Australian supports for workplace flexibility (principally the WorkChoices legislation), as well as election promises made by the new Labor government, will be analyzed in terms of these four indicators (note that the epilogue updates this chapter with reference to the Fair Work Act 2009 [Cth], which commenced in part on July 1, 2009, and implements Labor's election promises to provide greater support for working families and wind back problematic aspects of WorkChoices—namely the weighting towards employer-centric flexibility). These indicators will be considered within Australia's cultural context, particularly the concepts that (a) gender equity is a key driver of the work-family agenda; (b) part-time work is perceived as a key enabler of work-family balance (particularly for women); and (c) historically Australia has had a highly regulated industrial frame-work, which has been supportive of collective bargaining and centralized arbitra-tion. Each of these three factors influences expectations about the "right" kind of support for workplace flexibility, which is designed to promote work-family bal-ance, and therefore adds an additional layer to an evaluation of the current state of play in Australia.

Legal Policymaking: The Process

Between 2005 and 2007, several initiatives created policy development pressures relevant to the national work-family agenda. First, the federal Sex Discrimination Commissioner stimulated public discussion with the publication of her discussion paper *Striking the Balance: Women, Men, Work and Family* (Human Rights and Equal Opportunity Commission 2005), culminating in the 2007 report *It's About Time: Women, Men, Work and Family* (Human Rights and Equal Opportunity Com-mission 2007). The second initiative was launched by the House of Representatives' Standing Committee on Family and Human Services, which conducted a public inquiry into *Balancing Work and Family*,[3] culminating in the publication of the 2006 *Report on the Inquiry into Balancing Work and Family* (House of Representatives 2006). Both reports called on the previous conservative federal government to en-hance supports for working families, with broad recommendations touching on financial support, care services, and flexible work practices.

In addition, between 2005 and 2007 the Taskforce on Care Costs (an indepen-dent strategic alliance of forty-five business and nongovernmental organizations) released four major research reports on the relationship between work and the cost of care. The final 2007 report also highlighted the importance (and nature of) workplace flexibility for employees with responsibilities for the aged and people with a disability (Taskforce on Care Costs [TOCC] 2007c). Although the recom-mendations of each of these three stakeholders were largely ignored by the previous conservative federal government, they found fertile ground in the (then) Oppo-sition. Recommendations made in the Sex Discrimination Commissioner's 2007 report and by the Taskforce on Care Costs (2006b) were adopted by the Australian Labor Party in its 2007 election promises.

In contrast on May 26, 2005, the federal cabinet approved a proposal by Work-place Relations Minister Kevin Andrews to extend the scope of federal jurisdiction over state industrial laws (O'Neill 2005). This allowed the conservative federal gov-ernment to appropriate from state governments, many of them run by the Labor

Party, their traditional power to regulate employment arrangements, thus reducing the ambit of collective bargaining and central arbitration. Subsequently, the Workplace Relations Amendment (WorkChoices) Bill 2005 (Cth; "WorkChoices") was introduced into the House of Representatives on November 2, 2005, and approved only eight days later, on November 10, 2005. Following a brief Senate inquiry, the bill was passed by Parliament on December 7, 2005, and went into effect on March 27, 2006.

The introduction of these sweeping reforms was swift and merciless. The ruling conservative government provided minimal opportunity for consultation on the bill or the regulations, notwithstanding significant and vocal opposition from state governments, the Opposition, and unions. The nature of these reforms, and their potential impact on work-family flexibility, are discussed in detail later in the chapter. This lack of consultation may have contributed to the public's distrust of these reforms, as indicated by the subsequent election of the Labor government in late 2007. The scope of the backlash was certainly a stimulant for the conservative government to introduce amendments shortly before the 2007 election to limit the impact of WorkChoices by subjecting certain industrial agreements to a "fairness test"[4] and an impetus for the current Labor government to wind back WorkChoices via the Fair Work Act (Cth) in 2009.

Australia's Policy Position in Relation to Flexibility and the Work-Family Agenda

Australia does not have a national overarching or comprehensive statement of policy that identifies the country's position regarding workplace flexibility and the work-family agenda. Such a statement would assist in identifying and cohering work-family objectives, and in developing a strategic plan of action across government portfolios. This omission can be contrasted with the position taken by the New Zealand government in 2006, which released *Choices for Living, Caring and Working: A Ten-Year Plan to Improve the Caring and Employment Choices Available to Parents and Carers* (New Zealand Department of Labour 2006). In this document, the then Prime Minister of New Zealand Helen Clark asserted that her Government was "committed to creating more choice for all New Zealanders as they care for families and loved ones, and seek[s] to achieve personal, family and financial goals. The *Choices for Living, Caring and Working Plan of Action* aims to enhance caring and employment choices over the next decade" (2). Critically, the document was endorsed by the New Zealand Council of Trade Unions, the Equal Employment Opportunity Trust, and Business New Zealand, suggesting a uniformity of vision by all key stakeholders.

Given the absence of an overarching statement of policy, the previous Australian government's position on work-family flexibility must be inferred from statements of previous government ministers, as well as their initiatives (including legislation,[5] budget allocation, and discussion papers). The new federal government's position can be inferred from its election promises and initiatives implemented during its first eighteen months of power.

HOW AND WHY DID THE WORK-FAMILY AGENDA BECOME A GOVERNMENT FOCUS?

Australia's current commitment to workplace flexibility originated in a work-family agenda, which itself arose from a focus on gender equity. The history of gender equity can be said to have commenced in Australia in the early 1900s with women's gain of significant citizenship rights (including the right to own property, vote, and hold public office). I will highlight key legal/policy developments dating from the 1970s.[6] In summary the focus on gender equity has revealed that substantive equality requires more than access to work; it requires changes in work practices, to enable women (and men) to balance their work and family responsibilities. These changes have been characterized as "flexible work practices."

In the 1970s, the demand for gender equity was channeled into a politicized campaign for diverse social and economic reforms, including antidiscrimination legislation, equal pay, and industrial reforms. In 1972, after twenty-three years of conservative government, the Australian Labor Party was elected, and during its short period in office (1972–75) it implemented policies and bureaucratic machinery to promote gender equity. This included reopening the *Equal Pay* case (ensuring that women and men received equal pay for work of equal *value*, not just equal pay for doing the same *work* as men), appointing a ministerial adviser on women's issues, and, in 1974, requesting federal and state/territory premiers to prepare programs to improve women's status in accordance with International Women's Year.

In the 1980s, successive federal and state/territory governments built on these gender-focused initiatives by introducing broader antidiscrimination legislation (e.g., the Federal Sex Discrimination Act of 1984). The country also introduced affirmative action legislation to stimulate and proactively monitor gender equity programs in government agencies and among large private employers (e.g., via the Affirmative Action [Equal Opportunity for Women] Act, 1986). The Australian legislation does not compel an organization to meet quotas but to set their own targets and develop, implement, and report on their gender equity programs.[7]

Although complaints under federal and state discrimination legislation can only be brought to redress past discrimination and harassment, key cases have led to considerable publicity and widespread changes in employment practices. Women effectively challenged their exclusion from certain male-dominated industries (e.g., as pilots in the 1979 *Wardley v. Ansett Transport Industries* case); from studies (e.g., from technical studies in the 1986 *Leves v. Haines* case) and from promotional opportunities (e.g., as senior flight attendants in the 1985 *Squires v. Qantas Airways Limited* case, and as foreign correspondents in the 1988 *Styles v. The Secretary of the*

Department of Foreign Affairs and Trade case). At the same time, industrial test cases improved workplace conditions for women (e.g., the 1979 *Maternity Leave* case, which entitled women to twelve months unpaid maternity leave following birth or adoption). In effect, these discrimination cases helped open the door for women by eliminating formal occupational and hierarchical gender-based barriers, while industrial test cases held the door open during maternity leave. The outcome was a greater influx of women into the workplace prior to childbearing. Nevertheless, women continued to demonstrate a lower level of return during childrearing (i.e., postmaternity leave).

In the 1990s, concerns about women's inability to achieve equal representation at senior levels of public office and in management, notwithstanding "formal" equality, gave rise to the commissioning of numerous government and industry reports, notably the 1992 federal government report *Half Way to Equal: Report into Equal Opportunity and Equal Status for Women,* and the 1994 Law Reform Commission's report *Equality before the Law: Women's Equality.* These reports led to a deeper understanding of the hidden barriers to gender equity, and in particular the workplace norms and structures that separated work and family, and favored employees without significant caring responsibilities (usually men) over employees with such responsibilities (usually women). Hence these barriers were conceptualized as indirectly discriminating against women, and led to a wave of legal and industrial reforms to create more "family-friendly" workplaces. In 1990, Australia ratified the International Labour Organisation's Convention 156, "Workers with Family Responsibilities" (which came into force in 1991), and tellingly[8] amended the Sex Discrimination Act 1984 (Cth) in 1994 to prohibit dismissal from employment on the basis of family responsibilities. Further industrial reforms were introduced to enable employees to provide short-term care for an ill family or household member by accessing their sick leave or bereavement leave entitlements (through the 1994 *Family Leave* test case and 1995 *Personal/Carers' Leave* test case).

Finally, a new wave of discrimination cases questioned the "reasonableness" of employers limiting women's access to part-time work and job-share arrangements at more senior levels (e.g., as a law firm partner in *Hickie v. Hunt and Hunt* in 1998), and in certain occupations (e.g., as a local council finance officer in *FMSCEU [NSW] v. Nambucca Shire Council* in 1998).

In summary, a focus on gender equity in the 1970s and 1980s led to reforms that provided women with formal equality; that is, the right to enter and remain in the workplace. In the 1990s, with the greater influx of women into the workforce, women became numerically positioned to expose the more hidden barriers to equality. These barriers included the normative separation of work and family. Workplace flexibility—especially the mainstreaming of flexible work practices such as part-time work, job sharing, working from home, leave, and varying the start and finish times of the working day—has been the more recent goal of national reforms to promote work-family balance, and thus gender equity.

MORE RECENT APPROACHES TO THE NATIONAL
WORK-FAMILY AGENDA

The industrial reforms introduced by the previous federal government, which were promoted as enabling work-family balance, have served as the starting point for more recent approaches to workplace flexibility in the 2000s. The most significant of these was the introduction of WorkChoices legislation, which was formally operative until July 1, 2009, and is still impactful via the industrial agreements created under that legislation that are still in place. This section will describe WorkChoices and its relationship to workplace flexibility and work-family balance, then detail recent developments arising from election promises made by the Labor Party in 2007. Notably, election promises by the new federal government demonstrate an intention to provide greater employee entitlements to work-family-centered flexibility, and to achieve gender equity by expanding the work-family debate to explicitly include men.

When he announced the proposed introduction of the WorkChoices legislation, the then Prime Minister John Howard stated that the changes were "big, but they are fair" (Howard 2005, 1), and directly raised the connection to work-family balance. He argued that the government had sufficiently considered the interrelationship between the industrial reforms and family outcomes, as it had conducted "a detailed analysis of the impact of labour market policies on families, particularly labour market policies which address issues of workplace and family balance" (Howard 2005, 2). In response to questions from the media, Howard reiterated that the potential impact of the legislation on families had been considered by the cabinet as a result of the Family Impact Statement, and commented that "the best news for families is that their wages are higher, their jobs are more plentiful and their children are finding it easier to get jobs than they did ten years ago" (7). Hence, Howard assumed that low unemployment rates (and labor shortages) would provide employees with a high level of bargaining power to negotiate workplace flexibility. He seemed to believe that enabling industrial negotiations between *individual* employees and employers would facilitate greater levels of individually tailored workplace flexibility, and that this process would be employee-focused because "as never before we live in a worker's market. And that is something that has to be kept constantly in mind as we examine these reforms" (2).

The connection between WorkChoices, workplace flexibility, and the work-family agenda was more directly espoused by the Minister for Employment and Workplace Relations Kevin Andrews in a 2005 policy publication:

> The Australian Government recognises that flexible, family-friendly working arrangements are critical in assisting both men and women in finding an appropriate balance between their work and family responsibilities....The best way to ensure that [employees] have access to flexible and family-friendly working arrangements is through the promotion of agreement making at the individual

workplace level. (Department of Employment and Workplace Relations [DEWR] 2005b, 1)

In another publication by the Department of Employment and Workplace Relations, promoted by both Howard and Andrews, the previous government reiterated:

> Flexible work practices will help attract and retain the best people in a fiercely competitive market. Employers will be able to influence experienced workers to remain working longer by offering attractive working conditions and incentives. Employers who proactively provide an environment which supports work-life balance...will increase employee engagement, focus and productivity. (DEWR 2005c, 27)

When the previous treasurer, Peter Costello, announced the 2006/07 budget, he stated that "helping families is one of the highest priorities of this Government" (Costello 2006, 6). In addition, the objectives of the Workplace Relations Act (WRA) 1996 explicitly referred to work-family balance. The principal purpose of the WRA was "to provide a framework for cooperative workplace relations which promotes the economic prosperity and welfare of the people of Australia" (§ 3). The law's last three (of fourteen) objectives were:

(l) assisting employees to balance their work and family responsibilities effectively through the development of mutually beneficial work practices with employers; and

(m) respecting and valuing the diversity of the workforce by helping to prevent and eliminate discrimination on the basis of race, colour, sex, sexual preference, age, physical or mental disability, marital status, family responsibilities, pregnancy, religion, political opinion, national extraction or social origin; and

(n) assisting in giving effect to Australia's international obligations in relation to labour standards.[9]

All of these statements would lead one to the obvious conclusion that the previous government was cognizant and supportive of the work-family agenda, and that it considered workplace flexibility to be a key strategy to enabling work-family balance. The question, then, is whether the rhetoric was reflected in the previous government's policies and processes—and in particular, the WorkChoices legislation that, at its zenith, was said to govern the working arrangements of 85 percent of Australian workers (DEWR 2005a)—or whether the rhetoric was merely a cover for a hidden objective, namely employer-centered flexibility. This has been the criticism leveled by opponents of WorkChoices.

To a significant extent, the pre-2007 election assessment of Australia's position on work-family flexibility and on WorkChoices in particular was more of a reflection of the political affiliations of the analysts than an objective consideration of the legislation itself. The previous government's framework of analysis portrayed WorkChoices as enabling individual bargaining with safety nets and, in an economic environment of perceived employee power, the capacity to negotiate work-family flexibility without the previous restraint of awards.[10] Within this framework, Australia might have been seen as fully progressing the work-family agenda through workplace flexibility. It appears reasonable to argue that there were elements of WorkChoices that were positive in terms of this agenda. In contrast, critics, such as president of the Council of Trade Unions Sharan Burrow (2005), argued that, "On any measure the WorkChoices legislation will be bad law." Others contended that there was a "disconnect between Howard's political rhetoric about the diverse life experiences of Australia's families in the 21st century, the Government's role to 'support families in the choices they wish to make' (Howard, 2005) and the conservative ideology of gender that structures work and family policy initiatives" (Hill 2006, 1).

Hill identified apparent inconsistencies between the taxation system and benefits payments (e.g., the Maternity Payment[11] and Child Care Benefit[12]), which appeared to both penalize and support working parents, and suggested that these reflected the government's confusion about whether women should be regarded as workers, carers, or both. According to her view, this confusion flowed through WorkChoices as well.

In essence, the fundamental criticism of WorkChoices, in relation to enabling work-family balance, was that it relied too heavily on market forces, and in particular the low unemployment rate, to ensure that employees had equal bargaining power with employers. Although equality of bargaining positions might exist for high-income employees with scarce skills, that outcome is less available for vulnerable employees, such as youth and women. Furthermore, WorkChoices was criticized as providing insufficient legislative impetus for employees to facilitate work-family balance through flexible work practices. These criticisms were reflected in the Australian Labor Party's (ALP) preelection commitments to amend WorkChoices. In particular, the ALP was elected on a promise to wind back aspects of WorkChoices (e.g., the focus on individual bargaining) and reform perceived deficiencies (e.g., those relating to flexible work practices). In essence, the new federal government intends to leave less to market forces and provide a higher level of legislated employee entitlement. Tellingly, however, the ALP did not promise to repeal WorkChoices per se, but to modify its ambit, suggesting that some aspects of WorkChoices are beneficial to working families.

Legal Framework and Workplace Flexibility

The most significant event to affect workplace relations during the conservative government's thirteen years in power was the 2005 introduction of the WorkChoices legislation, which substantially amended the Workplace Relations Act of 1996 (Cth).

The significance of WorkChoices reforms was underlined by the fact that the then Prime Minister John Howard jointly announced the reforms together with the Minister for Employment and Workplace Relations, even though they strictly related to the subject area of employment and therefore fell within that minister's portfolio. In essence, the WorkChoices legislation reduced the capacity of state governments to continue their traditional role in regulating employment arrangements and created new rules for workplace bargaining.

Howard summarized WorkChoices as driving three major changes to the existing industrial environment: first, "the creation of a single national industrial relations system"; second (and euphemistically), "the simplification of the agreement making process"; and third (and disingenuously), "a better balancing of the Unfair Dismissal Laws" (Howard 2005, 1).[13] In relation to work-family flexibility, it is not the broad focus of these changes that is of particular interest, but the details in relation to (a) agreement-making; (b) minimum standards; and (c) discrimination law safety nets, as well as the broader framework necessary for implementation of work-family focused flexibility, namely, financial support (e.g., childcare) and communication strategies (i.e., knowledge of workplace flexibility).

AWARDS AND AGREEMENT-MAKING

Historically, "awards" and "agreements" have been the dominant industrial instruments used to regulate Australian workplace conditions. Traditionally awards are made following a collective process of industry negotiation between unions and employers and an independent review by an industrial agency or commission/ court, while agreements could be bargained at the individual or enterprise level (but referenced back to awards as a safety net). In 2005, approximately "half of the award-regulated workforce in Australia (and probably a greater proportion of the total workforce) [were] regulated in their employment by awards and industrial agreements made or approved by State industrial tribunals" (Punch 2006, 1–120).

Arising from the introduction of the WorkChoices legislation, if state employees were employed by a corporation, then (setting aside transitional provisions) they became governed by the operation of the Federal Workplace Relations Act 1996 (WRA). This change was not just an academic matter, since the WorkChoices legislation compelled employees and employers to enter into one of five specific types of agreements that were negotiated at the enterprise or individual level, and reduced the capacity for union-negotiated agreements. These agreements were required to include five minimum terms and conditions (known collectively as the Australian Fair Pay and Conditions Standard) and prohibited from including specific content (e.g., allowing for industrial action or encouraging trade union membership). Finally, these agreements were not vetted or approved by an independent agency. (At a federal level under the prereform WRA, individual and collective agreements were previously scrutinized by either the Office of the Employment Advocate [OEA] or the Australian Industrial Relations Commission [AIRC], respectively.) Instead, they become operational after being agreed upon by the parties and lodged (an administrative process) with the OEA.

Shortly after being elected Prime Minister, Kevin Rudd announced that his cabinet had approved the development of a bill to prevent the creation of new Australian Workplace Agreements (AWA; Gillard and Swan 2007) and Deputy Prime Minister Julia Gillard committed to establishing a new industrial umpire to facilitate collecting bargaining and collective agreements (Gillard 2007b). In February 2008 Gillard introduced the Workplace Relations Amendment (Transition to Forward with Fairness) bill into the parliament to begin the process of phasing out elements of WorkChoices. In effect, these amendments will shift the balance back to collective agreement-making, and step up the independent review process. In May 2009 the Fair Work Act was passed by Parliament and came into effect (in part) on July 1, 2009, finalizing that process of wind back on those issues.

MINIMUM STANDARDS

WorkChoices provided that agreements could not be less favorable than the five minimum terms and conditions that constituted the previous standard (although parties could bargain above these minima). The standard comprised (a) wages, (b) maximum hours of work, (c) annual leave, (d) personal and carer's leave, and (e) parental leave.

First, with respect to wages, WorkChoices set a federal minimum wage and provided that the Australian Fair Pay Commission could review and adjust this minimum.

Second, with respect to the ordinary hours of work, WorkChoices "guaranteed" that an employee could not be required to work more than thirty-eight hours a week (averaged across an applicable period, but not longer than twelve months), plus "reasonable additional hours" (WRA 1996, § 226[1]). In terms of the "reasonableness" of additional hours, WorkChoices provided that the employee's personal circumstances (including family responsibilities) were one of the factors to be considered (WRA 1996, § 226[4]).

Third, with respect to annual leave, all employees (except for casuals) were "guaranteed" up to four weeks leave per year (for full-time workers, and calculated on a pro-rata basis for fewer than full-time hours), with the capacity to cash out up to two weeks of that leave.

Fourth, with respect to personal and carer's leave, full-time, noncasual employees were entitled to ten days paid personal carer's leave per year (for part-time workers, leave is calculated on a pro-rata basis). Personal leave is accessible if the employee is sick, whereas carer's leave is accessible by employees who have responsibilities to care for an "immediate family member"[14] due to the illness of that family member. Two additional days of paid compassionate leave were available to employees if the employee's immediate family member had an illness or injury that is life threatening (WRA 1996, § 257). Two additional days of unpaid carer's leave were available to an employee to undertake their caring responsibilities for a family member if all paid leave has been exhausted (WRA 1996, § 250).

Fifth, with respect to parental leave, WorkChoices provided that employees who had been employed for twelve months (including casuals who had been employed on a regular and systematic basis for the preceding twelve months) were entitled to twelve months of unpaid maternity leave (WRA 1996, § 265), one week unpaid paternity leave to be concurrently taken with the spouse (WRA 1996, § 282[1a]), up to twelve months unpaid paternity leave to be the primary carer (WRA 1996, § 282[1b]), two days unpaid preadoption leave, three weeks unpaid adoption leave, or twelve months adoption leave (WRA 1996, §§ 301–303).

In February 2008, the new Labor government released an exposure draft of the proposed ten National Employment Standards for consultation (Australian Government Department of Education 2008). The draft National Employment Standards provided entitlements in relation to (a) hours of work, (b) parental leave, (c) flexible work for parents, (d) annual leave, (e) personal, carer's, and compassionate leave, (f) community service leave, (g) public holidays, (h) information in the workplace, (i) termination of employment and redundancy, and (j) long service leave. Additional conditions regulating employment will be included in new award provisions (e.g., wages).

Critically, in relation to flexibility and work-family balance, the two most innovative standards promised by the new federal government are:[15]

1. *Parental leave:* Twelve months' unpaid parental leave, for each parent, to be taken in conjunction with the birth or adoption of their child. One parent is entitled to request an additional twelve months leave from their employer, and refusal must be on "reasonable business grounds" (ibid., 14).
2. *Flexible work for parents:* A right for parents to request flexible work arrangements (e.g., part-time work, nonstandard start or finish times, working from home, and job sharing) from their employer, until their child reaches school age. Refusal must be on reasonable business grounds (ibid., 10).

Between promise and implementation (i.e., the introduction of legislation to give effect to the new standards), further support was introduced for working parents in relation to these two standards. In 2009 the government introduced eighteen weeks of paid maternity leave (effective January 1, 2011) and a right for parents of young children and children with a disability to request a flexible work arrangement (effective January 1, 2010).

Effectively, the new government has built upon the previous government's concept of minimum standards and made significant extensions in relation to workplace flexibility. These extensions reflect the new government's espoused commitment to provide "fresh ideas for work and family." As noted previously in discussing the work-family agenda as a government focus, this impetus is grounded in an underlying commitment to gender equity. The association between flexibility, work and family, and gender equity is evident from the following explanation given by the current deputy prime minister, Julia Gillard, during the election campaign:

> National surveys of work life outcomes tell us that long, unsocial hours of work, a lack of quality part-time work and traditional leave arrangements make it difficult for men and women to balance work and family life.…Women in their prime working age are taking on multiple roles, including paid and unpaid work, and voluntary work. (Gillard 2007a, 4)

The new Labor government's rhetoric is notably inclusive of men, in keeping with the findings from the Sex Discrimination Commissioner's 2007 report, *It's about Time: Women, Men, Work and Family;* namely, that the engagement (and acknowledgment) of men's participation in work and family is a pathway to gender equity outcomes (Human Rights and Equal Opportunity Commission 2007). This perspective follows a general shift in public debate about work and family, and suggests a more inclusive, government-led framework of reference going forward.

DISCRIMINATION LAW SAFETY NETS

Finally, in relation to discrimination safety nets, WorkChoices maintained the WRA's previous prohibition against unlawful termination (irrespective of the size of the organization) on prescribed grounds. These grounds included termination on the basis of a discriminatory reason (including family responsibilities; WRA 1996, § 659.2.f), and maternity or other parental leave (WRA 1996, § 659.2.h). In relation to the family responsibilities provisions, this jurisdiction has previously been enlivened in a case (*Laz v. Downer Group Ltd* 2000) concerning a female employee's capacity to control her working hours—or at least be given reasonable notice about variations to those hours—in order to meet her childcare responsibilities.

These safety nets are consistent with the Federal Sex Discrimination Act of 1984 and various pieces of state antidiscrimination legislation that prohibit discrimination on the basis of family/caring responsibilities. (However, the WRA provisions are more limited in scope than discrimination legislation because they relate only to termination.)

Although there are differences between these legislative protections, at the high water mark employees (i.e., both men and women) are protected from direct and indirect (disparate impact) discrimination on the basis of their caring responsibilities; under the Anti-Discrimination Act 1977 (NSW), employers may even be obliged to reasonably accommodate an employee's caring responsibilities (Anti-Discrimination Act 1977 [NSW], Part 4B; subject to limited defenses[16]). This backdrop of caring responsibilities discrimination legislation cannot be ignored when assessing the current state of play of workplace flexibility in Australia, as it has been used effectively by workers with caring responsibilities[17] to access flexible work practices (e.g., part-time work,[18] job-share arrangements,[19] and changes to the start and finish times of the workday[20]) and has helped to cement a cultural expectation that mothers returning from maternity leave should be able to work part-time when their children are young.

In 2007, the Sex Discrimination Commissioner recommended that this safety net should be further enhanced by the introduction of broad and explicit federal antidiscrimination legislation for working carers. Such legislation would shift the (federal) focus from women to carers (currently protections come under the Sex Discrimination Act 1984 [Cth]). It also would create consistent rights across federal and state jurisdictions by bringing all states up to the high water mark (Human Rights and Equal Opportunity Commission 2007, xvii). A Family Responsibilities and Carers' Rights Act would provide protection from discrimination for all Australian employees with caring responsibilities (not just parents), as well as the right to request access to (reasonable) flexible work practices. Critically, this act would create litigable rights for working carers who are denied access to workplace flexibility. Although the previous government declined to take up this recommendation, the Australian Labor Party noted the Sex Discrimination Commissioner's recommendation and made a preelection commitment to establish the Office of Work and Family, which has been fulfilled. This office is tasked with considering the introduction of such legislation (McLucas 2007). Although a commitment to "consider" the introduction of legislation is somewhat loose, it at least opens the door to discussions with the new federal government about creating litigable rights. At present the prohibition against an employer's refusal to provide reasonable flexibility to parents (which is proposed under the National Employment Standard) is not subject to review by an independent third party (Gillard 2007a). Given that this legislation appears to have a higher priority for implementation than the introduction of the Family Responsibilities and Carers' Rights Act, it seems reasonable to expect that the new federal government will focus on litigable rights once employers and employees have become more comfortable with the softer rights under the National Employment Standard.

As to the importance of these legislative imperatives, 77 percent of best practice organizations surveyed by the Equal Employment Opportunity Network of Australasia (2008) stated that legal requirements drive their diversity-related (including gender and caring) employment practices, and a recent international report suggested that this is a common experience in high-income countries (Hegewisch and Gornick 2008).

FINANCIAL SUPPORT

One of the key structural supports for work-family flexibility is access to affordable and quality care. Current financial supports for working carers include a range of benefits and allowances.[21] In 2004 and 2005, the conservative government introduced further financial and structural reforms to assist carers. In December 2004, the government introduced the Child Care Tax Rebate (CCTR) to refund 30 percent of out-of-pocket childcare expenses (capped at AUS$4,000 per year) to carers.

When announcing the CCTR, the treasurer commented that "this is going to be of benefit to all working women in Australia, it will be of enormous benefit to families" (Costello 2004). In relation to the accessibility of care, in the 2006–07 budget the treasurer announced that his government would "remove the limit on the number of subsidised outside school hours care and family day care," and that this would "generate an additional 25,000 places by 2009. In 1996 there were 300,000 child-care places in Australia. We are budgeting for over 700,000 in 2009" (Costello 2006, 7). With respect to elder and disability care, the treasurer allocated a bonus of between AUS$600 and $1,000 to each carer and commented, "Carers of people with disabilities—whether they are children or older people—make a special selfless contribution to our society" (Costello 2006, 7).

Between 2005 and 2007, the Taskforce on Care Costs (TOCC) published research demonstrating the inadequacy of the federal government's care-related financial commitments. Moreover, employees' inability to meet escalating care costs was jeopardizing their continued workforce participation (one in four workers with caring responsibilities was likely to leave the workforce, and another one in four was likely to reduce his or her hours of work; TOCC 2005, 2006a, 2006b). In support of this claim in 2006, TOCC published Australia's first Childcare Affordability Index (CAI). Based on data produced by the Australian Bureau of Statistics, the CAI tracked the cost of childcare against disposable income during the period 1990 to 2006. The CAI demonstrated that between 2001 and 2006, the average family's ability to afford childcare had decreased substantially. In particular, childcare costs had increased by 65 percent, while average household disposable income had increased by only 17 percent, creating a decrease in affordability of 52 percent (TOCC 2007b).

TOCC undertook economic modeling to identify a fair and sustainable economic solution to this challenge, and in October 2006 recommended that the government reimburse 50 percent of out-of-pocket care costs, capped at AUS$10,000 per year per family. TOCC demonstrated that the proposed reimbursement would provide an immediate 54 percent return on the investment by increasing parents' levels of workforce participation (and therefore income tax contributions), and by reducing levels of welfare dependency (TOCC 2006b, 4).

In relation to employees with caring responsibilities for the aged and people with a disability, in November 2007 (immediately prior to the election) TOCC (2007c) published a final report criticizing the very low level of financial support for these carers, as well as the branding of these supports as "welfare" rather than related to "workforce participation." TOCC concluded that this group of carers were extremely disadvantaged, and therefore at high risk of leaving the workforce or working below skill level.

The previous federal government responded to TOCC's data on childcare by announcing a small (10%) increase in Child Care Benefit payments (TOCC 2007a) in the 2007 budget, and ignored TOCC's data on aged and disability care. In contrast, as part of its election commitments, the Australian Labor Party adopted TOCC's childcare reimbursement proposal with a slight amendment (namely, that the cap was reduced to AUS$7,500 per child per year), and this promise was implemented in the new government's first budget in 2008. The Labor Party also promised to introduce fifteen hours per week free preschool or early learning for all four-year-olds, and to establish the Office of Work and Family with terms of reference that would include carers of the aged and people with a disability.

COMMUNICATION STRATEGY

Finally, communication about the nexus between flexibility, work-family balance, and gender equity is integral to its successful implementation. The previous federal government expended significant sums on a communication strategy about workplace flexibility in general and, more particularly, about the work-family connection. In 2005, the Prime Minister Howard and the Minister for Workplace Relations Andrews engaged in a national road show to personally educate employers about the business imperatives to adapt to current and predicted labor shortages by, in part, introducing flexible work practices and improving the work-family balance.

Furthermore, the previous government financed the development of "Workplace Flexibility Industry Projects" to "improve employer awareness and take-up of flexible working arrangements" and "Employment Demand Demonstration Projects" in relation to mature age workers and employees with a disability (DEWR 2005d). The Workplace Flexibility Industry Projects targeted three industries/sectors (hospitality, retail, and childcare) known for their high representation of women, and developed targeted publications. A case study publication, *Serving Up Flexibility,* was developed for the restaurant and catering industry; "Flexibility Works," a website on flexible work arrangements[22] was developed for the retail sector; and a training program for managers of center-based long daycare centers, *Flexibility Benefits,* was produced (DEWR, 2007a).

Finally, the previous federal government continued to support the National Work and Family Awards, which were commenced in 1992 to give "public recognition to significant achievement by business in the development and implementation of work and family policies" (DEWR 2007b, 1).

In summary, the previous federal government adopted multiple formats (i.e., face-to-face, Internet, and hard copy publications) and methodologies (i.e., information and awards) to communicate the value of workplace flexibility in terms of creating work-family balance. It did not evaluate its communication strategy; however, it is clearly perceived by the public to be of value because the new federal government was elected on promises to continue and extend key elements of the strategy. In particular the new federal government committed to promoting:

1. *Information:* Help small businesses to pursue workplace flexibility, which will enhance work-family balance by distributing business- and industry-specific

information and providing small grants to businesses to self-initiate family-friendly measures (e.g., developing policies; Gillard 2007a, 4).

2. *Awards:* Extend the National Work and Family Awards to include awards for specific industries. At present the awards are made for organizations of a certain size (i.e., small, medium, and large organizations) and sector (i.e., private, government, and community). Further, the awards will be promoted by the government funding a full-page advertisement in the employment pages of major Australian newspapers (Gillard 2007a, 3).

3. *Citation:* Introduce a special symbol to be used by National Work and Family Award winners and accredited employers (following accreditation by the Work and Family Award judges), indicating that an organization has attained a certain standard in relation to "the achievement of work/family balance" (Gillard 2007a, 3–4).

In measuring the effectiveness of the previous government's communication strategy, the first clear indicator is the level of public awareness of the importance of these issues in private and public debate. Prime Minister Howard described the topic of work and family as a "BBQ stopper" (Howard 2002; i.e., a controversial current affairs issue that is discussed among Australian families on social occasions), a term that has been adopted repetitively since then by the media and others to describe the private debate around work-family issues. The public debate on work and family (and workplace flexibility), as illustrated by the Australian Labor Party during the 2007 election, indicates its importance to the broad Australian population. The communication strategy to create workplace flexibility clearly fell short of public expectations, given that the previous government lost office in the 2007 federal election. The centrality of work-family and flexibility issues to the election outcome was underscored by the new prime minister in his acceptance speech on election night, when he stated that "[getting] the balance right between fairness and flexibility in the workplaces of the nation" is a key agenda item for his government, as it will ensure "by that and by other practical assistance to working families in Australia, that the great Australian 'fair go' has a future and not just a past" (Rudd 2007).

In summary, this section has identified the key pieces of legislation that regulate workplace flexibility in relation to work-family balance, and in particular, the relevant elements of WorkChoices and antidiscrimination legislation. It has also identified some of the key budgetary and communication supports for workplace flexibility. These initiatives suggest a match between the previous government's espoused support for work-family flexibility and reality, although room for improvement is clearly indicated by the new government's election. The following section provides a critical analysis of these initiatives in terms of the four criteria of mutual work-family flexibility, identified earlier in the chapter.

A Critical Analysis

In Australia, the four key indicators of workplace flexibility that enable work-family balance are (a) enabling access to flexible work practices (and leave) without disadvantage; (b) ensuring reasonable and predictable hours; (c) providing a legal safety net for noncompliant conduct; and (d) ensuring sufficient structural support to provide real choice. It is critical to have valid and specific indicators by which to measure the current state of play in Australia, since much of the current debate about flexibility, and in particular comment on WorkChoices, has been fallen more into the realm of political rhetoric and perception than considered analysis.

Enabling Access to Flexible Work Practices without Disadvantage

In relation to access to flexible work practices without disadvantage, Australian discrimination law cases, as well as academic/industry research, suggest that full-time work is still the normative mode of work in Australia and that attitudinal as well as structural barriers persist in relation to flexible work arrangements, particularly at senior levels within organizations, among professional or managerial occupations, and by gender.

The proportion of men and women working part-time has increased significantly over the past twenty years (by 9% each for men and women).[23] Nevertheless, in 2006, only a quarter (28.6%) of the total number of people employed work on a part-time basis (defined as working less than thirty-five hours per week), and females comprise 71.6 percent of the part-time workforce (Australian Bureau of Statistics [ABS] 2007). Furthermore, industry research suggests that part-time work is associated with lower quality work, restricted access to training (Industrial Relations Victoria 2005a), and career limitations (e.g., Victorian Women Lawyers 2005).

WorkChoices provided minimal leave entitlements and prohibited unlawful termination on the basis of family responsibilities (one characteristic of which is adjustments to working time arrangements). Thus, prima facie WorkChoices legislation, together with broader discrimination legislation, offers remedial protection to workers who are disadvantaged by using flexible work arrangements or leave to balance their work-family responsibilities. Furthermore, in terms of the match between government rhetoric about work-family balance and reality, there is a positive development in that, out of twenty "allowable award matters" included in awards[24] both pre- and post-WorkChoices, the previous government's standard enshrined five minimum terms and conditions for all agreements, four of which could be easily categorized as relating to work-family flexibility. (Under the prereform Act, these terms were globally no less favorable than the relevant award terms in agreements by virtue of the "no-disadvantage" test.[25])

This, however, is not the end of the story. The minimum leave standards in WorkChoices were in essence a codification of common practice, legislation, and award conditions. Some of these arose from the AIRC's previous decisions (which were adopted by state industrial commissions/courts) in relation to maternity leave (1979), adoption leave (1985), parental leave (1990), family leave (1994), personal/carer's leave (1995), and parental leave for casuals (2001). Hence, as a general statement, these standards do not *advance* the current state of play in relation to work-family flexibility.

Moreover, the standards in relation to personal/carer's leave are explicitly not applicable to casual employees. This position mirrors the pre-WorkChoices environment, and conforms to the provision that casuals receive a 20 percent higher hourly rate of pay above the basic wage periodic rate of pay to compensate for this omission (WRA 1996, §§ 182, 185, 186). WorkChoices reinforced the stratification of benefits according to permanent/casual status. This is of particular concern given the predominance of women casual employees (31%) over men (22%; ABS 2006b, 2), as women are traditionally more likely to seek access to carer's leave (Group of 151 Australian Industrial Relations, Labour Market and Legal Academics 2005, 34).

The only exception to these general comments about WorkChoices' failure to advance work-family balance relates to the leveling of the playing field for all employees. Before WorkChoices, 73 percent of employees had entitlements to paid annual and/or sick leave, and of this group, full-time workers were more likely (87%) than part-time workers (41%) to have access to these entitlements, and men (77%) were more likely than women (69%) (Australian Bureau of Statistics [ABS] 2006b, 3–4). Hence, for nearly a quarter (23%) of employees, these minimum conditions ensured access to paid annual and personal leave. In addition, for full-time and part-time workers who did not previously have access to carer's leave, the minimum standards represented a significant positive guarantee. In assessing the value of the minimum standards, the raising and leveling of the playing field should not be neglected.

Critically, however, for all employees, WorkChoices failed to codify significant[26] aspects of the most recent (and innovative) AIRC decision, the *Family Provisions* case (2005a). Prior to the *Family Provisions* case, employees were entitled to (a) one week of concurrent leave following the birth of a child, and three weeks' concurrent leave following adoption; and (b) one year of unpaid parental leave following the birth or adoption of a child. There were no entitlements for a parent to work part-time on returning from parental leave. In relation to working time and parental leave, in 2005 the AIRC decided that an employee had the right to request an employer to approve

1. the taking of a simultaneous period of unpaid parental leave by both parents of a child (following birth or adoption) for up to eight weeks;
2. 104 weeks of unpaid parental leave;

3. part-time work for a parent until a child reaches school age; and that the request may only be refused if the employer has reasonable grounds.

In summary, it could be said that the state of play in Australia prior to the November 2007 federal election had advanced slightly through the establishment of minimum standards, which created a level playing field (and a raised field for those employees who did not previously have access to such entitlements). At the same time, the failure to codify the innovative provisions of the *Family Provisions* case in relation to extended leave and part-time work was a significant step backward for workers with childcare responsibilities. The extension of the parental leave entitlements and the introduction of part-time work entitlements were significantly disputed before the AIRC, so the ultimate decision by the AIRC was perceived as considered and positive in terms of advancing the work-family agenda. As a mark of that high regard, the AIRC decision was substantially followed by the NSW Industrial Relations Commission in late 2005.[27] There was, therefore, a palpable sense that WorkChoices' failure to codify the full impact of the AIRC *Family Provisions* case was a reduction of entitlements, especially given that some state government workers were covered by the more extensive family provisions, and therefore regressive in terms of mainstreaming flexible work practices.

It is expected that these deficiencies will be largely remedied through the implementation of the new federal government's election promises, most notably in relation to the introduction of paid maternity leave and the right for (some) parents to request flexible work arrangements under the 2009 National Employment Standards. The realization of these commitments, albeit not applicable to all employees with caring responsibilities, means that the Australian government has taken a significant step toward providing concrete support for working parents rather than leaving outcomes to market forces.

Ensuring Reasonable and Predictable Hours

With respect to the indicator regarding ensuring reasonable and predictable hours, WorkChoices guaranteed the maximum hours of ordinary work (on average a thirty-eight-hour week) and limited overtime to a "reasonable" standard.

Average weekly hours for both full- and part-time workers have increased in recent decades—for example, between 1985 and 2005, average weekly hours for full-time workers increased from 40.2 to 41.9 hours (ABS 2006a, 126).[28] Thus, the establishment of a guaranteed maximum number of work hours was a positive step, particularly as the standard was in line with community expectations about the length of the standard working week. The limitation on overtime essentially codified the AIRC's decision in the *Working Hours* case (2002). This decision provided that an employee could refuse overtime if that would prejudice the employee's personal circumstances (including family responsibilities).

In relation to the predictability of hours, and a reduction in the proportion of employees working a standard week, however, WorkChoices provided no further prescription than the reasonable hours standard. This is of particular concern for workers with caring responsibilities, given that the regularity and predictability of hours is critical to making decisions about obtaining, retaining, and affording care arrangements (Industrial Relations Victoria 2005a, 41). This hollowing out of the standard working week has both positive and negative connotations. As observed above, the proportion of people working part-time has increased over the last twenty years; for those wishing to balance their work and family responsibilities through part-time work, this is a positive trend.[29] At the same time, however, working very long hours (defined as fifty hours or more per week) has become more common, with 30 percent of men working full-time putting in fifty hours or more per week (up from 22% in 1985; ABS 2006a, 127). Of this group, over half (59%) would prefer to work fewer hours (ABS 2006a, 128). In relation to the predictability of hours, a key trend has been the increasing proportion of casual labor (i.e., labor that is temporary and irregular).[30] In contradistinction to permanent part-time work, which connotes a regular pattern of shorter working hours, casual work is associated with unpredictability and irregularity.[31]

In summary, the work-family indicator of reasonable and predictable hours is partially fulfilled by the WorkChoices legislation, although the minimum standard does little more than codify existing expectations and provisions. WorkChoices essentially adopted a neutral position in relation to regulating the predictability of hours. WorkChoices did not reduce entitlements, since such regulations did not exist prior to WorkChoices, but neither did it advance the work-family agenda by attempting to balance the competing desires of business for employment at will with the needs of employees for predictability and regularity.

In terms of possible changes regarding hours of work since the 2007 election, the Australian Labor Party's election policy on industrial relations promised that (a) under the National Employment Standards "the standard working week for a full-time employee will be 38 hours. Employees may be required to work additional hours, but cannot be required to work unreasonable additional hours" (Rudd and Gillard 2007, 7); (b) new Awards will include conditions on "arrangements for when work is performed, including hours of work, rostering, rest breaks and meal breaks" (Rudd and Gillard 2007, 10); and (c) a model flexibility clause will be published for inclusion in collective agreements (Gillard 2007b, 4). Notwithstanding the implementation of these promises via the Fair Work Act 2009 (Cth), it is unclear whether these will cover, and be sufficient to address, the issue of predictability of hours.

Providing a Legal Safety Net for Noncompliant Conduct

The third indicator, providing a legal safety net for noncompliant conduct—in the sense of conduct that does not support mutual flexibility—attracted the most criticism from opponents of the WorkChoices legislation. In Australia legal safety nets, within the industrial law context, have been traditionally perceived as deriving from the collective and transparent nature of workplace bargaining, and the role of review processes. Discrimination law has been seen as a supplementary process because it is based on an individual complaint mechanism.

In relation to collective bargaining, WorkChoices promoted individual and enterprise bargaining, and while individual- and enterprise-based agreements were available before the WorkChoices reforms, WorkChoices reduced the opportunity for award-making and collective bargaining. Furthermore, WorkChoices limited both the external review of agreements by independent agencies by reducing the capacity of the AIRC to arbitrate, and it reduced the transparency of the agreements by removing the Office of the Employment Advocate vetting process.

In relation to the reduction of collective bargaining (particularly as negotiated by unions), the perceived negative impact of WorkChoices should not be overstated. As of 2005, only 22.4 percent of the population were trade union members, down from 32.7 percent in 1995(ABS 2006a, 115), and award coverage had declined significantly. Indeed, it has been estimated that only "20% of the workforce relied upon changes to award rates to obtain any regular wage increase, while more than double that number were being paid in accordance with registered workplace agreements" (Commerce Clearing House 2006, para. 9–090). Nevertheless, there are issues of concern about WorkChoices tacit coercion into (or at least the favoring of) individual bargaining.[32]

In support of individual bargaining, commentators suggested that WorkChoices created the opportunity for "more flexible workplace arrangements which can depart from award restrictions" (Colvin, Watson, and Ogilvie 2006, 99). In relation to work-family flexibility,[33] the chief executive of the Australian Industry Group argued that WorkChoices enabled those employees who seek a flexible work arrangement to bargain for that arrangement: "All employees should have the right to enter into an individual agreement with their employer. In a male-dominated workplace, flexible working arrangements may hold little attraction to the majority of employees, but they may be extremely important to a female worker—far more than a pay rise" (Ridout 2006, 63). There is some merit to the argument that women in particular have not always been advantaged by collective agreements negotiated by male-dominated unions in male-dominated workplaces. However, the individual bargaining option may not be a real alternative for vulnerable employees negotiating flexibility. This is because the individual bargaining argument rests on the assumption of equal bargaining power between the employee and employer, which was of course the Prime Minister Howard's perspective when he argued that the guarantee of harmonious workplace conditions was the existing labor shortage. However, labor shortages are not evenly dispersed throughout the market, and the evidence suggests that an employee's capacity to take advantage of individual bargaining is situationally dependent. In particular, the OECD has concluded that workplace support for work-family flexibility "is most common in the public sector and among large firms with a sig-nificant female workforce. These policies are more commonly associated with highly educated and high skilled workers." In contrast, the OECD has found that "women in less skilled occupations are therefore less likely to benefit from family-friendly poli-cies" (Organisation for Economic Co-operation and Development [OECD] 2005, 5). The OECD's finding suggests that not all workers who seek to access family-friendly workplace flexibility will be successful; and that the assumption of equal bargaining power, even in the face of low unemployment rates, is not supported. As a conse-quence, Pocock and Charlesworth (2006) suggest that WorkChoices created a "wid-ening dispersion in outcomes in different industries and occupations and amongst men and women and different classes of workers" (6).

In relation to the public review/arbitration of workplace conditions, as noted above, the AIRC has had a lengthy history of advancing work-family flexibility through test cases on leave and hours provisions. The AIRC arbitrated specific awards and subject issues, and then the decision would be "flowed on" to other federal awards and taken up in state industrial courts/commissions. In the absence of this mechanism, a significant opportunity for robust and considered debate has been removed from the public arena. Optimistically, Punch (2006) argues that

> in the medium term to long term, this stultification of the major aspects of the AIRC's jurisdiction could lead to a reduction in its relevance, influence and sta-tus. However, the AIRC is a hardy creature—in one form or another it has been around for 101 years, and it has survived many challenges to its role. (1–070)

In relation to the transparency of the negotiation and review process (which can be said to facilitate compliant conduct), pre-WorkChoices Australian Work-place Agreements were submitted to the Office of the Employment Advocate or the AIRC for approval. Under WorkChoices, agreements are generally "made" (WRA 1996, § 333) once they have been executed (i.e., signed, dated, and witnessed) by the parties (e.g., the employer and employee), and operative once they have been lodged with the Office of the Employment Advocate. The OEA operated in an ad-ministrative capacity and did not review or scrutinize the content of agreements. In particular, agreements no longer had to satisfy the "no disadvantage" test.[34]

However, this situation changed in July 2007, when the Federal Workplace Au-thority was tasked by the conservative government with implementing a "fairness test," by which collective agreements or Australian Workplace Agreements (lodged from May 7, 2007) would not be approved unless it could be demonstrated that the new agreement provided fair compensation for lost or changed conditions.[35] This change signaled a desperate attempt by the previous government to win back public support for a system of workplace relations regulation that was out of step with community expectations of fairness and balance.

Finally, in relation to the safety nets provided by discrimination law, as noted above, WorkChoices preserved the prohibition against termination for a discriminatory reason (including family responsibilities), and other federal and state discrimination laws continue to protect workers with caring responsibilities from discrimination. As argued elsewhere, discrimination laws have been used innovatively by administrative tribunals to create a relatively robust safety net in relation to work-family flexibility (Bourke 2004).[36]

In summary, the legal safety net for noncompliant conduct (supportive of work-family flexibility) has been indirectly diminished by the shifts in collective bargaining, transparency, review, and arbitration processes. This means that much more reliance must now be placed on direct protections for workers with caring responsibilities, which are to be found in discrimination laws.

This position, however, is likely to be remedied by election commitments from the new federal government, which (a) encourage enterprise-level collective bargaining, and halt individual bargaining via AWAs (Rudd and Gillard 2007, 13); (b) introduce Fair Work Australia to act as "an independent umpire to oversee Federal Labor's new industrial relations system" and promote "family friendly and flexible work arrangements" (Gillard 2007b, 2); and (c) reintroduce unfair dismissal laws for employees of small businesses (Rudd and Gillard 2007, 19).

In the event that these are not sufficient, more pressure will be placed on the new government to implement federal discrimination legislation, as recommended by the Sex Discrimination Commissioner, to give broader and litigable rights to all employees with caring responsibilities (i.e., beyond young children).

Ensuring Sufficient Structural Support to Provide Real Choice

With respect to ensuring sufficient structural support to provide real choice, the previous government devoted significant emphasis and budgetary resources to developing and implementing an employer-focused communication strategy, essentially informing employers of the imperatives for addressing work-family flexibility as well as creating implementation tools to facilitate workplace change, rather than extensively regulating the workplace itself. In addition, the government provided a measure of direct financial support for carers (e.g., the Child Care Tax Rebate).

The previous government's financial supports implicitly acknowledged that there are two sides to the work-family agenda—work flexibility and caring arrangements—both of which require adequate attention to enable workers to make real choices about work-family balance. As noted above, between 2004 and 2007 the Taskforce on Care Costs undertook a systematic research campaign to identify the relationship between work and the cost of care. In essence, TOCC concluded that financial supports for employees with caring responsibilities for children, the aged, and people with a disability were inadequate. This led to reduced levels of workforce participation (one in four employees with caring responsibilities had reduced their hours of work because of the cost of care) and increased the risk of further reductions (one in four employees with caring responsibilities said that they were likely to leave the workforce because of the cost of care; TOCC 2005, 2006a). Furthermore, in 2007 TOCC criticized the (previous) government's focus on employees with children, and suggested that greater weighting should be given to employees with aged and disability care needs as well, especially given the aging of Australia's population (TOCC 2007c).

Other community advocates also questioned the adequacy of places and quality assurances of care, particularly in relation to childcare (Pocock and Hill 2006). Leveraging this criticism, in early 2007 the Australian Labor Party released their *Care for Kids: Labor's Early Childhood Blueprint* (Beazley 2007), which promised increased numbers of available childcare places, as well as increased financial supports for carers.

One objective measure of the sufficiency of the supports introduced by the previous federal government is the labor force participation rates of women with children. Longitudinal data gathered between 1990 and 2003 show that, for women in couple relationships or alone, in their prime childbearing (twenty-five to thirty-four) and childrearing years (thirty-five to forty-four), labor force participation has declined by approximately 3 percent (Kelly, Bolton, and Harding 2005, 15). These findings offer a marked contrast to overall trend of increased women's participation in the labor force.[37] These data sit neatly with the Taskforce on Care Costs 2006 survey findings, which demonstrated that unemployment rates for carers are linked to the cost of care: "In 2006, affordability of care influenced the departure of 64% of employed carers from the workforce, and 60% of unemployed carers would return to the workforce if care was more affordable" (TOCC 2006a, 7).

In summary, the previous government took some positive steps toward ensuring the availability of structural support to provide carers with real choice as to how they manage their work-family flexibility. Key components of the previous government's approach included a targeted communication strategy, as well as the introduction of the CCTR. The question is whether those were sufficient. The Taskforce on Care Costs argued that the supports were narrowly focused and insufficient to address labor force shortages and an aging population. In 2006 TOCC concluded that "Australia is in the grip of a work/cost of care crisis and without significant policy change the situation will not improve" (TOCC 2006a, 6). Moreover, the Australian public obviously felt that more should be done, given that the Australian Labor Party was elected on a suite of promises concerning workplace flexibility and work-family balance.

Moving Ahead with Speed

The previous and current Australian governments both espouse a work-family agenda, and have promoted flexibility as a key pathway to work-family balance. This chapter has identified the rhetoric and reality of the current state of play in Australia in relation to work-family flexibility, and in particular the impact of the sweeping WorkChoices industrial reforms. Four key indicators of work-family flex-ibility have been identified that support a conceptual framework of mutual benefit (for employees and employers). Australian legal and policy frameworks were then evaluated against these four indicators, namely (a) enabling access to flexible work practices (and leave) without disadvantage; (b) ensuring reasonable and predictable hours; (c) providing a legal safety net for noncompliant conduct; and (d) ensuring sufficient structural support to provide real choice.

Overall, the previous federal government minimally advanced an agenda sup-portive of work-family balance and flexibility, particularly when measured against a concept of mutual flexibility, rather than one that is employer-centric. Clearly, its progress was insufficient to meet the aspirations of the Australian public. Ac-cordingly, in November 2007 the Australian Labor Party was elected on the basis of a suite of promises to reform perceived deficiencies in WorkChoices (namely an imbalance in employer-employee negotiations as well as a lack of transparency and review processes) and take the work-family agenda much further. Recent im-plementation of these initiatives, including the right for parents to request flex-ible work arrangements from their employer (indicator one), new avenues of legal redress for noncompliant conduct (indicator three), and the introduction of paid maternity leave and higher levels of childcare payments (indicator four) all suggest that Australia is manifesting renewed energy for work-family–centered flexibility.

Epilogue

In November 2007 the Labor government was elected on a platform of providing greater support to "working families." During the past eighteen months the govern-ment has progressively implemented its "working families" related election prom-ises, including the introduction of eighteen weeks paid maternity leave, financial grants to enable small businesses to implement work and family initiatives, and leg-islation to amend WorkChoices. The legislation is highly significant in terms of its impact on workplace flexibility. In particular the Fair Work Act 2009 (Cth) (FWA), which commenced in part on July 1, 2009, extends the WorkChoices' minimum standards (albeit reframed as ten "National Employment Standards") to include the right for employees with children under school age, or children with a disability, to request a flexible work arrangement. Such a request may only be refused on "rea-sonable business grounds." In addition the FWA provides employees with legislative protection from "adverse action" that arises from their caring or family responsi-bilities, unless that action relates to the "inherent requirements" of the job. These changes tip the balance from flexibility that is more employer-oriented and reliant on market forces to flexibility that is predicated on mutuality and a reasonable bal-ance between employer and employee needs.

15

FLEXIBLE EMPLOYMENT AND THE INTRODUCTION OF WORK-LIFE BALANCE PROGRAMS IN JAPAN

Machiko Osawa

Japan is at a crossroads. The post–World War II economic model, known as "Japan, Inc.," has been largely discredited, and is no longer seen as viable in the twenty-first century without substantial modification. Even as the underpinnings of Japan, Inc. are gradually abandoned, there is no consensus on cobbling together a new paradigm. For example, Japan's employment system is in transition. In the mid-1980s, the proportion of nonregular employment began to increase, accelerating during the 1990s (Houseman and Osawa 2003), but the movement toward such arrangements remains controversial. Firms have increasingly resorted to more flexible working arrangements in order to lower labor costs, subsidize existing employment arrangements, and facilitate incremental employment adjustment. The stable employment associated with Japan, Inc. is giving way to employment practices more commonly associated with the United States, generating unease about this transition. Some have argued that this new flexible employment model is creating a society of "haves" and "have-nots," while Japan's declining fertility rate is partially blamed on rising economic uncertainties as young people weigh their options (Tachibanaki 2006). Now, as they contemplate a looming labor shortage generated by this steep and ongoing fertility decline, policymakers recognize the importance of more fully integrating additional women into the labor force. However, this is problematic, given that women have multiple household responsibilities as wives, mothers, and caregivers for elderly parents.

In order for women to combine family and work responsibilities, it is necessary to introduce more flexible work arrangements on more favorable terms. Although flexibility has primarily been introduced to cut costs, it is time to rethink this approach, and share the fruits of flexibility by introducing family-friendly work arrangements that will enable women to balance their multiple roles. Society will gain from more productively tapping their talents; women will gain by having more responsible and better paying careers; and the tax base will benefit from the revenue they will provide, toward medical care and pension programs to meet the needs of Japan's rapidly aging society. In addition, to the extent that work-life balance arrangements can become the norm, Japan can also address its declining fertility. Currently, Japanese women must choose between raising families or pursuing careers, as very few can juggle both in the absence of necessary support from employers and government policies.

The concept of work-life balance in Japan faces an uphill battle, given the value placed on self-sacrifice for the company good. Japanese workers work excessive hours, including unpaid but mandatory overtime that does not show up in cross-national statistics (Ogura 2007). The misery index can be measured in terms of rising levels of depression, suicide, *karoshi* (death from overwork), dysfunctional families, and divorce (Cabinet Office 2007a). As Japanese firms restructured their workforces during the 1990s and limited new hires (Ministry of Health, Labour and Welfare 2002), workloads were shouldered by fewer full-time workers, who face greater anxiety about prospects for job stability. With mortgages to pay, children to educate, and elderly parents to care for, workers find that less stable employment translates into greater household stress. Work-life balance programs offer a means to alleviate some of this stress and raise productivity.

General Situation

During much of the post–World War II period, the job-centric approach to work went unquestioned and unchallenged. At weddings, senior executives in the groom's company often served as the go-between. They made speeches extolling the value of the groom's contributions to the firm, asking the bride to understand the husband's long hours and absences as a necessary and even desirable reflection of his expected devotion to work. Weekends could involve golfing and other outings, while entertaining customers during the week was an extension of work. It was also common for firms to divide families by requiring husbands to transfer to distant branch offices while their families remained behind, the so-called *tanshin funin* system. Clearly, there was little balance in the employment system associated with Japan, Inc. The costs of this imbalance, in terms of worker well-being, family instability, and declining fertility, are now better understood. Contemporary Japan is experiencing the tensions between long-established attitudes and practices and the widespread recognition that Japan needs less perspiration and more inspiration. It is a sign of the times that the governor of Iwate Prefecture launched a campaign called "Gambaranai Iwate" (Don't Try Too Hard, Iwate), clearly challenging and mocking the overemphasis on diligence that has been the bane of workers and their families.

Workaholics?

Work, like alcohol, can become an unhealthy obsession, and nowhere is this more evident than in Japan. In Japan, the proportion of workers working more than fifty hours a week increased between 1987 and 2000. In 1987, 26.8 percent fell into this category, while in 2000 this proportion increased to 28.1 percent (Messenger 2004). This percentage is one of the highest in the world (compared to 20% in the United States and 15.5% in the United Kingdom in 2000; ibid.). Again, it is important to bear in mind that obligatory unpaid overtime is not recorded in these official statistics. Workers' perceptions of employers' and managers' expectations, and related career concerns explain why workers often feel compelled to work such long hours, and why they come to see them as a normal occurrence and an important gesture of solidarity. Broken down by age group, the proportion of those working more than sixty hours a week is the highest in the thirty to thirty-nine age group. This is the age group most likely to have young children at home, meaning that childcare responsibilities cannot be shared.

Why are hours of work increasing among full-time workers? One of the reasons is that companies reduced new hires in the 1990s, filling the gap by hiring more part-time workers (Yamada 2004). As a result, from 1992 to 2002 the number of full-time workers actually declined by 3.5 million, while the number of nonregular workers increased by 5.67 million (Ministry of Internal Affairs and Communications 2002). This development means that the burden of work responsibilities has been shifted onto the shoulders of fewer full-time workers in their thirties, precisely at the time that they are most likely to have children (Osawa 2004).

In 1992, nonregular workers accounted for 20 percent of the labor force, but by 2008 they accounted for 34.1 percent of the workforce (National Women's Education Center 2006). Given that these workers are not required to work unpaid overtime, and are generally given fewer responsibilities than their full-time counterparts, this trend means that full-timers face even more difficult working conditions. While their hours of work are increasing, surveys indicate that an increasing proportion of nonregular workers desire to work full-time—similar to U.S. workers, as Jacob and Gerson (2004) show—but are not able to do so (Ministry of Health, Labour and Welfare 2007d). They wish to switch to full-time status because they face significant disadvantages in terms of pay, benefits, and job security. Those who are paid relatively well (full-timers) have no time, and those with time (nonregular workers) have relatively little money. Thus, both households with full-timers and those with nonregular workers face increasing stress.

Given the above situation, an increasing number of people want to have a more balanced life. For instance, 58.6 percent of mothers currently raising children say they want to balance both work and family duties, but only 12.4 percent realize a satisfactory balance. Among fathers, 51.6 percent desire a better work-life balance, but only 25.9 percent are able to realize it (Cabinet Office 2006a). Thus, among contemporary Japanese there is a huge gap between hopes and realities in terms of work-life balance.

The need for shorter working hours is not only related to family or elderly care. One of the reasons cited most often by workers is the desire for more education. In a survey conducted in 2004 regarding the desire for shorter working hours, 73.1 percent of male respondents and 70.1 percent female respondents said they would like to reduce working hours and spend more time for learning (Ministry of Health, Labor and Welfare 2004b). This reason outstrips the desire to assume greater family obligations.

Work-life balance is an imperative to addressing the challenges of Japan's demographic time bomb. Helping households better balance work and family obligations is not only good for the families but also can mobilize more effectively the human capital of women workers, boost the fertility rate, address the impending labor shortage, and restore the solvency of medical care and pension systems by generating considerable increases in tax payments. Belatedly, the government and firms are responding to the need to promote work-life balance as they come to understand the potential implications.

Fertility Trends

Women are bearing fewer children and increasingly shying away from marriage. From a high point of 4.3 babies in 1947, the birthrate dropped to a low of 1.26 children per woman as of 2005, and increased slightly to 1.32 in 2006 (Ministry of Health, Labour and Welfare 2007a). This decline in the birthrate reflects the decision by more women to postpone or forgo marriage altogether. Changes in the patterns of marriage and childbearing in Japan are ascribed to an increase in women's participation in the labor force, rising women's educational attainment, increasingly attractive single lifestyles, reluctance to accept more difficult lifestyles owing to marriage, and a major gap between the sexes in attitudes toward marriage and gender roles. The greater economic independence of women reduces their dependence on marriage and effectively allows increasing numbers of women to opt out of marriage. It seems that the proportion of women who never marry will continue to increase.

As of 1999, 54 percent of women in their late twenties had never married, while 20 percent in their thirties had also remained single. Women's average age at marriage has risen from 24.6 in 1970 to 29.4 in 2004 (National Women's Education Center 2009). The percentage of unmarried women in the 35–39 age cohort rose from 5.3 percent in 1975 to 10 percent in 1995. In 2002, NHK (Nippon Hosoō Kyokai, Japan Broadcasting Corporation) reported that in the previous decade the percentage of unmarried women in their thirties had nearly doubled, from 12 percent to 23 percent. Given how few children are born out of wedlock in Japan (Iwasawa 2004), the surge in nonmarriage suggests continuing declines in the birthrate.

In Japan the average age of marriage for men is thirty. For those between thirty and thirty-four years of age, the marriage rate for full-time workers is 60 percent, while that for temporary workers is 30 percent, and it is only 17 percent for freeters (part-timers who frequently change jobs; Higuchi and Ota 2004). Clearly the likelihood of marriage is strongly correlated with job status. This suggests that employment instability for both men and women is one of the main causes of fertility decline in Japan.

Fertility is in decline because women are finding the costs of marriage and childrearing to be unacceptably high. In 2003 the Cabinet Office reported that the projected lifetime loss of income for a typical working woman who quits her job to give birth and raise a child to university age amounts to 85 million yen ($720,000), even if she later returns to work (Cabinet Office 2003). Since raising a child through university is conservatively estimated to cost at least 25 to 30 million yen ($250,000–$300,000, and as high as 60 million yen [$600,000] for those educated in private institutions), the high price of parenting constitutes a significant disincentive. This stark projection of lost income is significant, since two-thirds of Japanese women quit their jobs upon giving birth to their first child and shoulder most of the childrearing responsibilities.

This pattern appears to occur because employment practices and policies tend to shunt women workers to the disadvantageous periphery of the labor market. Japan's industrial relations system is structured in ways that discourage women's careers and shape both labor demand and supply, such that women are concentrated in jobs covered by nonstandard work arrangements where the risk of dismissal is high and the pay and benefits low. Problematically, the logic of the lifetime employment system, seniority-based pay, and continuous on-the-job-training does not translate well in terms of the lifecycle needs of women workers. The failure to modify this system to accommodate the lifecycle needs and responsibilities of women workers often renders it an impossible or unattractive option for women rearing families.

Overall, only about one out of four women with children under the age of three continues working. The rigidities of the employment system make it difficult for mothers to remain employed full-time, explaining why 40 percent of working women do so on a part-time basis, and why so few become managers (Ministry of Health, Labour and Welfare 2007b). The key point is that once women quit their jobs to raise children, most are effectively excluded from good jobs thereafter. They have few alternatives to the part-time, dead-end track of low-paying, insecure jobs. However, with divorce rates rising, the growing reliance of families on two incomes, and rising job insecurity for husbands, women are reconsidering whether they can afford to interrupt their careers and devote themselves full-time to childrearing responsibilities.

Despite these pressures for change, attitudes toward women's "proper" roles in society remain deeply ingrained and patriarchal. Having babies means accepting significantly restricted freedom and much heavier household burdens. There are also strong social expectations that mothers will take care of their children until at least the age of three, meaning that they are expected to shelve their careers for this period. Effectively, this terminates many of their careers. In addition, most household work is done by women, whether or not they are working (Sato and Takeishi 2004).

Recent surveys indicate that on average men spend thirty-six minutes a day on housework, while working women average nearly four hours on top of their commuting and jobs (Ministry of Internal Affairs and Communications 2001). Some 70 percent of surveyed men report that they never prepare meals or do washing. This imbalance at home makes it difficult for women to work full-time, and helps explain why so many stop working after giving birth. The general unwillingness of husbands to participate in domestic duties also helps explain why so many women are leery of marriage.

Clearly the declining fertility rate in Japan is a consequence of a complex interplay of various factors. This chapter concentrates on how Japan's distinctive industrial relations system depresses fertility, by not providing job protection for part-time workers and not adopting the principle of equal pay for equal work, practices that are prevalent in Europe. In addition, flexible employment has not been adopted in a family-friendly manner; it is implemented chiefly to compensate for the high costs and rigidities of the prevailing system of industrial relations. The low birth rate symbolizes the failure to modify the industrial relations system in ways that would help women reconcile their multiple roles, and reduce the various direct and indirect costs of giving birth.

Work and Fertility

There has been a consensus among economists that women's labor force participation is negatively correlated with fertility. However, some countries experience fertility recovery despite increases in women's labor force participation rates (Cabinet Office 2006c), while in other countries (e.g., Japan) the fertility rate declines as women's employment rate increases. Different institutional arrangements in the labor market appear to be one factor influencing women's labor force participation and family formation decisions.

Employment adjustment mechanisms are one institutional arrangement that affects the peripheral workforce, which is dominated by youth and women who are entering or reentering the labor market. Those countries that continue to experience a fertility decline tend to have relatively strong job protection for the core labor workforce; thus, rigidity favoring stable employment for core workers comes at the expense of peripheral workers engaged on nonstandard employment terms. These peripheral workers act as the shock absorbers that cushion employment adjustments, in effect, subsidizing the stable jobs and better conditions enjoyed by core workers. Consequently, the benefits of flexible employment are enjoyed most by these core workers and their employers.

On the other hand, some countries introduce flexibility by changing the way regular workers work through providing choices about hours and places of work; these arrangements are often referred to as work-life balance labor practices. It appears that there is a correlation between pro-work-life balance employment practices and relatively high fertility rates.

Economic globalization is forcing Japanese companies to introduce nonstandard work arrangements to cut costs. Protectionism previously allowed countries to preserve stable employment, at the expense of a high cost of living and low productivity growth (Houseman and Osawa 2003). As companies adjust to the greater competition of globalization, relatively rigid and expensive employment systems have come under siege and are seen as unviable. However, job security is important to motivate workers, improve productivity, and maintain competitiveness. Thus, there is growing debate about *how* to balance the need to introduce employment flexibility and provide stability, as the *manner* of striking a balance influences fertility. The process of adjusting the balance between job security and flexibility is influenced by industrial relations practices, labor laws, tax policies, and social security systems. In this context, specific features of Japan's industrial relations system and public policies are key factors explaining Japan's low fertility rate.

Industrial Relations, Taxes, and Employment Adjustment

Japan's Industrial Relations System

Two prominent features of Japanese industrial relations are lifetime employment and *nenko* (seniority-based) wages that first emerged prior to World War II and subsequently became the norm in large firms after the war (Houseman and Osawa 2003). These norms also strongly influenced working conditions in medium- and small-size firms. Under the *nenko* wage system, in theory workers are initially paid wages below their marginal revenue product, but as their tenure rises they eventually are paid more than their marginal revenue product. For war-devastated Japan, *nenko* wages depressed initial wage outlays, thereby freeing up funds for capital investment. The system was sustainable because the workforce was young and the economy was growing rapidly, thus assuring that the age structure of a firm's workforce would be pyramid-shaped. Workers favored this system because wages rose just as workers' family-related expenditures increased.

The structure of financial markets also supported these postwar industrial relations practices. Under cross-share holding arrangements, related *keiretsu* firms, or friendly firms, would control large blocks of a firm's shares. The prevalence of this practice, plus access to bank loans at low rates (Iwasawa 2004; Iwai 2003), allowed firms to focus on expanding market share and long-term profits without worrying about pressures to boost quarterly earnings. Thus, financial markets exerted little pressure on companies to trim the labor force during business cycle downturns.

Some of the forces that gave the Japanese employment system its logic for much of the post–World War II period have changed, generating pressures on businesses to adopt new practices. One is the changing demographic composition of the workforce. The birthrate in Japan has been steadily falling since World War II, and the decline has been accompanied by a graying workforce with longer job tenure. The increase in tenure increases companies' wage costs because, under the *nenko* system, wages rise sharply with tenure and this rise is not matched by increases in productivity. Because the number of 20–25-year olds is declining dramatically, from 7.3 million in 2005 to an estimated 5.1 million in 2030 (National Institute of Population and Social Security Research 2008), the problem of an aging workforce will not be alleviated in the near future.

At the same time that employers' wage costs have been rising, Japanese businesses have come under tremendous pressure to lower labor costs in the face of increased international competition with the opening of Japanese markets. Trade liberalization has resulted not only in the growth of imports but also in an increase of foreign direct investment, with leading banks, insurance companies, and auto companies coming under foreign control. In the past, the close relationship between Japanese companies and banks allowed them to focus on long-term growth and market share, but now Japanese businesses face foreign shareholders and banks that expect short-run profitability (Alexander 2000). As a result, firms are under pressure to cut costs. Thus, by far the most common reason businesses cite for increasing the number of part-time workers is to save personnel costs.

In sum, firms employ workforces that are top-heavy with older, highly paid, but less productive workers at a time when cutting costs and raising productivity are necessary due to heightened global competition. Japanese firms have responded by trimming bonuses, cutting overtime, dispatching workers to subsidiaries, and pressuring older workers into early retirement. To make wages more responsive to performance, some companies have begun determining wages on an annual basis (*Nenposei*) while introducing merit-based wages. However, the implicit social contract that has developed over the years makes it difficult for companies to introduce sweeping changes to their industrial relations practices in rapid fashion, without causing loss of morale and risking productivity declines among regular workers. The government and courts have also impeded a wholesale restructuring. As a result, many companies have continued to protect their core workforce, while expanding the size of their nonstandard workforce, especially part-time workers, who do not receive *nenko* wages and implied commitments of job security.

Tax Policy

Public policies have encouraged growth in part-time employment in Japan by providing significant tax incentives to businesses to hire part-time workers and to workers to accept part-time positions. If the part-time worker is married and earns less than 1.3 million yen ($13,000) in a year, he or she can be regarded as a dependent. A dependent is not required to pay the social security or health insurance premium, but is still entitled to health insurance and a basic pension upon retirement.

Similarly, workers earning up to 1,030,000 yen ($10,000) per year do not pay taxes on their income, and if they are married their spouses may claim a dependent deduction from income taxes (currently 380,000 yen—$3,800) and may receive a dependent allowance from the employer. If a worker's income exceeds this level, not only must she or he pay income taxes but, if married, the spouse will lose his or her dependent tax deduction, and may have to forfeit (in about 40% of the cases) the family allowance paid by the employer. This tax and compensation structure creates a significant financial incentive for married women to work part-time and earn less than this income threshold. Many part-time working women in Japan reduce their hours of work specifically to avoid exceeding the annual income threshold.

The tax thresholds should also have the effect of depressing the hourly earnings of part-time workers relative to full-time workers. Because women workers restrict their earned income within these thresholds, there is no incentive for the workers to increase their labor supply, or for employers to raise wage rates. In 2004, female part-time workers earned 45.2 percent of male regular workers' hourly pay.

Low wage rates for part-time workers help explain why reentry to the labor market is negatively correlated with women's level of educational attainment, since there are so few options for highly educated women who have a higher reservation wage. The low wages offered by these positions, however, belie the actual need for women in part-time professional and other high-status positions.

Employment Adjustment

Under the current structure of the labor market, the burden of employment adjustment due to structural changes in the economy is shouldered largely by nonregular workers. Before 1990, the internal labor market had some flexibility, such that regular workers could be dispatched by headquarters to their related companies, a practice known as *shukko*. However, since the 1990s, for a variety of reasons, Japanese companies are finding it more difficult to adjust their workforce in this fashion (Genda and Nakata 2002). Thus, the internal labor market is losing its capacity to serve as a shock absorber, and firms have shifted employment adjustments to nonregular workers.

However, many of these nonregular workers are no longer married women enjoying a measure of security provided by their employed spouses. Now, many of these insecure, poorly paying jobs without benefits are held by young people who have not yet married or had children. Thus, the focus on protecting the older core labor force at the expense of the younger peripheral workforce is depressing fertility. Young people are delaying or avoiding marriage; even if they do marry, they are likely to have fewer or no children, since their economic situation is tenuous, their prospects for improvement bleak, and they are not accumulating seniority or skills. Shunting so many young workers into the disadvantageous labor market periphery thus carries enormous implications for society, including the prospects for further declines in fertility that will amplify the consequences of Japan's demographic time bomb.

Japanese Industrial Relations System and Flexible Employment

These distinctive patterns among women workers can be understood in the context of the industrial relations and social security systems in Japan. In exchange for strong job protection, regular full-time workers are expected to perform a wide variety of tasks beyond their normal work duties, including unpaid overtime, and to accept family-dividing transfers to distant offices (*tanshin funin*) (Sato, Fujimura, and Yashiro 1999). This phenomenon of *tanshin funin*, which almost invariably involves male workers, carries strong implications for working women, in that absentee husbands/fathers do not share in household duties. This makes it very difficult for such women to pursue full-time careers, because they need flexible schedules in order to assume the full burden of family obligations. Thus, this common corporate employment policy shifts the burden of household duties onto women and makes it very difficult for them to pursue careers.

This is one of the reasons why Japanese women, especially highly educated ones, tend to postpone marriage or remain single. Only 27.6 percent of women think that their standard of living will improve after marriage, only 10 percent expect that their work life will be improved, and about 30 percent expect that their sex life will improve.

In general, part-time workers are hired for relatively routine tasks requiring little training; they are not expected to work overtime and they are not subject to transfers (Sato, Fujimura, and Yashiro 1999). Thus, for women who need or want to work, part-time jobs are the only opportunity that affords them the flexibility they need to raise families and care for elderly parents.

Japanese corporations have failed to provide flexibility for full-time women workers, unlike the policies in place in many other countries. This means that many who wish to pursue careers involving full-time work, more responsibility, better pay, and benefits have no choice: work and family are an either/or proposition. In addition, the seniority-based employment system also means it is difficult to interrupt and resume careers; once a woman withdraws from the labor force to raise an infant, relatively few are able to resume careers (Ministry of Health, Labour and Welfare 2005a). Thus, women's lifecycle family responsibilities require a flexible work schedule that is not well accommodated by the relatively inflexible employment practices of Japanese firms. These employment practices are geared to married male workers who rely on their wives to take care of the family while they concentrate on their careers. Women workers do not have the same option.

For working wives and mothers, part-time work is the best option, because it offers them flexible schedules, and they do not face the same obligations and expectations as full-time workers in terms of transfers and mandatory unpaid overtime. On the other hand, they are paid relatively low hourly wages and have no job protection. When employment adjustment is necessary, they are the first to be dismissed (Sato, Fujimura, and Yashiro 1999).[1]

In this way, the definition of part-timers in Japan is quite different from that in other advanced countries. Essentially, in terms of job protection and pay, part-time and temporary work are similar in Japan, whereas they are quite different categories and treated differently in other countries. In addition, the difference between full-time and part-time employment in Japan is not based on hours of work. In fact, nearly 30 percent of part-timers work the same hours as their full-time counterparts. Some even assume responsible positions. However, there are clear differences in job security, promotion, wage rates, and benefits among these two categories of workers. In some European countries, part-timers are treated as if they are part of the regular workforce that chooses to work shorter hours or flexible work schedules. They get equal pay, benefits, and job security. In Japan, employers designate workers as part-time chiefly as a way of reducing labor costs and circumventing job dismissal protections and social security payments. Part-timers in Japan, like temporary workers in other countries, are treated as peripheral workers. Given that about 90 percent of part-time workers in Japan are women, the implications for fertility are significant.

The Reason for the Growth of Nonregular Work

Growth of Nonregular Workers

The most notable recent change in the Japanese labor market is the growth of nonstandard work arrangements. In 1984, nonregular workers accounted for 15.3 percent of the total labor force, but by 2008 this ratio had risen to 34.1 percent (Ministry of Internal Affairs and Communications 2009). Japan has gone from being a country known for stable, lifetime employment to one where one-third of the workforce is made up of nonregular workers.

This trend is even more pronounced among women workers. In 1988, 35.1 percent of women workers were engaged as nonregular workers, but by 2008 this figure had increased to 53.6 percent. Thus, over only fifteen years, nonregular employment among women quickly rose from slightly more than one-third to more than one half of the total. In 1982, most of the fifteen to twenty-five-year-old cohort were classified as regular workers, However, by 2002 this proportion had declined substantially, suggesting that an increasing number of single women are entering the labor force as nonregular workers (Ministry of Internal Affairs and Communications 2002).

Reasons for the Growth of Nonstandard Work

Using a shift-share analysis to decompose whether this increase is due to supply-side factor (demographic shift) or demand-side factors, it was found that 93 percent of the growth of nonregular workers was due to an increase in the surge in demand for nonregular workers by employers.[2] Between 1992 and 2002, the ratio of non-regular workers in the 20–24-year-old age cohort has steadily risen from 15.2 percent to 32.4 percent. The same figures are calculated for both part-time workers and student temporary part-time (*arubaito*) workers separately. The results are more dramatic among *arubaito* workers. Since the youth population is declining in Japan, almost all of the increase in nonregular employment is demand-driven, as firms slash costs by reducing regular employment and shift toward recruiting nonregular workers. This has created the so-called *freeter* phenomenon in Japan, a controversial issue that is prominent in public debate about the socioeconomic consequences of contemporary employment trends. Although initially romanticized as young rebels rejecting conformity and corporate culture, freeters are now seen as victims of the shift toward nonregular employment for new hires, aimed at protecting the jobs and perquisites of older core employees. The problem is that freeters remain in the poorly paid, insecure labor market periphery because they are unable to accumulate skills that will facilitate mobility to regular jobs (Osawa 2006).

Among nonregular workers, one-third of the growth is explained by supply-side factors. The increase in the labor force participation rate of married women over the last ten years explains one-third of the growth of nonregular employment. However, as pointed out above, this supply-side behavior is influenced by the fact that workers who need flexible schedules have no other option. Demand-side factors account for two-thirds of the growth in nonregular employment; these reflect employment adjustments by firms struggling to cut costs in the face of heightened competition and difficult economic conditions during the "lost decade" of the 1990s, when the economy remained mired in recession. The incidence of part-time employment grew dramatically among young men and women. For instance, between 1982 and 2002 the incidence of part-time employment grew from 19 percent to 34.2 percent among working men age fifteen to nineteen, and from 15 percent to 75.4 percent among working women age fifteen to nineteen (Ministry of Internal Affairs and Communications 2002). It was also found that the growth in job vacancies for part-time workers exceeded the growth in part-time job applicants during the 1980s, a period of economic expansion in Japan.

It is generally argued in Japan that the rapid growth of part-time workers in the 1990s during Japan's severe recession was demand-driven, which is consistent with this analysis. However, the vacancy data suggest that the growth in nonregular employment began earlier, during the expansionary years of the late 1980s, the so-called bubble economy; this was also demand-driven (Houseman and Osawa 2003).

This finding suggests that the steady growth of nonregular employment reflects structural changes in the Japanese economy (i.e., globalization, changing financial markets, and changes in demographic composition). In *The System That Soured: The Rise and Fall of the Japanese Economic Miracle*, Katz (1998) argues that the Japanese government and companies postponed needed structural adjustments by adopting a series of stopgap measures. Within this context, the shift toward greater part-time employment was aimed at preserving the prevailing employment system and compensating for its high cost and inflexibility. Structural changes have made the policies and practices associated with Japan, Inc. even less sustainable, and are forcing corporate Japan to incrementally jettison its rigid and costly employment system. This translates into a shift in demand away from regular workers to non-regular workers, introducing a higher degree of employment instability, especially among younger workers.

Women, Nonstandard Employment, and Low Fertility

In 2000, there was a positive correlation between women's labor force participation and fertility among OECD countries. One of the reasons for this correlation is that some countries succeeded in arresting their fertility decline (United Kingdom) and in some cases experienced increased fertility (Scandinavian countries and the United States). In contrast, there has been an inverse correlation between fertility rates and women's labor force participation in Mediterranean countries, Japan, and Korea (McDonald 2000).

To hypothesize, it appears that this difference can be explained by differences in industrial relations, tax, immigration, and social security systems. The fertility decline is most pronounced in countries that have a dual labor market—an internal labor market consisting of the core workforce, and an external labor market consisting of a peripheral labor force, wherein the core workers' jobs are protected by the industrial relations system. In such countries, economic shocks and structural adjustments are mostly absorbed by the peripheral labor force in the external labor market.

It is clear that the rise of nonstandard work arrangements in Japan has led to lower fertility, because such jobs involve greater risk of dismissal and more uncertainty about future economic prospects. In Japan, an inflexible industrial relations system has been subsidized and sustained by growing reliance on nonstandard workers. Women are disproportionately represented among nonstandard workers, because public policies tend to encourage them to seek part-time work and corporate policies make these poorly paid and less secure jobs the only options for women who need flexible work schedules. Women are thus still serving as shock absorbers for the Japanese economy, which has the effect of depressing fertility rates.

Given that there is a structural shift toward expanding the proportion of workers engaged under nonstandard work arrangements in Japan, further declines in fertility can be expected. These are bound to continue, to the extent that public policies fail to lower risks, boost job protection and compensation for such workers, and more equitably distribute the fruits of flexibility in ways that enable working women to balance the demands of careers and families.

16

GOVERNMENT POLICIES SUPPORTING WORKPLACE FLEXIBILITY

The State of Play in Japan

Sumiko Iwao

When the Japanese refer to workplace flexibility, they can choose between many different expressions. The terms "workplace flexibility" and "flexible working," which are considered subsets of the broader topic of "work-family compatibility," are occasionally used by Japanese policymakers, but the public is less familiar with them. "Workplace flexibility" primarily refers to the practice of providing leave time for childcare and eldercare and implies that it is the employee who primarily benefits (to date, this is where policymakers have placed more importance); "flexible working" is used to indicate institutional adjustments to work schedules and is considered more beneficial to the employer. "Work-family compatibility" covers a range of measures, including flexible work schedules, nontraditional workdays, and nontraditional work locations, as well as the other revisions to traditional employment practices deemed necessary by the government to secure a more satisfied citizenry and to better position the country to contend in the age of global competition.

Flexible employment has been formally addressed by the Ministry of Health, Labour and Welfare through a working group created on the subject. The group's findings were published in June 2004. Legal measures for securing fairness under a flexible employment system are being considered, and a new law is to be proposed to the National Diet dealing especially with employers' and employees' conflicting interests on this subject. News reports in Japan originally claimed that the ministry hoped to submit the law to the Diet in 2007 (e.g., Ikuji ryouritsushien apiiru 2006), but the reform bill was put on hold because of strong opposition from labor unions.[1]

Because this chapter deals with currently available measures supporting workplace flexibility, flexible working schedules and practices under discussion to support flexible work are excluded. The government's stated reason for supporting workplace flexibility is its potential to combat Japan's declining birthrate, which is now seen as a national crisis. Government predictions of a 20 percent reduction in Japan's population over the next fifty years (National Institute of Population and Social Security Research 2002) have sounded the alarm on this issue in the media and among the general public. Although the government undoubtedly hopes that improvement in workplace flexibility will reap many benefits for Japanese society— including enhancing Japan's competitiveness in global markets and securing higher rates of satisfaction among the electorate—public and private statements by policy-makers suggest that the declining birthrate is the government's primary motive.

The conventional wisdom among policymakers is that Japanese women are increasingly reluctant to have children because of the tremendous demands on their time and energy. It is hoped that a friendlier workplace might make child-raising less burdensome, and therefore more appealing. This perceived link between a friendlier workplace and the birthrate is quite evident in some municipalities, where childcare leave, eldercare leave, daycare services, and after-school clubs are even classified as "countermeasures against the falling birthrate" (Health, Labour and Welfare Minister Jiro Kawasaki, as cited in "Japan Population," para. 6).

Although work-family compatibility is the government's overall goal, thus far policy measures have aimed only to specifically counter the population crisis (e.g., Ministry of Health, Labour and Welfare n.d, 2005b).[2] The general public understands the government's efforts very narrowly,[3] as childcare leave and eldercare leave programs designed to encourage more working women to have children. There is a shared understanding in government circles and among the public that unless it becomes easier for women to work *and* raise a family at the same time, there will be no improvement in the birthrate.

The government's policy measures to make working and raising a family more attractive to women were announced on June 14, 2006.[4] They have two pillars: the Work Style Reform Initiative and direct monetary assistance to cover costs related to childrearing. The Work Style Reform Initiative includes four policy agendas: (a) improving the treatment of part-time workers; (b) promoting childcare leave and supporting reentry into the labor force; (c) providing financial support to employers who offer assistance for childcare and providing preferential treatment to such employers in bidding for government work; and (d) altering the practice of long working hours and encouraging workers to take annual leave.

The purpose of this chapter is twofold: to provide information regarding Japanese government policy for promoting workplace flexibility, and to contribute to the pool of information regarding how governments are meeting the needs of workplace flexibility, as well as the currently perceived effects of these measures, so that readers can utilize a "best-practices" framework to promote workplace flexibility in their own countries. Because measures taken by the Japanese government to promote workplace flexibility are relatively new, they are not well known even among Japanese citizens, with the exception of childcare leave by eligible mothers (Cabinet Office 2007c). These measures are virtually unknown outside the country, as information about such actions is usually not available in English. In addition, stereotypical assumptions and insufficient information about Japanese society seem to hinder non-Japanese researchers from looking into and understanding the facts objectively. This chapter aims to correct some of these misconceptions and add to the limited knowledge of Japan's workplace flexibility policies.

Background for Government Policy Endeavor

Women in the Labor Force

As of 2005, the labor participation rate of Japanese women was 48.4 percent (73.3% for men), and women made up 41.4 percent of the total labor force. The 2005 labor participation rate of married women ages 25–29 was 49.7 percent; 30–34 was 48.1 percent; 35–39 was 55.3 percent; 40–44 was 67.3 percent; and ages 45–49 was 71.9 percent (Ministry of Internal Affairs and Communications 2006). Undoubt- edly, most of these women also had family responsibilities while performing their duties as employees. Men certainly have family responsibilities as well, and many are eager to share in household chores and childrearing. Yet, in reality, their long work hours make it difficult for them to do so, leaving the bulk of domestic work and childcare squarely on the shoulders of women, regardless of the duties they also assume at work.[5] Therefore, the government's policy agenda has been aimed primarily at women's needs, in an effort to make work and family more compat- ible. The implementation of various family-care leave laws is such an example.

Today, an increasing number of women and men in Japan are engaged in non- regular employment, such as part-time work or contract work, which means they do not enjoy the pay or benefits to which full-time regular employees are entitled. Data from the employment status survey conducted by the Ministry of Internal Affairs and Communications (2007) shows that the share of nonregular employ- ees among all employees rose from 21.9 percent in 1996 to 35.3 percent in 2006. Among women workers, the ratio rose from 31.9 percent to 52.7 percent during the same period. In Japan, regular employees and nonregular employees are usually delegated to different career tracks, resulting in widening wage and benefit gaps. Many employees will only agree to work as nonregular workers when no regular jobs are available, since they understand that this decision will result in a lower- trajectory career path. Workers responding to family needs are often forced into this nonregular category, and as such must work at lower wages than full-time workers. In terms of working hours, part-time workers generally do have shorter workweeks. However, contract workers, who also fall into the nonregular worker category, often work the same number of hours or more than regular workers. Therefore, being hired as a nonregular worker does not necessarily mean shorter working hours, nor a more flexible work schedule. Not all nonregular workers in Japan can be simply equated with part-time workers.

The Ministry of Health, Labor and Welfare (2006a) reported gross differences in earnings related to employment status and sex. Among "full-time" employment status workers, women's earnings are about 68 percent of men's earnings. Compared to male workers with "full-time" status, part-time men's earnings are approximately 51 percent, and part-time women's earnings are approximately 45 percent. These differences are a function of both hours worked and full-time/part-time status. Efforts are needed to fill these wage gaps.[6]

From the employers' point of view, nonregular employment practices enable them to reduce personnel costs, a high priority given Japan's prolonged economic slump, amid heightened global competition. As noted earlier, the hiring of permanent employees has been severely constrained by the fact that the dismissal of these workers is very difficult in Japan. Labor unions are opposed to granting more flexibility in dismissing permanent, full-time workers (Nariai 2007). Unless Japan's economy recovers, it seems doubtful that both employers and employees will agree to more flexibility in employment practices, and the conflict between employers and employees will not be resolved. The employees in these nonregular jobs are on a highly unstable career track, and are therefore hesitant to voice demands for a more flexible workplace. This situation sends a message to regular workers to hold on to their jobs at all costs, and even to put demands from the workplace ahead of their family's needs.

Seventy percent of women drop out of the labor force at the time of giving birth to their first child (Cabinet Office 2007a). This creates a loss of trained workers for employers and results in high opportunity costs for women. The government has advanced the Plan of Support for Women's Renewed Challenges policy initiative (Gender Equality Bureau 2005a) to provide comprehensive assistance to these women. The assistance includes vocational training and skill development to help women who have temporarily stopped working, for childrearing and other reasons, to find suitable jobs again.[7]

Many of these women return to the labor force, but only as part-time workers, because the workplace does not provide the flexibility they need. The treatment part-time workers must endure in the Japanese workplace has created a situation whereby women are hesitant to leave the labor force at all, even to have children.[8]

Declining Birthrate

Japan's ongoing demographic shift (i.e., a declining birthrate and a growing elderly population) and the resultant decline in labor participation is undoubtedly the most significant factor behind the Japanese government's push to create a more flexible workplace. The speed of these demographic shifts has been much faster in

Japan than similar shifts occurring in other countries. Japanese believe that their country's human resources are the only way Japan has been able to overcome its scarcity of many important natural resources. This fundamental understanding of Japan's place and history has aroused a strong sense of concern about the dwindling population (Cabinet Office 2004, 90).

In fact, the declining birthrate has become an issue of highest importance for the government, and there has been much discussion about the causes and effects of this demographic shift. Policy is being expressly devised to stop the decline. The government and its agencies have conducted many public opinion surveys attempting to determine why efforts have thus far failed to reverse the trend, and why women are having fewer children than they state they would like to have. Survey findings have repeatedly shown that many women think managing both work and family is exceedingly difficult, especially without the assistance of men with household chores and childcare (e.g., "Survey on Support Measures for Work and Child Care," conducted and reported by Dai-Ichi Life Research Institute 2007). Although compared to older generations, young fathers are eager to participate in household chores and childcare, an increasing number of men in their thirties and forties are working more than sixty hours a week, leaving little time to spend with their families (Ministry of Health, Labour and Welfare 2007c).

In 2005, in the face of these dramatic demographic shifts and the resulting societal problems, Prime Minister Junichiro Koizumi[9] created a new cabinet-level post to deal with matters related to the declining birthrate and gender equality. This is indicative of the government's sense of crisis over the demographic shifts now clearly in motion. At the same time, however, the government has been remarkably cautious in its public statements about both proposed and enacted policies designed to halt the declining birthrate. Politicians have repeatedly emphasized, as reflected in the Preface of Basic Law for Birth-declining Society (Law 133 of 2003), that having children or not is a private affair, and that the government's job is merely to create a desirable environment for those who wish to have children and to create a situation of greater work-family compatibility.[10]

The government has already enacted various measures, including those directly related to workplace flexibility. These sometimes costly measures were made in the face of a severe budgetary deficit, by a government clearly concerned about the long-term implications of the demographic trends. Unfortunately, even with these efforts, the trends are continuing and the latest available figure for birthrates in 2005 was 1.25 children per woman, the lowest in Japanese history (Ministry of Health, Labour and Welfare 2006b). This has generated an even stronger sense of crisis by both the government and the general public. Presently, the most intense discussions in history are being carried out in Japan to determine why the efforts to date have done nothing to halt the decline.

It should be noted that the focus of recent discussion has shifted more toward reviewing work styles in general, as opposed to the narrow focus of providing direct

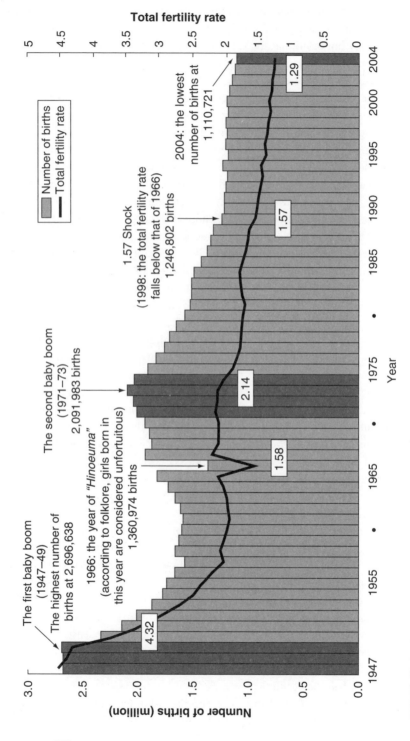

FIGURE 16.1. Declining birthrate (Ministry of Health, Labour and Welfare 2008)

financial support for the care of young children and services such as daycare centers. In National Diet meetings, Prime Minister Koizumi (in a cabinet ministers' meeting in March 2003) emphasized the importance of creating "family-friendly workplace environments." Similarly, when major newspapers have addressed this issue, they have tended to emphasize the importance of reviewing the overall workplace to make it work-life compatible for all workers (e.g., Kobayashi 2005). Figure 16.1 graphically illustrates Japan's declining birthrate.

Aging Population

At present, 20 percent of the Japanese population is over sixty-five years of age, and this percentage is increasing, due to the world's highest longevity: men, 78.64 years; women, 85.59 years (National Institute of Population and Social Security Research 2005). Many middle-aged workers, both men and women, are caring for their elderly parents. This situation has directly resulted in the eldercare leave policy and the public eldercare insurance scheme.

Many organizations in both the public and private sectors have a mandatory retirement age of around sixty (Horioka 2001). Starting in 2007, baby boomers began retiring in an unprecedented mass, creating a keen labor shortage. According to a recent government forecast, the labor force in 2030 will be 56 million—10.5 million less than in 2007 (Cabinet Office 2007d). Two groups that can possibly fill in the shortage domestically are women and the elderly. However, in order to induce women to remain in the labor force while fulfilling family responsibilities, the work environment must be made more flexible.

Some employers, especially larger corporations, are already planning to hire more elderly workers. *Kourei shakai hakusho* [White paper on our aging society], a survey conducted by the Cabinet Office (2006b), revealed that 75.9 percent of corporations with more than five thousand employees are planning to expand hiring to include elderly workers, while only 24.0 percent of smaller companies currently have a strategy to hire elderly workers. It is undeniable that Japan will need increasingly larger numbers of elderly workers. However, since many of the elderly can only work under flexible work conditions, accommodations by employers must and will be made beyond those required by the current childcare and eldercare leave measures.

Government Policy Measures

The government does not classify its support measures into categories. In order to better understand the measures enacted thus far, they can be viewed as legal, educational, or financial in nature.

Legal Measures

LAWS

The government has attempted to make workplace flexibility on several key issues a matter of law through a number of measures. These include the Child-Care Leave Law (1991); the Child-Care/Elder-Care Leave Law (1999); the Basic Law for Gender Equal Society (1999); Government Guidelines for Supporting Work and Child-Care (Ministry of Health, Labour and Welfare 2001); the Child-Care, Elder-Care and Sick Child-Care Leave Law (2005); and the Part-time Labor Law (2008). Initially, only leave for mothers was a legal right for employees under the Equal Employment Opportunity Law of 1986. The right of parental leave was then granted to both parents through the 1991 Child-Care Leave Law. In 1999, the law was expanded to cover eldercare.[11]

The most recent version, enacted in April 2005, has expanded the length of basic childcare leave to twelve months, with a possible extension for special circumstances until the child is eighteen months old. The current law grants five days a year in sick childcare leave for workers with preschool children. It also gives workers a total of ninety-three days of eldercare leave for each elder in need of care. Therefore, if a worker had two gravely ill parents, he or she could conceivably take six months of leave.

Unfortunately, these laws established no clearly stated penalties for employers who are not in compliance. Companies are merely obliged to comply with the law. In a highly competitive marketplace, many employers are reluctant to comply with a powerless set of new legal requirements that will cost them considerable money upfront. Other employers, however, recognize that there is also great competition for certain sought-after workers. These firms have eagerly provided workplaces that go well beyond the minimum leave requirements set by law.

Regarding wages during leave, 50 percent of a worker's normal wage is now picked up by unemployment insurance.[12] Originally, workers received no compensation while on leave. However, in 1995, workers on leave were granted compensation of 25 percent of normal wages. This was raised to 40 percent in 2001, and to the current level of 50 percent in 2007, effective for three years only (Employment Insurance Law 2007). In reality, some employees feel pressure not to take advantage of these leave laws. Employers are to blame for allowing such a hostile environment, as it appears that the government has quite favorably enacted these leave laws. These legal measures have been enacted to respond to the perceived needs of workers. Therefore, a lag between the needs of contemporary workers and corresponding government measures cannot be avoided.

It seems that only one of the legal measures listed above was specifically designed to anticipate perceived employment trends: the Basic Law for a Gender Equal Society. Passed and enacted in 1999, this law states clearly that building a gender equal society is Japan's most important task for the new century. In such a society, every individual can express his or her talents fully as he or she wishes in activities both in and outside of home (this includes the workplace and the community at large). Wording used in similar basic laws has tended to be quite abstract. However, the Basic Law for a Gender Equal Society has, and will continue to have, broad policy implications for promoting work-life compatibility, based on the freely made choices of individuals.[13]

MEASURES FOR SHORTENING WORKING HOURS

In the current childcare/eldercare leave law revised in 2005, both of the following measures for shortening working hours are included: Article 23, for workers with children under three years old, and Article 24, for workers with other family members in need of care. They are combined in the following list, as their contents are redundant:[14] Employers must take *one* of the following measures for workers with children under three years old, or with family members in need of care (Article 23 and 24): (a) reduced working hour system (fewer working hours per day, per week, or per month; fewer working days per week or per month; give workers the right to request certain hours or certain days off); (b) flextime system; (c) earlier start or later finish of work period; (d) limitation on overtime work; (e) on-site daycare or equivalent financial support for childcare; or (f) financial support for eldercare services.

To reduce the number of working hours, employers may choose any measure from the above list that they find most suitable to their workplace. The law requires employers to take at least one of these actions to reduce overall working hours; however, employers are strongly encouraged to exceed the minimum requirement. Employers undoubtedly appreciate the flexibility of having several options on how they can become compliant with the leave laws; however, having so many options available does make noncompliance more difficult to identify.

Two specific articles within the childcare/eldercare leave law that deserve special note are Articles 26 and 27. Although reasons for compliance with the two issues addressed in these articles may seem self-evident, lawmakers felt it necessary to spell them out and give them the force of law. Article 26 states that employers must make an effort to not transfer a worker to another office if such a transfer would hinder the worker's care of a family member. Article 29 mandates employers to select and designate someone within the company to coordinate work-life compatibility issues and to liaise with the local equal employment office. The law expects the work-life compatibility coordinator to be responsible for implementing and certifying compliance on behalf of the employer.

Educational Support Measures for Employers

Essential governmental supports through education include "work-life compatibility" seminars to help employers better understand the various support measures available to them, and seminars explaining the diagnostics available to human resource managers to evaluate their company's work-life support system and offer ways the managers can facilitate further improvement. There is also a website publicizing specific efforts made by various employers to promote work-life compatibility.

Many of the seminars are conducted by local government labor offices that earnestly see it as their mandate to get a large turnout for the events. The labor offices rely on employers to send staff members to these seminars, though it seems likely that many who do attend are not necessarily eager participants. Even though there is no penalty for noncompliance with the various leave laws, these local labor offices have the authority and the power to give guidance and report infractions. Ultimately, the threat of public disclosure of noncompliance and the public relations damage that such a disclosure might cause are perhaps the biggest incentives for most companies to fully comply.

Financial Support Measures for Employers

Economic assistance through the government is available for the provision of care at the workplace. For starting or running on-site daycare, the government reimburses up to approximately $2,000 (or 50%) of total costs, whichever is greater, for the establishment and/or operation of on-site daycare.[15] The government has also agreed to reimburse from 33 percent to 50 percent of the cost employers cover for their employees to secure care providers, depending upon the size of the company. The total amount the government will pay is capped at approximately $3,000 per worker and $34,000 per workplace per year.

Governmental support varies from approximately $1,000 to $5,000 per worker for the hiring of temporary staff to cover workers taking childcare leave, for workers to return to their previous posts when the leave terminates, and for creating a work environment that encourages fathers to take childcare leave; the approximate amount of support is $5,000 per year per workplace for a maximum of two years. The approximate amount of support is from $1,200 to $3,500 per workplace for providing additional childcare leave in excess of three consecutive months for workers with preschool children above the age of three.[16] The same amount is available for employees who use a short working time system for a period of more than six months, to spend more time at home with a child under three years of age. (This applies only to companies with fewer than one hundred employees.)

Financial support is available in the amounts of approximately $5,500, $7,300, or $9,100. Actual amounts are dependent on the length of use of the system by the first qualified worker; then $1,800, $3,600, or $5,500 is available for use by the second qualified worker. This measure was created in 2006, and is expected to remain in place for five years, through 2011.

When there is a range in the available financial support, the larger amount is designated for smaller companies. If a qualified employer wishes to obtain any of these financial support measures, he or she must download application forms from the government's website and apply.

The instructions for applicants are rather detailed. Therefore, it is very useful to attend the seminars held by the government at its offices and at the offices of independent agencies around the country. One of the independent agencies, called 21 seiki shokugyou zaidan (Institute for Workers' Evolution), was set up by the Ministry of Health, Labour and Welfare to provide the sort of assistance applicants might need in securing financial support measures.

Of course, the government hopes that these measures will act as incentives for employers to promote its policy directives. It is expected that once employers implement the various flexibility schemes, more and more workers will take advantage of the schemes that ensure permanent employee benefits, and no monetary incentive from the government will be necessary. For instance, in the above-mentioned measure for smaller companies, the government support is extended only for the first two employees, and none for the third.

How New Measures Are Implemented in Japan

The Process of Implementation

Different measures have different levels of priority, and will consume different amounts of the budget to accomplish. Two ministries handle almost all of the measures relating to workplace flexibility: the Ministry of Health, Labour and Welfare and the Gender Equality Bureau in the Cabinet Office. Among the measures cited above, most are handled by the Ministry of Health, Labour and Welfare, except for the Basic Law for a Gender Equal Society.

The standard procedure by which a policy measure comes to exist is as follows: first, consultation with an advisory council, then the interim report of the advisory council is made public; public comments are then sought, after which there is further discussion among advisory council members, taking public comments into consideration; a new policy measure is then announced, and, if necessary, a new law is proposed to the National Diet; the new measures are then enforced and their effectiveness is evaluated; if necessary, revisions are then made.

It is quite common that a research team or a committee is formed within a ministry to conduct a discussion that will yield a policy proposal. The research teams and committees are usually comprised of scholars and experts in the field, with the secretariat role filled by personnel from the ministry. If different interest groups have opposing views, representatives from each camp are invited to join. The minutes of the meetings are published for the general public to observe the process as it unfolds.

Enforcement of Policies

As already noted, there are no penalties for companies failing to comply with the government's flexible work policies. Employers are obliged to comply with the law, but it remains ineffectual with only civil sanctions. Enforcement is further compromised by the historic weakness of labor unions in Japan and the general cultural aversion toward asserting worker rights. Labor union participation is less than 20 percent of the working population. Therefore, the government must rely on other means to encourage adoption of its workplace flexibility policies. Toward this end, the Ministry of Health, Labour and Welfare has taken steps to hasten compliance with the flexible work policies by using Japan's unique corporate culture to the government's advantage.

GRIEVANCE

Upon a complaint from employees, the local government labor office has been instructed to investigate and give necessary guidance to the employer. This first technique requires the employee to summon his or her courage; an employee should not lose his or her job by making a complaint, but in reality he or she may feel uncomfortable in the workplace after making a complaint to the labor office. Eventually he or she may choose to resign. If rumor circulates about the offending company receiving "guidance" for noncompliance, company officials may be shamed into taking corrective action. Despite the positive end result, it is the *employee* who must initially risk his or her job by coming forward.

AWARDS

Ministry officials will honor and publicize those companies that are promoting workplace flexibility measures beyond the standards set by the government. This second technique to encourage compliance is more of a "carrot approach," and will result in some companies offering flexibility measures to their employees that significantly exceed the minimum requirements set by law. Since 1999, twenty-five companies have received the Family Friendly Award from the Minister of Health, Labour and Welfare, and 245 companies have received awards from the directors of the local labor offices. The list of companies receiving awards is widely publicized, along with an itemization of the concrete measures these companies are taking to promote workplace flexibility, and both the ministry and the recipient companies have received considerable PR mileage from the award process. In reality, however, not many companies will want to provide employees much more than is required by law. Therefore, this technique is likely to leave out a majority of workplaces.

PUBLIC DISCLOSURE

Some companies eager to attract able applicants for their job openings may be lured into compliance by the ministry's third technique, since working conditions at various companies and their treatment of employees are made easily visible to the public for discussion and judgment. These companies may reason that they would be more successful at attracting premier employees if applicants could easily compare their working environment with that of their competitor's. Outside of the potential benefit to job applicants, this technique will only have efficacy if the public begins to take a greater interest and involvement in issues of workplace flexibility. Given the general time pressures of ordinary life, this seems unlikely, unless the ministry can successfully tie workplace flexibility issues to broader and more pressing concerns of the citizenry, and make the comparisons between companies even easier to access than they are via their website.

Although these Japanese-style inducements for compliance have certain limitations, on the whole they seem to work fairly well. Many employers tend to oppose the exertion of control through these legal measures. If so, as long as these companies comply, it may be better for the government to get their cooperation by leaving the responsibility for compliance up to the employers. At the same time, strategies must be in place to address employers who continue to defy the law despite public admonishment.

Effectiveness of Available Measures and an Assessment of the Current Situation

The Ministry of Health, Labour and Welfare (n.d.) has translated some of its public documents into English. Those that describe the current state of workplace flexibility in Japan state that "while measures have been implemented from various angles, they have not been sufficient to fully respond to the changes in society." The document goes on to add:

> Little progress has been made on the review of working styles. One in four men in their 30s who have children work more than 60 hours a week and do not have enough time to spend with their children. The time Japanese men spend on domestic work and child rearing is at the lowest level in the world, and the burden is concentrated on women. Because of this "pervasive atmosphere in the workplace," the childcare leave system has not been sufficiently utilized.[17]

The childcare support service is not available to everyone who needs it.

Efforts have been made to improve and expand childcare services cited in the Initial and New Angel Plans and the "strategy for the zero-waiting list for day-care centers" (a recommendation made by the Specialists Committee on Support Measures for Work and Child Care), which was implemented in 2000. Despite these efforts, many children are still on the waiting list due to an increased demand for childcare services.

It is clear that the government does not regard its policy measures as very effective. Officials often use acquisition rates of childcare leave as an indication of their success or failure. The rate of women taking childcare leave was 70.6 percent, and for men it was 0.56 percent in 2004. Financial considerations are perhaps of greatest consequence, as only about 50 percent of regular wages are compensated through childcare leave. Men may also refuse childcare leave to avoid inconveniencing their co-workers, because of uncooperative superiors or deferred promotions ("Daddies on Leave" 2007). Without a doubt, this leaves much room for improvement, and the government assessment of its own policy measures seems to be fair and modest.

It is true that the average number of working hours in Japan has been on the decline, with males now averaging 46.7 hours of work per week. The average time fathers with preschool children return home each night is 8:00 p.m., while 33 percent of fathers come home between 9:00 and 11:00 p.m. (Ministry of Health, Labour and Welfare 2005c).

Although the customs of making work the highest priority and remaining in the office until late are still taken as signs of loyalty in Japan and place a great burden on employees, it seems these customs belie the ever-increasing burden of the dual-career-track system. Because an increasing number of companies now utilize cheaper, nonregular workers, there is often an increase in work for regular workers, especially for the ones attempting to prove their loyalty by staying late into the evening. Unless employers change the basic dual-track-employment system, many regular workers will be unable to take advantage of flexible work opportunities, no matter how many of them the company proudly proclaims that they will offer.

According to a survey reported by the Ministry of Health, Labour and Welfare (2004a), 41.9 percent of workplaces are offering flexible work measures, such as shorter working periods. The effectiveness of these available measures can be examined by looking at the actual use of work flexibility measures. However, one must be cautious in reviewing the figures. As noted earlier, the law requires employers to provide at least one of the measures listed, but some of the measures cannot be used unless an employee is in a situation to use them, such as having a child in need of care. Also, an employee must wish to use them in the first place. If the workplace does not have a qualified employee, the number of actual users remains low. According to a study of workplaces conducted by the Cabinet Office's Gender Equality Bureau (2005b), 28.6 percent of companies have either had in the past, or currently have, some employees using the flexible work measures. However, most companies (54.6%) have available measures but have had no employee use them.

The percentage figures given here were compiled from those workplaces that have self-evaluated, using the scheme provided and operated by the government. Because only a limited number of workplaces are currently using the self-evaluation scheme to evaluate the state of their work flexibility measures, the results shown below are not strictly scientific, and the figures should be taken only as reference indicators. Measures used include shorter working hours (used by 28% of workplaces self-reporting online); flextime system (used by 9%); earlier start or later finish of working time while keeping the total amount of working hours unchanged (used by 11%); exemption from overtime work (used by 19% of workplaces for childcare purposes, by 27% for eldercare purposes); on-site daycare services (used by 4%);

financial assistance to defray childcare cost or eldercare cost (used by 5% of workplaces for childcare; 3% for eldercare); and work-at-home for workers with small children or elders in need of care (1%) (Family Friendly Site n.d.).

These results indicate that among measures employers are obliged to offer (i.e., at least one), shorter working hours and exemption from overtime work seem to be used more than others. Also, there is still little flexibility in terms of the physical location for working (i.e., working at home is an option that is not widely available). This is perhaps due to the large number of jobs that are not easily done outside of the office, because jobs in Japan tend to lack clear job specifications.

Schemes for Employers to Evaluate Their Own Support Measures

The Japanese government encourages individual employers to diagnose and evaluate their own support measures, by using an online scheme the government established on the Internet.[18] The scheme is very easy to follow, and the feedback, which comes in the form of an overall score, will instantly show companies how they rank against the national average.

This method assigns the monitoring function to the employers themselves, so that they can gauge the relative degree to which their organization has introduced workplace flexibility measures into their corporate culture. Monitoring in this way satisfies the employers' need for confidential social comparison, that is, to know where they stand in terms of flexibility measures versus other companies, without being identified. If, after learning the results of the self-evaluation, an employer feels compelled to improve workplace flexibility, then the impetus for the scheme will have been fulfilled.

There are two sets of evaluation schemes available. One is called a "trial diagnosis," and the other is referred to as the "main diagnosis," offering comments and advice based upon the results of the diagnosis. Each evaluation scheme consists of sixty-one questionnaire items, making a score of 410 points full marks. There are the five main categories in the trial diagnosis: work-life compatibility support (leaves), work-life compatibility support (flexible work such as shorter work period), actual number of users (of leave), creating an appropriate workplace environment, and personnel management. Upon responding to all sixty-one items in the thirty-minute "trial diagnosis," the scores are automatically calculated and displayed to the employer numerically, as well as in a radar chart, exemplified in figure 16.2. The radar chart shows where the employer's company stands in comparison to the national average on each of the five pillars. Employers who seek additional comments or advice from the agency on issues revealed by the diagnostic exam are encouraged to visit the diagnostic website.

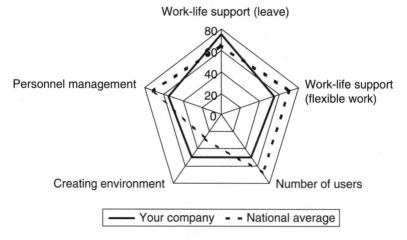

FIGURE 16.2. Scheme for evaluating support measures (Japan Institute of Worker's Evolution n. d.)

Policies and Goals Set by the Government for the Next Ten Years

Five-Year Goals

When implementing major policy measures, the Japanese government often sets five- or ten-year targets. The ongoing flexibility support measures cover a five-year period through 2009 with three main goals.

SUPPORT COMPANIES

The government plans to support companies to draw up and implement action plans toward compliance with current law, and to provide a certification process that will likely acknowledge approximately 20 percent of those companies as fully compliant. Companies with more than 301 employees will be mandated to submit their action plans, but medium and small companies with fewer than three hundred employees will only be encouraged to submit plans. Ninety-seven percent of large companies had already submitted their action plans by year-end 2005. Employers are also able to voluntarily register their action plans online, on a site maintained by the government and accessible to the general public. As of June 2006, 189 companies were registered on the site; one could quickly learn about measures they have implemented to enhance workplace flexibility.[19] Some companies listed on the website will undoubtedly benefit in terms of community goodwill, recruiting, and so forth. There is currently ongoing discussion in Japan about whether or not to require all companies to make their action plans available to the public.

DISSEMINATE INFORMATION ON BEST PRACTICES

The government aims to give Family Friendly Awards to a total of seven hundred companies during the five-year target period (2004–09), as was announced by the government as a part of Child and Childrearing Support Programs in December 2004. When giving the awards, government officials have been providing fairly detailed descriptions of the variety of workplace support initiatives the winning companies have created. Undoubtedly, this is expected to act as good public relations for the companies without any cost in terms of disclosure of proprietary information, as the descriptions of the support initiatives have been widely disseminated by the government. It is believed that companies do gain some marketing advantage through the enhancement of their image in the eyes of the public, and they also probably gain a recruiting advantage, as job applicants tend to be highly interested in workplace flexibility. This certainly will be a great asset for companies preparing for the upcoming labor shortage.

PROMOTE VOLUNTARY EFFORTS BY LABOR UNIONS AND MANAGEMENT TO SHORTEN WORKING HOURS AND REDUCE OVERTIME WORK

The target is a 10 percent reduction in the number of workers now working in excess of sixty hours per week.

Ten-Year Goals

In addition to these five-year goals, the Japanese government has recently announced its ten-year objectives for workplace flexibility. Fulfilling the five-year goals remains the government's priority, and it is under political pressure to be evaluated favorably on these goals when the initial five-year period concludes in 2009. Based on progress so far in achieving the five-year goals, some of the ten-year objectives may be unrealistic. They are as follows: (a) allow anyone who wishes to take childcare leave (it is estimated that by 2014 10% of men and 80% of women will do so); (b) reduce working hours for employees with preschool children (this is expected to apply to 25% of workers); (c) review and modify the working styles of employees with children; and (d) increase productivity by making the workplace more diversified.

Limitation of Current Measures and Unaccomplished Tasks

Realistically speaking, both the Japanese political situation and economic environment are not conducive to enactment of costly measures. Politically, the House of Representatives is dominated by the Liberal Democratic Party and the House of Councilors is dominated by opposition parties, which makes it very difficult for controversial laws such as a employment flexibility law to get passed. Economically,

Japan is burdened by a large budget deficit, which makes it difficult for both employers and the government to carry out costly measures.

At the same time, the growing number of young workers, especially males, in nonregular employment has alarmed the government and the public because of the serious social instability this development may cause, given the implied widening income disparities. Currently, this issue has taken precedence over the nagging problem of a large number of women in nonregular employment. Having stated these problems, it is clear that there are many support measures that the Japanese government ought to implement to promote both flexible work and workplace flexibility. These suggested measures offered below are not necessarily totally independent; some are closely related or overlap.

IMPROVE TREATMENT OF WORKERS

The treatment of nonregular employees and part-time workers (even if they are classified as regular employees) should be improved. Wages for these workers are usually lower than regular or full-time workers, as already noted. Their jobs are often unstable, and they have few career or financial options available to them. Management, implicitly aware of the powerless situation in which these workers find themselves, subject the workers to a working style that is different from "flexible work," where employees enjoy various choices. Given the coming shortage of skilled workers in Japan, the plight of these workers must be resolved. A small step in the right direction is the revised part-time labor law enacted in April 2008. Complicating an immediate solution is the misunderstanding in Japan that flexible work is equal to part-time work. This sort of misunderstanding needs to be corrected.

FINANCIAL SUPPORT

Economic measures are needed to fill the gap created by the reduction in working hours and lower incomes. Although this objective may be difficult to achieve, it was one of the most frequently expressed requests from employees who responded to the study of fathers who had taken childcare leave. These fathers are caught in a vicious cycle of needing a higher salary in order to shoulder the financial burden of more children, so they agree to ever more overtime overwork. More children arrive, and with them comes a mounting desire by these fathers to leave work early to be home with their burgeoning families, yet they cannot. The family now truly needs the overtime salary.

A complete solution to this systemic problem is difficult, but some practical improvements can be made. For example, some companies encourage fathers to leave to be with their families by topping off the payments the government gives the fathers while they are away from work. Whereas the government will pay 50 percent of the salary for the father on leave, some companies will provide an additional

15 percent of the father's salary as an added incentive for the fathers to take the leave.

INTRODUCE PENALTIES OR STRENGTHEN THE ENFORCEMENT OF EXISTING LEGAL MEASURES

It is not clear what potential penalties would be most effective in encouraging employers to comply with existing laws. In Japan, perhaps the threat of public disclosure of the names of all firms failing to comply with laws related to workplace flexibility would be enough to get the vast majority of companies to correct their illegal behavior. The government's needs for cooperation from employers to promote workplace flexibility in order to achieve the utmost effect cannot be ignored. Therefore, instead of prematurely levying harsh financial penalties for noncompliance with these laws, the government must listen to employers' voices and collaborate with them to produce the best results.

MAINSTREAM AND NORMALIZE FLEXIBLE WORK

Currently, employees choosing a flexible work schedule are considered somewhat abnormal, and there is a common perception that a flexible work schedule is only for those who are uninterested in promotion. This situation must be changed. A flexible workplace can be the norm, and no employee should be made to feel career or peer pressure not to choose flexible work. Highlighting the benefits flexible work brings to the workplace is one way to hasten its normalization.

ADJUST ESTABLISHED WORK POLICIES

The traditional assumptions and expectations of employers and employees must be modified to more properly value a flexible work style. New measures are needed for evaluating workers' loyalty, performance, and contribution to the workplace, other than tenure in the office or number of hours logged per week. Also, it is vital that employers put into place policies whereby employees cannot be negatively evaluated merely for adopting a flexible work schedule.

LIFESTYLE CONSIDERATIONS

Workplace, home, and community should be considered as being closely connected. Convincing evidence ought to be presented to employers that they benefit from providing a more flexible workplace.

INFORMATION AWARENESS

There are many detailed and segmented measures that are not widely known or in use. The low accessibility rate of these measures is partly due to lack of appropriate information dissemination by the government. At the same time, the government should periodically assess and review their policy measures, and publicize the findings so that current policies can be revised to suit people's actual needs.

BROADEN GOVERNMENTAL FOCUS

Japanese government officials are generally considered to be quite able, but they have a tendency to myopically focus on segmented tasks at hand, without giving sufficient consideration to their wider policy implications and applicability. By widening their perspectives on the tasks at hand, and considering issues that are seemingly unrelated to the planning of workplace flexibility, the probable result would be greater comprehensive reform and more effective promotion of workplace flexibility.

REPLACE THE DEMOGRAPHIC FOCUS

Finally, and most important for Japan, is the need to shift the premise for promoting workplace flexibility and its implementation away from a solution to demographic problems (i.e., a declining birthrate and an aging population) and toward a solution to more fundamental issues, including how to bring a more meaningful life to citizens and promote work-family well-being. Clearly, the nation's demographic problems should be addressed while there is a shared sense of crisis in society in order to promote workplace flexibility, being mindful of the responsibilities to more fundamental issues, as well.

As a final note, government policy measures relevant to promoting workplace flexibility are often categorized as something else, and therefore are not easily identified. Also, many relevant measures are now under consideration, including flexible employment practices. In other words, workplace flexibility is an ongoing issue in Japan, and new measures or revisions of current measures can be expected, albeit slowly.

CONCLUSIONS

Solving the Workplace/Workforce Mismatch

Kathleen Christensen and Barbara Schneider

Most U.S. workers are employed in rigidly structured work environments where they have to make difficult and, oftentimes, undesirable choices between meeting the demands of work and the needs of their families. Being expected to work long hours, with minimal control over when and where to work and few opportunities for any type of leave from work, results in a situation in which workers often, and unwillingly, privilege work over family. This situation is one that applies to all types of workers, including low-income, hourly workers and high-income, salaried professionals, as well as all family types, most notably single working mothers and dual-earner parents. As the chapters in this book show, the tensions between work and family that so many Americans experience emanate from a serious mismatch between the way that the U.S. workplace is organized in time and space and the needs of an increasingly diverse workforce.

Over the last seventy years, while the workplace largely has retained the structure of full-time, full-year work, with no time off for family or personal needs, the lives of American workers have become more complicated. The majority of women did not work for pay in the late 1930s, whereas today mothers of infants and young children not only join the workforce but stay in it. Over 60 percent of families with children under the age of eighteen have two employed parents or an employed single parent. With women's deep engagement with paid work, both men and women now are shouldering more responsibility for the care of sick and aging parents and relatives. One in four employed men and women have eldercare responsibilities (American Business Collaboration for Quality Dependent Care 2002).

As the responsibility for paid work has shifted from only men's work to men's and women's work, the arithmetic of the family has changed from a two-job–two-parent family to a three-job–two-parent one. In the traditional two-job–two parent households, the demands of the one paid and one unpaid job are sufficiently met by the resources of two adults. In a three-job–two-parent family, the demands of the three jobs (two paid, one unpaid) outstrip the resources of the two adults. Even if there is complete gender equity with the third job being equally shared by the man and woman, each ends up with 1.5 jobs.

An obvious solution to the workplace/workforce mismatch is for one of the workers to give up paid work and return to the two-job–two-parent family structure of the past. But the solution is unlikely and, for many, undesirable. The economic realities of American life are such that in most dual-earner families both parents have to work to keep their combined incomes in line with inflation and other additional costs of modern living, including their children's college tuition, which has far outpaced inflation (Immerwahr and Johnson 2007). Economists show that in adjusted dollars, the average family income has barely increased over the past twenty years. It is important to point out that if women did not work, most family incomes would not have risen at all in the 1980s and 1990s. For many male workers there has been a persistent erosion of income since the 1970s.

Although the workplace can be draconian, work remains an enjoyable, intellectually engaging activity for many, if not most, workers. In addition to issues of maintaining a reasonable lifestyle, work has been shown to increase self-esteem, independence, social contacts, and new experiences. For many people there is a cognitive challenge and sense of fulfillment when working at one's job that does not occur at other times in their lives. While working parents enjoy being at home, when at work both mothers and fathers experience a different and rewarding psychic satisfaction unparalleled in other instances such as during quality time with children or in leisure activities (Koh 2005; Sexton 2005).

For those adults who need and want to work, but who also have significant family responsibilities, flexibility in the time, timing, and location of work provides one way to realign the structure of work to their needs. Workplace flexibility involves a commitment to organizing work in time and space in ways that give employees greater control over when and where they work, while at the same time helping employers achieve business objectives.

Flexible work arrangements (FWAs) alter the time and/or place that work is conducted on a regular basis—in a manner that is as manageable and predictable as possible for both employees and employers. FWAs provide:

- flexibility in the scheduling of hours worked, such as alternative work schedules (e.g., nontraditional start and end times, flextime, or compressed workweeks) and arrangements regarding overtime, predictable scheduling, and shift and break schedules;
- flexibility in the amount of hours worked, such as part-time work, job shares, phased retirement, or part-year work; and

- flexibility in the place of work, such as working at home, at a satellite location, or at different locations.

Time Off in Short Increments. Short-Term Time Off (STO) addresses the ordinary, predictable and unpredictable needs of life (e.g., a sick employee, a sick child, a child's school conference, a death in the family, a home repair). *Episodic Time Off (EPTO)* addresses a recurring, predictable need for time off from work (e.g., an employee who has—or cares for a family member who has—an illness or chronic health condition that flares up sporadically, an employee who volunteers regularly in the community, an employee who is obtaining advanced training).

Time Off in Long Increments. Extended Time Off (EXTO) addresses a need for time off from work for a single reason that extends for more than five days but less than one year (e.g., caring for a newborn or newly adopted child, having a serious health condition or caring for a family member with a serious health condition, or serving in the military).

Career Exit, Maintenance, and Reentry addresses the needs of employees who, out of necessity or personal choice, leave the workforce completely for a period of time, but need and/or want to reenter the workforce later.

Flexibility, to be successful, has to be carefully designed and implemented. Research reveals that often does not occur. Among some companies that have flexibility policies on the books, employees are implicitly discouraged from using them for fear of risking denial of promotion, termination, and disdain from co-workers who resent having to pick up extra work (Blair-Loy and Wharton 2002; Clarkberg and Moen 2001; Hays 1996; Jacobs and Gerson 2004). For women who desire to take longer-term leaves, the situation is even more problematic, as changing jobs or returning to the labor force after voluntarily leaving full-time, stable, well-paying jobs has proven to be extremely difficult, as the time away is often viewed as an employment liability (Budig and England 2001; Weeden 2001). The companies that do provide usable and workplace flexibility options for both women and men find that such provisions tend to increase productivity (Burud and Tumolo 2004).

The United States is not alone in experiencing structural workplace/workforce mismatch, nor in turning to flexibility as a way to realign the structure of work to the needs of workers. Other industrialized nations face similar situations. Some countries, such as Japan, have linked low fertility to workplace problems such as gender discrimination and inadequate childcare. Yet the United States is alone in relying heavily on voluntary efforts by employers to provide flexibility. As noted in chapters by Gornick and den Dulk and Lewis, European countries have turned to both the public and private sectors to create flexibility policies and practices to alleviate work and family imbalances. The solutions offered by these countries also highlight the problems and challenges of implementation, a question that continues to plague even the most progressive and cost-savings initiatives. This raises questions, such as, To what extent can there be a public-private partnership in developing flexibility policies? What policies are needed? Only then can the complementary roles that the public and private sectors should play in meeting the needs of today's workers and their families be understood.

Problems of Today's Workers

U.S. workers spend more time on the job than do workers in other countries, although there is some controversy as to whether these increased hours translate into greater economic gains for companies or the national GDP (Jacobs and Gerson 2004). Overworking creates enormous burdens on families and it has been argued that instead of increasing American productivity, the present structure of the workplace is having detrimental effects on the recruitment, retention, and promotion of talented employees (Corporate Voices for Working Families 2005).

As the first two sections of this book show, several demographic changes related to the number of mothers in the workplace, the aging baby boomers and their increased responsibilities for eldercare, as well as their limited employment options, and stagnating (if not decreasing) income are transforming traditionally private, individual work/family concerns into a major societal concern.

Long hours spent working late, coming in early, and bringing work home take a major toll on families. Bianchi and Wight's findings and those of others (Schneider and Waite 2005) show increased stress and anxiety among mothers and fathers who work long hours. These feelings of stress spill over into family life where parents often multitask to stretch out work time when at home (see Offer and Schneider, chapter 2). The challenges of arranging the schedules and obligations of children and parents coupled with the demands of working at home have disrupted one of the few remaining sacred aspects of American family life—the dinner hour (see Ochs et al., chapter 3). Eating alone with the company of a phone, Blackberry, or computer screen signals an ominous future for family cohesion and child well-being.

It is not only the families with young children and adolescents who feel the brunt of an antiquated work environment. As Moen and Huang discuss in chapter 4, formal retirement policies are practically nonexistent, and when they can be found they are inconsistent with today's workers' expectations and desires for when and how to retire from their careers. For elder workers, as Haider and Loughran show in their analysis, those most likely to remain in the workforce (albeit for lower wages) are those workers who have the most education, enjoy good health, and have considerable assets. The elderly leaving the labor force appear to be more constrained in their employment opportunities that those who continue to work.

Numerous surveys and studies report that most mothers working full-time would prefer to work part-time. They often see part-time work as the solution for releasing families from the three-job–two-person dilemma. Yet this option is rarely workable. Few managers implement such policies and employees are often afraid to use them, fearing that they will be perceived as disloyal, nonproductive, and not fit for advancement in the organization. Most workers view work as a full-time proposition and leaving work early means you are not serious about your job, are not committed to the organization, and have let down the other members of your work team.

For women, especially those in managerial and professional jobs, decisions to move to part-time work or take paid leave from the workforce carry enormous economic penalties both for the present and the future (Glass 2004). Some have suggested that recent increases in the number of highly qualified women leaving the workplace can be explained by the fact that they are "opting out" of the career track to have or care for their children. Research, however, indicates that declines in labor force participation rates among women are a consequence of the weakness of the labor market rather than the decision to be a "stay at home mom" (Boushey 2005). Hewlett, in chapter 5, describes how some firms are providing various options to women needing to go to part-time work, take leaves, and work nonstandard hours. Working from home, job sharing, telecommuting, and spending fewer hours at the office are solutions for accommodating both the female and male workers who need greater workplace flexibility options for a variety of reasons, not only child care.

Flexible work schedules and access to paid leave are key components for allowing workers to meet their family and job responsibilities. Although the case for such provisions appeared to be increasing with some momentum in the 1990s and early 2000s, by 2004 the trend had reversed and now fewer companies offer flexible scheduling than they did in 2001 (U.S. Bureau of Labor Statistics 2005). According to the Levin-Epstein (2006), only 28 percent of all full-time wage and salary workers had flexible schedules that allowed them to vary the time they began or ended work. The majority of workers (57%) have no control over when they can start or end their times at work (Galinsky, Bond, and Hill 2004) and slightly less than half of full-time workers have access to paid sick days. Paid leave for sick days, paid holidays, and paid vacations have also fluctuated from the 1990s to today in both the private and public sectors, with most employees having less access to them.

Finding Solutions

The relationship between business productivity and workplace flexibility is intertwined, perhaps now more than ever. Research shows that workplace flexibility has substantial benefits to both individuals and businesses (Christensen and Staines 1990; Glass and Estes 1997; Yasbek 2004). Although the evidence in some instances is case-based or primarily statistically associative rather than causal, the evidential material that exists strongly suggests that workplace flexibility can have positive effects on businesses and individuals. In general flexible work hours have resulted in increased employee productivity. A Watson Wyatt (2008) study showed a 3.5 percent increase in returns to flexible work arrangements, with the increase largely attributable to workers using time more efficiently and to increased employee retention. Without flexibility, employees are more likely to leave their jobs (Eaton 2001; Galinsky and Johnson 1998). There are other benefits beyond retention. Workplace flexibility has also been associated with lower recruitment and training costs (Evans 2001), improved corporate image (Center for Ethical Business Culture 1997), a larger and highly qualified recruitment pool (Dex and Scheibl 1999; Evans 2000), reduced absenteeism and sick leave (Managing Work/Life Balance 2003), and higher morale (Comfort, Johnson, and Wallace 2003; Galinsky and Johnson 1998).

At the individual level, workplace flexibility has been associated with reductions in worker stress, depressive symptoms, a general reduction in work/family conflict, and increases in the amount of time families spend together (Glass and Estes 1997). Levin-Epstein (2006) reports that in a recent MetLife Survey, workers rank relationships on the job as the most important factor for joining or staying at a firm; work-life balance was second. Galinsky, Bond, and Hill (2004) found that employees with few flexibility options were less satisfied with their jobs compared to worker in companies with more flexibility (23% versus 67%).

The situation is not entirely bleak and there are places in both the private and public sector that are attempting to change the structure of the workplace. A number of U.S. firms have led the way in implementing promising flexibility practices including opportunities for part-time work, job sharing, work at home, and compressed workweeks. There are examples of part-time work and part-time careers that belie the stereotype of part-time workers as uncommitted or unproductive workers. There are accounting and law firms that have not only permitted part-time work but have also created opportunities for part-time partners.

The capacity to "make the case" to business and point out successful business practices associated with flexibility has been enhanced by the work of Ellen Galinsky and her colleagues who have been working on issues of work and family for nearly three decades. Galinsky has shown that employees with high-quality jobs and more supportive workplace environments are more likely to go home in better moods and with more energy to give to their families and other important people in their lives. In her chapter, she profiles several alternatives for restructuring the workplace and the effects such initiatives are having on workers. One of the difficulties in implementing some of the promising practices cited by Galinsky, Sakai, Eby, Bond, and Wigton is the fact that companies are not the same and issues of coordination and implementation vary by size, function, and sector. Hutchens and Nolen, taking on the issue of childcare, underscore how important it is that workplace flexibility be customized to the business and industry. This argument is also made in the Christensen, Weinshenker, and Sisk chapter, where they describe the federal governments' flexibility practices for its thousands of employees, providing a model for other not-for-profits.

The question is whether a case can be made in the United States for flexibility. As Williams argues in chapter 10, in contrast to other industrialized countries, in the fiercely individualistic culture of the United States, where too much government control is perceived as a threat to entrepreneurial capitalism, it is difficult to make a case for more federal control of the workplace. Although many other countries have adopted strong flexibility practices (see Gornick, chapter 11), U.S. workers are still cautious about them, worrying about losing their jobs or not being promoted (see Lewis and den Dulk, chapter 12). In instances where there are strong unions (as in Australia), flexibility practices have been supported, although the gender inequities there are as problematic, if not more so, than in the United States. Although part-time work is more available in Australia, the type of work that women can pursue tends to be gender-specific and targeted at low skill levels (see Drago and Wooden, chapter 13, and Bourke, chapter 14). Japan's government intervention into workplace flexibility stems from a different incentive than the United States, as much of what is being proposed directly relates to declining fertility and gender inequity (see Osawa, chapter 15, and Iwao, chapter 16). What is interesting is that, in a crisis situation, the government intervention package has been one that benefits both employees and employers.

Given this situation, what is the take-away message for the United States? Certainly workplace flexibility can carry costs related to the costs of covering for leaves, providing training for managers, scheduling for periods of unexpected reductions in productivity from worker absences, and monitoring to be sure that policies are carried out. Another message has to do with how the culture actually supports overwork and how flexibility can fit into that culture of long work hours. When mothers and fathers explain why they overwork, some of it is due to fear of not being promoted or of being let go—but some is also due to feeling a sense of community and relationship with other employees, who they do not want to let down by not pulling their weight. It is these norms of the business workplace that reinforce the notion that overworking makes one fit into the office culture. The culture and normative environment is extremely difficult to change, as it requires both that policies are put in place and that a new mind-set is developed—not only on the part of higher management but the workers themselves. Any efforts to implement flexibility have to take into account these normative structures.

Statistics alone cannot make the business case. The relationship between work and personal life requires focusing on the overall firm culture, norms, and values, not only programs or practices. Some of the benefits are intangibles, but one might expect that work flexibility options would improve morale and enhance recruitment. Firms could engage in more systematic ways of determining the actual effects on the balance sheet (e.g., by measuring employee retention, absenteeism, health-related time off, and enhanced productivity). The fear is that these programs are expensive and some individuals are likely to take advantage of leave policies, using them for reasons other than for what they were intended, extending the period of leave beyond the allotted time, returning with a noncooperative attitude, or simply not returning at all. In reality, workplace flexibility may well encourage these undesirable behaviors and attitudes among some employees, but most people are unlikely to engage in such behaviors. A firm culture that discourages such actions helps to maintain a trustworthy environment that reinforces the implementation of intended flexibility practices.

Solving the Problems

The chapters in this book clearly show that workplace flexibility addresses a societal problem that can only be solved by creating strong partnerships between employees and their employers, and with governmental support. Solving the mismatch problem requires ingenuity, but most of all it requires a forum in which ideas and practices can be shared and the costs for such alternatives thoughtfully estimated and shared across multiple sectors. The first step is increasing public awareness of the need for workplace flexibility. With 80 percent of U.S. workers reporting that they want flexibility, while only 29 percent have it, there is no question that workplace flexibility is a compelling national issue.

A number of organizations have taken up the banner for workplace flexibility, but undoubtedly the most concerted and well-developed initiative has been created by the Alfred P. Sloan Foundation. In 2003 the Foundation established the Workplace Flexibility Initiative, which serves as a model with its multipronged approach to the problem. First, it has provided grants to researchers, lawyers, and public policy analysts to develop case studies on the costs and benefits of workplace flexibility, and to analyze business data on the costs and benefits to employers and employees of workplace flexibility options. Second, it has engaged in an active plan to increase public awareness of the need for workplace flexibility. Third, it has forged a bipartisan dialogue among policymakers where the issues of workplace flexibility can be discussed and cooperative solutions that involve both private industry and the government can occur.

The Foundation has taken the perspective that workplace flexibility requires voluntary employer and employee action as well as public policy reforms. For policy change to occur, it should be directed at the federal, state, and local levels. The resulting practices must benefit not only employees but employers as well. Workplace flexibility should be available to employees at every stage of the life course and to both men and women, so that they can attend to issues that include child care, but that it certainly extends beyond it to other professional and personal dimensions of workers' lives. Currently, definitions of workplace flexibility abound in the literature and popular media. Taking a first step toward a consensual dialogue where ideas can be translated into action, the Workplace Flexibility Initiative has articulated a bounded definition of workplace flexibility that includes the ability of all workers to have the flexibility arrangements discussed earlier.

Creating a Discourse

One place that Sloan has concentrated its efforts is in the media. Too often researchers ignore the media, yet it constitutes an important vehicle for transporting information and thereby increasing awareness. Coverage has increased significantly since Sloan began supporting targeted dissemination of research findings to the media; over thirteen thousand stories featuring flexibility keywords have been found in print since 2003, according to data from the National Press Club. In addition to the printed word, researchers working on topics related to flexibility have appeared on major television networks, including NBC, ABC, CNN, and PBS (Sloan Initiative on Workplace Flexibility 2006).

Investigators reviewing what type of work is now being cited by the press regarding flexibility have found interesting trends. Rather than stories on specific practices (such as examples of individuals who job share or work compressed weeks), the media has turned to broader issues of career flexibility or workplace flexibility. This suggests several distinctive changes in the discourse. One is that the problem is not just one of individuals solving their own personal job flexibility needs. Instead, the coverage has been more on how businesses are re-creating workplaces. The most telling evidence for this is that stories on workplace flexibility have moved off the style page to the business section; for example, the *Wall Street Journal* has a column that directly focuses on workplace issues, with a reporter whose "beat" is to report stories on families and work issues.

Working with Business

A second major initiative of the Foundation is to build empirical case studies of businesses that use flexible work practices. As stated earlier, the work of Galinsky has been very instrumental in this initiative. Additionally, Sloan has funded the BOLD Initiative, a pilot demonstration project designed to implement workplace flexibility in major companies in the United States that began with a pilot study that included Weyerhauser, Gannet, Chubb, Prendial, Johnson & Johnson, and others. The focus of the program was to institute a team-based and results-oriented approach that was specifically designed to benefit both employees and employers.

The BOLD Initiative took on one of the most difficult, yet typical, problems that face many businesses: scheduling worker time consistent with the demands of the market. In many work environments, workload cycles vary across units so that companies must staff for peak periods or pay overtime. Employees often are expected (or volunteer for overtime) to work long hours when there are deadlines—but when deadlines are in the future, workloads may decrease substantially, sometimes resulting in layoffs. Fixed weekly or annual schedules are inconsistent with such work demands and can affect company profits. The problem posed to the company is how a more productive workplace can be created that allows for greater flexibility with respect to these high and low periods of labor demand.

Essentially the plan for BOLD is for companies to identify work teams, which are invited to set performance goals, identify personal needs for flexibility, devise innovative work schedules, and improve the work process to accomplish both performance goals and flexibility needs. The results-focused goal is to identify a unit within the company for which it would be economically advantageous to introduce workplace flexibility and make it available to all team members. Teams are expected to set performance goals, develop and implement plans for achieving them, and create a strategy for expanding the approach to other parts of the company (provided it proved to be successful for both employees and employers).

Reports from the pilot BOLD Initiative are impressive, including greater productivity and attendance. Fewer attendance problems and higher productivity have been reported around periods that tended to be subject to backlogs and customer delays in service. Workers have also responded positively to the program, reporting higher levels of trust and support, and most important of being able to have control over their time at work. The successful implementation of BOLD is now scheduled to be brought to several other companies.

Another business initiative of the Foundation is being conducted by the Families and Work Institute in cooperation with the Institute for a Competitive Workforce (an affiliate of the U.S. Chamber of Commerce) and the Twiga Foundation (Galinsky and Backon 2007). Beginning in 2005, the Institute set out to find what employers were doing to make work "work" for themselves and their employees. Eight communities participated in the first year, growing to seventeen in 2006 and thirty in 2009. The purposes of the initiative are to identify best workplace flexibility practices in small, midsized, and large workplaces; create practical flexibility resources for employers, community leaders, policymakers, and employees; and provide recognition to top employers in an awards program, whereby winners are publicly recognized. Winners are selected in a two-round process. In the first round employers self-nominate, completing a questionnaire regarding their organization's flexibility initiatives. These responses are contrasted with those from a nationally representative sample of employers. Round two selects the top 20 percent of employers and then asks a stratified sample of employees within the company (in small companies of fewer than 250 workers, all employees are surveyed) to complete a questionnaire about their use of and experiences with flexibility. The final score is determined by a ratio of employer and employee responses on two major issues: use of flexibility and supportiveness for using it. Winners of this initiative are publicly announced in major media outlets and their practices are widely distributed through print and electronically. As of today, there are nearly 500 winners of these awards.

Many of the flexibility practices these award-winning companies engage in are described in Galinsky et al., chapter 7. The public awareness of these initiatives represents another facet of bringing workplace flexibility into national focus. This type of attention to "best practices" stimulates not only discussion of exemplary practices but a reality check on how things can be accomplished within the context of very different types of organizations. The importance of highlighting how different industries and companies of various sizes customize their flexibility options helps to create a range of choices for restructuring businesses to make them more compatible with employee needs and profitability.

The other strategy the Sloan Foundation has taken is to examine how legislative actions can ensure that workplace flexibility benefits employees and employers. Georgetown's University's Workplace Flexibility 2010 is providing a forum for members of the House of Representatives and Senate to expand their knowledge base on workplace flexibility by translating academic research into accessible formats, and engaging stakeholders holding diverse political and advocacy positions in discussions that hopefully lead to new strategies for dealing with these issues. Translation of academic findings is conducted by policy staff to provide policymakers with summaries of research on the need for and the costs of workplace flexibility. Additionally the staff has worked on organizing bipartisan briefings on specific workplace issues, such as the importance of workplace flexibility for an aging workforce, healthy child development, and family well-being.

The notion that a discourse is vital to change is perhaps one of the key components to Sloan's National Workplace Flexibility Initiative. The summaries of materials on workplace flexibility abstracted by the News Roundup of Workplace 2010 is a compilation of the latest news articles, reports, and other materials related to workplace flexibility published twice-weekly online, http://www.law.georgetwon. edu/workplaceflexibility2010/. Most recently the Foundation has supported a Center on Aging and Work/Workplace Flexibility at Boston College that complements the Georgetown center in affecting public discussion and the dissemination of information about aging and work. Part of the new Boston College center is a Global Initiative in partnership with Middlesex University in London to focus on quality of employment cross-nationally, specifically to examine the twenty-first-century multigenerational workforce in different countries. This underscores the message of the last section of this book: workplace flexibility is not only a national, but a global concern.

Approximately 120 million dollars have been expended in support of these and related Sloan Foundation initiatives—an amount that does not capture all of the hidden costs, including labor and the indirect support of the universities and organizations that are part of this agenda for change. Many of the larger organizations involved in the Sloan initiatives have been mentioned in this book; there are many others. Although these organizations addressed problems of families, issues of aging, and workplace concerns before Sloan's involvement, Sloan became a catalyst and umbrella by which these efforts could be coordinated for the purpose of making a difference in the lives of workers and their workplaces. There are certainly other organizations outside the Sloan network involved in these efforts; we highlighted those that are most relevant to the issues and problems discussed in this book.

When we began writing this book, the global economic crisis was not anticipated. In fact, in the financial services industry one of the companies singled out for praise at that time now no longer exists. We do not know what the long-term effects of the financial crisis will be on workers and workplaces; however, it does raise a series of questions that warrant further study.

The Sloan initiatives point to the fact that how we answer these questions will undoubtedly affect workers and workplace flexibility practices and policies in the future. Answers for enhancing workplace flexibility, however, are complicated and not easily resolved. Sloan has provided a blueprint for how to move forward on changing policies and practices. The Foundation initiatives underscore the importance of (a) bringing to the table all parties with interests in constructing attainable solutions; (b) funding high-quality evidential research to make the economic and personal case for workplace flexibility more compelling; and (c) making more short-term goals on a defined set of criteria, the intent of which is, in part, to stimulate discussion among key stakeholders. Such efforts may make it easier to continue the positive initiatives undertaken by Sloan as well as replicate the steps taken by other countries and avoid some of the problems they are also encountering.

Government Solutions

Sloan demonstrates how private funds can be used to lay the foundations for a social movement. This is a societal function that foundations have played in the past and it is unclear that without their support such social movements could be initiated and sustained. The launching and commitment to a social reform of this magnitude and complexity is particularly important because the U.S. government's efforts to foster flexibility have been relatively weak, particularly with respect to scheduling. In the United States, unlike other industrialized nations, there are not federal laws that provide for universal paid sick days, parent leaves, or vacation days in the private sector. Although the United States has supported paid leave for full-time workers, issues such as compensatory time off and safeguards regarding working overtime are not part of the political agenda. To move these efforts forward requires political bipartisan support, yet workplace flexibility has typically been seen as a woman's issue.

As the chapters in this book have shown, workplace flexibility can be strategically used to address the structural workplace/workforce problem that affects most American workers: men, women, old, and young. American workers are working longer, are carrying a greater burden of care, and are not being recognized for their dual burden of work and family. We need to move away from seeing these burdens as private, individual problems and see them for what they genuinely are, which are public, social problems that require public attention. To do so requires the concerted efforts of both employers and government.

The government has a unique role in leveling the playing field regarding flexibility across different types of companies. It is difficult for medium-sized companies to take on flexibility practices because of labor costs and profit margins. However, these are precisely the places where potential economic growth is likely. The efforts in the private sector have to reward the most progressive companies in hopes of a trickle down effect. But if we are serious about stimulating economic growth, a more concerted effort needs to be directed at these smaller and midsize companies.

One of the key messages from our international authors is that just because the government implements a set of policies there are no assurances that such regulations will be followed, especially if they have short-term negative cost implications. The aging of our workforce and the looming picture of shortages of skilled workers suggests that we need to restructure the workplace to cope with these demographic changes (Pitt-Catsouphes and Smyer 2005). Levin-Epstein (2006) has suggested a number of federal government actions that could foster better flexibility conditions. Her list includes a number of actions that are consistent with the central argument of this book: (a) establishing minimum standard for paid leave, paid sick days, paid family and medical leave, and annual leave; (b) continuing to use itself as a model of workplace flexibility arrangements; (c) encouraging other governmental units at the state and local levels to implement such policies; (d) building public awareness of the benefits of responsive scheduling; and (e) offering tax breaks as incentives for quality jobs.

If workplace flexibility is going to happen, it will require committed efforts by multiple players, including business, government, the foundation world, and the will of the people to make a change in our lives. The current situation is untenable; it is having a negative impact on the very individuals the United States needs for its future, its families, and their children. We cannot continue under the present structure. We need to construct a more workable solution that brings the twentieth-century workplace in line with the lives of its twenty-first-century workers.

Notes

INTRODUCTION

1. For more information, see http://www.sloan.org/programs/stndrd dualcareer.shtml.

2. In July 2004, California became the first state to offer a comprehensive paid family leave program that allows works to receive up to six weeks per year of partial wage replacement for leave taken to care for a seriously ill family member. The program does not guarantee an employee the right to take leave nor does it require an employer to hold an employee's job open when he or she is on leave.

3. Compressed work schedule programs are available for U.S. government employees. The Federal Employees Flexible and Compressed Work Schedules Act (FEFCWA) allows for two specific types of alternative work schedules (AWS): flexible work schedules (FWS) and compressed work schedules (CWS). The FEFCWA authorizes but does not require AWS programs for U.S. government employees. Georgetown University Law Center reports that employee usage of AWS programs is inconsistent across and within federal agencies. However, employers and employees consider it a success, raising morale and agency efficiency. Those agencies that are involved with AWS maintain that the program should be supported and expanded (see Workplace Flexibility 2010 [2006a]).

4. See Galinsky and Backon 2007. One such firm is Kaye/Bassman International, an executive recruiter firm with more than one hundred employees. Over 85% of the firm's employees are recruiters who can move from part-time to full-time work and then back to part-time work. About 10% of the employees have made use of the Reduced Hours option, available to all employees regardless of their level in the company (the only exception are employees whose performance is viewed as marginal). The company has one job-sharing situation, but the president envisions that this number will increase as he employs a number of young women who are interested in having children and sharing positions. The philosophy of Kaye/ Bassman is that it makes good business sense to treat the needs of employees on an individual basis with respect to reduced hours, compressed time, and flexible schedules.

1. THE LONG REACH OF THE JOB

1. For question wording and response categories for these items, please contact the authors.

2. For information about the classification of the daily activities captured in the time diary and definitions of the activities included in childcare, housework, free time, and so forth, please contact the authors.

3. Diary estimates of paid work hours shown in figure 1.1 are lower than in the CPS "usual work" hours estimates used to classify couples. Hence, the diary hours of paid work average forty-eight hours, not fifty-five hours per week, for mothers in the group in which both spouses work fifty or more hours a week.

4. When considering the total workloads of all two-parent families, the total workloads of mothers and fathers are more similar—sixty-four hours per week for mothers, versus 64.6 for fathers. (This includes the 8% of couples where the mother is employed but the father is not employed or is employed part-time, and the 2% where neither spouse is employed.)

5. Data not shown, available from the authors.

6. One caveat on these estimates is that they are based on very small numbers.

3. COMING TOGETHER AT DINNER

This research was generously supported by funding from the Alfred P. Sloan Foundation program on the Workplace, Workforce, and Working Families. The study is part of an interdisciplinary collaborative research endeavor conducted by members of the UCLA Sloan Center on the Everyday Lives of Families (CELF). The authors are indebted to the working families who participated in this study for opening their homes and sharing their lives. The authors are also grateful to our research team members Alex Black, Yanira Lemus, and Justin Catalan for their careful preparation and coding of the dinnertime corpus. Colleagues Karin Aronsson, Mara Buchbinder, Linda Garro, and Jeffrey Good influenced the direction of the study through their valuable contributions.

1. Two weekday dinners and four weekend dinners were not recorded. The family either ate before researchers arrived or ate at a location where they could not be observed without the additional permission of nonparticipants (e.g., a meal eaten at a softball game, a sit-down restaurant dinner).

4. CUSTOMIZING CAREERS BY OPTING OUT OR SHIFTING JOBS

Direct correspondence to Phyllis Moen, McKnight Presidential Endowed Chair, Sociology Department, University of Minnesota, 909 Social Sciences Building, 267 19th Avenue South, Minneapolis, MN 55455, 612-625-5483, phylmoen@umn.edu. We thank the Alfred P. Sloan Foundation, which provided support for every phase of this research, including collection of the Ecology of Careers data, and Jane Peterson for manuscript preparation and bibliographic work.

5. KEEPING ENGAGED PARENTS ON THE ROAD TO SUCCESS

Direct all correspondence to Sylvia Ann Hewlett, Center for Work-Life Policy, 1841 Broadway, Suite 400, New York, New York 10023, cwlp@worklifepolicy.org. We would like to acknowledge the corporations whose examples of "best practices" are featured in this chapter: Booz Allen Hamilton, BT Group, Lehman Brothers, and Unilever. A special thanks to Kathleen Christensen and the Alfred P. Sloan Foundation for a grant that supported case study research underlying these best practices. Grant #2005-5-34 WPF.

1. Research participants who requested privacy are referred to by first name only.

2. Survey participants were given a list of factors for reentry, and were asked to select whether or not they considered each factor important to them.

3. Survey participants were given a list of job characteristics, and were asked to select whether or not they considered this attribute important to them.

6. ELDERLY LABOR SUPPLY

This chapter is an abridged version of Haider and Loughran (2001), which was supported by the Center for Retirement Research at Boston College and the U.S. Social Security Administration. The opinions and conclusions are solely those of the authors and should not be construed as representing the opinions or policy of the Social Security Administration or any agency of the federal government or the Center for Retirement Research at Boston College.

1. Haider and Loughran (2008) provide a discussion and detailed analysis of this policy change specifically and the Social Security retirement earnings test more generally.

2. See Hurd (1990) for a review of this lengthy literature.

3. HRS98 includes the fourth wave of the original HRS cohort of individuals born between 1931 and 1941, first surveyed in 1992. The HRS98 also includes the third wave of the Asset and Health Dynamics among the Oldest Old cohort (AHEAD, born 1923 and earlier) and the first waves of the Children of the Depression Age (CODA, born 1924–30) and the War Baby (WB, born 1942–47) cohorts. See http://hrsonline.isr.umich.edu/ for more information.

4. This adjustment is based on the implicit adjustment to the federal poverty line between couples and individuals of 0.79. A lower rate of 0.75 is used because Social Security benefits are reduced by a larger fraction when a spouse dies. A household with a widow will receive 0.50 to 0.67 of the benefits the household received before the death of a spouse.

5. Educational attainment is categorized as follows: dropout (<12 years), high school (twelve years), some college (thirteen to fifteen years), college (sixteen years), advanced (>16 years).

6. Six ADLs are included in this analysis: walking one block, climbing several flights of stairs, stooping, kneeling, or crouching, extending arms above shoulder level, lifting weights over ten pounds, and picking up a dime from a table.

7. The regressions also include a quadratic in age and dummy variables for male, black, and currently married.

8. Percentages can only be calculated after 1974, because hours worked per week are unavailable before then in the CPS.

7. EMPLOYER-PROVIDED WORKPLACE FLEXIBILITY

1. The 1992 NSCW survey was conducted by Mathematica Policy Research, using a questionnaire developed by Families and Work Institute. Hour-long telephone interviews were completed with a national cross-sectional sample of 3,381 employed men and women ages eighteen through sixty-four, as well as 337 women who had dependent children and who were not in the labor force by their own choice, for a total of 3,718. Of the total sample, 2,958 were wage and salaried workers. Data were collected from late March through September 1992. Cash incentives ranging from $10 to $15 were offered, and up to ten phone calls were made to determine household eligibility. Interviewers coded all open-ended responses. Sample eligibility was limited to people who (a) worked at a paid job or operated an income-producing business (b) were eighteen years or older (c) were in the civilian labor force (d) resided in the contiguous forty-eight states and (e) lived in a noninstitutional residence (i.e., household) with a telephone. In addition, workers sixty-five or more years old were not eligible for inclusion and workers eighteen through twenty-four, minority workers, and women not in the labor force were oversampled. In households with more than one eligible person, one was randomly selected to be interviewed. Among 4,493 eligible households, 3,718 interviews were completed—a completion rate of 83%. Dividing the number of completed interviews (3,718, including nonemployed women with children) by the number of households of known eligibility (4,493) plus the estimated number of eligible households among those where eligibility could not be determined (.634*4,537) yields an *overall response rate* of 50.5% for potentially eligible households.

2. The 2002 NSCW survey was conducted by Harris Interactive, Inc. (formerly Louis Harris and Associates) using a questionnaire developed by Families and Work Institute. A total of 3,504 interviews were completed with a nationwide cross-section of employed adults between October 2002 and June 2003. Interviews, which averaged forty-five minutes in length, were conducted by telephone using a computer-assisted telephone interviewing (CATI) system. Calls were made to a regionally stratified unclustered random probability sample generated by random-digit-dial methods. As necessary, thirty or more calls were made per telephone number to determine eligibility and complete interviews if appropriate. Coding of open-ended responses was done by interviewers, with the exception of occupation and industry, which were coded by the U.S. Bureau of the Census using 1990 three-digit occupation and industry classifications. Sample eligibility was limited to people who (a) worked at a paid job or operated an income-producing business, (b) were eighteen years or older, (c) were in the civilian labor force, (d) resided in the contiguous forty-eight states, and (e) lived in a noninstitutional residence (i.e., household) with a telephone. In households with more than one eligible person, one was randomly selected to be interviewed. Interviewers offered cash honoraria of $25 as incentives. Of the twenty-eight

thousand telephone numbers called, 3,578 were determined to represent eligible households, and interviews were completed for 3,504 of these—a *completion rate of 98%*. However, eligibility or ineligibility could not be determined for 6,035 cases—for which there were no answers or for which screening questions could not be asked. Using conservative response rate estimates recommended by the Council of American Survey Research Organizations and the American Association for Public Opinion Research, the response rate among eligibles and potential eligibles was estimated at slightly more than 52%. Adjusting for the growing number of residential and nonresidential telephone lines that are not used for voice communications, the overall response rate is estimated somewhere between 52% and 61%. Of the total sample interviewed, 2,810 are wage and salaried employees who work for someone else, 179 are employed persons who operate their own incorporated businesses and, therefore, work for themselves, and 515 are self-employed workers who do not have incorporated businesses. The average sampling error for wage and salaried sample statistics (n = 2,810) is approximately +/– 1%. Unless otherwise noted, findings are reported as statistically significant only when the probability of their occurring by chance is less than 1 in 100 (p < .01).

3. The 2005 NSE surveyed a representative national sample of 1,092 for-profit and not-for-profit companies with fifty or more employees using telephone interviews with human resource directors. Harris Interactive staff conducted the interviews from September 23, 2004 to April 5, 2005. Employers were selected from Dun and Bradstreet lists, using a stratified random sampling procedure in which selection was proportional to the number of people employed by each company to ensure a large enough sample of large organizations. The response rate was 38%, based on the percentage of all companies on the call list that completed interviews. Considerable effort was made to achieve a response rate equal to or better than that obtained in 1998 (45%). This included offering a $50 incentive to company representatives, many call backs over an extended interview period, and special efforts to convert refusals and complete partial interviews. Despite these efforts, we were unable to achieve the 1998 response level. The problem of relatively low response rates is growing in survey research involving both individuals and organizations. However, because of these efforts, a much better response rate has been achieved than that of the 10% to 20% rate that is typical of organizational research today. When analyzing data to make generalizations about the universe of organizations with fifty or more employees in the United States, the sample was weighted to the distribution of companies of different sizes in the United States. The questionnaire was developed to complement the Families and Work Institute's 2002 National Study of the Changing Workforce (NSCW), which surveyed a representative national sample of employees in the U.S. labor force.

4. Beginning in 2005, Families and Work Institute, the Institute for a Competitive Workforce, an affiliate of the U.S. Chamber of Commerce, and the Twiga Foundation have given this community-based award. In 2005, the award was conferred in eight communities, expanding to sixteen in 2006 and twenty-four in 2007. The process for granting this award is as follows: in Round I, employers self-nominate, completing a questionnaire about their organization's flexibility policies and practices at their worksite. To qualify for Round II, employers must rank among the top 20% of employers nationally, based on the 2005 National Study of Employers. For those who advance, employees must complete a questionnaire that asks about their individual use of and experiences with flexibility, the supportiveness of the workplace culture, and the presence or absence of job jeopardy for using flexibility. A 40% response rate by employees is required. (Response rates averaged 48% in 2006.) To calculate final scores, individual items in each questionnaire are scored on 0 to 5 scales; then, multi-item category scores are calculated on 1 to 100 scales. One-third of the final score depends on the employers' responses and two-thirds on the employees' responses—with equal weighting given to employees' reports of (a) access/use of flexibility and (b) supportiveness and lack of

job jeopardy for using flexibility. There is no minimum or maximum number of award re-
cipients or honorable mentions within a community. The winning organizations (39 winners
from 103 applicants in 2005, and 89 winners from 247 applicants in 2006) receive local and
national recognition, including an award presentation at a well-publicized local ceremony
hosted by the regional chamber; a citation in the *U.S. Congressional Record;* and congratula-
tions in a full-page ad in *USA Today* that includes a downloadable report on the accomplish-
ments of the winners.

5. Professional educators in the seasonal workforce are not included, even though many
do not work during the summer months. Professional educators at postsecondary levels are
excluded from the estimates of voluntary part-year work since many, but not all, work year-
round. Professional educators at pre-kindergarten through high school levels are classified
as voluntary "part-year employees," since most, though not all, have nine-month contracts
and take the summers off. Although the estimate of the proportion of voluntary part-year
employees is imperfect, it is deemed sufficiently accurate to portray the current extent of
voluntary part-year employment in the U.S. workforce.

8. WILL THE REAL FAMILY-FRIENDLY EMPLOYER PLEASE STAND UP

1. On part-time work, see Rosen (1978) and Montgomery (1988). On fringe benefits, see
Ehrenberg and Smith (1983) and Lazear (1998, chap. 15).

2. In particular, see Ingram and Simons (1995) and Goodstein (1994). Wood (1999) provides a good review.

3. See Wood (1999) for a discussion of institutional theory and a useful empirical test.

4. The emphasis on internal labor markets in Osterman (1995) yields a similar hypothesis.

5. The focus is on formal training because informal training is so ubiquitous that a question about informal training would have little content. Note also that formal training is not
included in the list of proxies for minimum hours constraints. This is because there are good
proxies for whether or not firms impose minimum hours constraints (e.g., whether workers
can job share and the percentage of workers who are part-time). Here we are especially interested in the effect of training conditional on those proxies.

6. Several authors note that due to differences in technology, the economic cost of implementing work-family policies can differ across employers (Barringer and Milkovich 1998,
317; Ingram and Simons 1995, 1470; Osterman 1995, 692). Minimum hours constraints
could be viewed as a logical consequence of such cost differences. Similarly, the fourth hypothesis, with its focus on long-term relationships between workers and firms, is at least implicit in the sociological literature. For example, Ingram and Simons (1995, 1469) argue that
if an organization fails to exhibit sufficient work-family responsiveness, it may have difficulty
recruiting and retaining employees. In making their argument they cite several sociological
sources.

7. To implement the restriction to white-collar employees, the interviewer indicated that
white-collar means professionals, including technical workers, managers and administrators,
sales personnel, and clerical and office workers. The restriction to white-collar workers was
due to the need for detailed information in a relatively brief survey. A thorough treatment
of both blue- and white-collar workers would have required a longer survey and resulted in
lower response rates.

8. Although the latter restriction is ideal for a study of phased retirement (ensuring that
questions about phased retirement are relevant to the establishment's current situation), it
could conceivably complicate a study of establishment-level work-family practices. In particular, if establishments with two or more white-collar employees over age fifty-five have
unobserved characteristics associated with their handling of work-family issues, then there
could be a problem with sample selection bias. Since there is no way to know whether this is

a problem, we checked for robustness by reestimating models in samples that are restricted to large (more than one hundred employees) establishments. Sample selection should be less of a problem in large establishments, since most large establishments will pass the test of having two or more older white-collar workers. The reestimated models were, in fact, quite similar to those estimated in the full sample. In particular, a test of the null hypothesis that coefficients in the 100+ sample are the same as those in model 5 of table 8.3 fails to reject the null at a .20 level.

9. The response rate was 64% in the Educational Quality of the Workforce National Employers Survey, which was administered by the U.S. Bureau of the Census as a telephone survey in August and September 1994 to a nationally representative sample of private establishments with more than twenty employees (Lynch and Black 1998). The response rate was 65.5% in Osterman's 1992 telephone survey of establishments with more than fifty employees (Osterman 1994). Holzer and Neumark (1999) report a response rate of 67% for establishments that were successfully screened in a telephone survey undertaken between June 1992 and May 1994.

10. We are indebted to Eileen Trzcinski for pointing this out.

11. See Allison (2002) for a discussion of the advantages of listwise deletion. Hutchens and Grace-Martin (2006) use multiple imputation to address missing data issues in the survey that underlies this chapter. Those results indicated that missing data are not causing serious bias in the coefficients.

9. WORKPLACE FLEXIBILITY FOR FEDERAL CIVILIAN EMPLOYEES

1. According to the Economic Policy Institute, the 2003 bill to extend comp time to the private sector, H.R. 1119, contained provisions to which labor objected that were different from the federal guidelines. Most notably, the bill would have allowed employers to defer disbursing overtime pay for up to thirteen months (Wenger 2001).

2. Both H.R. 1722, the Telework Improvements Act of 2009, and S. 707, the Telework Enhancement Act of 2009, would require agencies to develop telework training programs and also would create a full-time telework manager position in every agency.

3. Today, part-time employees' weekly hours may exceed these boundaries as a result of earning and spending credit hours, as described in the section on alternative work schedules.

10. THE ODD DISCONNECT

Direct all correspondence to Distinguished Professor of Law, University of California Hastings College of the Law, 200 McAllister Street, San Francisco, California, 94102; williams@uchastings.edu. The author would like to thank Claire-Therese Luceno, Matthew Melamed, Angela Perone, Liana Sterling, and Emily Stratton for their expert research assistance, and Donna Adkins and Stephanie Bornstein for their invaluable editing and proofreading help.

1. Scenarios adapted from those originally published in "The Public Policy of Motherhood," by Joan C. Williams and Holly Cohen Cooper, *Journal of Social Issues* 60 (2004): 849–65.

2. Delivering health insurance though employers drives up the hours of both nonexempt workers, who are entitled to overtime, and managers and professionals, who are exempt from the overtime requirements of the FLSA. To preserve access to health coverage, professional-managerial class families have to retain one parent in a full-time job, fueling the "neotraditional" trend (Moen 2003) of men working fifty-plus hours per week in "full-time" positions, while women work (if at all) in short hours jobs, for low pay and no benefits.

3. Among the experts cited were the author (Joan Williams) and Deputy Director of the Center for WorkLife Law Cynthia Calvert.

11. LIMITING WORKING TIME AND SUPPORTING FLEXIBILITY FOR EMPLOYEES

Janet C. Gornick is Professor of Political Science and Sociology at the Graduate Center, at the City University of New York. She is also Director of the Luxembourg Income Study. Please direct all correspondence to Professor Janet Gornick, Luxembourg Income Study at the CUNY/GC: The Graduate Center, City University of New York, Room 6203.08, 365 Fifth Avenue, New York, NY, USA 10016–4309.

1. The 1993 EU Working Time Directive specified that maximum working hours, on average, must not exceed forty-eight per week. However, the meaning of maximum hours varies. In most cases, maximum-hour policies mean that workers may not work above the set ceiling, while in others workers may not exceed the ceiling unless they opt to do so.

2. This is also the case in Germany and the Netherlands, but collective bargaining coverage is much greater in those countries.

3. In addition, many workers are granted public holidays off, both in Europe and in the United States. Although the number of public holidays affect total time spent at work each year, those days are not reported in this comparison. First, it is not always clearly specified that holidays are considered to be paid days. Second, holidays are less useful than vacation days, from the workers' perspective, in that workers do not have discretion as to when to take them.

4. The rules covering self-insured health plans can be found in section 105(h) of the Code, and the regulations can be found at 26 CFR 1.105–11. The standards related to pensions can be found in section 202 of ERISA and section 410 of the Internal Revenue Code. The regulations under ERISA can be found at 29 CFR 2530.202–1 and 2530.202–2, and the regulations under the Code can be found at 26 CFR 1.410(a)-3 and 1.410(a)-3T. Thanks to Deborah Forbes at the Pension Benefits Guaranty Corporation for providing this information. See Gornick and Meyers (2003) for more information.

5. "Weeks of leave" presented in figure 3 reflects a combination of duration and benefit generosity. In other words, ten weeks at 80% of wages and eight weeks at 100% of wages would receive the same value: eight weeks.

6. Note that this figure reports only *earnings-related components* of family leave and assumes earnings below any existing earnings caps. Some of these countries, including France and Germany, also offer additional periods of leave paid at a low flat rate. These low-paid benefits are excluded here for a few reasons. One is that these benefits are not always conditioned on employment, so characterizing them as wage replacement is not fully accurate. Furthermore, take-up is much lower than in the earnings-related programs, so including them exaggerates the level of provision. Also, note that, in the United States, maternity benefits paid under the state-based Temporary Disability Insurance programs are not included, because these programs operate in only five states.

7. Across these countries, the wage replacement rates for these *earnings-related leaves* are high, so the maximum number of "fully paid" weeks of leave is the same as, or similar to, the maximum number of weeks at any rate of replaced wages. The actual maxima are approximately fifty-two weeks in Sweden, Norway, Denmark, and Canada; approximately forty-four weeks in Finland; eighteen weeks in the United Kingdom; and 12–16 weeks in the five Continental countries, where wage replacement rates are generally 100%.

8. Maternity leave rights in the United Kingdom, however, have been increased recently, although they still remain relatively modest. The duration of the "maternity allowance" (the program with the broadest eligibility) was recently increased from eighteen to twenty-six weeks, but the benefit, in most cases, is still paid at a flat rate rather than as a fraction of earnings—which translates to comparatively few "fully paid weeks." The recent reforms are not reflected in figure 3, so as to keep the figure comparable at a point in time.

9. For more information on this scale, and to see the scoring of a larger set of countries, see Gornick and Meyers (2003).

10. Since the time point of this comparison—approximately 2002—France and the United Kingdom both instituted a modest number of paid paternity days for fathers.

11. Public measures that would increase access to flexible options would especially benefit low-wage workers, as more highly skilled workers typically have substantially more access granted voluntarily by their employers (Levin-Epstein 2006).

12. For a more detailed discussion of the possible effects on nonstandard schedules and on gender inequality, see Gornick and Heron (2006).

13. At the same time, the directive includes a number of other components, many of which are clearly advantageous to workers. It requires minimum provisions related to daily rest breaks, weekly rest periods, and, as noted, annual leave.

14. These studies and others establish that parents perceive that shortening their working hours reduces their work-family conflict. Whether, and to what extent, parents spend those "freed-up" hours with their children is an empirical question that has received much less attention. One study that addresses this directly is also from the French case. According to a 2001 survey, among parents with children under age twelve, 43% of French parents say that, since the enactment of the thirty-five-hour week, they spend more time with their children (see Kamerman et al. 2003 for a review of research on the effects of the French law).

15. Whether women's working time preferences are different from men's—in some fundamental and enduring way—is a contested question. Hakim (1997), for example, has long argued that while many women are career-oriented, substantial numbers are not—and it is their preferences, not constraints or institutional factors, that explain their relatively low hours compared to men's. Others argue that women's intrinsic preferences cannot be identified until gendered expectations and institutional constraints erode (Gornick and Meyers 2003).

12. PARENTS' EXPERIENCES OF FLEXIBLE WORK ARRANGEMENTS IN CHANGING EUROPEAN WORKPLACES

Portions of this chapter previously appeared in "Parents' Experiences of Flexible Work Arrangements in Changing European Workplaces: A Multi-layer Contextual Approach," *Sociological Problems* (IL-II/2008): 5–28. Reprinted with permission of the Institute of Sociology, Bulgarian Academy of Science.

1. This project was funded by the European Union. See www.workliferesearch.org/transitions.

2. The other two phases included mapping the national context and individual biographical interviews with working parents.

3. Partners were Suzan Lewis, Janet Smithson, Christina Purcell, and John Howarth, Manchester Metropolitan University; Julia Brannen and Michaela Brockmann, Thomas Coram Institute, University of London; Ann Nilsen, Sevil Summer, and Lise Granlund, University of Bergen; Margareta Bäck-Wiklund and Lars Plantin, University of Göteborg; Nevenka Černigoj Sadar, Jana Nadoh, and Polona Kersnik, University of Ljubljana; Anneke van Doorne-Huiskes, Laura den Dulk, Bram Peper, and Marijke Veldhoen–van Blitterswijk, Utrecht University; Siyka Kovacheva, Atanas Matev, and Paissii Hilendarski, State University, Bulgaria; Maria das Dores Guerreiro, Pedro Abrantes, Inês Pereira, and Inês Cardoso, Instituto Superior de Ciências do Trabalho e da Empresa, Lisbon, Portugal; Jeanne Fagnani, Centre d'Economie de la Sorbonne, University of Paris.

4. Pseudonyms are used for each company.

13. WORK HOURS MISMATCH IN THE UNITED STATES AND AUSTRALIA

1. Medium hours refers to working 30–40 hours per week.

2. The OECD (2004) report data on the proportion of employees working long usual weekly hours for a much longer list of countries, but using a weekly hours cutoff of forty-five

rather than fifty hours. In this list Iceland, Japan, New Zealand, and the United Kingdom all show up as having more male employees working longer hours than both Australia and the United States.

3. Data on trade union membership are regularly compiled by the Australian Bureau of Statistics and reported on in ABS, *Employee Earnings, Benefits and Trade Union Membership* (ABS cat. no. 6310.0).

4. Source: ABS, *Employee Earnings, Benefits and Trade Union Membership, August 2005* (ABS cat. no. 6310.0). Part-time employment is defined by the ABS as including any person who usually works less than thirty-five hours a week (in all jobs) and either did so during the survey reference week or was not at work in the reference week.

5. Source: OECD, *Employment Outlook 2005*, Statistical Annex: table B.

6. The source for these data is OECD, *Employment Outlook 2005*, Statistical Annex: table E. Note that while the OECD does its best to convert data for each member country into a comparable format, there are differences in definitions that could not be dealt with. Most obviously, the U.S. data are for wage and salary earners only whereas the Australian data relate to all employed persons. Further, the definition of part-time employment in the U.S. data relates to usual hours below thirty in the main job, while in the Australian data it is based on actual hours below thirty-five worked in all jobs.

7. Australia has had a national state-funded age pension since 1909. Since 1992, all employers have been required to make contributions into privately funded schemes for retirement, known as superannuation. Since these require employer contributions, they are included in the more general discussion on the cost of pensions to employers.

8. The 2002 NSCW survey administration is described in *National Study of the Changing Workforce, Guide to Public Use Files*, May 2004, a file provided with the *2002, 1997 and 1992 National Study of the Changing Workforce, Public-Use Files Version 1.0* (New York: Families and Work Institute, 2004).

9. It is not obvious that the time divide theories discussed earlier will apply to the self-employed, so they are excluded from the analysis.

10. See Wooden and Watson (2007) for a discussion of the design and administration of the HILDA Survey.

11. In addition, all usual work hours values of ninety-nine per week or above are set to missing.

12. The precise wording of the usual and preferred hours questions, the means and standard deviations of variables used in the regression analyses, and subsidiary regression results discussed but not shown are provided in an appendix available at http://lser.la.psu.edu/work fam/mismatch.doc.

13. The HILDA includes an income caveat discussed below. To make the NSCW data more comparable, this study excludes fifty-two respondents who (a) claimed to prefer fewer hours; (b) responded to a follow-up question regarding whether a reduction would alter their income with the answer "no"; and (c) were employed on an hourly basis. Salaried employees who believed that an hours reduction would not alter their income, as might well be the case, are not excluded. For hourly employees, hours reductions should translate directly into income reductions.

14. A check with reestimation using the zero hours cutoff (not reported) yields very similar results.

15. Educational attainment could instead proxy ideal worker status, an approach we reject on empirical grounds. The simple correlation between a dummy variable for holding a bachelor's degree or higher qualification and usual work hours is .124 in the NSCW and .013 in the HILDA Survey. For the correlation between managerial or professional occupation and usual hours, the coefficients are .132 in the NSCW and .156 in the HILDA Survey.

16. The constant is 21.04, and the usual hours coefficient is -.640, with an adjusted R^2 of .488 and an N of 2367.

14. RENEWED ENERGY FOR CHANGE

Juliet Bourke, Juliet.Bourke@aequus.com.au. Aequus Partners, Office 3, 332 Darling Street, Balmain, 2041 NSW, Australia.

1. The term "balance" has been heavily criticized as aspirational (rather than practical), and as "a conservative expression of a radical impulse" (see Connell 2005). Nevertheless, I use the term "work-family balance" because it has general currency, and is therefore readily understood to represent the desire to negotiate and achieve an holistic work-family arrangement.

2. For an examination of twenty high-income countries' statutory response to flexibility, refer also to Hegewisch and Gornick (2008).

3. http://www.aph.gov.au/house/committee/fhs/workandfamily/media/media16.pdf.

4. In June 2007, the government introduced a "fairness test" by which collective agreements or Australian Workplace Agreements, lodged from May 7, 2007, would not be approved by the Federal Workplace Authority unless it could be demonstrated that the new agreement provided fair compensation for lost or changed conditions.

5. Although the subject lies beyond the scope of this chapter, some commentators have focused on inferring Australia's work-family policy position through an examination of the taxation system (e.g., Hill 2006).

6. For a brief history of gender equity prior to the 1970s, see Squirchuk and Bourke 2000 (118–20).

7. The AAA is now known as the Equal Opportunity for Women in the Workplace Act 1999.

8. Tellingly, because family responsibilities were seen as primarily an issue of sex discrimination against women.

9. Australia is a signatory to the ILO Workers with Family Responsibilities Convention (1981) and the Convention of the Elimination of All Forms of Discrimination Against Women (which is a schedule to the Sex Discrimination Act 1984).

10. Awards are collective agreements negotiated between unions and employers which regulate the employment conditions of certain industry groups of workers.

11. Australia does not provide paid maternity leave (scheduled to commence in 2001), but does provide a Maternity Payment to working and nonworking mothers. The Maternity Payment is a one-time payment available to assist with the extra costs of a new baby, and is payable for babies born or adopted on or after July 1, 2004.

12. The Child Care Benefit is available to assist with the costs of approved childcare fees (i.e., for long [7 a.m. to 6 p.m.] daycare, family daycare, occasional care, outside school hours care, vacation care, and in-home care) and registered care (TOCC 2006a, 48).

13. In fact, WorkChoices removed an employee's right to contest an "unfair" dismissal if the employee is employed in a small to medium enterprise (one with less than one hundred employees).

14. An immediate family member is defined as a (a) spouse, child, parent, grandparent, grandchild, or sibling of the employee, or (b) child, parent, grandparent, grandchild, or sibling of the spouse of the employee (WRA 1996, § 240).

15. Only those standards are noted that relate to work-family balance and which differ from the existing five standards; for example, the new "Hours of work" standard does not differ in substance from the existing standard.

16. Namely, that the employee's caring responsibilities mean that they would be unable to perform the "inherent requirements" of the job, or in order to carry out those requirements, would need accommodation that "would impose an unjustifiable hardship on the employer" Anti-Discrimination Act 1977 [NSW] (§ 49V.4.a.b).

17. Under the most expansive legislation (e.g., the Anti-Discrimination Act 1977 [NSW], § 49S), the definition of caring responsibilities is wider than in the WRA and also includes de facto (i.e., nonmarried) and homosexual relationships.

18. E.g., *Tleyji v. The TravelSpirit Group Pty Ltd* (2005) NSWADT 294.

19. E.g., *Bogle v. Metropolitan Health Service Board* (2000) 93–069 EOC 74,200.

20. E.g., *Community Public Sector Union v. CSL* (2002) C2002/2562 AIRC.

21. For a summary of the full range of benefits and allowances in relation to carers of children, the elderly, and people with a disability, see Taskforce on Care Costs (2005, 2006a).

22. http://www.flexibilityworks.dewr.gov.au/ http://www.flexibilityworks.dewr.gov.au/.

23. The increase for men was from 6% to 15% between 1985 and 2005, while for women was from 37% to 46% in the same period (ABS 2006a).

24. This amount was reduced to fifteen under WorkChoices (§ 513).

25. In essence, the "no-disadvantage" statutory test provided that approval of industrial agreements was contingent on them being measured "globally" against the relevant award and found to create "no disadvantage" for employees. That test was removed by WorkChoices.

26. In the *Family Provisions* test case, the AIRC decided that an employee is entitled to access up to ten days of personal leave, including accrued leave, to care for a member of the employee's immediate family or household who is sick or requires care due to an unexpected emergency. This was codified in the WorkChoices minimum standards.

27. State government employees not employed by a corporation were not covered by WorkChoices. On December 19, 2005, the NSW Industrial Relations Commission substantially adopted the AIRC *Family Provisions* case in the *Family Provisions Case* 2005 (2005b) and gave a general order that (subject to some exceptions) the decision applied to NSW state government employees.

28. Although note that the ABS *Australian Social Trends 2006 Data Cube,* which was updated in August 2007, shows that average weekly hours had reduced to forty in 2006 (ABS 2007, table 1).

29. The data are not uniformly positive, however, with 31% of part-time workers preferring to work more hours per week (ABS 2006a, 129).

30. Using the ABS definition of casual labor, although the proportion of casual labor has remained steady since 1998, there was a slight increase between 2004 (24%) and 2006 (26%; ABS 2006c, 2).

31. Although the Australian Bureau of Statistics agrees with this "common understanding" of the difference between permanent part-time and casual employment, it has also noted that "many casuals have long-term regular jobs." Accordingly, the ABS notes that "the nature and level of casual employment in Australia continues to be debated"; we (the ABS) use the definition for research purposes that distinguishes between ongoing employees (who have access to paid sick and/or annual leave) and casuals (who do not have access to paid leave; ABS 2006c, 1–2).

32. WorkChoices legitimized an employer's refusal to employ a prospective employee if he or she fails to enter into an agreement provided by the employer (WRA 1996, § 400.6).

33. For more generalized concerns about the impact of WorkChoices beyond work-family flexibility, see Thew (2005).

34. For a more comprehensive review of the agreement making and approval procedures, see Thew (2006).

35. See note 8.

36. Against this trend of robust and broad interpretation by administrative tribunals, two appeal courts have recently taken a narrow approach to interpreting the carers' responsibilities provisions under discrimination and industrial law respectively (see *State of Victoria v. Schou* [2004] VSCA 71 and *State of NSW v. Amery* [2006] HCA 14).

37. 45.7% in 1985, compared with 56.7% in 2005 (Kelly, Bolton, and Harding 2005, 4).

15. FLEXIBLE EMPLOYMENT AND THE INTRODUCTION OF WORK-LIFE BALANCE PROGRAMS IN JAPAN

1. Recently, some Japanese court decisions have granted job security to part-time workers and compelled retroactive salary adjustments, but this development does not yet

mean that part-time workers can expect the same treatment accorded to regular, full-time workers.

2. Contact the author for information on shift-share analyses.

16. GOVERNMENT POLICIES SUPPORTING WORKPLACE FLEXIBILITY

Sumiko Iwao; siwao@gmail.com; 1-20-14 Momoi, Suginami-ku, Tokyo Japan 167-0034.

1. Unions are concerned that a move to a more flexible employment system will jeopardize existing labor regulations that currently make it difficult for employers to dismiss permanent employees. Furthermore, by granting employers more flexibility in adjusting employment contracts freely to fit a variety of job formats, union leaders worry the reform bill will result in companies hiring fewer regular, full-time employees.

2. As indicated in the report *Basic Directions of Promoting Work/Life Balance,* issued in July 2007 by the Cabinet Office (2007b). However, this initial report merely outlines the issues and illustrates their importance. Concrete policy measures to dramatically overhaul the workplace have yet to be taken.

3. The results of a government public opinion survey conducted in August 2007 show that only 27% of respondents "have ever seen or heard the term 'work-life balance.'" The phrase is even less known by women than by men. For example, only 12% of women in their twenties and only 19% of those in their thirties "have heard or seen the term" (Cabinet Office, 2007c).

4. http://www8.cao.go.jp/shoushi/taisaku.pdf.

5. According to the White Paper on Gender Equality, 2006, the average amount of time fathers with working spouses spend for household chores and child- or eldercare is 25 minutes per day, while the average working spouse spends 4 hours and 12 minutes a day on the same tasks (Cabinet Office 2007).

6. To complicate the scene even further, a recent study by Hiroki Sato of the University of Tokyo shows that a majority of nonregular female employees are more satisfied than regular employees with their working conditions and wages. This can be taken as evidence that many regular employees do not have flexibility regarding their work and, therefore, are not in a position to be envied by women in nonregular employment.

7. The government has been promoting its Support Plan for Women's Renewed Challenges since 2005. However, the support plan does not mention or address workplace flexibility directly, and it is not considered a measure to promote workplace flexibility, so it will not be discussed further in this chapter.

8. The revised part-time labor law went into effect in April 2008. This law requests that employers treat part-time workers in more equal terms compared to permanent, full-time employees. The revised law does allow for an adjustment to the general equality standard, based on the number of working hours and responsibilities assumed by the part-time employees. Employers will also be asked to provide opportunities to part-time workers to switch to permanent employee status.

9. This chapter was prepared while Mr. Koizumi was the prime minister.

10. See also http://www8.cao.go.jp/shoushi/suisin/se-mokuji.html.

11. In addition to the aforementioned laws, the Labour Standards Law (2007) stipulates that employers must exempt pregnant women from work for six weeks prior to expected delivery upon the pregnant women's request, and they usually are obliged to exempt them from work for eight weeks after delivery (Article 65). This is called Pre/Post Delivery Leave and is different from childcare leave, which is for both mother and father.

12. www.mhlw.go.jp/bunya/koyou/koyouhoken05/pdf/02.pdf.

13. The author was the chair of the Gender Equality Council in the Cabinet Office that discussed the need for the Basic Law for a Gender Equal Society, and proposed its framework to the government.

14. *Ikuji kaigo kyuugyouhou no aramashi* (Summary of Child-care/Elder-care Leave Law; Ministry of Health, Labour and Welfare, and Japan Institute of Workers' Evolution 2005).

15. The amount in dollars fluctuates according to the exchange rate.

16. Providing childcare for children younger than three is already an obligation designated by law.

17. What the government means by "this pervasive atmosphere in the workplace" is not explained in the material; they may be referring to the dominant corporate mentality that loyalty to a job is measured by the number of hours worked each week, and the priority an employee gives to his company over all other interests.

18. http://www.familyfriendly.jp/~ff/top/tr/en_1.php through http://www.familyfriendly.jp/~ff/top/tr/en_5.php.

19. The government's website is most helpful in researching a company with a known name. A list of the names of all registered companies is not yet available to facilitate cross-referencing.

References

Acemoglu, D., and J. Angrist. 2001. Consequences of employment protection? The case of the Americans with Disabilities Act. *Journal of Political Economy* 109: 915–57.

Adams, S. 2000. Three essays on the economics of aging. PhD diss., Michigan State University.

Age Discrimination Act. 29 U.S.C. §§ 621–634. 1967.

Albelda, R., and C. Cosenza. 2000. *Choices and trade-offs: The parent survey on child care in Massachusetts.* Boston: Parents United for Child Care.

Albiston, K. T. 2008. *The institutional context of civil rights: The FMLA in the courts and in the workplace.* Paper presented at the annual meeting of the Law and Society Association, Denver.

Alexander, A. J. 2000. *What happened to Japan's economy in the 1990s?* Japan Economic Institute Report 27. Washington, D.C.: Japan Economic Institute of America.

Allard, M. D., S. M. Bianchi, J. Stewart, and V. R. Wight. 2007. Comparing childcare in the ATUS and earlier time-diary studies. *Monthly Labor Review* 130(5): 27–36.

Allison, P. D. 2002. *Missing data.* Thousand Oaks, Calif.: Sage Publications.

Altobelli, J., and P. Moen. 2007. Work-family spillover among dual-earner couples. In *Advances in the Life Course,* vol. 7, *Interpersonal relations across the life course,* ed. T. Owens and J. J. Suitor, 361–82. New York: Elsevier.

Altonji, J. G., and J. Oldham. 2003. Vacation laws and annual work hours. *Economic Perspectives—Federal Reserve Bank of Chicago* 27(3): 19–29.

American Business Collaboration for Quality Dependent Care. 2002. *10th Anniversary Report, 1992–2002.* http://www.abcdependentcare.com/docs/abc-10th-anniversary-report.PDF.

American Federation of Labor–Congress of Industrial Unions [AFL-CIO]. n.d. *Work and family: Family-friendly work schedules.* http://www.aflcio.org/issues/workfamily/worksched ules.cfm.

Andreassi, J., and C. A. Thompson, C. A. 2008. Work-family culture: Current research and future directions. In *Handbook of work-family integration: Theories, perspectives and best practices,* ed. K. Korabik, D. Lero, and D. Whitehead, 331–52. New York: Academic Press.

Appelbaum, E., T. Bailey, P. Berg, and A. L. Kalleberg. 2001. *Shared work, valued care: New norms for organizing market work and unpaid care work.* Washington, D.C.: Economic Policy Institute.

Ashenfelter, O., and D. Card. 2002. Did the elimination of faculty retirement affect faculty flows? *American Economic Review* 92: 957–80.

Aspen Publishers. 2007. State's FMLA applies to company's sick leave policy. *Fair Employment Practices Guidelines* 629: 7.

Attkisson, S. 2004. Maternity: A job hazard? *CBS Evening News,* November 11.

Australian Bureau of Statistics (ABS). 2006a. *Australian social trends 2006: Trends in women's employment.* ABS Cat No. 4102. Canberra: Australian Bureau of Statistics.

——. 2006b. *Employee earnings, benefits and trade union membership, Australia 2005.* ABS Cat No. 6310. Canberra: Australian Bureau of Statistics.

——. 2006c. *Year book Australia 2006, casual employees.* ABS Cat No. 1301. Canberra: Australian Bureau of Statistics.

——. 2007. *Australian social trends 2006 data cube.* ABS Cat No. 4102. August 7. Canberra: Australian Bureau of Statistics.

Australian Government Department of Education, Employment and Workplace Relations. 2008. *Discussion paper: National employment standards exposure draft.* Canberra: Commonwealth of Australia.

Australian Industrial Relations Commission (AIRC). 1979. *Maternity leave.* Print D9579. Melbourne: Australian Industrial Relations Commission.

——. 1985. *Adoption leave.* Print F9582. Melbourne: Australian Industrial Relations Commission.

——. 1990. *Parental leave.* Print J3596. Melbourne: Australian Industrial Relations Commission.

——. 1994. *Family leave.* Print L6900. Melbourne: Australian Industrial Relations Commission.

——. 1995. *Personal/carers' leave.* Print M7000. Melbourne: Australian Industrial Relations Commission.

——. 2001. *Parental leave for casual employees.* PR904631. Melbourne: Australian Industrial Relations Commission.

——. 2002. *Working hours.* PR072002. Melbourne: Australian Industrial Relations Commission.

——. 2005a. *Family Provisions case.* PR082005. Melbourne: Australian Industrial Relations Commission.

——. 2005b. *Family Provisions case.* NSWIRComm 478. Melbourne: Australian Industrial Relations Commission.

Aycan, Z. 2008. Cross-cultural approaches to work-family conflict. In *Handbook of work-family integration: Theories, perspectives, and best practices,* ed. K. Korabik, D. Lero, and D. Whitehead, 353–70. New York: Academic Press.

Back v. Hastings on Hudson Union Free Sch. Dist. 365 F.3d 107. 2d Cir. 2004.

Bailyn, L. 1993. *Breaking the mold: Women, men, and time in the new corporate world.* New York: Free Press.

——. 2006. *Breaking the mold: Redesigning work for productive and satisfying lives.* Ithaca: Cornell University Press.

Baird, M. 2006. *Employment relations: What's new?* Paper presented at the Women, Management and Employment Relations Conference, Sydney.

Ballenstedt, B. 2008. House revisits paid leave for federal parents. *GovernmentExecutive.com.* http://www.govexec.com/dailyfed/0308/030608b2.htm.

Bardasi, E., and J. C. Gornick. 2003. Women's part-time employment across countries: Workers' 'choices' and wage penalties. In *Women in the labour market in changing economies: Demographic issues,* ed. B. Garcia, R. Anker, and A. Pinnelli, 209–43. Oxford: Oxford University Press.

Barnett, R. C. 1998. Toward a review and reconceptualization of the work/family literature. *Genetic, Social, and General Psychology Monographs* 124: 125–82.

——. 2004. Work hours as a predictor of stress outcomes. Paper presented at the Conference on Long Working Hours, Safety, and Health, Baltimore.

——. 2006. Relationship of the number and distribution of work hours to health and QOL outcomes. In *Research in occupational stress and well being, vol. 5,* ed. P. L. Perrewe and D. C. Ganster, 99–138. New York: Elsevier.

Barr, S. 2008. A plea for paid parental leave. *Washington Post,* March 7, D4.

Barringer, M. W., and G. T. Milkovich. 1998. A theoretical exploration of the adoption and design of flexible benefit plans: A case of human resource innovation. *Academy of Management Review* 23: 305–24.

Basic Law for a Gender Equal Society. Law No. 78 of 1999.

Batt, R., and P. M. Valcour. 2003. Human resources practices as predictors of work-family outcomes and employee turnover. *Industrial Relations* 42: 189–220.

Bauman, Z. 1998. *Globalisation: The human consequences.* New York: Columbia University Press.

BBC. Japan population starts to shrink. 2005. http://news.bbc.co.uk/2/hi/asia-pacific/4552010.stm.

Beazley, K. 2007. Care for kids—Labor's early childhood blueprint. July 28. http://www.alp.org.au/download/now/blueprint,_childcare,_060728.pdf.

Becker, G. S. 1985. Human capital, effort, and the sexual division of labor. *Journal of Labor Economics* 3: S33–S58.

Becker, P. E., and P. Moen. 1999. Scaling back: Dual-career couples' work-family strategies. *Journal of Marriage and the Family* 61: 995–1007.

Belkin, L. 2003. The opt-out revolution. *New York Times Magazine,* October 26, 42.

———. 2006. Life's work: Family needs in the legal balance. *New York Times,* July 30.

Benitez-Silva, H. 2000. Micro determinants of labor force status among older Americans. Unpublished manuscript, State University of New York at Stony Brook.

Benko, C., and A. Weisberg. 2007. *Mass career customization: Aligning the workplace with today's nontraditional workforce.* Boston: Harvard Business School Press.

Bianchi, S. M. 2000. Maternal employment and time with children: Dramatic change or surprising continuity? *Demography* 37: 401–14.

Bianchi, S. M., M. A. Milkie, L. C. Sayer, and J. P. Robinson. 2000. Is anyone doing the housework? Trends in the gender division of household labor. *Social Forces* 79: 191–228.

Bianchi, S. M., and S. B. Raley. 2005. Time allocation in families. In *Work, family, health, and well-being,* ed. S. M. Bianchi, L. M. Casper, and R. B. King, 21–42. Mahwah, N.J.: Lawrence Erlbaum.

Bianchi, S. M., J. P. Robinson, and M. A. Milkie. 2006. *Changing rhythms of American family life.* New York: Russell Sage.

Bianchi, S. M., V. R. Wight, and S. B. Raley. 2005. *Maternal employment and family caregiving: Rethinking time with children in the ATUS.* Paper presented at the ATUS Early Results Conference, Bethesda, Md.

Biernat, M., F. J. Crosby, and J. C. Williams, ed. 2004. The maternal wall: Research and policy perspectives on discrimination against mothers. *Journal of Social Issues* 60: 675–83.

Bird, C. E., and A. M. Fremont. 1991. Gender, time use, and health. *Journal of Health and Social Behavior* 32: 114–29.

Bispinck, R. 2005. Trade unions and the organisation of individual working time flexibilisation in Germany: What contribution does collective bargaining policy make to work-life balance? In *Working time for working families: Europe and the United States,* ed. A. Hegewisch, 186–209. Washington, D.C.: Friedrich Ebert Stiftung.

Bittman, M. 1995. Changes at the heart of family households: Family responsibilities in Australia, 1974–1992. *Family Matters* 40: 10–15.

Bittman, M., and J. Wajcman. 2000. The rush hour: The character of leisure time and gender equity. *Social Forces* 79: 165–89.

Blair-Loy, M. 2003. *Competing devotions: Career and family among women financial executives.* Cambridge: Harvard University Press.

Blair-Loy, M., and A. Wharton. 2002. The "overtime culture" in a global corporation: A cross-national study of finance professionals' interest in working part-time. *Work and Occupations* 29: 32–63.

———. 2004. Mothers in finance: Surviving and thriving. *Annals of the American Academy of Political and Social Science* 596: 151–71.

Blau, D. 1994. Labor force dynamics of older men. *Econometrica* 62: 117–56.

Bogle v. Metropolitan Health Service Board. 93–069 EOC 74,200. 2000.

Bohen, H. H., and A. Viveros-Long. 1981. *Balancing jobs and family life: Do flexible work schedules help?* Philadelphia: Temple University Press.

Bond, J. T., E. Galinsky, S. S. Kim, and E. Brownfield. 2005. *National study of employers.* New York: Families and Work Institute.

Bond, J. T., E. Galinsky, M. Pitt-Catsouphes, and M. A. Smyer. 2005. *Context matters: Insights about older workers from the national study of the changing workforce.* http://agingandwork.bc.edu/documents/RH01_InsightOlderWorker.pdf.

Bond, J. T., E. Galinsky, and J. E. Swanberg. 1998. *The 1997 National Study of the Changing Workforce.* New York: Families and Work Institute.

Bond, S., J. Hyman, J. Summers, and S. Wise. 2002. *Family friendly working? Putting policy into practice.* York, U.K.: Joseph Rowntree Foundation.

Bond, J. T., C. Thompson, E. Galinsky, and D. Prottas. 2003. *Highlights of the National Study of the Changing Workforce.* New York: Families and Work Institute.

Booth, A., and M. Wood. 2008. Back-to-front down-under? Part-time/full-time wage differentials in Australia. *Industrial Relations* 47: 114–35.

Bound, J., M. Schoenbaum, T. Stinebrickner, and T. Waidmann. 1999. The dynamic effects of health on the labor force transitions of older workers. *Labour Economics* 6: 179–202.

Bourdieu, P. 1977. *Outline of a theory of practice.* Cambridge: Cambridge University Press.

——. 1979. *La distinction: Critique sociale du jugement* [Distinction: A social critique of the judgment of taste]. Paris: Les Éditions de Minuit.

——. 1990. *The logic of practice.* Stanford: Stanford University Press.

Bourke, J. 2000. *Corporate women, children, careers and workplace culture.* IRRC Monograph No. 15. Sydney: Industrial Relations Research Centre, University of Studies in Organisational Analysis and Innovation.

——. 2004. Using the law to support work/life issues: The Australian experience. *American University Journal of Gender, Social Policy, and the Law* 12(1): 19–69.

Boushey, H. 2005. *Family friendly policies: Helping mothers make ends meet.* Washington, D.C.: Center for Economic and Policy Research.

Bradley, R. H., R. F. Corwyn, H. P. McAdoo, and C. García Coll. 2001. The home environments of children in the United States. Part 1: Variations by age, ethnicity, and poverty status. *Child Development* 72: 1844–67.

Briscoe, F. 2006. Temporal flexibility and careers: The role of large-scale organizations for physicians. *Industrial and Labor Relations Review* 60: 88–104.

——. 2007. From iron cage to iron shield? How bureaucracy enables temporal flexibility for professional service workers. *Organization Science* 18: 297–314.

Bruce, W., and C. Reed. 1994. Preparing supervisors for the future workforce: The dual-income couple and the work-family dichotomy. *Public Administration Review* 54: 36–43.

Buchmueller, T. C., J. DiNardo, and R. G. Valletta. 2002. Union effects on health insurance provision and coverage in the United States. *Industrial and Labor Relations Review* 55: 610–27.

Budig, M. J., and P. England. 2001. The wage penalty for motherhood. *American Sociological Review* 66: 204–25.

Bulow, J. I., and L. H. Summers. 1986. A theory of dual labor markets with application to industrial policy, discrimination, and Keynesian unemployment. *Journal of Labor Economics* 4: 376–414.

Burchall, B., D. Lapido, and F. Wilkinson, ed. 2002. *Job insecurity and work intensification.* London: Routledge.

Burkhauser, R., J. Butler, Y. Kim, and R. Weathers II. 1999. The importance of accommodation on the timing of male disability insurance application. *Journal of Human Resources* 34: 589–611.

Burlington Northern and Santa Fe Ry. v. White. 126 S. Ct. 2405. 2006.

Burrow, S. 2005. Speech on WorkChoices legislation. http://www.actu.asn.au/public/news/files/monash_uni_seminar_oct2005.doc.

Burud, S., and M. Tumolo. 2004. *Leveraging the new human capital: Adaptive strategies, results achieved, and stories of transformation.* Palo Alto, Calif.: Davies-Black Publishing.

Cabinet Office. 2003. *Kokumin seikatsu hakusho* [White paper on national life]. Tokyo: Gyosei.

——. 2004. *Shoshika shakai hakusho* [White paper on birthrate-declining society]. Tokyo: Gyosei.

——. 2006a. *Danjo kyodo sankaku hakusho* [White paper on gender equality]. Tokyo: Kokuritsu Insatsukyoku.

——. 2006b. *Kourei shakai hakusho* [White paper on the aging society]. Tokyo: Gyosei.

——. 2006c. *Shoshika to danjo kyodo sankaku ni kansuru ishiki chosa* [Opinion survey on gender equality]. Tokyo: Gyosei.

——. 2007a. *FY2006 annual report on the state of formation of a gender-equal society* (White paper). Tokyo: Cabinet Office.

——. 2007b. *Basic directions of promoting work-life balance.* Tokyo: Cabinet Office.

——. 2007c. *Public opinion survey on gender equality.* Tokyo: Cabinet Office.

——. 2007d. *White paper on the labor economy 2007.* Tokyo: Cabinet Office.

California Federal S. and L. Assn. v. Guerra. 479 U.S. 272. 1987.

California Labor Code. §§ 230.7, 230.8, 233, 513. 2006.

Calta, M. 2005. *Barbarians at the plate: Taming and feeding the modern American family.* New York: Pedigree Books.

Cantor, D., J. Waldfogel, J. Kerwin, M. McKinley-Wright, K. Levin, J. Rauch, T. Hagerty, and M. Stapleton-Kudela. 2001. *Balancing the needs of families and employers: Family and medical leave surveys, 2000 update.* Rockville, Md.: Westat.

Cao, H. 2000a. AHEAD95 Imputations: Documentation. Unpublished manuscript, University of Michigan.

——. 2000b. HRS 1998 preliminary imputations. Unpublished manuscript, University of Michigan.

Carlson, D. S., and J. G. Grzywacz. 2008. Reflections and future directions on measurement in work-family research. In *Handbook of work-family integration: Theories, perspectives, and best practices,* ed. K. Korabik, D. Lero, and D. Whitehead, 57–74. New York: Academic Press.

Casey, J. 2006. Why are flexible work schedules an important workplace issue? *Effective Workplace Series: Flexible Work Schedules* (no. 2): 1.

Casper, L. M., and S. M. Bianchi. 2002. *Continuity and change in the American family.* Thousand Oaks, Calif.: Sage Publications.

Casper, L. M., and M. O'Connell. 1998. Work, income, the economy, and married fathers as child-care providers. *Demography* 35: 243–50.

Center for Ethical Business Culture. 1997. *Creating high performance organizations: The bottom-line value of work/life strategies.* http://www.cebcglobal.org/KnowledgeCenter/Publica tions/WorkLife/CreatingHighPerformanceOrganizations.htm.

Chamallas, M. 1999. Mothers and disparate treatment: The ghost of Martin Marietta. *Villanova Law Review* 44: 337–54.

Chatzky, J. 2006. Stop getting eaten alive by grocery bills. *Money* 34: 36.

Chesley, N., and P. Moen. 2006. When workers care: Dual-earner couples' caregiving strategies, benefit use, and psychological well-being. *American Behavioral Scientist* 49: 1248–69.

Chicago Transit Authority. Case no. 96–080. Goldstein 1997.

——. Case no. 97–0166. Hayes 1999.

Child Trends. Family meals: Child Trends Data Bank Survey. http://www.childtrendsdatabank. org/pdf/96_PDF.pdf.

Child-Care Leave Law. Law No.76 of 1991.

Child-Care, Elder-Care and Sick Child-Care Leave Law 2005.

Child-Care/Elder-Care Leave Law 1999.

Christensen, K. 1989. *Flexible staffing and scheduling in U.S. corporations.* Research Bulletin No. 240. New York: Conference Board.

——. 2005. Achieving work-life balance: Strategies for dual-earner families. In *Being together, working apart: Dual-career families and the work-life balance,* ed. B. Schneider and L. Waite, 449–57. Cambridge: Cambridge University Press.

——. 2006. Foreword to *Working couples caring for children and aging parents: Effects on work and well-being,* by M. B. Neal and L. B. Hammer. Mahwah, N.J.: Lawrence Erlbaum.

Christensen, K. E., and G. L. Staines. 1990. A viable solution to work/family conflict? *Journal of Family Issues* 11: 455–76.

Cinotto, S. 2006. "Everyone would be around the table": American family mealtimes in historical perspective, 1850–1960. *New Directions for Child and Adolescent Development* 111: 17–33.

Clarkberg, M., and P. Moen. 2001. Understanding the time-squeeze: Married couples preferred and actual work-hour strategies. *American Behavioral Scientist* 44: 1115–36.

Clearinghouse on International Developments in Child, Youth, and Family Policies at Columbia University. 2002. *Mother's Day: More than candy and flowers, working parents need paid time-off.* http://www.childpolicyintl.org/issuebrief/issuebrief5.pdf.

Cohen, A. R., and H. Gadon. 1978. *Alternative work schedules: Integrating individual and organizational needs.* Reading, Mass.: Addison-Wesley.

Coleman, M., and J. Pencavel. 1993a. Changes in work hours of male employees, 1940–1988. *Industrial and Labor Relations Review* 46: 262–83.

——. 1993b. Trends in market work behavior of women since 1940. *Industrial and Labor Relations Review* 46: 653–76.

Coltrane, S. 2000. Research on household labor: Modeling and measuring the social embeddedness of routine family work. *Journal of Marriage and the Family* 62: 1208–33.

Colvin, J., G. Watson, and N. Ogilvie. 2006. *An introduction to the industrial relations reforms.* Chatswood, N.S.W.: Freehills and Lexis Nexis Butterworths.

Comfort, D., K. Johnson, and D. Wallace. 2003. *Part-time work and family-friendly practices in Canadian workplaces.* Ottawa: Statistics Canada.

Commerce Clearing House, ed. 2006. *Australian master workplace relations guide–The WorkChoices edition.* Sydney: CCH.

Committee for Economic Development. 1999. *New opportunities for older workers.* New York: Committee for Economic Development.

Committee on Ways and Means, Subcommittee on Human Resources. 2006. *A decade since welfare reform: 1996 welfare reforms reduce welfare dependence.* http://waysandmeans.house.gov/media/pdf/welfare/022706welfare.pdf.

Community Public Sector Union v. CSL. C2002/2562 AIRC. 2002.

Congressional Budget Office (CBO). 2007. *Characteristics and pay of federal civilian employees.* Pub. No. 2839. Washington, D.C.: CBO.

Connell, W. 2005. A really good husband: Work/life balance, gender equity and social change. *Australian Journal of Social Issues* 40: 369–83.

Convention on the Elimination of All Forms of Discrimination Against Women. G.A. res. 34/180, 34 U.N. GAOR Supp. No. 46 at 193, U.N. Doc. A/34/46. 1981.

Corporate Voices for Working Families. 2005. *Business impacts of flexibility: An imperative for expansion.* Washington, D.C.: Corporate Voices for Working Families.

Correll, S. J., S. Benard, and I. Paik. 2007. Getting a job: Is there a motherhood penalty? *American Journal of Sociology* 112: 1297–1338.

Costa, D. 1999. Has the trend toward early retirement reversed? Paper presented at the First Annual Joint Conference for the Retirement Research Consortium, Boston.

Costello, P. 2004. *Child care rebate.* http://www.treasurer.gov.au/DisplayDocs.aspx?doc=transcripts/2004/173.htmandpageID=004andmin=phcandYear=2004andDocType=2.

——. 2006. Budget speech 2006–07, on the second reading of the Appropriation Bill No. 1, 2006–07. http://www.smh.com.au/pdf/speech.pdf.

Counihan, C. M. 1988. Female identity, food, and power in contemporary Florence. *Anthropological Quarterly* 61(2): 51–62.

Craig, L. 2006. Does father care mean fathers share? A comparison of how mothers and fathers in intact families spend time with children. *Gender and Society* 20: 259–81.

Crittenden, A. 2001. *The price of motherhood: Why the most important job in the world is still the least valued.* New York: Metropolitan Books.

Crompton, R., S. Lewis, and C. Lyonette, ed. 2007. *Women, men, work and family in Europe.* Basingstoke, U.K.: Palgrave Macmillan.

Crouter, A. C., F. F. Bumpus, M. R. Head, and S. M. McHale. 2001. Implications of overwork and overload for the quality of men's family relationships. *Journal of Marriage and Family* 63: 404–16.

Crouter, A. C., H. Helms-Erikson, K. Updegraff, and S. M. McHale. 1999. Conditions underlying parents' knowledge about children's daily lives in middle childhood: Between- and within-family comparisons. *Child Development* 70: 246–59.

Crouter, A. C., and S. M. McHale. 2005. Work, family, and children's time: Implications for youth. In *Work, family, health, and well-being,* ed. S. M. Bianchi, L. M. Casper, and R. B. King, 49–66. Mahwah, N.J.: Lawrence Erlbaum.

Csikszentmihalyi, M., and R. Larson. 1987. Validity and reliability of the Experience Sampling Method. *Journal of Nervous and Mental Disease* 175: 526–36.

Cummins, H. J. 2006. Family obligation is growing field of discrimination law: A lawsuit against IBM is part of a burst of complaints that companies punish people who have family responsibilities. *Minneapolis Star Tribune,* August 3, 1D.

Daddies on Leave. 2007. January 9. *Web Japan.* http://web-japan.org/trends/lifestyle/lif 070109_02.html.

Dai-Ichi Life Research Institute. 2007. *Life design report.* Tokyo: DLRI.

Daly, M., and J. Bound. 1996. Worker adaptation and employer accommodation following the onset of a health impairment. *Journal of Gerontology* 51B: S53–60.

Davidoff, L., and C. Hall. 2002. *Family fortunes: Men and women of the English middle class, 1780–1850.* Rev. ed. London: Routledge.

Davis, E. M., and R. D. Lansbury. 1998. Employment relations in Australia. In *International and comparative employment relations,* 3rd ed., ed. G. J. Bamber and R. D. Lansbury, 110–43. London: Sage.

DeBare, I. 2007. Law now entitles all workers in San Francisco to paid sick leave. *San Francisco Chronicle,* February 6, A1.

DeLeire, T. 2000. The wage and employment effects of the Americans with Disabilities Act. *Journal of Human Resources* 35: 693–715.

De Matos Viegas, S. 2003. Eating with your favourite mother: Time and sociality in a Brazilian Amerindian community. *Journal of the Royal Anthropological Institute* 9: 21–37.

Demerouti, E., and S. Geurts. 2004. Towards a typology of work-home interaction. *Community, Work and Family* 7: 285–309.

den Dulk, L., B. Peper, and A. van Doorne-Huiskes. 2005. Work and family life in Europe: Employment patterns of working parents across welfare states. In *Flexible working and organisational change: The integration of work and personal life,* ed. B. Peper, A. Van Doorne-Huiskes, and L. den Dulk, 3–12. Cheltenham, U.K.: Edward Elgar.

den Dulk, L., and A. van Doorne-Huiskes. 2007. Social policy in Europe: Its impact on families and work. In *Women, men, work and family in Europe,* ed. R. Crompton, S. Lewis, and C. Lyonette. Basingstoke, U.K.: Palgrave Macmillan.

den Dulk, L., A. van Doorne-Huiskes, and J. J. Schippers, ed. 1999. *Work-family arrangements in Europe.* Amsterdam: Thela-Thesis.

Department of Consumer and Employment Protection. 2005. *Work/life Balance Survey 2004: A snapshot of Western Australian workplaces.* West Perth, Western Australia: Department of Consumer and Employment Protection.

Department of Employment and Workplace Relations. 2005a. *How will the changes affect you?* https://www.workchoices.gov.au/ourplan/workchoices/Howwillthechangesaffectyou.htm.

———. 2005b. *Work and family: The importance of workplace flexibility in promoting balance between work and family.* Canberra: Department of Employment and Workplace Relations.

———. 2005c. *Workforce tomorrow: Adapting to a more diverse Australian labour market.* Canberra: Department of Employment and Workplace Relations.

——. 2005d. *Workplace flexibility industry projects.* http://www.workplace.gov.au/workplace/ Programmes/WorkFamily/WorkplaceFlexibilityIndustryProjects.htm.

——. 2007a. *Flexibility benefits: Creating flexible workplaces in the childcare industry.* Canberra: Department of Employment and Workplace Relations.

——. 2007b. *A history of the National Work and Family Awards since 1992.* http://www.work place.gov.au/workplace/Programmes/WorkFamily/AhistoryoftheNationalWorkand FamilyAwardsSince1992.htm.

DeVault, M. L. 1991. *Feeding the family: The social organization of caring as gendered work.* Chicago: University of Chicago Press.

Dex, S., and F. Scheibl. 1999. Business performance and family-friendly policies. *Journal of General Management* 24(4): 22–37.

Dickens, W., and S. Lundberg 1993. Hours restrictions and labor supply. *International Economic Review* 34: 169–92.

Dinges, D. F. 2005. *Time use for sleeping in relation to waking activities.* Paper presented at the ATUS Early Results Conference, Bethesda, Md.

Drago, R. 2000. Trends in working time in the U.S.: A policy perspective. *Labor Law Journal* 51: 212–18.

——. 2007. *Striking a balance: Work, family, life.* Boston: Dollars and Sense.

Drago, R., R. Scutella, and A. Pirretti. 2007. Work and family directions in the U.S. and Australia: A policy research agenda. *Journal of Industrial Relations* 49: 49–66.

Drago, R., Y. Tseng, and M. Wooden. 2005. Usual and preferred working hours in couple households. *Journal of Family Studies* 11:46–61.

Drago, R., and J. Williams. 2000. A half-time tenure track proposal. *Change* 32(6): 46–51.

Draznin, Y. 2001. *Victorian London's middle-class housewife: What she did all day.* Westport, Conn.: Greenwood Press.

Dumont, L. 1980. *Homo hierarchicus: The caste system and its implications.* Rev. English ed. Chicago: University of Chicago Press.

Duxbury, L., S. Lyons, and C. Higgins. 2008. Too much to do, and not enough time: An examination of role overload. In *Handbook of work-family integration: Research theory and best practices,* ed. K. Korabik, D. S. Lero, and D. L. Whitehead, 125–40. London: Elsevier.

Dye, J. L. 2008. *U.S. Census Bureau, Fertility of American women: 2006, Population Characteristics.* http://www.census.gov/prod/2008pubs/p20-558.pdf.

Eaton, S. C. 2001. *If you can use them: Flexibility policies, organizational commitment, and perceived productivity.* KSG Working Paper No. 01–009. Cambridge: John F. Kennedy School of Government, Harvard University.

Eckes, T. 2002. Paternalistic and envious gender prejudice: Testing predictions from the stereotype content model. *Sex Roles* 47: 99–114.

Economic Policy Institute. n.d. Minimum wage issue guide: Facts at a glance. http://www.epi. org/content.cfm/issueguides_minwage_minwagefacts.

Economist. Women and the world economy: A guide to womenomics. 2006. http://www. economist.com/finance/displaystory.cfm?story_id=6802551.

Ehrenberg, R. G., and R. S. Smith. 1983. Estimating wage-fringe trade-offs: Some data problems. In *The measurement of labor costs,* ed. J. E. Tripplett, 347–67. Chicago: University of Chicago Press.

Elias, N. 2000 [1939]. *The civilizing process: Sociogenetic and psychogenetic investigations.* Trans. E. Jephcott. Oxford: Blackwell.

Employee Benefits Research Institute (EBRI). 1998. *Employment-based health care benefits and self-funded employment-based plans: An overview.* Washington, D.C.: Employee Benefits Research Institute.

Employee Retirement Income Security Act. 29 U.S.C § 1001 et seq. 1974.

Employment Insurance Law. Law No. 116 of 1974, as revised. 2007.

England, P. 2006. Calculations from 2001 current population survey. Unpublished raw data on file with author.

Equal Employment Opportunity Law of 1986.

Equal Opportunity Act 1984 (SA).

Equal Opportunity Amendment (Family Responsibilities) Bill 2007 (VIC).

Equal Opportunity for Women in the Workplace Act 1999 *(Cth).

Equal Employment Opportunity Network of Australasia. 2008. *Status report on diversity and flexibility.* http://www.eeona.org/ADES_2008_Report_25_July_2008.pdf.

Esping-Anderson, G. 1990. *The three worlds of welfare capitalism.* Princeton: Princeton University Press.

EU Expert Group on Gender, Social Inclusion and Employment (EGGSIE). 2005. Reconciliation of work and private life: A comparative review of thirty European countries. http://europa.eu.int/comm/employment_social/gender_equality/docs/2005/reconciliation_report_en.pdf.

EU Fifth Framework Programme. 2003. *Households, work and flexibility: Final scientific report.* HPSE-CT-1999–0030. Brussels: EU Fifth Framework Programme.

Europa. 1993. *Council Directive 93/104/EC, of 23 November, concerning certain aspects of the organisation of working time.* http://eur-lex.europa.eu/smartapi/cgi/sga_doc?smartapi!celexapi!prod!CELEXnumdocandlg=enandnumdoc=31993L0104andmodel=guichett.

———. 2004. *Part-time working.* http://europa.eu.int/scadplus/leg/en/cha/c10416.htm.

European Foundation for the Improvement of Living and Working Conditions. 2004. *Part-time work in Europe.* http://www.eurofound.eu.int/working/reports/ES0403TR01/ES0403TR01.pdf.

European Union Online. n.d. European Union Council Directive 93/104/EC concerning certain aspects of the organization of working time. *Official Journal of the European Union* L 307, 13.12.1993 and European Union Council Directive 97/81/EC concerning the Framework agreement on part-time work. *Official Journal of the European Union* 20.1.98 L14/9–11.

Evans, J. 2000. "*Family-friendly" firms: An international view.* Oxford: Family Policy Studies Centre.

———. 2001. *Firm's contribution to the reconciliation between work and family life.* Labour Market and Social Policy Occasional Paper No. 48. Paris: Organisation for Economic Cooperation and Development.

Executive Office of the President of the United States. 2008. *Economic report of the president.* Washington, D.C.: U.S. Government Printing Office.

Expedia. 2004. *Refill the commuter coffee mug: Expedia.com survey reveals Americans will forfeit 415 million vacation days this year.* http://www.travelantium.com/travel00789i.htm.

Ezra, M., and M. Dickman. 1996. Balancing work and family responsibilities: Flextime and child care in the federal government. *Public Administration Review* 56: 174–79.

Fagan, C., A. Hegewisch, and J. Pillinger. 2006. *Out of time: Why Britain needs a new approach to working-time flexibility.* London: Trades Union Congress.

Fagnani, J., G. Houriet-Ségard, and S. Bédouin. 2004. *Transitions research report no. 1: Context mapping for the EU Framework 5 funded study "Gender, parenthood and the changing European workplace".* Manchester: Research Institute for Health and Social Change, Manchester Metropolitan University.

Fagnani, J., and M-T. Letablier. 2004. Work and family life balance: The impact of the 35-hour laws in France. *Work, Employment, and Society* 18: 551–72.

Fair Labor Standards Act. 29 U.S.C. § 8. 1938.

Families and Work Institute. 2007. *Making work "work:" New ideas from the winners of the Alfred P. Sloan awards for business excellence in workplace flexibility.* New York: Families and Work Institute.

Family and Medical Leave Act. 29 U.S.C. § 2601. 1993.

Family Friendly Site. n.d. http://www.familyfriendly.jp/~ff/index.php.

Feldblum, C. 2005. Definition of workplace flexibility. Washington, D.C.: Workplace Flexibility 2010, Georgetown University Law School.

Fels, A. 2004. *Necessary dreams: Ambition in women's changing lives.* New York: Pantheon Books.

Fiske, S. T., A. J. C. Cuddy, P. Glick, and J. Xu. 2002. A model of (often mixed) stereotype content: Competence and warmth respectively follow from perceived status and competition. *Journal of Personality and Social Psychology* 82: 878–902.

Flanders, J. 2003. *The Victorian house: Domestic life from childbirth to deathbed.* London: HarperCollins.

Fleming, D. 2003. *The state of California telework-telecommuting program, 1983–21st century.* Sacramento: California Department of Personnel Administration.

Folbre, N. 2001. *The invisible heart: Economics and family values.* New York: New Press.

Fredricksen-Goldsen, K. I., and A. E. Scharlach. 2001. *Families and work: New directions in the twenty-first century.* New York: Oxford University Press.

Freeman, R. B. 1981. The effect of unionism on fringe benefits. *Industrial and Labor Relations Review* 34: 489–509.

Friedberg, L. 2000. The labor supply effects of the Social Security Earnings Test. *Review of Economics and Statistics* 82: 46–63.

Friedman, D. E., and E. Galinsky. 1992. Work and family issues: A legitimate business concern. In *Work, families, and organizations,* ed. S. Zedeck, 168–207. San Francisco: Jossey-Bass.

Fulkerson, J. A., M. Story, A. Mellin, N. Leffert, D. Neumark-Sztainer, and S. A. French. 2006. Family dinner meal frequency and adolescent development: Relationships and developmental assets and high-risk behaviors. *Journal of Adolescent Health* 39: 337–45.

Fullerton, H., Jr. 1999. Labor force participation: 75 years of change, 1950–98 and 1998–2025. *Monthly Labor Review* 122(12): 3–12.

Galinsky, E. 2001. Toward a new view of work and family life. In *Working families: The transformation of the American home,* ed. R. Hertz and N. L. Marshall, 168–86. Los Angeles: University of California Press.

Galinsky, E., and L. Backon. 2007. *When Work Works: Making work "work".* New York: When Work Works.

Galinsky, E., and J. T. Bond. 1998. *The 1998 business work-life study: A source book.* New York: Families and Work Institute.

Galinsky, E., J. T. Bond, and D. E. Friedman. 1993. *The changing workforce: Highlights of the [1992] national study.* New York: Families and Work Institute.

Galinsky, E., J. T. Bond, and J. Hill. 2004. *When work works: A status report on workplace flexibility.* New York: Families and Work Institute.

Galinsky, E., J. T. Bond, S. S. Kim, E. Brownfield, and K. Sakai. 2005. *Overwork in America: When the way we work becomes too much.* New York: Families and Work Institute.

Galinsky, E., and A. Johnson. 1998. *Reframing the business case for work-life initiatives.* New York: Families and Work Institute.

Galinsky, E., S. S. Kim, and J. T. Bond. 2001. *Feeling overworked: When work becomes too much.* New York: Families and Work Institute.

Gambles, R., S. Lewis, and R. Rapoport. 2006. *The myth of work-life balance: The issue of our time for men, women and societies.* London: Wiley.

Genda, Y., and Y. Nakata, ed. 2002. *Risutora to tenshoku no mekanizumu* [Restructuring middle-aged workers in Japan]. Tokyo: Toyokeizai Shinposha.

Gender Equality Bureau. 2005a. *Plan of Support for Women's Renewed Challenges.* Tokyo: Cabinet Office. http://www.gender.go.jp/english_contents/pamphlet/gender-equality 07/04.pdf (in English), p. 28. http://www.gender.go.jp/saisien/siryo/p-1.pdf (in Japanese).

———. 2005b. *Survey of managers' attitudes towards support measures.* Tokyo: Cabinet Office.

Giard, L. 1994. Seconde partie: Faire-la-cuisine. In *L'invention du quotidien,* ed. M. De Certeau and L. Giard, 213–349. Paris: Gallimard.

Gillard, J. 2007a. *Fresh ideas for work and family.* Canberra: Australian Labor Party.

———. 2007b. *Labor's new industrial umpire: Fair work Australia.* Canberra: Australian Labor Party.

Gillard, J., and W. Swan. 2007. Joint press conference with the Hon Julia Gillard, MP, and the Hon Wayne Swan, MP Prime Minister's courtyard, Parliament House, Canberra. http://www.pm.gov.au/news/interviews/2007/interview_00010.cfm.

Gillis, J. R. 1989. Ritualization of middle-class family life in nineteenth-century Britain. *International Journal of Politics, Culture, and Society* 3: 213–35.

Glass, J. 2004. Blessing or curse? Work-family policies and mother's wage growth over time. *Work and Occupations* 31: 367–406.

Glass, J., and S. B. Estes. 1997. The family responsive workplace. *Annual Review of Sociology* 23: 289–313.

Glass, J., and L. Riley. 1998. Family responsive policies and employee retention following childbirth. *Social Forces* 76: 1401–35.

Gold, D. M. 1998. Flex time for everyone? It's closer every day. *New York Times,* November 1, BU11.

Golden, L. 2006. Overemployment in the U.S.: Which workers are willing to reduce their work hours and income? In *Decent working time: New trends, new issues,* ed. J.-Y. Boulin, M. Lallement, J. C. Messenger, and F. Michon, 209–61. Geneva: International Labour Organization.

Golden, L., and H. Jorgensen. 2002. *Time after time: Mandatory overtime in the U.S. economy.* January. EPI Briefing Paper No. 120. http://www.epi.org/publications/entry/briefingpapers_bp120/.

Golden, L., and B. Wiens-Tuers. 2005. Mandatory overtime work in the United States: Who, where, and what? *Labor Studies Journal* 30: 1–25.

———. 2006. To your happiness? Extra hours of labor supply and worker well-being. *Journal of Socio-Economics* 35: 382–97.

Goldin, C. 2004. The long road to the fast track: Career and family. *Annals of the American Academy of Political and Social Science* 596: 20–35.

Gonzales, G. 2006. Family care bias suits rise as workers assert rights. *Business Insurance* 14: 11–15.

Goodstein, J. D. 1994. Institutional pressures and strategic responsiveness: Employer involvement in work-family issues. *Academy of Management Journal* 37: 350–82.

Gornick, J. C. 2001. Cancel the funeral: Reports of the demise of the European welfare state are premature. *Dissent* 48(3): 13–18.

———. 2007. Social expenditures on children and the elderly, 1980–1995: Shifting allocations, changing needs. In *Allocating private and public resources across generations: Riding the age waves, vol. 2,* ed. A. H. Gauthier, C. Chu, and S. Tuljapurkar. New York: Springer Publishing.

Gornick, J. C., and A. Heron. 2006. Working time regulation as work-family reconciliation policy: Comparing Europe, Japan, and the United States. *Journal of Comparative Policy Analysis* 8: 149–66.

Gornick, J. C., and J. A. Jacobs. 1998. Gender, the welfare state, and public employment: A comparative study of seven industrialized countries. *American Sociological Review* 63: 688–710.

Gornick, J. C., and M. K. Meyers. 2001. Lesson-drawing in family policy: Media reports and empirical evidence about European developments. *Journal of Comparative Policy Analysis* 3: 31–57.

———. 2003. *Families that work: Policies for reconciling parenthood and employment.* New York: Russell Sage Foundation.

Gray, M., L. Qu, D. Stanton, and R. Weston. 2004. Long work hours and the well-being of fathers and their families. *Australian Journal of Labour Economics* 7: 255–73.

Green, F. 2004. Work intensification, discretion, and the decline in well-being at work. *Eastern Economic Journal* 30: 615–25.

Grieshaber, S. 1997. Mealtime rituals: Power and resistance in the construction of mealtime rules. *British Journal of Sociology* 48: 649–66.

Grossman, K. 2001. Getting off supermom track. *Chicago Sun-Times,* May 27, 17.

Group of 151 Australian Industrial Relations, Labour Market and Legal Academics. 2005. Research evidence about the effects of the "WorkChoices" Bill: A submission to the Senate inquiry into the Workplace Relations Amendment (WorkChoices) Bill 2005. http://www.aph.gov.au/SENATE/committee/eet_ctte/wr_workchoices05/submissions/sub175.pdf.

Grubb, D., and W. Wells. 1993. Employment regulation and patterns of work in EC countries. *OECD Economic Studies* 21: 7–58.

Gruber, J., and P. Orszag. 2003. Does the Social Security Earnings Test affect labor supply and benefits receipt? *National Tax Journal* 56: 755–73.

Grzywacz, J. G., and B. L. Bass, 2003. Work, family, and mental health: Testing different models of work-family fit. *Journal of Marriage and Family* 65: 248–61.

Grzywacz, J. G., D. S. Carlson, K. M. Kacmar, and J. H. Wayne. 2007. A multilevel perspective on the synergies between work and family. *Journal of Occupational and Organizational Psychology* 80: 559–74.

GTE California, Inc. Case no. 11-91-86. Miller 1992.

Gustman, A. L., and T. L. Steinmeier. 1983. Minimum hours constraints and retirement behavior. *Contemporary Policy Issues* 3: 77–91.

——. 1986. A disaggregated structural analysis of retirement by race, difficulty of work, and health. *Review of Economics and Statistics* 68: 509–13.

Gutek, B. A., S. Searle, and L. Klepa. 1991. Rational versus gender role explanations for work-family conflict. *Journal of Applied Psychology* 76: 560–68.

Guthrie, D., and L. M. Roth. 1999. The state, courts, and equal opportunities for female CEOs in U.S. organizations: Specifying institutional mechanisms. *Social Forces* 78: 511–42.

Haas, L., K. Allard, and P. Hwang. 2002. The impact of organizational culture on men's use of parental leave in Sweden. *Community, Work and Family* 5: 319–42.

Haider, S. J., and D. Loughran. 2001. *Elderly labor supply: Work or play?* CRR WP 2001–4. Chestnut Hill: Center for Retirement Research at Boston College. http://crr.bc.edu/working_papers/elderly_labor_supply_work_or_play_.html.

——. 2008. The effect of the Social Security Earnings Test on male labor supply: New evidence from survey and administrative data. *Journal of Human Resources* 43: 57–87.

Hakim, C. 1997. A sociological perspective on part-time work. In *Between equalization and marginalization: Women working part-time in Europe and the United States of America,* ed. H-P. Blossfeld and C. Hakim, 22–70. Oxford: Oxford University Press.

Han, S-K., and P. Moen. 1999. Clocking out: Temporal patterning of retirement. *American Journal of Sociology* 105: 191–236.

Hanson, G. C, L. B. Hammer, and C. L. Colton. 2006. Development and validation of a multidimensional scale of perceived work-family positive spillover. *Journal of Occupational Health Psychology* 11: 249–65.

Harkness, S., and J. Waldfogel. 1999. *The family gap in pay: Evidence from seven industrialised countries.* CASE Paper 29. London: Centre for Analysis of Social Exclusion, London School of Economics.

Hartmann, H. 2003. IWPR president's response to "The Opt-Out Revolution." http://www.iwpr.org/rnr/archives/nov03.htm.

Hays, S. 1996. *The cultural contradictions of motherhood.* New Haven: Yale University Press.

Hayward, M., E. Crimmins, and L. Wray. 1994. The relationship between retirement life cycle changes and older men's employment rates. *Journal of Gerontology* 49(5): S219–30.

Hayward, M., and W. Grady. 1990. Work and retirement among a cohort of older men in the United States, 1966–1983. *Demography* 27: 337–56.

Healy, M. 2004. We're all multitasking but what's the cost? *Los Angeles Times,* July 19, F1.

Hegewisch, A. 2005. *Employers and European flexible working rights: When the floodgates were opened.* Issue Brief. San Francisco: WorkLife Law, University of California Hastings College of Law.

Hegewisch, A., and J. C. Gornick. 2008. *Statutory routes to workplace flexibility in cross-national perspective.* San Francisco: WorkLife Law, University of California Hastings College of Law.

Heinz, W. R. 2003. From work trajectories to negotiated careers: The contingent work life course. In *Handbook for the life course,* ed. J. Mortimer and M. Shanahan, 185–204. New York: Kluwer Academic/Plenum Publishers.

Hemel, D. J. 2005. Summers' comments on women and science draw ire. http://www.thecrimson.com/article.aspx?ref=505349.

Herz, D. 1995. Work after early retirement: An increasing trend among men. *Monthly Labor Review* 118(4): 13–20.

Hessing, M. 1994. More than clockwork: Women's time management in their combined workloads. *Sociological Perspectives* 37: 611–33.

Hewlett, S. A. 2002. Executive women and the myth of having it all. *Harvard Business Review* 80(4): 66–73.

——. 2007. *Off-ramps and on-ramps: Keeping talented women on the road to success.* Boston: Harvard Business School Press.

Hewlett, S. A., and C. B. Luce. 2005. Off-ramps and on-ramps: Keeping talented women on the road to success. *Harvard Business Review* 83(3): 43–54.

Hewlett, S. A., C. B. Luce, P. Shiller, and S. Southwell. 2005. *The hidden brain drain: Off-ramps and on-ramps in women's careers.* Boston: Harvard Business School Publishing.

Hewlett, S. A., and N. Vite-León. 2002. *High-achieving women, 2001.* New York: Center for Work-Life Policy.

Heymann, J. 2000. *The widening gap: Why America's working families are in jeopardy and what can be done about it.* New York: Basic Books.

——. 2006a. *Forgotten families: Ending the growing crisis confronting children and working parents in the global economy.* Oxford: Oxford University Press.

——. 2006b. We can afford to give parents a break. *Washington Post,* May 14, B07.

Higuchi, Y., and K. Ota. ed. 2004. *Joseitachino Hesei Fukyo* [Women in economic recession]. Tokyo: Nihon Keizai Shinbunsya.

Hill, E. 2006. Howard's "choice": The ideology and politics of work and family policy 1996–2006. *Australian Review of Public Affairs,* February 26.

Hochschild, A. R. 1989. *The second shift: Working parents and the revolution at home.* New York: Viking.

——. 1994. Inside the clockwork of male careers. In *Gender and the academic experience,* ed. K. P. Meadow Orlans and D. C. Knill, 125–40. Lincoln: University of Nebraska Press.

——. 1997. *The time bind: When work becomes home and home becomes work.* New York: Metropolitan Books.

Hofferth, S. L. 1996. Effects of public and private policies on working after childbirth. *Work and Occupations* 23: 378–404.

Holden, K. 1988. Physically demanding occupations, health, and work after retirement: Findings from the New Beneficiary Survey. *Social Security Bulletin* 51(11): 3–15.

Holzer, H. J., and D. Neumark. 1999. Are affirmative action hires less qualified? Evidence from employer-employee data on new hires. *Journal of Labor Economics* 17: 534–69.

Hoogstra, L. 2005. Design and sample characteristics of the 500 Family Study. In *Being together, working apart: Dual-career families and their work-life balance,* ed. B. Schneider and L. J. Waite, 23–48. Cambridge: Cambridge University Press.

Horioka, C. Y. 2001. Japan's public pension system in the twenty-first century. In *Japan's new economy: Continuity and change in the twenty-first century,* ed. M. Blomström, B. Gangnes, and S. J. La Croix, 99–119. Oxford: Oxford University Press.

House of Representatives, Standing Committee on Family and Human Services. 2006. *Balancing work and family: Report on the inquiry into balancing work and family.* Canberra: House of Representatives.

Houseman, S., and M. Osawa, ed. 2003. *Nonstandard work in developed economies: Causes and consequences.* Kalamazoo, Mich.: W. E. Upjohn Institute.

Howard, J. 2002. Prime Minister's address to Federal Women's Forum, Liberal Party Federal Council. http://pandora.nla.gov.au/pan/10052/20020521–0000/www.pm.gov.au/news/speeches/2002/speech1594.htm.

———. 2005. *Howard announces details of industrial relations changes.* http://pandora.nla.gov.au/pan/10052/20051121–0000/www.pm.gov.au/news/interviews/Interview1620.html.

HRHero.com. 2002. Discrimination: A glass ceiling for parents? http://www.hrhero.com/pregnancy/parents_print.html.

Hughes, D. L., and E. Galinsky. 1994. Gender, job, and family conditions, and psychological symptoms. *Psychology of Women Quarterly* 18: 251–70.

Hughes, D. L., E. Galinsky, and A. Morris. 1992. The effects of job characteristics on marital quality: Specifying linking mechanisms. *Journal of Marriage and Family* 54:31–42.

Human Rights and Equal Opportunity Commission. 2005. *Striking the balance: Women, men, work and family.* Discussion paper. Sydney: Human Rights and Equal Opportunity Commission.

———. 2007. *It's about time: Women, men, work and family.* Final paper. Sydney: Human Rights and Equal Opportunity Commission.

Hurd, M. D. 1990. Research on the elderly: Economic status, retirement, and consumption and saving. *Journal of Economic Literature* 28: 565–637.

———. 1996. The effect of labor market rigidities on the labor force behavior of older workers. In *Advances in the economics of aging,* ed. D. Wise, 11–58. Chicago: University of Chicago Press.

Hurd, M. D., and K. McGarry. 1993. *The relationship between job characteristics and retirement.* NBER Working Paper No. 4558. Cambridge, Mass.: National Bureau of Economic Research.

Hutchens, R. M. 1986. Delayed payment contracts and a firm's propensity to hire older workers. *Journal of Labor Economics* 4: 439–57.

Hutchens, R. M., and K. Grace-Martin. 2006. Employer willingness to permit phased retirement: Why are some more willing than others? *Industrial and Labor Relations Review* 59: 525–46.

Iams, H. 1987. Jobs of persons working after receiving retired-worker benefits. *Social Security Bulletin* 50(11): 4–19.

Ikuji ryouritsushien apiiru [Making the appeal for expanded childcare and work-family support] 2006. *Nihon Keizai Shimbun,* April 17.

Immervoll, H., and D. Barber. 2005. *Can parents afford to work? Childcare costs, tax-benefit policies and work incentives.* OECD Social, Employment and Migration Working Paper No. 31. Paris: Organisation for Economic Cooperation and Development.

Immerwahr, J., and J. Johnson. 2007. *Squeeze play: How parents and the public look at higher education today.* San Jose, Calif.: National Center for Public Policy and Higher Education.

Industrial Relations Victoria. 2005a. *Quality part-time work: Working better for everyone.* Report from the Quality Part-time Work Project. Victoria: Industrial Relations Victoria.

———. 2005b. *Work and family balance action agenda report card, April 2005.* Victoria: Industrial Relations Victoria.

Ingram, P., and T. Simons. 1995. Institutional and resource dependence determinants of responsiveness to work-family issues. *Academy of Management Journal* 38: 1466–82.

Interlake Material Handling Div., Interlake Conveyors Inc. 113 LA 1120. Lalka 2000.

International Labour Organization. 2003a. *Yearbook of labour statistics, 2003.* Geneva: ILO.

———. 2003b. New ILO study highlights labour trends worldwide: US productivity up, Europe improves ability to create jobs. http://www.ilo.org/global/About_the_ILO/Media_and_public_information/Press_releases/lang—en/WCMS_005291.

ITT Industries, NightVision Roanoke Plant. 118 LA 1504. Cohen 2003.

Iwai, K. 2003. Kaisya wa Korekara donarunoka [What's to become of the (Japanese) firm?]. Tokyo: Heibonsya.

Iwasawa, M. 2004. Changing male-female relationship and fertility decline. In *Shoshika no Jinkougaku* [Demographic decline], ed. H. Obuchi and S. Takahashi. Tokyo: Harashobo.

Jacobs, J. A., and K. Gerson. 2000. Who are the overworked Americans? In *Working time: International trends, theory and policy perspectives,* ed. L. Golden and D. Figart, 89–105. London: Routledge.

———. 2004. *The time divide: Work, family, and gender inequality.* Cambridge: Harvard University Press.

Jacobs, J. A., and S. Winslow. 2004. Overworked faculty: Job stresses and family demands. *Annals of the American Academy of Political and Social Science* 596: 104–29.

Japan Institute of Worker's Evolution. n.d. *Shigoto to katei no ryouritsu* [Work and family compatibility]. http://www.familyfriendly.jp/~ff/top/nm/sample.php.

Javid, F. and A. Varney. 2007. The grand seduction of multitasking. *ABC News.* http://abcnews. go.com/2020/Story?id=3474058&page=1.

Jencks, C. 1992. *Rethinking social policy: Race, poverty, and the underclass.* Cambridge: Harvard University Press.

Joesch, J. M. 1997. Paid leave and the timing of women's employment before and after birth. *Journal of Marriage and the Family* 59: 1008–21.

Johnson, J. H. I. 2004. Do long work hours contribute to divorce? *Topics in Economic Analysis and Policy* 4: 9–23.

Joice, W. 1993. *Telecommute America report: The federal flexible workplace pilot project work-at-home component.* Washington, D.C.: U.S. Office of Personnel Management.

———. 2000. *The evolution of telework in the federal government.* Washington, D.C.: U.S. General Services Administration.

———. 2001. *Federal telework topics.* Washington, D.C.: U.S. General Services Administration.

Joint Economic Committee. 2008. *Paid family leave at fortune 100 companies: A basic standard but still not the gold standard.* Washington, D.C.: Joint Economic Committee.

Joint Governments' Submission. 2000. *Safety Net Review—Wages: 1999–2000.* Canberra: Commonwealth Department of Employment, Workplace Relations and Small Business.

Jones, P., P. Shears, D. Hillier, D. Comfort, and J. Lowell. 2003. Return to traditional values? A case study of slow food. *British Food Journal* 105: 297–304.

Jordan, T. E. 1987. *Victorian childhood: Themes and variations.* Albany: State University of New York Press.

Kahn, A. J., and S. B. Kamerman. 1980. *Social services in international perspective.* New Brunswick, N.J.: Transaction Books.

———, ed. 2002. *Beyond child poverty: The social exclusion of children.* New York: Institute for Child and Family Policy.

Kaiser Family Foundation. 2005. *Survey finds steady decline in businesses offering health benefits to workers since 2000.* http://www.kff.org/insurance/chcm091405nr.cfm.

Kalleberg, A. L., B. F. Reskin, and K. Hudson. 2000. Bad jobs in America: Standard and non-standard employment relations and job quality in the United States. *American Sociological Review* 65: 256–78.

Kamerman, S. B. 2005. Europe advanced while the United States lagged. In *Unfinished work: Building equality and democracy in an era of working families,* ed. J. Heymann and C. Beem, 309–47. New York: New Press.

Kamerman, S. B., and A. J. Kahn. 1978. *Family policy: Government and families in fourteen countries.* New York: Columbia University Press.

———. 1987. *The responsive workplace: Employers and a changing labor force.* New York: Columbia University Press.

Kamerman, S. B., M. J. Neuman, J. Waldfogel, and J. Brooks-Gunn. 2003. *Social policies, family types, and child outcomes in selected OECD countries.* OECD Social, Employment and Migration Working Papers No. 6. Paris: Organisation for Economic Cooperation and Development.

Katz, R. 1998. *Japan: The system that soured; The rise and fall of the Japanese economic miracle.* Armonk, N.Y.: M. E. Sharpe.

Keith, P. M., and R. B. Schafer. 1980. Role strain and depression in two-job families. *Family Relations* 29: 483–88.

Kelly, E. L. 2005. *Explaining non-compliance with the Family and Medical Leave Act.* Paper presented at the annual meeting of the American Sociological Association, Philadelphia.

———. 2006. Work-family policies: The United States in international perspective. In *The work and family handbook: Multi-disciplinary perspectives and approaches,* ed. M. Pitt-Catsouphes, E. E. Kossek, and S. Sweet, 99–123. Mahwah, N.J.: Lawrence Erlbaum.

Kelly, E. L., and A. Kalev. 2006. Managing flexible work arrangements in U.S. organizations: Formalized discretion or "a right to ask." *Socio-Economic Review* 4: 379–416.

Kelly, E. L., and P. Moen. 2007. Rethinking the clockwork of work: Why schedule control may pay off at home and at work. *Advances in Developing Human Resources* 9: 487–506.

Kelly, S., T. Bolton, and A. Harding. 2005. *Changing face of the Australian labour force 1985–2005, May the labour force be with you.* AMP.NATSEM Income and Wealth Report Issue 12. Canberra: AMP National Centre for Social and Economic Modelling.

Knapp, K., and C. Muller. 2001. *Productive lives: Paid and unpaid activities of older Americans.* New York: International Longevity Center.

Knauf Fiber Glass. 81 LA 333. Abrams 1983.

Kobayashi, K. 2005. Roudoukeiyaku meguru shingi honkakuka [Discussion on initiating labor contracts]. *Nihon Keizai Shimbun,* November 7.

Koh, C. 2005. The everyday emotional experiences of husbands and wives. In *Being together, working apart: Dual-career families and the work-life balance,* ed. B. Schneider and L. Waite, 169–189. Cambridge: Cambridge University Press.

Kohn, M. L., and C. Schooler. 1982. Job conditions and personality: A longitudinal assessment of their reciprocal effects. *American Journal of Sociology* 87: 1257–86.

Kornbluh, K. 2003. The parent trap. *Atlantic Monthly,* January–February, 111–14.

Kossek, E. E., B. A. Lautsch, and S. C. Eaton. 2005. Telecommuting, control, and boundary management: Correlates of policy use and practice, job control, and work-family effectiveness. *Journal of Vocational Behavior* 68: 347–67.

Kouzis, G., and L. Kretsos. 2003. *Annualised hours in Europe.* Dublin: European Industrial Relations Observatory (EIRO).

Kovatcheva, S. 2000. The "old red woman" against the "young blue hooligan": Gender stereotyping of economic and political processes in post-communist Bulgaria. In *Gender, agency and change: Anthropological perspectives,* ed. V. A. Goddard, 195–220. London: Routledge.

Kreiger, L., and P. Cooney. 1983. The Miller-Wohl controversy: Equal treatment, positive action, and the meaning of women's equality. *Golden Gate Law Review* 13: 513–72.

Labor Standards Law. Law 49 of 1947 as revised. 2007.

Lareau, A. 2002. Invisible inequality: Social class and childrearing in black families and white families. *American Sociological Review* 67: 747–76.

Law Concerning the Improvement of Employment Management, Etc. of Part-Time Workers (Part-Time Work Law), Law No. 76 of 1993.

Laz v. Downer Group Ltd. FCA 1390, 108 IRR 244, 2000 FCA 1390. 2000.

Lazear, E. P. 1979. Why is there mandatory retirement? *Journal of Political Economy* 87: 1261–84.

———. 1981. Agency, earnings profiles, productivity, and hours restrictions. *American Economic Review* 71: 606–20.

———. 1998. *Personnel economics for managers.* New York: John Wiley and Sons.

Lee, Y-S. 2006. Measuring the gender gap in household labor: Accurately estimating wives' and husbands' contributions. In *Being together, working apart: Dual-career families and their work-life balance,* ed. B. Schneider and L. J. Waite, 229–47. Cambridge: Cambridge University Press.

Legal Momentum. n.d. Legal Momentum's history. http://www.legalmomentum.org/about/history.html.

Lehndorff, S. 2000. Working time reduction in the European Union. In *Working time: International trends, theory, and policy perspectives,* ed. L. Golden and D. M. Figart, 38–55. New York: Routledge.

Leslie, D. W., and N. Janson. 2005. *Phasing away: How phased retirement works for college faculty and their institutions.* Williamsburg, Va.: School of Education, College of William and Mary.

Levin-Epstein, J. 2006. *Getting punched: The job and family clock; It's time for flexible work for workers of all wages.* Washington, D.C.: Center for Law and Social Policy.

Lévi-Strauss, C. 1963. *Structural anthropology.* New York: Basic Books.

———. 1969 [1964]. *The raw and the cooked.* Trans. J. Weightman and D. Weightman. New York: Harper and Row.

Lewis, J. 1997. Gender and welfare regimes: Further thoughts. *Social politics: International studies in gender, state and society* 4(2): 160–77.

Lewis, K. R. 2005. Want better work-life balance? Negotiate reduced hours. *Newhouse News Service,* August 24.

Lewis, S. 1991. Motherhood and/or employment: The impact of social and organisational values. In *Motherhood, meanings, practices and ideologies,* ed. A. Phoenix, A. Woolett, and E. Lloyd, 195–215. London: Sage.

———. 1997. Family friendly policies: Organisational change or playing about at the margins? *Gender, Work and Organisations* 4: 13–23.

———. 2001. Restructuring workplace cultures: The ultimate work-family challenge? *Women in Management Review* 16(1): 21–29.

Lewis, S., M. das Dores Guerreiro, and J. Brannen. 2006. Using case studies in work-family research. In *The work-family handbook: Multi-disciplinary perspectives and approaches,* ed. M. Pitt-Catsouphes, E. Kossek, and S. Sweet, 489–502. Mahwah, N.J.: Lawrence Erlbaum.

Lewis, S., and J. Smithson, J. 2001. Sense of entitlement to support for the reconciliation of employment and family life. *Human Relations* 55: 1455–81.

Living Wage Resource Center. n.d. The living wage movement: Building power in our workplaces and neighborhoods. http://www.livingwagecampaign.org/index.php?id=2071.

Lumsdaine, R., J. Stock, and D. Wise. 1996. Why are retirement rates so high at age 65? In *Advances in the economics of aging,* ed. D. Wise, 61–82. Chicago: University of Chicago Press.

Lundberg, S. 1985. Tied wage-hours offers and the endogeneity of wages. *Review of Economics and Statistics* 67: 405–10.

Lundberg, S., and E. Rose. 2002. The effects of sons and daughters on men's labor supply and wages. *Review of Economics and Statistics* 84: 251–68.

Lupton, D. 2000. "Where's me dinner?" Food preparation arrangements in rural Australian families. *Journal of Sociology* 36: 172–86.

Lynch, L. M., and S. E. Black. 1998. Beyond the incidence of employer-provided training. *Industrial and Labor Relations Review* 52: 64–81.

Lynd, R. S., and H. M. Lynd. 1929. *Middletown: A study in contemporary American culture.* London: Constable.

Malinowski, B. 1935. *Coral gardens and their magic: A study of the methods of tilling the soil and of agricultural rites in the Trobriand Islands.* London: G. Allen and Unwin.

Managing Work/Life Balance. 2003. *About us.* http://www.worklifebalance.com.au/about.html.

Marcus, R. 2006. The family as firing offense. *Washington Post,* May 14, B1.

Marshall, N. L., and R. C. Barnett. 1993. Work-family strains and gains among two-earner couples. *Journal of Community Psychology* 21: 64–78.

Mattingly, M. J., and S. M. Bianchi. 2003. Gender differences in the quantity and quality of free time: The U.S. experience. *Social Forces* 81: 999–1030.

McCann, D. 2004. Regulating working time needs and preferences. In *Working time and workers' preferences in industrialised countries: Finding the balance,* ed. J. Messenger, 10–28. Oxford: Routledge.

McDonald, P. 2000. Gender equity in theories of fertility transition. *Population and Development Review* 26: 427–39.

McLucas, J. 2007. *Disability and carers.* http://www.alp.org.au/download/now/071107_disability_and_carers_policy_doc___with_header.pdfwww.alp.org.au.

Meiksins, P., and P. Whalley. 2002. *Putting work in its place: A quiet revolution.* Ithaca: Cornell University Press.

Mellor, E. F. 1986. Shift work and flextime: How prevalent are they? *Monthly Labor Review* 109: 14–21.

Messenger, J., ed. 2004. *Working time and workers' preferences in industrialised countries: Finding the balance.* Oxford, UK: Routledge.

Metcalfe, B., and M. Afanassieva. 2005. Gender, work and equal opportunities in central and eastern Europe. *Women in Management Review* 20: 397–411.

Meyer, J. W. 1986. The institutionalization of the life course and its effects on the self. In *Human development and the life course: Multidisciplinary perspectives,* ed. F. E. Weinert and L. R. Sherrod, 119–216. Hillsdale, N.J.: Lawrence Erlbaum.

Meyers, M. K., D. Rosenbaum, C. Ruhm, and J. Waldfogel. 2004. Inequality in early childhood education and care: What do we know? In *Social inequality,* ed. K. Neckerman. New York: Russell Sage Foundation.

Milkie, M. A., M. J. Mattingly, K. M. Nomaguchi, S. M. Bianchi, and J. P. Robinson. 2004. The time squeeze: Parental statuses and feelings about time with children. *Journal of Marriage and Family* 66: 739–61.

Milkie, M. A., and P. Peltola. 1999. Playing all the roles: Gender and the work-family balancing act. *Journal of Marriage and Family* 61: 476–90.

Ministry of Health, Labour and Welfare. 2001. *Government guidelines for supporting work and child-care.* Tokyo: Ministry of Health, Labour and Welfare.

——. 2002. *Rodo keizai hakusho* [White paper on labor]. Tokyo: Gyosei.

——. 2004a. *Basic survey of employment management of women.* Tokyo: Ministry of Health, Labour and Welfare.

——. 2004b. *Danjo kyodo sankaku* [Gender equality data book]. Tokyo: Gyosei.

——. 2008. Jinkou dotai chousa [Population dynamics survey]. Tokyo: Ministry of Health, Labour and Welfare.

——. 2005a. *Josei rodo hakusho* [White paper on working women]. Tokyo: 21seiki Shkugyo Zaidan.

——. 2005b. *Ryoritsu shien jigyou no goannai* [Introduction to compatibility support measures]. Tokyo: Ministry of Health, Labour and Welfare.

——. 2005c. *Trends and features of the labour economy in 2004.* http://www.mhlw.go.jp/english/wp/l-economy/2005/dl/02–02-03.pdf.

——. 2006a. *Basic survey on wage structure.* Tokyo: Ministry of Health, Labour and Welfare.

——. 2006b. *Diversification of employment and working life.* Tokyo: Ministry of Health, Labour and Welfare.

——. 2007a. *Jinko dotai tokei* [Population statistics]. Tokyo: Gyosei.

——. 2007b. *Josei rodo hakusho* [White paper on working women]. Tokyo: 21seiki Shkugyo Zaidan.

——. 2007c. *Labor economic analysis.* Tokyo: Ministry of Health, Labour and Welfare.

——. 2007d. *Rodo keizai hakusho* [White paper on labor]. Tokyo: Gyosei.

——. 2008. Jinkou dotai chousa [Population dynamics survey]. Tokyo: Ministry of Health, Labour and Welfare.

———. n.d. *Declining birthrate and next generation nurturing support measures.* Tokyo: Ministry of Health, Labour and Welfare.

Ministry of Health, Labour and Welfare and Japan Institute of Workers' Evolution. 2005. *Ikuji kaigo kyuugyouhou no aramashi* [Summary of childcare/eldercare leave law]. Tokyo: Ministry of Health, Labour and Welfare and Japan Institute of Workers' Evolution.

Ministry of Internal Affairs and Communications. 2001. *Shakai seikatsu kihon chosa* [Basic survey of lifestyles]. Tokyo: Statistics Bureau.

———. 2002. *Shugyo kozo kihon chosa* [Basic survey of employment structure]. Tokyo: Statistics Bureau.

———. 2006. *Labor force survey.* Tokyo: Ministry of Internal Affairs and Communications.

———. 2007. *Labor force survey.* Tokyo: Ministry of Internal Affairs and Communications.

———. 2009. *Labor force survey.* Tokyo: Ministry of Internal Affairs and Communications.

Mintzberg, H. 1979. *The structuring of organizations: A synthesis of the research.* Englewood Cliffs, N.J.: Prentice-Hall.

Mishel, L., J. Bernstein, and S. Allegretto. 2005. *The state of working America: 2004–2005.* Washington, D.C.: Economic Policy Institute.

Mitchell, O. 1990. Aging, job satisfaction, and job performance. In *The aging of the American workforce,* ed. I. Bluestone, R. Montgomery, and J. Owen. Detroit: Wayne State University Press.

Mitchell, R. 2006. Pregnancy bias in the workplace on the rise. *CBS Evening News,* May 24.

Moen, P., ed. 2003. *It's about time: Couples and careers.* Ithaca: Cornell University Press.

———. 2007. Not so big jobs and retirements: What workers (and retirees) really want. *Generations* 31: 31–36.

———. 2008. It's constraints, not choices. *Science* 319 (5865): 903–4.

Moen, P., and N. Chesley. 2008. Toxic job ecologies, time convoys, and work-family conflict: Can families (re)gain control and life-course "fit"? In *Handbook of work—family integration: Research, theory, and best practices,* ed. K. Korabik, Donna S. Lero, and D. L. Whitehead, 95–122. New York: Elsevier.

Moen, P., and D. I. Dempster-McClain. 1987. Employed parents: Role strain, work time, and preferences for working less. *Journal of Marriage and the Family* 49: 579–90.

Moen, P., V. Fields, H. Quick, and H. Hofmeister. 2000. A life course approach to retirement and social integration. In *Social integration in the second half of life,* ed. K. Pillemer, P. Moen, E. Wethington, and N. Glasgow, 75–107. Baltimore: Johns Hopkins Press.

Moen, P., and C. B. Howery. 1988. The significance of time in the study of families under stress. In *Social stress and family development,* ed. D. Klein and J. Aldous, 131–56. New York: Guilford.

Moen, P., and E. Kelly. 2009. Working families under stress: Socially toxic job time cages and convoys. In *Handbook of families and work,* ed. E. J. Hill and D. R. Crane. Lanham, Md.: University Press of America.

Moen, P., E. Kelly, and R. Magennis. 2009. Gender strategies: Socialization, allocation, and strategic selection processes shaping the gendered adult life course. In *Handbook of research on adult learning and development,* ed. M. C. Smith, 378–411. New York: Routledge.

Moen, P., and P. Roehling. 2005. *The career mystique: Cracks in the American dream.* New York: Rowman and Littlefield.

Moen, P., S. Sweet, and R. Hill. 2009. Risk, resilience, and life-course fit: Older couples' strategic adaptations to job displacement. In *New frontiers in resilient aging,* ed. P. S. Fry and C. L. M. Keyes. New York: Cambridge University Press.

Moen, P., and Y. Yu. 2000. Effective work-life strategies: Working couples, work conditions, gender, and life quality. *Social Problems* 47: 291–326.

Montgomery, M. 1988. On the determinants of employer demand for part-time workers. *Review of Economics and Statistics* 70: 112–16.

Moos, B. 2008. Older workers are turning to government for second careers. *Dallas Morning News,* January 17.

Munnell, A. H. 2006. *Policies to promote labor force participation of older people.* CRR WP 2006–2. Chestnut Hill, Mass.: Center for Retirement Research at Boston College.

Murcott, A. 1982. The cultural significance of food and eating. *Proceedings of the Nutrition Society* 41: 203–10.

———. 1995. Social influences on food choice and dietary change: A sociological attitude. *Proceedings of the Nutrition Society* 54: 729–35.

Mutari, E., and D. M. Figart. 2001. Europe at a crossroads: Harmonization, liberalization, and the gender of work time. *Social Politics* 8: 36–64.

Nariai, O. 2007. Dealing with diversity in employment. *Japan Echo* 34(3): 7–9.

National Alliance for Caregiving and AARP. 2004. *Caregiving in the U.S.* http://www.caregiving.org/data/04finalreport.pdf.

National Institute of Population and Social Security Research. 2002. *Population projection for Japan 2001–2050.* Tokyo: National Institute of Population and Social Security Research.

———. 2005. *Population statistics of Japan.* Tokyo: National Institute of Population and Social Security Research.

———. 2008. *Jinko tokei shiryoshu* [Databook of population statistics]. Tokyo: Statistics Bureau.

National Partnership for Women and Families. n.d. Paid leave. http://www.nationalpartnership.org/Default.aspx?tabid=43.

National Women's Education Center. 2006. *Danjo kyodo sankaku* [Gender equality data book]. Tokyo: Gyosei.

———. 2009. *Danjo kyodo sankaku* [Gender equality data book]. Tokyo: Gyosei.

National Women's Law Center. n.d. Lower your taxes or increase your refund: The National Women's Law Center Tax Credits Outreach Campaign; 2006 tax filing season. http://www.nwlc.org/details.cfm?id=2493andsection=tax.

Neumark, D. 2003. Age discrimination legislation in the United States. *Contemporary Economic Policy* 21: 297–317.

Neumark, D., and W. Stock. 1999. Age discrimination laws and labor market efficiency. *Journal of Political Economy* 13: 736–61.

Neumark-Sztainer, D., M. Wall, M. Story, and J. A. Fulkerson. 2004. Are family meal patterns associated with disordered eating behaviors among adolescents? *Journal of Adolescent Health* 35: 350–59.

Nevada Dept. of Human Resources v. Hibbs. 538 U.S. 721. 2003.

New Zealand Department of Labour. 2006. *Choices for living, caring and working: A ten-year plan to improve the caring and employment choices available to parents and carers.* http://www.dol.govt.nz/PDFs/Choices-for-Living.pdf.

Nickell, S. 1997. Unemployment and labor market rigidities: Europe versus North America. *Journal of Economic Perspectives* 11(3): 55–74.

Nock, S. L. and P. W. Kingston. 1984. The family work day. *Journal of Marriage and Family* 46: 333–43.

———. 1988. Time with children: The impact of couples' work-time commitments. *Social Forces* 67: 59–85.

Nollen, S. D., B. B. Eddy, and V. H. Martin. 1977. *Permanent part time employment: The manager's perspective.* PB-268–390, Employment and Training Administration, Office of Research and Development. Washington, D.C.: School of Business Administration, Georgetown University.

———. 1978. *Permanent part time employment: The manager's perspective.* New York: Praeger.

Nollen, S. D., and V. H. Martin. 1978. *Alternative work schedules part 1: Flextime.* New York: Amacom.

Nomaguchi, K. M., M. A. Milkie, and S. M. Bianchi. 2005. Time strains and psychological well-being: Do dual-earner mothers and fathers differ? *Journal of Family Issues* 26: 756–92.

Ochs, E., C. Pontecorvo, and A. Fasulo. 1996. Socializing taste. *Ethnos* 6: 7–46.

Ochs, E., and M. Shohet. 2006. The cultural structuring of mealtime socialization. *New Directions for Child and Adolescent Development* 111: 35–49.

Office of Federal Housing Enterprise Oversight. 2005. *House price appreciation slows from record-setting pace, but remains strong.* Washington, D.C.: Office of Federal Housing.

Ogura, K. 2007. *Endless workers.* Tokyo: Nihon Keizai Shinbunsha.

Olmsted, B., and S. Smith. 1994. *Creating a flexible workplace: How to select and manage alternative work options.* 2nd ed. New York: Amacom.

Olson, D. H., D. G. Fournier, and J. M. Druckman. 1987. *PREPARE/ENRICH counselor's manual.* Rev. ed. Minneapolis: PREPARE/ENRICH Inc.

O'Neill, S. 2005. Workplace relations legislation: Bills passed, rejected or lapsed, 38th—40th Parliaments (1996–2004). Parliament of Australia. http://www.aph.gov.au/library/intguide/ECON/workplace_relations.htm.

Organisation for Economic Cooperation and Development (OECD). 1998. Working hours: Latest trends and policy initiatives. In *Employment Outlook, 1998,* 153–88. Paris: OECD.

———. 2001. Balancing work and family life: Helping parents into paid employment. In *Employment Outlook 2001,* 129–66. Paris: OECD.

———. 2004. Recent labour market developments and prospects. Special focus on clocking in (and out): Several facets of working time. In *Employment Outlook 2004,* 17–59. Paris: OECD.

———. 2005. Babies and bosses: Balancing work and family life. *OECD Policy Brief,* March.

Osawa, M. 2004. Women's employment and cost of children. In *Changing family norms among Japanese women in an era of lowest-low fertility,* ed. Mainichi Newspapers Population Problems Research Council. Tokyo: Mainichi Shinbunsya.

———. 2006. *Towards a work-life balanced society.* Tokyo: Iwanami Shoten.

Osberg, L. 2002. *Time, money and inequality in international perspective.* Luxembourg Income Study Working Paper No. 334. Luxembourg: Luxembourg Income Study.

Osterman, P. 1994. How common is workplace transformation and who adopts it? *Industrial and Labor Relations Review* 47: 173–88.

———. 1995. Work/family programs and the employment relationship. *Administrative Science Quarterly* 40: 681–700.

Parnes, H., and D. Sommers. 1994. Shunning retirement: Work experience of men in their seventies and eighties. *Journal of Gerontology* 49(3): S117–S124.

Partnership for Public Service (PPS). 2008. *A golden opportunity: Recruiting baby boomers into government.* Washington, D.C.: PPS.

Part-time Labor Law. 1993. As amended by Law 12 of 2007.

Pienta, A., Burr, J., and Mutchler, J. 1994. Women's employment in later life: The effects of early work and family experiences. *Journal of Gerontology* 49(5): S231–S239.

Pierce, J. L., J. W. Newstrom, R. B. Dunham, and A. E. Barber. 1989. *Alternative work schedules.* Boston: Allyn and Bacon.

Pisano, M. 2006. Cooking v. carryout a hot topic for scholars. http://www.mysanantonio.com/salife/stories/MYSA022106.01P.Home_Cooking.c605848.html.

Pitt-Catsouphes, M., and M. A. Smyer. 2005. *Businesses: How are they preparing for the aging workforce?* http://agingandwork.bc.edu/documents/IB02_BusinessPreparing.pdf.

Pleck, J. H., and G. L. Staines. 1985. Work schedules and family life in two-earner couples. *Journal of Family Issues* 6: 61–82.

Pocock, B., and S. Charlesworth. 2006. Work and family beyond "WorkChoices": Establishing partnership. Paper presented to the "Work, family and industrial relations: Making it work" roundtable. Melbourne, Australia.

Pocock, B., and E. Hill. 2006. Summary of Academy of Social Science workshop "Child-care: A better policy framework for Australia": Ten Policy Principles for a National System of Early Childhood Education and Care. http://www.familypolicyroundtable.com.au/pdf/Final%20Policy%20Principles.doc.

Pope, J. 2006. *College costs keep rising.* http://www.boston.com/news/education/higher/ articles/2006/10/24/college_costs_top_inflation/.

Portegijs, W., B. Hermans, and V. Lalta. 2006. *Emancipatiemonitor 2006, veranderingen in leefsituatie en levensloop* [Changes in life situations and course of life]. The Hague: *Sociaal en Cultureel Planbureau, Centraal Bureau voor de Statistiek.

Powell, G. N., and L. A. Mainiero. 1999. Managerial decision making regarding alternative work arrangements. *Journal of Occupational and Organizational Psychology* 72: 41–56.

Pre-K Now. n.d. Fact sheet: Pre-K across the country. http://www.preknow.org/advocate/ factsheets/snapshot.cfm.

Presser, H. B. 1988. Shift work and child care among young dual-earner American parents. *Journal of Marriage and the Family* 50: 133–48.

——. 2000. Nonstandard work schedules and marital instability. *Journal of Marriage and Family* 62: 93–110.

——. 2003. *Working in a 24/7 economy: Challenges for American families.* New York: Russell Sage Foundation.

Pugh, D. S., D. J. Hickson, C. R. Hinings, and C. Turner. 1969. The context of organization structures. *Administrative Science Quarterly* 14: 91–114.

Punch, P. 2006. *Australian master workplace relations guide: The WorkChoices edition.* Sydney: Commerce Clearing House.

Purcell, P. 2000. Older workers: Employment and retirement trends. *Monthly Labor Review* 123(10): 19–30.

——. 2003. Older workers: Employment and retirement trends. CRS Report for Congress. RL30629. Washington, D.C.: Congressional Research Service.

Quinn, J. 1999. Has the early retirement trend reversed? Paper presented at the First Annual Joint Conference of the Retirement Research Consortium, Boston.

Quinn, R. P., and G. L. Staines. 1979. *The 1977 quality of employment survey.* Ann Arbor: Institute for Social Research, University of Michigan.

Radloff, L. S. 1991. The use of the Center for Epidemiological Studies Depression Scale in adolescents and young adults. *Journal of Youth and Adolescence* 20: 149–67.

Rapoport, R., L. Bailyn, J. K. Fletcher, and B. H. Pruitt. 2002. *Beyond work-family balance: Advancing gender equity and workplace performance.* San Francisco: Jossey-Bass.

Reynolds, J. 2005. In the face of conflict: Work-life conflict and desired work hour adjustments. *Journal of Marriage and Family* 67: 1313–31.

Reynolds, J., and L. Aletraris. 2006. Pursuing preferences: The creation and resolution of work hour mismatches. *American Sociological Review* 71: 618–38.

Ridout, H. 2006. ACTU plan is a step backwards. *Australian Financial Review,* September 14.

RMC Research Corporation. 2005. *Washington state healthy youth survey 2004.* Portland, Ore.: RMC Research Corporation.

Robinson, J. P. 1999. The time-diary method: Structures and uses. In *Time use research in the social sciences,* ed. W. Pentland, A. Harvey, M. Lawton, and M. McColl, 47–89. New York: Kluwer Academic/Plenum.

Robinson, J. P., and G. Godbey. 1999. *Time for life: The surprising ways Americans use their time.* 2nd ed. University Park: Pennsylvania State University Press.

Rodgers, J. R. 2004. Hourly wages of full-time and part-time employees in Australia. *Australian Journal of Labor Economics* 7: 231–54.

Rombauer, I. S. 1931. *The joy of cooking.* St. Louis: A. C. Clayton Print Co.

Rones, P. L., R. E. Ilg, and J. M. Gardner. 1997. Trends in hours of work since the mid-1970s. *Monthly Labor Review* 120(4): 3–14.

Rose, S. J., and H. I. Hartmann. 2004. *Still a man's labor market: The long-term earnings gap.* http://www.iwpr.org/pdf/C355.pdf#search=%22Rose%2C%20Stephen%20and%20 Heidi%20Hartmann%20still%20a%20man's%20labor%20market%22.

Rosen, S. 1978. Substitution and division of labour. *Economica* 45(179): 235–50.

——. 1986. The theory of equalizing differences. In *Handbook of Labor Economics,* ed. O. Ashenfelter and R. Layard, 641–92. New York: North-Holland.

Ross Phillips, K. 2004. *Getting time off: Access to leave among working parents.* New federalism: National survey of America's families Series No. B-57. Washington, D.C.: Urban Institute.

Rubery, J., M. Smith, and C. Fagan. 1998. National working time regimes and equal opportunities. *Feminist Economics* 4(1): 71–101.

Rubin, B. A., and B. T. Smith. 2001. Re-employment in the restructured economy: Surviving change, displacement, and the gales of creative destruction. In *Working in restructured workplaces,* ed. D. B. Cornfield, K. Campbell, and H. McCammon, 323–42. Thousand Oaks, Calif.: Sage Publications.

Rubinstein, J. S., D. E. Meyer, and J. E. Evans. 2001. Executive control of cognitive processes in task switching. *Journal of Experimental Psychology: Human Perception and Performance* 27: 763–97.

Rudd, K. 2007. "Election victory speech." Brisbane, Australia. http://www.alp.org.au/media/1107/spepme240.php.

Rudd, K., and J. Gillard. 2007. *Forward with fairness: Labor's plan for fairer and more productive Australian workplaces.* http://www.kateellis.com.au/files/downloads/New_Directions_IR_Forward_with_Fairness.pdf.

Ruhm, C. 1990. Bridge jobs and partial retirement. *Journal of Labor Economics* 8: 482–501.

——. 2000. Parental leave and child health. *Journal of Health Economics* 19: 931–60.

Sandberg, J. F., and S. L. Hofferth. 2001. Changes in children's time with parents: United States, 1981–1997. *Demography* 38: 423–36.

Sato, H. 2006. *Shuugyoukeitai tayouka no nakadeno nihonjin no hatarakikata: nihonjin no hatarakikata chousa* [Support for balancing work and childcare: Cooperation among companies, families, and communities]. JILPT Research Report No. 50. Tokyo: Japan Institute for Labour Policy and Training.

Sato, H., H. Fujimura, and A. Yashiro. 1999. *Atarashii jinji romu kanri* [New human resource management]. Tokyo: Yuhikaku.

Sato, H., and E. Takeishi. 2004. *Dansei no ikuji kyugyo* [Childcare leave of Japanese men]. Tokyo: Iwanami Shoten.

Sayer, L. C., E. Passias, and L. M. Casper. 2006. Are single mothers time poor? Living arrangement differences in mothers' housework, child care, and free time. Paper presented at the annual meeting of the American Sociological Association, Montreal.

Scattergood, A. 2006. Simplicity: Let it rule; Insanely good dishes that are a snap to make? We kid you not. *Los Angeles Times,* March 15.

Schneider, B. 2006. In the moment: The benefits of the Experience Sampling Method. In *The work and family handbook: Multi-disciplinary perspectives and approaches,* ed. M. Pitt-Catsouphes, E. E. Kossek, and S. Sweet, 469–88. Mahwah, N.J.: Lawrence Erlbaum.

Schneider, B., and L. Waite, ed. 2005. *Being together, working apart: Dual-career families and the work-life balance.* Cambridge: Cambridge University Press.

Schor, J. B. 1991. *The overworked American.* New York: Basic Books.

Scrivani, A. 2005. Real food doesn't hold still. *New York Times,* December 7.

Segalen, M. 1986. *Historical anthropology of the family.* Cambridge: Cambridge University Press.

Senior Citizens' Freedom to Work Act. 42 U.S.C. § 403. 2000.

Senior Executive Service. n.d. *USA Jobs FAQ.* http://www.seniorleaders.gov/EI35.asp.

Sennett, R. 1998. *The corrosion of character: The personal consequences of work in the new capitalism.* New York: W. W. Norton.

Sered, S. S. 1988. Food and holiness: Cooking as a sacred act among Middle-Eastern Jewish women. *Anthropological Quarterly* 61: 129–39.

Severson, K., and J. Moskin. 2006. Meals that moms can almost call their own. *New York Times,* March 26.

Sex Discrimination Act 1984. *Cth, No. 4. 1984.

Sexton, H. R. 2005. Spending time at work and at home: What workers do, how they feel about it, and how these emotions affect family life. In *Being together, working apart: Dual-career families and the work-life balance,* ed. B. Schneider and L. Waite, 49–71. Cambridge: Cambridge University Press.

Shellenbarger, S. 2008. Some companies rethink telecommuting trend. *Wall Street Journal,* February 28, D1.

Sherriff, R. L. 2007. *Balancing work and family.* Sacramento: California Senate Office of Research.

Skocpol, T., and R. C. Leone. 2001. *The missing middle: Working families and the future of American social policy.* New York: W. W. Norton.

Skolverket. n.d. *Child care in Sweden.* http://www.skolverket.se/content/1/c4/09/44/00-531.pdf.

Sloan, A. E. 2006. What, when, and where America eats: A state-of-the-industry report. *Food Technology* 60: 19–27.

Sloan Initiative on Workplace Flexibility. 2006. *Workplace, work force, and working families: History of the Workplace, Work Force, and Working Families Program.* http://207.57.17.137/programs/Working_Families_History.shtml.

Small Business Encyclopedia. n.d. Comp time. *Answers.com.* http://www.answers.com/topic/comp-time?cat=biz-fin

Smith, K., B. Downs, and M. O'Cornell. 2001. *Maternity leave and employment patterns: 1961–1995.* Current population reports P70–79. Washington, D.C.: U.S. Census Bureau.

Smithson, J. 2000. Using and analysing focus groups: Limitations and possibilities. *International Journal of Social Research Methodology: Theory and Practice* 3(2): 103–19.

———. 2006. Using focus groups to study work and family. In *The work and family handbook: Multi-disciplinary perspectives and approaches,* ed. M. Pitt-Catsouphes, E. E. Kossek, and S. Sweet, 435–450. Mahwah, N.J.: Lawrence Erlbaum.

Sobal, J., C. F. Bove, and B. S. Rauschenbach. 2002. Commensal careers at entry into marriage: Establishing commensal units and managing commensal circles. *Sociological Review* 50: 378–97.

Social Security Administration, Westminster Teleservice Ctr. 93 LA 687. Feigenbaum 1990.

Squirchuk, R., and J. Bourke. 2000. Gender equity: From equal opportunity in employment to family-friendly policies and beyond. In *Organisational change and gender equity: International perspectives on fathers and mothers at the workplace,* ed. L. Haas, P. Hwang, and G. Russell, 117–32. San Francisco: Sage Publishing.

Staines, G. L., and J. Pleck. 1983. *The impact of work schedules on the family.* Ann Arbor: University of Michigan, Institute for Social Research.

Stark, B. 2006. Picking on moms in the workplace: Parents and caregivers face professional hurdles but strike back in court. *ABC News,* July 6.

State of New York, Rochester Psychiatric Center. 87 LA 725. Babiskin 1986.

State of NSW v. Amery, 2006 HCA 14.

State of Victoria v. Schou, 2004 VSCA 71.

Steinhauer, J. 2006. The way we eat: Ode to Joy. *New York Times Magazine,* October 15, 81–82.

Still, M. C. 2006. *Litigating the maternal wall: U.S lawsuits charging discrimination against workers with family responsibilities.* http://www.uchastings.edu/site_files/WLL/FRDreport.pdf.

Stone, P. 2007. *Opting out? Why women really quit careers and head home.* Berkeley: University of California Press.

Stone, P., and M. Lovejoy. 2004. Fast-track women and the "choice" to stay home. *Annals of the American Academy of Political and Social Science* 596: 62–83.

Sutton, D. 2001. *Remembrance of repasts: An anthropology of food and memory.* New York: Berg.

Sutton, K., and R. Noe. 2005. Family friendly programs and work-life integration: More myth than magic? In *Work and life integration: Organizational, cultural and individual perspectives,* ed. E. E. Kossek and S. Lambert, 151–68. Mahwah, N.J.: Lawrence Erlbaum.

Sweet, S., P. Moen, and P. Meiksins. 2007. Dual earners in double jeopardy: Preparing for job loss in the new risk economy. In *Research in the sociology of work: vol. 17, Workplace temporalities,* ed. B. A. Rubin, 445–69. New York: Elsevier.

Swody, C., and G. Powell. 2007. Determinants of employee participation in organizations' family-friendly programs: A multi-level approach. *Journal of Business and Psychology* 22: 111–22.

Tachibanaki, T. 2006. *Kakusashakai naniga mondai nanoka* [Have and have-not society: What is the problem?]. Tokyo: Iwanami Shoten.

Taskforce on Care Costs (TOCC). 2005. *Creating choice: Employment and the cost of care.* Sydney: Taskforce on Care Costs.

——. 2006a. *Where are we now? 2006 interim review of the 2005 Creating Choice: Employment and the cost of care report.* Sydney: Taskforce on Care Costs.

——. 2006b. *Where to now? 2006 TOCC final report.* Sydney: Taskforce on Care Costs.

——. 2007a. "2007 Budget response by the Taskforce on Care Costs: Getting with the program." Sydney: Taskforce on Care Costs.

——. 2007b. *Childcare Affordability Index, February 2007: Frequently asked questions.* Sydney: Taskforce on Care Costs.

——. 2007c. *The hidden face of care: Combining work and caring responsibilities for the aged and people with a disability.* Sydney: Taskforce on Care Costs.

Taylor, P., C. Funk, and A. Clark. 2007. *From 1997 to 2007: Fewer mothers prefer full-time work.* Washington, D.C.: Pew Research Center.

Tenneco Packaging Burlington Container Plant. 112 LA 761. Kessler 1999.

Thew, P. 2005. *The effect of the second wave reforms on vulnerable workers.* Sydney: Commerce Clearing House.

——. 2006. *Australian workplace agreements.* Seminar paper presented to the College of Law, Sydney.

Thompson, B. W. 1994. Food, bodies, and growing up female: Childhood lessons about culture, race, and class. In *Feminist perspectives on eating disorders,* ed. P. Fallon, M. Katzman, and S. Wooley, 355–78. New York: Guilford Press.

Thurow, L. C. 1984. 63 cents to the dollar: The earnings gap doesn't go away. *Working Mother,* October.

Tilly, C. 1991. Reasons for the continuing growth of part-time employment. *Monthly Labor Review* 114(3): 10–18.

Tleyji v. The TravelSpirit Group Pty Ltd 2005 NSWADT 294.

Toosi, M. 2004. Labor force projections to 2010: The graying of the U.S. workforce. *Monthly Labor Review* 127(2): 37–57.

Trezza v. The Hartford, Inc. 1998 U.S. Dist. LEXIS 20206. S.D.N.Y. 1998.

Trzcinski, E. 1991. Employer's parental leave policies: Does the labor market provide parental leave? In *Parental leave and child care: Setting a research and policy agenda,* ed. J. S. Hyde and M. J. Essex, 209–28. Philadelphia: Temple University Press.

UK Low Pay Commission. 2005. *National minimum wage: Low Pay Commission Report 2005.* London: HMSO.

U.S. Bureau of Labor Statistics. 2005. *Workers on flexible and shift schedules in 2004 summary.* Washington, D.C.: U.S. Department of Labor.

——. 2008. *The employment situation: May 2008.* http://www.bls.gov/news.release/pdf/empsit.pdf.

U.S. Census Bureau. 1997. *Current Population Survey, May 1997: Work schedules and work at home supplement file.* Washington, D.C.: U.S. Census Bureau.

——. 2004. *Current Population Survey, May 2004: Work schedules and work at home supplement file.* Washington, D.C.: Bureau of the Census.

——. 2005. *Current population survey, 2005 annual social and economic (ASEC) supplement.* Washington, D.C.: Bureau of the Census.

——. 2006a. *Current population survey: 2006 March supplement.* Washington, D.C.: Bureau of the Census.

——. 2006b. Fact sheet for Los Angeles County: 2004 American Community Survey. http://factfinder.census.gov.

——. 2006c. *Statistical abstract of the United States: 2006.* Washington, D.C.: U.S. Government Printing Office.

U.S. Congress. 2008. *Family-Friendly Workplace Act.* 110th Cong., 2nd sess. H.R. 6025. May 13.

——. 2009. *Telework Enhancement Act of 2009.* 111th Cong., 1st sess. S. 707. March 25.

——. 2009. *Telework Improvements Act of 2009.* 111th Cong., 1st sess. H.R. 1722. March 25.

——. 2009. *Federal Employees Paid Parental Leave Act of 2009.* 111th Cong., 1st sess. H.R. 626. Jun 8.

U.S. Department of Labor. 2006. National Compensation Survey: Employee benefits in private industry in the United States, March 2006. Summary 06–05. Washington, D.C.: U.S. Department of Labor.

U.S. General Accounting Office (GAO). 1994. *Alternative work schedules: Many agencies do not allow employees the full flexibility permitted by law.* GAO/GGD-94–55. Washington, D.C.: GAO.

——. 2001a. *Private health insurance: Small employers continue to face challenges in providing coverage.* GAO 02–8. Washington, D.C.: GAO.

——. 2001b. *The use of alternative work arrangements at GAO.* Washington, D.C.: GAO.

U.S. House of Representatives, Special Committee on Aging. 2000. Now hiring: The rising demand for older workers: Hearing before the Special Committee on Aging, 106th Cong.

U.S. Merit Systems Protection Board. 1991. *Balancing work responsibilities and family needs: The federal civil service response.* Washington, D.C.: U.S. Government Printing Office.

——. 2008. *Attracting the next generation: A look at federal entry-level new hires.* Washington, D.C.: U.S. Merit Systems Protection Board.

U.S. Office of Personnel Management (OPM). 2001. *Report to Congress on paid parental leave.* CPM-2001–11. Washington, D.C.: OPM.

——. 2004. *Status of telework in the federal government 2004: Report to the Congress.* Washington, D.C.: OPM.

——. 2006. *Career patterns: A 21st century approach to attracting talent.* Washington, D.C.: OPM.

——. 2007. *Status of telework in the federal government: Report to the Congress.* Washington, D.C.: OPM.

——. 2008. *Human resource flexibilities and authorities in the federal government.* Washington, D.C.: OPM.

——. n.d.a. *FedScope: Federal human resources data.* http://www.fedscope.opm.gov/index.asp.

——. n.d.b. *Leave administration.* http://www.opm.gov/oca/leave.

——. n.d.c. *Part-time employment and job-sharing guide.* http://www.opm.gov/employment_and_benefits/worklife/officialdocuments/handbooksguides/pt_employ_jobsharing/index.asp.

U.S. Steel Corp. 95 LA 610. Das 1990.

USA Jobs. n.d. *Federal employment information fact sheet,* EI 35. http://media.newjobs.com/opm/www/usajobs/pdf/ei35-15.pdf.

Valcour, M. 2007. Work-based resources as moderators of the relationship between work hours and satisfaction with work-family balance. *Journal of Applied Psychology* 92: 1512–23.

Van Dyne, L., E. E. Kossek, and S. Lobel. 2007. Less need to be there: Cross-level effects of work practices that support work-life flexibility and enhance group processes and group-level OCB. *Human Relations* 60: 1123–54.

Veciana-Suarez, A. 1994. Bringing up baby on one paycheck: Compromise, reducing lifestyle crucial. *Times Union* (Albany, N.Y.), June 17, C4.

Victorian Women Lawyers. 2005. *A 360° Review: Flexible work practices, confronting myths and realities in the legal profession.* Melbourne: Victorian Women Lawyers.

Visser, M. 1989. A meditation on the microwave. *Psychology Today* 20: 38–41.

Voydanoff, P. 1988. Work role characteristics, family structure demands, and work-family conflict. *Journal of Marriage and the Family* 50: 749–61.

Wachovia. n.d. *If you're from Venus, why get your financial advice from Mars?* http://www.wachovia.com/personal/page/0,505_513_1091_1099_1252,00.html.

Waldfogel, J. 1995. The price of motherhood: Family status and women's pay in a young British cohort. *Oxford Economic Papers* 47: 584–611.

——. 1998. Understanding the "family gap" in pay for women with children. *Journal of Economic Perspectives* 12: 137–56.

——. 2001. Family and medical leave: Evidence from the 2000 surveys. *Monthly Labor Review* 124(9): 17–23.

——. 2006. Work-family policies. In *Reshaping the American workforce in a changing economy,* ed. H. J. Holzer and D. Smith Nightingale. Washington, D.C.: Urban Institute.

Walker, K. H. 2007. Making the federal government work for women. *Public Manager* 36(1): 63–66.

Wallis, C. 2006. The multitasking generation. *Time Magazine,* March 27.

Warner, J. 2005. *Perfect madness: Motherhood in the age of anxiety.* New York: Riverhead Books.

Warner, R. 1986. Alternative strategies for measuring household division of labor: A comparison. *Journal of Family Issues* 7: 179–95.

Washington v. Illinois Dept. of Revenue. 420 F.3d 658. 7th Cir. 2005.

Watson Wyatt. 2008. *The business case for superior people management.* http://www.watsonwyatt.com/strategyatwork/article.asp?articleid=9521.

Weeden, K. 2001. Is there a flexiglass ceiling? The impact of flexible work arrangements on wages and wage growth. Unpublished manuscript, Cornell University.

Weinstein, M. 2005. *The surprising power of family meals: How eating together makes us smarter, stronger, healthier, and happier.* Hanover, N.H.: Steerforth Press.

Wenger, J. 2001. *The continuing problems with part-time jobs.* EPI Issue brief No. 155. Washington, D.C.: Economic Policy Institute.

White, M., S. Hill, P. McGovern, C. Mills, and D. Smeaton. 2003. "High performance" management practices, working hours and work-life balance. *British Journal of Industrial Relations* 41: 175–95.

Wight, V. R., S. B. Raley, and S. M. Bianchi. 2008. Time for children, one's spouse, and oneself among parents who work nonstandard hours. *Social Forces* 87: 243–71.

Wilensky, H. 1981. Family life cycle, work, and the quality of life: Reflections on the roots of happiness, despair, and indifference in modern society. In *Working life: A social science contribution to work reform,* ed. B. Gardell and G. Johansson, 235–65. New York: John Wiley and Sons.

Williams, J. C. 1989. Deconstructing gender. *Michigan Law Review* 87: 797–845.

——. 2000. *Unbending gender: Why family and work conflict and what to do about it.* New York: Oxford University Press.

——. 2006. *One sick child away from being fired: When "opting out" is not an option.* San Francisco: WorkLife Law, University of California Hastings College of Law.

Williams, J. C., and S. Bornstein. 2008. The evolution of "FReD": Family responsibilities discrimination and developments in the law of stereotyping and implicit bias. *Hastings Law Journal* 59: 1311–58.

Williams, J. C., and H. C. Cooper. 2004. The public policy of motherhood. *Journal of Social Issues* 60: 849–65.

Williams, J. C., J. Manvell, and S. Bornstein. 2006. *Opt out or pushed out? How the press covers work/family conflict.* San Francisco: Center for WorkLife Law, University of California Hastings College of the Law.

Williams, J. C., and N. Segal. 2003. Beyond the maternal wall: Relief for family caregivers who are discriminated against on the job. *Harvard Women's Law Journal* 26: 77–162.

Williams J. C., and V. A. Zelizer. 2006. To commodify or not to commodify: That is *not* the question. In *Rethinking commodification: Cases and readings in law and culture,* ed. M. M. Ertman and J. C. Williams, 362–82. New York: New York University Press.

Winegarden, C. R., and P. Bracy. 1995. Demographic consequences of maternal leave programs in industrial countries from fixed effects models. *Southern Economic Journal* 61: 1020–35.

Wood, S. G. 1999. Family-friendly management: Testing the various perspectives. *National Institute Economic Review* 168: 99–116.

Wood, S. G., and A. B. Sevison. 1990. Flexible working hours: A preliminary look at the phenomenon of flexibility in the American workplace. *American Journal of Comparative Law* 38: 325–40.

Wooden, M., and N. Watson. 2007. The HILDA survey and its contribution to economic and social research (so far). *Economic Record* 83(261): 208–31.

Work Style Reform Initiative. n.d. http://www8.cao.go.jp/shoushi/taisaku.pdf.

Workers with Family Responsibilities Convention 1981. ILO 156, 67th Session. 1983.

Workplace Flexibility 2010. 2006a. *Workplace Flexibility 2010 Legal Memo.* Washington, D.C.: Georgetown University Law Center.

———. 2006b. *The Federal Employees Flexible and Compressed Work Schedules Act (FEFCWA) Spring 2006 Legal Memo.* Washington, D.C.: Georgetown University Law Center.

Workplace Relations Act 1996 *(Cth).

Workplace Relations Amendment (A Stronger Safety Net) Act 2007 *(Cth).

Workplace Relations Amendment (WorkChoices) Bill 2005 *(Cth).

Workplace Relations Amendment Regulations 2006 No. 2 *(Cth).

Yamada, M. 2004. *Kibo kakusa shakai* [A society with a disparity in hope]. Tokyo: Chikuma Shobo.

Yasbek, P. 2004. *The business case for firm-level work-life balance policies: A review of the literature.* Wellington, New Zealand: Department of Labour.

Yin, R. K. 2003. *Case study research: Design and methods.* 3rd ed. London: Sage.

Zahn, P. 2006. *Paula Zahn NOW* (television series), May 2.

Zeitlin, J. 2000. Preface to *Organisational change and gender equity: International perspectives on fathers and mothers at the workplace,* ed. L. Haas, P. Hwang, and G. Russell, ix–x. San Francisco: Sage Publishing.

Zick, C. D., and W. K. Bryant. 1996. A new look at parents' time spent in child care: Primary and secondary time use. *Social Science Research* 25: 260–80.

Zweig, M. 2000. *The working class majority: America's best-kept secret.* Ithaca: Cornell University Press.

Contributors

Margaret Beck is assistant professor in the Department of Anthropology at the University of Iowa, and formerly served as a postdoctoral scholar at the Center on Everyday Lives of Families (CELF) at the University of California, Los Angeles. Beck is an archaeologist and anthropologist interested in food preparation and cuisine. In addition to her archaeological research in the U.S. Southwest and Great Plains, she has studied modern food habits and cooking techniques in the Philippines and the United States. Her publications on CELF project data include "Dinner Preparation in the Modern United States" (*British Food Journal* 2007) and "Gendered Time Use at Home: An Ethnographic Examination of Leisure Time in Middle-Class Families" with Jeanne E. Arnold (*Leisure Studies* 2009).

Suzanne M. Bianchi is distinguished professor of sociology and Dorothy Meier Chair in Social Equities at UCLA. She has served as coeditor of *Demography* and is a past president of the Population Association of America (PAA). Her recently published book (with John Robinson and Melissa Milkie), *Changing Rhythms of American Family Life* (2006), analyzes changing time-use patterns in working families over the 1965–2000 period. Her research interests include family change, women's employment, gender inequality, and child well-being.

James T. Bond is vice president for research and director of Work Life Research at the Families and Work Institute (FWI). Bond has coauthored numerous FWI publications including *Youth and Employment: What Do Young People Expect from the World of Work?*, the 2005 National Study of Employers, the 1997 and 2002 National Study of the Changing Workforce, *Beyond the Parental Leave Debate: The Impact of Laws in Four States*, and *The Changing Workforce: Highlights of the 1992 National Study*.

Juliet Bourke is an employment lawyer and partner with Aequus Partners of Australia, where she works with leading organizations to develop and implement organizational change strategies to promote equity and diversity, deliver training programs, and conduct workplace investigations and mediations. She is recognized nationally and internationally as an expert author and speaker on diversity, flexibility, and gender equity. Bourke has published widely on employment–related issues, including *Corporate Women, Children, Careers and Workplace Culture* (2000), and is coauthor of *Age Discrimination: Mitigating Risk in the Workplace* (2005).

Belinda Campos is assistant professor in the Department of Chicano/Latino Studies and the Department of Psychology and Social Behavior at the University of California, Irvine. A former postdoctoral scholar at CELF, she is a social-personality psychologist whose research examines how culture shapes relationship experience and health outcomes.

Kathleen Christensen founded and directs the Program on the Workplace, Work Force, and Working Families at the Alfred P. Sloan Foundation. Under her leadership, the program has played a vital role in developing work-family scholarship and in supporting effective workplaces that meet the needs of working parents and older workers. Christensen has published extensively on the changing nature of work and its relationship to the family. Her books include *Contingent Work: American Employment Relations in Transition* (1998); *Turbulence in the American Workplace* (1991); *Women and Home-Based Work: The Unspoken Contract* (1988); and *The New Era of Home-Based Work: Directions and Policies* (1988).

Laura den Dulk is assistant professor in the Department of Public Administration, Erasmus University Rotterdam, the Netherlands. Her main area of expertise is cross-national research regarding work-life policies in organizations in different welfare state regimes. Den Dulk's publications include *Work-Family Arrangements in Europe,* with Anneke van Doorne-Huiskes and Joop Schippers (1999); *Work-Family Arrangements in Organizations* (2001); and *Flexible Working, Organisational Change: The Integration of Work and Personal Life,* with Anneke van Doorne-Huiskes and Bram Peper (2005). Her research interests include the attitudes, opinions, and behavior of top managers toward work-life policies and the social quality in European workplaces. She participates in various European Community research projects, including Quality of Life in a Changing Europe (QUALITY) and Gender, Parenthood, and the Changing European Workplace: Young Adults Negotiating the Work-Family Boundary (TRANSITIONS).

Robert Drago is professor of labor studies and women's studies at Pennsylvania State University and a professorial fellow at the University of Melbourne, Australia, and he moderates the work/family newsgroup. He holds a PhD in economics from the University of Massachusetts at Amherst, and held a fellowship in 2008 from the ASA/NSF/BLS to study time use. Drago's most recent book is *Striking a Balance: Work, Family, Life* (Dollars & Sense 2007). He is a cofounder of the Take Care Net, past president of the College and University Work-Family Association, the 2001 recipient of the R.I. Downing Fellowship from the University of Melbourne, and a member of the Council on Contemporary Families and the International Association for Feminist Economics, and he serves on the advisory board for Take Our Daughters and Sons to Work Day.

Sheila Eby is president of Eby Communications. Using insights and skills developed through twenty years as a communications manager at JPMorgan Chase and eight years writing for publications ranging from the *New York Times* to *Vogue,* she now drafts features, reports, speeches, and Web materials for clients in fields ranging from finance to consumer products to leading not-for-profits.

Ellen Galinsky is president and cofounder of Families and Work Institute, a Manhattan-based nonprofit organization that conducts research on the changing family, changing workforce, and changing community. Galinsky is the author of over forty books and reports, including the groundbreaking book *Ask the Children,* selected by the *Wall Street Journal* as one of the best work-life books of 1999. She is also author of *Mind in the Making* (HarperStudio 2010). She has published more than one hundred articles in academic journals, books, and magazines. At the Institute, Galinsky codirects the ongoing National Study of the Changing Workforce, When Work Works, the National Study of Employers, and directs the annual Work Life Conference with the conference board. She is the recipient of the 2004 Distinguished Achievement Award from Vassar College.

Janet C. Gornick, a political economist, is professor of political science and sociology at the Graduate Center of the City University of New York (CUNY). She also is director of the Luxembourg Income Study (LIS), a cross-national research institute and data archive based in Luxembourg. Most of Gornick's research is comparative across the industrialized countries and concerns social welfare policies and their impact on family well-being and gender equality. Her core interest is in public programs that affect parents' capacity to combine employment with caregiving, such as childcare, paid family leave, the regulation of working time, and income supports targeted at families with children. She has published numerous academic articles on the subject of work-family policies, and a book, *Families that Work: Policies for Reconciling Work and Family,* coauthored by Marcia Meyers (2003). She also has published her work in popular venues, including the *American Prospect, Dissent,* and *Challenge Magazine.* She serves on several advisory boards, including "A Better Balance: The Work and Family Legal Center" and the *Journal of European Social Policy.*

Steven J. Haider is associate professor in the Department of Economics at Michigan State University. His research generally focuses on topics related to labor markets, the elderly, and poverty. In addition to his work on elderly labor supply, he recently has published papers on the preparedness of the elderly for retirement, the effects of school nutrition programs on children, and life-cycle variation in the relationship between annual and lifetime earning, and has published numerous papers on welfare reform.

Sylvia Ann Hewlett is an economist and the founding president of the Center for Work-Life Policy, a nonprofit think tank where she directs the "Hidden Brain Drain" task force, a group of fifty global companies and organizations committed to fully realizing female and multicultural talent. She also is the director of the Gender and Policy Program at the School of International and Public Affairs, Columbia University. Hewlett is the author of six *Harvard Business Review* articles and nine critically acclaimed nonfiction books including *When the Bough Breaks, Creating a Life, The War Against Parents* (coauthored with Cornel West), and *Off-Ramps and On-Ramps.* Her most recent book is *Top Talent: Keeping Performance Up When Business is Down* (Harvard Business Press, 2009). Her articles also have appeared in the *New York Times,* the *Financial Times,* and the *International Herald Tribune.* She is a featured blogger on HarvardBusiness.org and ForbesWoman.com. Hewlett has taught at Cambridge, Columbia, and Princeton universities and held fellowships at the Institute for Public Policy Research in London and the Center for the Study of Values in Public Life at Harvard University. In the 1980s she became the first woman to head the Economic Policy Council—a think tank of 125 business and labor leaders. A Kennedy Scholar and graduate of Cambridge University, she earned her PhD degree in economics at London University.

Qinlei Huang is a PhD candidate in the Department of Sociology at University of Minnesota. She received her MS in biostatistics from the School of Public Health at UMN. Her research interests include work, occupation, and organizations; the life course; health and well-being; gender and family; quantitative methods; social psychology; and international comparison.

Robert Hutchens is a professor in the Department of Labor Economics at Cornell University's School of Industrial and Labor Relations. His teaching focuses on labor economics and on the economics of government tax and transfer programs. His recent research has concentrated on long-term implicit contracts and on employer policy toward older workers. As part of this research focus, Hutchens recently completed a survey of employers that examines employer policies toward phased retirement. He has published in such leading journals as the *American Economic Review, Journal of Labor Economics, Journal of Human Resources, International Economic Review,* and *Mathematical Social Sciences.*

Sumiko Iwao is a social psychologist and a professor emeritus of Keio University (Japan). She received her MS and PhD in psychology from Yale University. Iwao has held numerous public positions, especially in the area of women and children. She chaired the Committee on Basic Issues of Gender Equality in the Cabinet Office and was the chair of the Gender Equality Council in the Prime Minister's Office. As a member of the Social Securities Council and the chair of its Task Force on Children in the Ministry of Health, Welfare, and Labour, Iwao worked toward providing nurturing environments for children and caregivers and ran a three-year research project promoting fathers taking childcare leave. She received a Prime

Minister's award in 2006 for her contribution to gender equality. Her English publications include *The Japanese Woman: Traditional Image and Changing Reality* (1993).

Suzan Lewis is professor of organizational psychology at Middlesex University Business School, London. Her research and consultancy focus on work and family issues, particularly workplace practice, culture, and change and the relationships between national social policy, workplace practices, and employee experiences, and she has led many national and international research projects on these topics. Lewis is founding editor of the international journal *Community, Work and Family* and is a member of an EU Expert Group on Women in Science and Technology. Her numerous publications include *The Work Family Challenge: Rethinking Employment,* with Jeremy Lewis (1996); *Work-Life Integration: Case Studies of Organisational Change,* with Cary Cooper (2005); *The Myth of Work-Life Balance: The Challenge of Our Time for Men, Women and Societies,* with Richenda Gambles and Rhona Rapoport (2006), *Women, Men, Work and Family in Europe,* with Rosemary Crompton and Claire Lyonette, (2007); and *Work, Families and Organizations in Transition: European Perspectives,* edited with Julia Brannen and Ann Nilsen (2009). She has advised governments and worked with employers and policymakers on work-life issues in Britain, the United States, and Japan.

David S. Loughran is a senior economist at the RAND Corporation and professor at the Pardee RAND Graduate School. His research focuses on applied topics in labor economics and demography. In addition to his work on elderly labor supply, Loughran maintains active research agendas related to family structure, fertility, and the effects of military service on economic and health outcomes.

Phyllis Moen holds a McKnight Presidential Endowed Chair and has served as professor of sociology at the University of Minnesota since 2003. Prior to that Moen held the Ferris Family Chair of Life Course Studies at Cornell University, where she founded and directed the Cornell Work and Family Careers Institute, established in 1996 as the first Alfred P. Sloan Working Families Center, as well as the Bronfenbrenner Life Course Center, established in 1992. Moen's research focuses on the dynamic interface between career pathways, working conditions, family conditions, health, and well-being over the (gendered) life course. She studies women's, men's, and couples' adaptive strategies in the face of a changing workforce and a global economy, together with obsolete workforce policies and practices constraining their options. Her two most recent books report findings from the Ecology of Careers Study, a multimethod, multilevel panel investigation of working families and gendered careers: *The Career Mystique: Cracks in the American Dream,* with Patricia Roehling (2005), and *It's about Time: Couples and Careers* (2003). Earlier books include *Women's Two Roles: A Contemporary Dilemma* (1992) and *Working Parents: Transformations in Gender Roles and Public Policies in Sweden* (1989). She also coedited *Examining Lives in Context: Perspectives on the Ecology of Human Development,* with Glen Elder and Kurt Luescher (1995); *The State of Americans: This Generation and the Next,* with Urie Bronfenbrenner and others (1996); *A Nation Divided: Diversity, Inequality, and Community in American Society,* with Donna Dempster-McClain and Henry A. Walker (1999); and *Social Integration in the Second Half of Life,* with Karl Pillemer, Elaine Wethington, and Nina Glasgow (2000). Dr. Moen now codirects (with Erin Kelly) the Flexible Work and Well-Being Center, part of an interdisciplinary NIH/CDC research network focusing on work, families, and health. She was recipient of the 2008 Work-Life Legacy Award from the Families and Work Institute.

Patrick Nolen received his PhD in economics from Cornell University in 2006, with a concentration in development and behavioral economics, and is a lecturer in the Department of Economics at the University of Essex in Colchester, United Kingdom. Recently he conducted experiments in South Africa and the United Kingdom to examine gender and racial differences in competition and performance. Nolen's current research focuses on issues in South Africa and China: his research in South Africa includes examining the effects of cell phones on rural labor markets; in China he is conducting a survey in rural Sichuan to investigate how individuals recovered from the 2008 earthquake.

Elinor Ochs is UCLA Distinguished Professor of Anthropology and Applied Linguistics and director of the UCLA Sloan Center on Everyday Lives of Families, which documents how working parents and their children sustain everyday family life across a spectrum of activities that reflect and construct valued ways of acting, communicating, thinking, and feeling. Drawing upon fieldwork in the United States, Samoa, Italy, and Madagascar, Ochs copioneered the field of language socialization, which analyzes how novices are apprenticed through and into socioculturally organized communicative practices. Ochs also has conducted research on the relation between language practices and psychopathology. Selected honors include Honorary Doctorate, Linköping University (2000); MacArthur Fellow (1998–2003); and Fellow of the American Academy of Arts and Sciences (1998).

Shira Offer is assistant professor in the Department of Sociology and Anthropology at Bar-Ilan University, Israel. She received her PhD in sociology from the University of Chicago, where she worked as a research associate at the Alfred P. Sloan Center on Working Families. Her research focuses on family and community processes in the urban context, with an emphasis on social support networks. She also has been studying work-family balance in poor and middle-class communities.

Machiko Osawa is professor of economics at Japan Women's University. She received her doctorate from Southern Illinois University with a major in Japanese literature. Osawa serves on advisory boards of the Ministry of Health, Welfare and Labour, the Prime Minister's Office, and the Ministry of Economy and Trade and Industry. She is the author of various books, including *Economic Change and Women Workers: Japan-U.S. Comparison* (1993), *Economics of New Family* (1998), *Non-Standard Work in Developed Economies,* with Susan Houseman (2003), *Towards a Work-Life Balanced Society* (2006), and *Work-Life Synergy* (2008).

Kelly Sakai is senior technology associate and communications coordinator at Families and Work Institute. She staffs the When Work Works project, managing the data collection, scoring, analysis, and reporting for the Alfred P. Sloan Awards for Business Excellence in Workplace Flexibility and is the communications contact for members of the media. Previous project work has included 9/11 As History and Salute to Educators.

Barbara Schneider is the John A. Hannah Chair University Distinguished Professor in the College of Education and the Department of Sociology at Michigan State University. She continues to hold an appointment as a university faculty research associate at the University of Chicago and as senior fellow at the National Opinion Research Center, where she previously worked for eighteen years. Her research focuses on how the social contexts of schools and families influence the academic and social well-being of adolescents as they move into adulthood. Schneider has published fifteen books and over one hundred articles and reports on the family, the social context of schooling, and the sociology of knowledge.

Merav Shohet is a PhD candidate in linguistic and psycho-medical anthropology at the University of California, Los Angeles. Her dissertation research concerns family life in Vietnam, focusing on the management of emotional expression and experience, and on socialization into and memories and practices of sacrifice, virtue, and devotion at home. Her recent publications include "Narrating Anorexia: 'Full' and 'Struggling' Genres of Recovery" in *Ethos* (2007) and "The Cultural Construction of Mealtime Socialization," with Elinor Ochs, in *New Directions in Child and Adolescent Development* (2006).

Blake Sisk is a doctoral student in sociology at Vanderbilt University. His research interests include immigration, race and ethnicity, and urban sociology. Sisk holds an MA in sociology from Fordham University.

Matthew Weinshenker is assistant professor of sociology at Fordham University. His current and recent research projects investigate the effects of dual-earner parents' nonstandard work schedules on young children's well-being, the difference age makes in the impact of becoming a father on married men's employment, and whether the prevalence of single-parent families explains the high child poverty rates in the United States compared with other developed nations.

Vanessa R. Wright is a senior research associate at the National Center for Children in Poverty in the Mailman School of Public Health, Columbia University. Her research is situated on the intersection of gender, work, and family, with a focus on the causes and consequences of poverty for children and families.

Tyler Wigton is a senior program associate at the Families and Work Institute, focusing on workforce and workplace issues. She is project manager of FWI's When Work Works project, an ongoing national initiative on workplace effectiveness and flexibility funded by the Alfred P. Sloan Foundation. She also works on the Supporting Work Project, funded by The Ford Foundation, and coordinates Families and Work Institute's annual Work Life Conference.

Joan C. Williams is 1066 Foundation Chair, Distinguished Professor of Law, and founding director of the Center for WorkLife Law at University of California, Hastings College of the Law. A noted expert on work-family issues, she is the author of *Unbending Gender: Why Family and Work Conflict and What to Do about It*, winner of the 2000 Gustavus Myers Outstanding Book Award. Williams has authored or coauthored five books and over fifty law review articles; "Beyond the Maternal Wall: Relief for Family Caregivers Who Are Discriminated Against on the Job" (with Nancy Segal; *Harvard Women's Law Review* 2003) was cited in *Back v. Hastings on Hudson Union Free School District*, 2004 U.S. App. Lexis 6684 (2d Cir. April 7, 2004). Williams also has played a central role in organizing social scientists to document maternal wall bias, notably in a special issue of the *Journal of Social Issues* (2004), which was awarded the Distinguished Publication Award by the Association for Women in Psychology. In 2006, Williams received the American Bar Association's Margaret Brent Award for Women Lawyers of Achievement. In 2008, she delivered the Massey Lectures in American Civilization at Harvard University.

Mark Wooden is a professorial fellow with the Melbourne Institute of Applied Economic and Social Research at the University of Melbourne, Australia, and the Director of the Household, Income, and Labour Dynamics in Australia (HILDA) Project, Australia's first large-scale household panel survey. He has developed a reputation as one of Australia's leading commentators on contemporary developments in the labor market. His current research interests are primarily in the areas of applied labor economics, the changing nature of work, employee relations, and survey methodology.

Index

Page numbers in *italics* refer to tables and figures.

Social Security Administration, 180
social welfare provisions
    economy, impact on, 241–243
Sommers, D., 112
spouse, time with. *See* marital quality
Spurlin, Leigh Ann, 153–154
standard workweek
    Europe, comparison to, 227, *227*
State of New York, Rochester Psychiatric Center
    (1986), 204
Steffen-Cope, Ilona, 95–96
Stock, W., 113
Stone, P., 82
Striking the Balance (Human Rights and Equal
    Opportunity Commission), 279
Study of Time Use (1981), 19
Summers, Larry, 96
supervisory costs, 161
Support Plan for Women's Renewed Challenges
    (Japan), 362n7
Survey of Income and Program Participation, 22
Swaziland, 211
Sweden, 196, 223–224, 226, *227*, 242
    annual leave, *227*
    family leave, 234, 235, *235*
    hours worked, 223, *224*
    part-time employment and, 198, *231*, 232
    part-time/full-time wage differentials, 238
The System That Soured (Katz), 315

tanshin funin (Japanese transfer system), 304, 312
Taskforce on Care Costs (Australia), 279, 291,
    300–301
team production, 160–161
telecenters, 184
telecommuting, 6, 98, 102, 185
    See also telework
telework, 188
    history and policy, 183–184
    utilization and availability, 184–186
    See also telecommuting
Telework Enhancement Act, 356n2
Telework Improvements Act, 356n2
Tenneco Packaging Burlington Container Plant
    (1999), 204
Texas Monthly, 144
Third European Working Conditions
    Survey, 240
"three job-two adult" work overload, 2–3
Tilly, C., 187
time mismatch
    Australia, comparison to, 266–267, 269,
        271–274, *272, 273*, 274–275
    determinants, 263–265
    gender and, 264–265, 271–274, 274–275
    ideal worker norm and, 263–265, 271, 274
    policy recommendations for, 275

unions and, 271, 274
    See also work-family mismatch
time off and leaves, 133, 137–142
time squeeze, 44–45
Trades Union Council (UK), 211
traditional families, 265
Transitions project, 11, 245, 250–259
    analysis of data, 251–252
    methodology, 250–251, *251*
    parents' experiences, 255–259
    policy recommendations, 261
    workplace flexibility, organizational support
        for, 252–254
Transition to Forward with Fairness bill
    (Australia), 287
Treasury Department, 193
Trezza v. The Hartford, Inc. (1998), 214
Tseng, Y., 269
two-parent families
    children, time with, *32–33, 35*, 36, *37*, 38
    employment status within, 28, *29*
    selected characteristics by work hours,
        28, *30*, 31
    subjective time-use experiences by
        employment, 38, *39*, 40
    time allocations, *35*, 35–36, *37*
    work hour trends, 26, *27*
    workloads, 31, *32–33*, 34–35

underemployment, 17
Unilever (consumer products
    company), 107–108
unions, 12, 208, 211–212, 226–227
    Australia, 12, 266
    credit hours system, opposition to, 181–182
    Europe, 226
    Japan, 320, 328, 362n1
    time mismatch and, 271, 274
United Kingdom, 223–224, 226, 227, *227*, 247,
    248, 253
    annual leave, *227*
    family leave, 234, *235*
    hours worked, 223, *224*, 237, 247
    maternity leave rights, 357n8
    part-time employment and, 198, *231*, 232, 233
    part-time/full-time wage differentials, 238
    unions and, 211, 226
UK Low Pay Commission (2005), 267
U.S. Census, 111
U.S. Merit Systems Protection Board, 186, 193
UCLA Sloan Center of Everyday Lives of
    Families (CELF), 8
"unsocial hours," 203

vacation. *See* annual leave
Viveros-Long, A., 182
voluntary employer practices, 10–11